COMPUTERS: AUDITING AND CONTROL

Edited by ELISE G. JANCURA, Ph.D., C.P.A.
and ARNOLD H. BERGER, Ph.D.

FIRST EDITION

AUERBACH publishers
philadelphia
new york
london

AUERBACH Publishers Inc.,
Philadelphia, 1973

AUERBACH Management and Communication Series

George Vardaman, General Editor

Sang M. Lee, *Goal Programming for Decision Analysis*
Elise G. Jancura and Arnold H. Berger, eds., *Computers: Auditing and Control*

Published simultaneously in the United Kingdom by AUERBACH Publishers Inc., Wallington, Surrey, England.

First Printing

Printed in the United States of America

Library of Congress Cataloging in Publication Data

Jancura, Elise G 1938- comp.
Computers: auditing and control.

(Auerbach management and communication series)
1. Electronic data processing--Accounting.
2. Electronic data processing--Auditing. 3. Electronic data processing--Business. I. Berger, Arnold H., 1931- joint comp. II. Title. III. Series.
HF5679.J288 658'.05'4 73-3043
ISBN 0-87769-153-5

Computers:
Auditing and
Control

Contents

PART TWO CONTROLLING COMPUTERIZED APPLICATIONS

PART FOUR IMPROVING EDP EFFECTIVENESS

Preface

The decade of the 1960s brought remarkable advances in computer technology, improved economics, and greater numbers of persons willing to attempt to apply the computer to the advancement of their organizational goals. One result has been a tenfold increase in the number of computers and a corresponding increase in both the number and variety of applications.

In many instances the projected benefits of computer use have been realized. But in recent years there has been a noticeable increase in concern about the effectiveness of computer utilization. Many applications have not yielded the expected benefits. Often the estimated costs and time of implementation were exceeded. Frequently the results proved unreliable and of little value.

As a result, persons who have (or intend to have) accounting and auditing responsibilities find themselves faced with two conditions:

1. A large portion of the organization's accounting and operating information flow, and at times even much of its decision making, are embodied in the computer applications. To effectively perform their responsibilities, accountants must adjust to this new technology and, at times, force this new technology to adjust to their needs.
2. A major opportunity to achieve improved utilization of the computer is now open to them. There is a wide and growing appreciation, one which we hope will be furthered by this volume, that the skills and objectivity of accountants and auditors are vital components in effective selection, design, implementation, and evaluation of computer applications.

Concern with control of computer and data security, changes in internal control, and the evaluation of the results of computerized activities are not exclusively the province of accountants and auditors, however. Certainly the management that uses information produced by the data processing departments and the management of these departments themselves must also evaluate the results produced and exert proper control over the assets entrusted to them. The authors whose works are included in this book represent a wide variety of skills and responsibilities. They include certified public accountants, internal auditors, controllers, systems analysts, installation managers, and data processing and management consultants.

We hope this book will be useful and of interest to readers from many areas. It is intended for professional accounts, but we expect that computer and management professionals will find it equally valuable. We are grateful for the contribution to the field made by each of the authors included and express our appreciation to those who have made this collection possible.

PART ONE

Perspective on Computers

1

The Computer Revolution

Early computer applications tended to replicate manual or unit record procedures for the major, routine information-handling tasks such as payroll, accounts receivable, and financial statement preparation. These applications had little impact on organizational practices. Generally, "hard" savings, in the form of clerical cost reductions, were obtained.

As the data processing staff grew in size and experience and improved computer capabilities were available, interest moved to more demanding applications. Data processing systems now initiated transactions and management messages, affected several types of data files, and generated accounting and operational data. The computer had changed from a passive recorder of historical events to an active participant in business operations. The organization began to feel the impact of the computer.

The natural tendency to discuss the "new state of the art" applications probably exaggerates the present importance of "total systems." These all-embracing applications, integrating data from all parts of the organization and providing fast response to managers' information needs, are more vision than reality. The basic, batch processed applications still dominate the computer workload.

But there is no doubt about the trend to integrate systems, to provide faster response, and to incorporate more functions in computer applications.

Increased systems comprehensiveness and complexity require new approaches to development and implementation. All components of the systems planning effort, particularly the preprogramming phases, become more demanding. Audit and control considerations are now recognized as a vital component of this development process.

"The Coming Age of Management Information Systems" suggests an even greater role for computer-based systems. The reader may well conclude that the functions of auditing and control in that new age will be performed largely through the development and use of advanced information systems. The computer system may be more than a new responsibility or a new tool; it may become the new environment for auditing and control.

THE COMING AGE OF MANAGEMENT INFORMATION SYSTEMS

by Earl C. Joseph

By the mid-1970s, unless managers use management information systems in their daily conduct of business, they will find themselves incapable of performing management tasks.

Tomorrow's managers at all levels and for all functions will be deeply involved in the use of computers. They will make daily use of computers in carrying out their management responsibilities. This involvement will be the result partially of the greater knowledge of the computer's power possessed by the young men entering corporate financial management and partially of the many programs that will become available to help executives.

Today's educational institutions have a special need to prepare their students for the age when the computer will serve as a partner in the management of any business. Industry must also educate its managers and professionals to use computers. The opportunities to use computers effectively, with their tremendous capabilities for assisting management, represent a real challenge to managers and computer system designers alike. Here, in the implementation of the computer for management use, is the future promise for curing the problems and ills now facing the professional manager.

The computer's role is to help management executives organize and manage as they desire. There is little doubt that computers will become increasingly important in helping executives achieve their goals. This trend is clearly visible today by the greatly expanding range of computer applications currently being implemented and used. It is especially encouraging to see these management aids evolve into systems that are really being used.

Reprinted by permission of the publisher from *Financial Executive,* August 1969, pp. 45-52.

Indicative of the expanding role of computers is the placement of computer operations and decisions at higher levels in the organization. The trend is to move EDP management away from its traditional assignment under the controller or financial officer and to give it executive status of its own. This movement is an assertion that the computer can help all areas of management rather than just the traditional areas. The shift upward clearly points to management's awareness of the computer's importance. Such movement merges computerized information systems, placing financial and operational levels closer together.

A question that has been often asked in the last year or so is, "Is MIS practical today?" The answer is yes, because:

• Computers are now large enough and fast enough.

• Memories have sufficient capacity and have become economical;

• Time sharing, which permits multiple access computing, allows many users (managers) to use the computer at the same time;

• Multiprogramming and multiprocessing systems have been developed;

• A basic set of computer programs to support the needs of MIS are now available.

Today, terminals connected to a remote computer can be used by a number of managers at a cost of $10 to $20 an hour. It's not very much, is it? In fact, in many cases, it is less than it would cost to add a man to your staff. We also have large computers that have been around a few years and which we have learned how to use. They are fast enough to accommodate many managers on line at the same time. And we now have the economical mass storage that makes management information systems feasible.

What about the future? What will happen in the 1970s that will make it even easier to use the computer for management information systems? First let's look at programs. We are going to have total operating systems to support the computer system operation. One of the most important types of programs we are going to have is the packaged program—packages of application programs and packages of systems programs, where the manager requesting information can piece together his management information systems when he needs them. We can't do that very easily today, because today's computers do not adapt to our language. The next generation of computers will adapt to man's language.

Another thing holding management information systems back is the cost of the terminal. Computer graphic terminals are somewhat costly, but their cost will come down drastically in the near future. In fact, in the late 1970s we can expect to be able to afford the graphic terminal on just about every manager's desk. Bell Telephone Laboratories expects to have 100,000 picture phones in use before 1975, and over a million in use between 1975 and 1980. That's a powerful lot of picture phones! And picture phones make nice computer terminals for presenting graphic real-time data of what is going on in the company.

We can also expect some breakthrough in the mass memory area from about 1972 to 1974. These breakthroughs will lead to extremely large memories of 100 billion bits or more at very low cost. The storage will be random access—we will be able to get at the data in microseconds.

All of this taken together is going to make it almost impossible *not* to use management information systems. Today, if your company were to implement MIS for your business from scratch by piecing together parts of programs, designing and programming other parts, it would be very costly—sometimes millions of dollars.

REAL-TIME ASSISTANT

By 1975, to do the same thing will cost tens of thousands. The cost to the on-line user, to you as the manager, for having a computer assist in making decisions, will be measured in pennies.

This is why we won't be able to get along without the computer in business. The computer will have such an effect on business that we will not be doing business as we are today. Managers will not be making decisions as they are today. It will bring about a tremendous revolution in business, perhaps one of the largest.

Not only is equipment changing, but the concept of management information systems itself is changing. Another word is being added—"control." Management information and control systems. In this type of system, management is going to have an assistant to control the business in real-time and provide a service on-line to its people and its customers.

In the past, management information systems meant programs to handle the administrative details. Most management information systems are like that today. There are other types, however. MIS aid is needed for planning and scheduling; for assisting managers in the decision-making process; and for management control—the current awareness function. If the manager has to dig out the information manually, he usually cannot dig it out in time to make use of it. So what we need is a system, a type of exception reporting system, that makes the manager aware of information at the time he needs to know it.

In this type of system there is the environmental feedback on how the total business is operating—the total company including the customer. It will operate in a closed-loop fashion, where the computer decides what to run as a result of the information it is getting. Today, practically all of our computer operations are triggered by specific commands for specific tasks. In the type of system we are looking for in the future (it is projected by 1975), the computer will decide what program should be run.

I am not talking about a type of system where the computer is going to take over, but strictly a type of system that is an aid to the people in the system—an aid to the managers and professionals. I am talking about a system that will tie in all the people in an organization, on-line. It will keep in its files updated profiles of the information needs of each person in the system. Each has changing needs (changes from day to day, month to month year to year) and, therefore, each profile of information requirements needs to be kept up to date. The computer itself will keep track of these changes for each individual as they occur.

The system will allow the user to question the system by asking, "What happens if I do this?" The "what if" question requires a powerful programming system to back it up. The computer needs to run a simulation of the total operation of the company, including the customers. That is a pretty big order.

But these types of simulations are now becoming available. When the manager is allowed to ask the computer, "What happens if I do this?" the computer runs a simulation which will give him a tested answer or a tested set of alternatives. Thus, a manager can test out a decision before he implements it by getting from the computer the probable outcome. Imagine how important it would be for managers to be able to ask that type of question.

We have a few such systems in the research stage already. Such systems will call managers—dial them up on the telephone and speak to them—to pass on high priority information and to trigger managers into action. These elaborate systems will make management by exception a reality. I think from this you can see how powerful management information systems will be in the coming decade.

To illustrate how these systems work, I would like to set up a hypothetical example. Suppose I am the manager and put into the computer my PERT updating information. (PERT is a planning tool that allows the computer to determine whether I will meet my schedule. The information I put in is my best guess of where I am and of how long it will take me to do certain items.) If I put in my current input this week and the computer runs the analysis program and determines I am going to have 13 weeks negative slack, I am going to miss my schedule by almost three months! If I am working on a six-month project, three months late is pretty bad. What does the computer do? It calls me up on the telephone and makes me painfully aware of this fact.

Next week I put in my PERT input (if I try to beat the system by not putting it in, the computer is going to run the PERT assuming that there is no change), and supposing I don't do a very good job of improving my situation, I will still have a negative slack. Instead of calling me up and telling me that I am going to be late, the computer also calls my boss. You can see how the computer is starting to control its environment!

Let's say the following week I put in my input and I still didn't improve enough. Instead of calling up just me and my boss, it calls up my bosses' boss. 1984? No; it is the opposite. It allows the manager to do the job of management in real time; it tells him when he must do something to help the situation—like how to keep me from getting fired.

Another example: A foreman comes in in the morning—quite a bit earlier than the people working for him. What does ho do? He goes to the stockroom to see what stocks are available; he goes around to each machine to see which ones are operating; he goes to the time clock to see who has punched in; and then he assigns the jobs. In the meantime, he has to look at the planning chart to see what he has planned out and what things have to be done that day rather than the next or next week. He has to do these things over and over again each day. It is a lot of leg work. He does not have a lot of time to do the things that any foreman or any manager should do—to interface with people. He shouldn't have to do the same thing over and over again.

DAILY ROUTINE CHANGES

With the aid of an MIS, the foreman's day would start differently. The computer would have printed out the itinerary for the day when the foreman arrives at work; it would keep track of what is in the stockroom; it would keep track of what machines are operable; it would keep track of people as they punch in. And so the computer has all the information it needs to print out the itinerary after looking over the planning chart to see what the foreman previously planned. The foreman is left with details of interfacing with the people—the thing he should be doing.

But the day isn't over yet. At 10:00 machine "B" breaks down, and Mary Jo goes home because she has a toothache. What does the foreman have to do? He has to re-do completely the morning cycle. He must go back to the crib to see what materials are there, what machines are available, whom he can reassign, and so forth.

With an on-line management information system, what would he have to do? The computer would already know that Mary Jo went home because she punched out. The computer, depending upon the type of system you have, may or may not know that the machine broke down. If it doesn't, the foreman puts that information in. The computer then types out or calls up on the telephone, depending on the type of system you have, what the alternatives are for the foreman, thereby saving him considerable time.

For still another example, let us suppose I am a computer designer and I get a new assignment: I have to design a new, medium-scale computer, and I have to design the program address counter. Program address counters have been designed thousands of times. Why should I have to design it over again?

If I had a system such as an on-line MIS where I could retrieve the information, the system would know even ahead of me that I am going to get this assignment. It could then send through the mail, instead of calling me up on the telephone, the possible designs that I might use. Then I make a selection from the possibilities described by the computer rather than run to various other designers and the libraries, ending up not finding anything I can use and redesigning the counter. The computer would then tell me what part needs to be changed or optimized.

So I can save a lot of time by using management information systems. They do the leg work that I am currently required to do today.

Computers designed specifically for management information systems are non-existent today. We are using computers designed for application to general purposes. What about the future? We are starting to design for MIS. Future systems will be more modular, allowing both hardware and software to be pieced together and tailored for MIS.

What specifically do we need for MIS? We need lots of memory capacity. We need hardware in our computer systems that assists with the task of file protection and security—many levels of locks and keys. We need a fast mass memory.

What is happening in the area of fast mass memory is rather dramatic. Memory units are speeding up and coming down in cost by a factor of more than 10 every 10 years. This trend is still continuing. The cost of memory, in the mid-1950s was about $1 per bit; in the mid-1960s it was about 10 cents per bit; and by the mid-1970s, if this progression continues, we can expect it to be about one tenth of a cent.

THINGS WILL BE DONE DIFFERENTLY

There is going to be an even bigger cost reduction for random-access high-speed memory. The cost for such memory is going to come down to considerably less than one cent per bit. The improvement in costs for this type of memory will be a factor of 10 or 100. You can't imagine what this going to do for the computer field. We just won't do things the way we used to.

In the mid-1950s the average speed of the main memory was about 10 microseconds; by the mid-1960s, about one microsecond; and by the mid-1970s a tenth to a hundredth of a microsecond is predicted. Capacity of memories? Here again we see a breakthrough—one of the reasons why the cost is coming down. Memory capacity has been increasing by a factor of 10 per 10 years. In the mid-1950s the central memory capacity of the computer was about 100 thousand bits; in the mid-1960s, one million to 10 million bits. By the mid-1970s the capacity of the central memory will be close to a billion bits of memory. This is exactly what we need to make management information systems economically feasible. The cost of the memory and the speed at which information can be processed are the main things holding back MIS. But this will soon change.

Before 1960, the cost of a single logic gate was $2.00. Today, with the advent of integrated circuits and MSI (medium scale integration of circuits), a gate cost about 10 cents. In the early 1970s, between 1970 and 1971, we can expect that the cost will be about a penny or so per gate. Soon thereafter they will be considerably less costly, and programs with built-in logic will be feasible.

Another trend is occurring in the input-output areas: the use of computers via remote computer terminals. Terminals, especially the cathode-ray tube terminal, need to become less expensive— and they will. Storage near to the terminal will be necessary. In fact we are approaching the era of the "intelligent terminal"—terminals that will do a number of things that computers now do. These terminals can be located at the source of the data and at data dissemination points. It is at these points that we need some of the computer's capabilities, and the future "intelligent terminals" will provide us with these capabilities.

COMPUTERS STILL MAKE MISTAKES

The main thing that has held up the time-sharing portion of the MIS system, and time sharing in general, has been the low reliability of systems. Computers are considerably more reliable than they were in the past, but they still make mistakes. The mean-time between failures in the early to mid-1950s was measured in a few hours; in other words, one error every hour or two. In the mid-1960s the mean-time is considerably longer. For the central processing unit, the computer, mean-time between failures is measured in thousands to ten thousands of hours.

In the total system—the peripherals, the memory, and the CPU—it is again down to a few hours. A few tens of hours in most cases. This is not reliable enough when you have hundreds or thousands of people on-line using the computer.

Univac is making a breakthrough in this area. We have improved the reliability of our total system so that the mean-time between failures is measured in years. Greater reliability has been accomplished by implementations of such things as self-repair—the capability of switching from a failing component to a good component. In other words, the system has built-in spare parts.

The biggest problem in the computer field is programming. The problem arises because computers do not use the language that you and I would like to use.

Language—computer language and the language with which we communicate with one another—has developed along similar lines. Languages start out with a few number of words. For example, early computers had from 15 to 60 instructions.

The next stage in development of any language is to make the basic words more complete. Latin is a very good example. Latin words have a lot of beginnings and endings and sentences have complex structures. Today's computers are like that. We have maybe 100 to 200 instructions in the repertoire with many thousands of variations on those instructions. In fact, we built one computer which had 64 instructions with a total of 30,000 variations.

What would happen if writers were restricted to 100 different words? You can imagine how long it would take them to express their ideas. This is part of the problem we have in communicating with computers: it takes a long time to program them.

Thus, the next step—one that we are beginning now with our software—is to get rid of some of the complexity and add words as they are needed. Computers will be designed to allow the user to specify the words or the instructions that he needs.

Such systems are called extensible or enhanceable language systems. They give the computer the ability to adapt to language, whether it is English or Russian, the language of a manager, a chemist, a manufacturing foreman, or the top executive. Many different languages can be conditioned in at the same time.

PROGRAMMING—THE BIGGEST COST

The primary purpose of such systems is to avoid the expense of lengthy programming. At present we spend more than 75 per cent of our total system cost for programming. In the early 1950s we spent only about 5 per cent. In the 1965 era we hit the half-way mark; 50 per cent of our cost was in the hardware and 50 per cent was in the software. But today, only four years later, we are up to 75 percent, and we are projecting that by 1970 about 80 to 85 per cent of the total cost of the system will be attributable to programming. This makes it mandatory that we use our old or current programs on our next generation system.

With language enhanceable systems, we can capitalize on past software investments. Specifically, we can tell our new computer to imitate the languages of the old computers that the programs we want to use were written for. This will save billions of dollars of software (currently in the neighborhood of $3 to $5 billion of software is in use). In the past, we threw away our software investment when we went to the next generation system. There was no way of capitalizing on it. We can't afford that any longer, and our next generation's systems must be able to capitalize on this software investment—and they will.

In spite of the many changes coming in the field, computers are going to stay in the field, a lot longer. The average life of a computer in the 1950s and 1960s was about three to five years. In the 1970s we are predicting up to 10 years for the life of the computer system. This is both good and bad: we can evolve into the system we are using, and thus make the programs more useful and less costly. It allows us to get our applications working so that we will not have to re-do them as the next piece of hardware comes out, as we did in the past. But, if our computers are going to stay out in the field longer, it is going to take longer for new innovations to get into the hardware. In other words, we will sort of batch the new "goodies" before we put them into our computers.

The longer life predicted for future computer systems is especially nice for the management information system. It will allow us to evolve these applications rather than to revolutionize them, and more managers will evolve into using MIS. But, as a company starts to use management information systems, it soon learns it never really had any problems before. Why is this? The answer is simply that you don't really know your problems until you see them in real-time. With management information systems, however, we have one big difference: we have the tool to do something about the problems that are newly made visible.

We can also expect that in the 1970s we are going to have some new communication systems. In fact, the technology might allow us to get out of the Gutenberg rut that we have been in for many hundreds of years. Some people, myself included, are predicting that sometime in the late 1970s we will be going to "paperless books." In some senses, we are almost there now. A lot of people don't read newspapers any longer. Most of our young people do not rely upon the newspapers or magazines or journals for news. They rely on TV. We can expect that because of the cost and problems of getting technical information, we are going to go on-line with the computer to disseminate such information.

The number of steps which an author must tread to get an idea to the reader is tremendous today. In my experience, which I think is typical, I go through maybe three or four drafts, with my secretary typing each. Maybe two or three editors go through it in a hurry a number of times.

THE COMPUTER—JACK-OF-ALL-TRADE

Just think how the process would be speeded up if I had a computer that would take over these secretarial and editing functions, in real-time, with my input to the computer. Suppose I have an interactive system where I can get a dialogue going with the computer, in real-time, where the computer helps the total process. It corrects the spelling, edits, takes out or tells me about redundant information, tells me that I should reorder the information to connect up this thought with that thought, etc. Can you imagine how easy it would be to be an author when we have such an aid? It would considerably speed up the way we get thoughts down so other people can use them.

Instead of printing out the edited manuscript, the computer can send it on-line to some publisher. Which publisher? It is not somebody who is going to produce a book or a journal. It is somebody who is going to distribute the information completely by electronic means to the user. So, the main purpose of the publisher here is to decide whether this piece of material is worth publishing. Once that decision is made, it goes out in real-time.

Suppose major cities have computers that are communicating with many users—an information utility. The users' first look at the author's information would not be the total material but an abstract of the material (located by title or key words or something like that). For some users there would be kept profile files of the material they want or are interested in. So the system would be set up to make these individuals aware of the new information that is available. And when information of interest is generated, the utility makes them aware of it. However, most users would query the system. They would actually see something that they like or think they can use, then they would look at the textual material.

Future picture phones and the current CRT terminals are good enough to do some browsing in this type of information utility system. In fact, we can envision even flat types of display devices that can be carried just like a book and probably weigh no more. These devices allow us to be on-line with the computer/communications systems in the 1970 decade. Can you imagine how much quicker ideas would be passed out. Can you imagine how the business of transmitting information and the publishing business would change? Can you imagine how much cheaper it would be to the user to get information if he did not have to go through all the steps that we go through now, of printing the material and distributing it?

PROGRAM CHANGES COMING

Programs are going to change quite a bit in the next generation. They are going to be modular, first of all. With the third generation computer system, we have quite a bit of modular hardware with which the user pieces together the system. The fourth generation computer will have modular programs—both system and applications programs. But most importantly, we are going to have application packages, such as MIS.

In summary, MIS systems and the computers to run them will be bigger, more economical, and easier to use. Future computer systems will contain many new features, commonly called "bells and whistles." And as always, some will prove to be useless and others will lead to new problems as time marches on. Hopefully, most of them will be found to be useful. They will also be more reliable, less costly, and have more built-in features, there will be more application programs for management use, more memory capacity, and greater efficiency.

No fact of contemporary life is more challenging to society than the present rapidly advancing technology and continual managerial change. These changes are speeded by the computer and communications industries. We could never go back to the pre-computer era—our dependence on computers is now far too great. Not only are the material and economic conditions of life enhanced and affected by this advanced tool of the cyberated age; it has and will continue to effect far-reaching changes in the way we manage.

Those of us working in the computerized management information system field are predicting that such systems certainly will evolve and come into mass use by executives. We further predict that those managers, companies, politicians, and governments who do not use such systems by 1975 to 1980 will simply not be able to compete in a society which does.

WHERE ARE WE GOING?

I have tried to put on tomorrow's glasses in order to see where we can go, rather than wear yesterday's glasses and see only how bad it was. I have fixed primarily on the period five to ten years hence. Because of the high cost of programming and the need to capitalize on the costly investment in programs, new advances and ideas will tend in the future to rest on the shelf much longer than advances have in the past. The state of the economy that surrounds programming will govern our actions more than we would like; it will inhibit our ability to advance into the future as promptly as we know we could. Thus, there should, of course, be some skepticism concerning the certainty of these predictions. The era that we thought we had entered when yesterday's advances sparked heated controversy, only to drop in importance as even more revolutionary hardware changes were thrust upon us, now appears to have been altered into an era where today's problems could be with us for a long time to come.

2

The Accountant's Role in the Computer Revolution

The increase in computers from an estimated 5,000 in the United States in 1960 to 52,000 in 1970, with a value in excess of $20 billion, is evidence of the growth of computerized activities and consequently of the very real need for accountants to be well prepared to use and evaluate computer systems. The impact of this growth affects both the management accountant and the public accountant. The ability of the computer to make truly management-oriented information systems feasible provides an outstanding opportunity for the individual who can work with these systems. It is hoped that accountants will see the opportunities and grow with them.

The personal auditing standards established by the AICPA Code of Professional Ethics require that the public accountant also be well versed in computerized techniques and activities. Specifically, the first and third standards apply:

1. The examination is to be performed by a person or persons having adequate *technical* training and proficiency as an auditor.
3. Due professional care is to be exercised in the performance of the examination and the preparation of the report.

This does not mean that all auditors must become EDP experts, but it does require that an auditor who is to be engaged in auditing where a computer is heavily used must have a sufficient knowledge of the techniques involved to evaluate their adequacy. As these techniques increase and change, the auditor's knowledge of them must keep pace. As the use of computers extends to more and more companies and at the same time becomes an ever more important part of each individual firm's information system, the requirement for this knowledge on the part of the auditor will increase.

THE COMPUTER, THE ACCOUNTANT, AND THE NEXT DECADE

by Felix Kaufman

Not too many years ago prophets of doom predicted that computers were destined to take over all information processing. If accountants didn't have a deep understanding of what was going on in computer development, they said, they would be pre-empted by those who did. These predictions proved to be a substantial exaggeration of what was really happening. In fact most CPAs, notably those in small and medium-sized firms, observed little or no impact on their day-to-day affairs. Thus the danger is that they may now be lulled into feeling that the computer, notwithstanding its power and pervasiveness, is not going to have much effect on their lives.

I am convinced that the computer *will* have a significant, basic impact on the CPA, even in serving small clients. It is therefore in his best interest to manage promptly the changes in his education, training and attitude that are required by this major technological development.

And there is evidence already that the accountant's role in data processing is being pre-empted by others. Al Zipf, executive vice president of the Bank of America, a person with impressive experience in the computer field, recently observed that "data processing was, thank God, emerging from an obscure niche in the controller's department." This view is shared by a lot of people with similar vantage points.

It's time to reconsider the impact of the computer on certified public accountants and to speculate on what may happen in the next few years. Computer technology moves at a dizzy pace and it seems prudent to look at the cumulative impact.

How might we conduct a reassessment?

First, let's examine current technical developments as so to determine whether their nature bears on the question.

Second, let's ask ourselves again what CPAs do, examine the computer's effects to date on these roles and consider prospective outcomes.

Third, let's conclude by asking whether CPAs are likely to adapt to forecasted changes and what happens if they do not.

Reprinted by permission of the publisher from *The Journal of Accountancy*, August 1971, pp. 33-39, copyright 1971 by the American Institute of Certified Public Accountants, Inc.

RECENT TECHNOLOGICAL DEVELOPMENTS

During the last half of 1970, computer manufacturers announced that a new price performance dimension was available if you had enough work to put through new, more powerful devices. This continued the tendency to provide hardware that can process a transaction at a lower cost than could its predecessor, although frequently at a greater total cost. In any case, the machines continue to be described by specifications that boggle the mind.

For example, we went through a period trying to understand what a microsecond was. (That's a millionth of a second and no mortal can really quite comprehend a second divided into a million parts.) Now our friends who make computers ask us to contemplate what a billionth of a second is, a so-called nanosecond.

The second development of significance is the burgeoning market for small computers. The IBM System 3 is a case in point. A large number of the several thousand customers for the system are companies with no previous computer experience. A related development involves the so-called mini computer. The mini computer appeared on the scene about ten years ago as a small-scale, relatively inexpensive computer, surrounded by very primitive peripheral capability. Although the mini increased in popularity through the 1960's, its uses were confined to the scientific and engineering environment. For example, it was frequently used in process control situations. In recent years, there have been improvements in the input-output devices that can be attached to mini computers. Input-output devices include card readers, paper tape readers, magnetic tape handlers, disk packs and card punches as well as line printers. These machines behave just like the peripherals we are accustomed to using with conventional business computers, but they tend to have abbreviated capabilities and accordingly are more modest in price.

The important point is this—it is now possible to attach devices to a mini computer that cause it to behave like a full-fledged machine in the sense that it can perform all of the functions of a business data processor.

In addition, the minis are now appearing in the market place, set up to be operated like accounting machines in the conventional sense. These are operated by a keyboard with arrangements for handling one or more ledger cards and their running speed is a function of the operator's speed. *Probably, all accounting machines in the next few years will really be small computers with appropriate keyboard and forms adaptation.*

In the data entry environment, we are moving rapidly toward a variety of methods for capturing transactions in machine-sensible condition at the point of origin. It follows that our incentive to use automatic data processing methods is increased substantially if we are favored with a variety of inexpensive data capturing devices. If the cost of converting a transaction to computerized processing is substantially reduced, it follows that another large chunk of the data processing environment becomes eligible for automation.

The prospective user is presented with an array of data processing options. He can have his own machine on his premises, he can transport data by conventional means to remote computers or he can communicate directly with remote computers.

Now it may be feasible to get data to remote computers even when it is only economically practical to operate in the batch mode. In one intriguing arrangement, a time-sharing facility provides a billing package which allows for the transmission of charges and credits to customer accounts through the use of conventional teletype terminals. When monthly statements are required, the time-sharing facility provides a magnetic tape of the statements to a collaborating bank. The bank prints and mails the statements, receives the remittances, converts the remittances to magnetic tape on its own system and dispatches that magnetic tape to the time-sharing facility so that its master files may be updated.

Another development of merit involves those technological changes that can cut the cost of programming. Perhaps it will be cheaper to turn out programs for specific applications that do not have to be customized to any significant extent by each user. The mini computer employed as an accounting machine represents this tendency. In the case of one manufacturer, programs can be written for a conventional machine of substantial power and automatically converted to the language of the mini computer. Then, the mini computer manufacturer produces a wired version of the program which literally plugs in whenever it is required.

WHAT THE CHANGES MEAN

What are the implications of these technical tendencies?

• Equipment costs continue to decrease. This means a wider range of use and, of course, a wider range of users.

• The number of processing options now available indicates a movement toward being able to select the amount of power appropriate to each job. Too often in the past hardware had to be geared to the most demanding assignment; this meant under-utilization on many tasks.

• Computer power is not portable. It's as close as the telephone. You can now go from place to place carrying a terminal and when the terminal is plugged into a telephone and the computer is called, you are on the air. *These possibilities in the time-shared environment also mean that the charge for using the computer has become a variable cost.* You pay when you're connected.

Some of these developments should reduce the serious difficulties encountered in designing and operating computer systems. This is because the spread of the small economical machine to thousands of new users rationalizes a greater effort to develop package programs, and the cumulative experience of thousands of man-years of mistakes has to finally turn into an advantage.

We can summarize by saying that the cost of making computer power available has reached levels that could hardly have been anticipated a few years ago; that the raw data processing power of this capability cannot be rivaled, and that we are reaching a condition where large low-volume sectors of data processing may now be economically attractive. To CPAs, the meaning of all this is fairly evident. In the due course a great many of your clients will use this capability in one form or another. For some of you this is true now.

IMPACT ON AUDITING

The CPA is first and foremost an auditor. Where he does not choose, or is not called upon, to perform the attest function, he also may be a keeper of records, and thus he may be doing his client's data processing. When he counsels his client, he helps to assemble, present and interpret information used for decision making. He also may be a designer of systems, advising his client as to how to organize and how to link methods and procedures so that information processing takes place efficiently.

The computer's impact on auditing has been very gradual and should continue to develop in an undramatic way. It's hard to understand how people can think that the attest function can be automated. Auditing has mechanical features and it has formality, but it is not a cookbook process. It cannot be programmed as a set of explicit steps to be followed on successive occasions in the same manner. Auditing cannot be accomplished by the numbers.

The opportunity for computerizing auditing depends to some extent on the auditor's ability to examine the attest function and, in specific situations, to separate activity which is structured, objective and explicit from that which is unstructured and subjective. The elements in the former segment are receptive to computer programming.

To be more specific, here are some audit activities that can be done by computer:

1. Whenever the client's files are in machine-sensible form, those files can be queried for what we want via the use of our own programs. This capability is the basis for software packages which have been developed by a number of CPA firms.
2. It is now relatively easy to analyze information using powerful statistical techniques. One does not have to be a statistician in order to be able to do this, but a knowledge of where the programs are and how to call on them is required. It now becomes possible to take a stream of information—a series of account balances, for example—and analyze their trends on a sophisticated basis.
3. There are interesting possibilities that relate to a consideration of materiality. It is now easier to analyze account relationships rapidly and to determine the sensitivity of profits, for example, to the behavior of specific accounts. Further investigation and experience in this area might help us do a better job when we write audit programs by ranking the significance of accounts, thereby facilitating the allocation of effort.
4. It follows that to the extent that one can automate the process of examining files, the size of the sample—the number of accounts observed—will be larger than it was likely to have been under other mechanical and manual methods. Given some of the characteristics of file updating, there will be situations where it is practical, using your own programs, to examine every record in a large file.

THE ACCOUNTANT AS A RECORD-KEEPER

The second role that was referred to earlier involved the accountant as a data processor. Perhaps this was the role that engendered the attitude that the computer might make CPAs obsolete. Such reasoning, although probably correct, treats the CPA in the context of a role that is not important to him professionally, notwithstanding its importance to some of the members of the profession. Therefore, I feel that the profession at large has no basis for worrying about this aspect of the accountant's activities, although it is likely that the "worst" will happen. No one who pushes a pencil to keep records can, in the long run, compete with the computer. Therefore the act of picking up data, storing it in the right place and returning it as required is no longer a job that ought to or will be done manually.

Some of the time-sharing arrangements mentioned earlier and the new type of accounting machines witness the accelerating displacement of manual activity. We should not be concerned that this role is being usurped from those accountants who do this sort of thing. They can preserve their relationship with clients and maintain responsibility for data processing by learning how to use the new tools.

TAX PREPARATION

Another data processing role worth mentioning is tax return preparation. Readers are aware of the extent to which computerized tax return packages have become available in the last few years. We can expect tax return packages to improve from year to year in terms of the scope of the tasks they are able to handle at the federal level, and the number of state returns that they are gradually able to comprehend. Also, time-sharing packages are being developed to facilitate financial counseling on a range of matters involving cash management, investments, tax planning, tax return preparation, estate planning and other matters. The CPA will have interesting possibilities for expanding his purview through the use of such programs.

HELPING CLIENTS USE INFORMATION

With the premise that the CPA is involved in helping his client to use information more effectively, let's examine the potential of the computer for improving and expanding the performance of this role. The computer probably enlarges the CPA's role as a presenter and interpreter of information which is really part of the process of facilitating the making of business decisions. Then, the decision-making process becomes a way of assembling information, a method of interpretation once it has been assembled and the loop in which the process is repeated. Because of new capabilities that can be implemented by the computer, it is likely that CPAs must know a lot more about ways in which information can be developed than they have heretofore. This idea has to be elaborated carefully.

THE BUDGET AS A FINANCIAL MODEL

The accountant has always understood that he could provide interpretive assistance by examining the figures presented in a conventional set of accounts by relating one account to another in order to produce meaningful ratios, by comparing an account to a standard in order to detect a variance and by comparing an account to comparable values in the past in order to detect a trend.

The accountant also knows that he can synthesize a set of transactions by making assumptions as to what will happen in the future. By "processing" these transactions so as to come up with pro forma financial statements he creates a budget. Since all of these activities could only be effected at occassional intervals, the accountant could not be aware of the latent power inherent in the fact that the accounting system—particularly the manifestation we call the budget—is in fact a model of the business. The model is a representation, other than reality itself, that can be employed to study the effect of certain assumptions as if these things had really happened. This can be accomplished without having to complete these events in a normal time framework.

To repeat, a model is a representation of reality. Models which are effective for planning purposes compress time and space and dramatically decrease the cost of testing various propositions. The budgeting process has two aspects. First, we process certain assumptions as to what will happen by "passing" the transactions representing these assumptions through the budget system. This allows us to perceive what the financial effects will be. Then we determine whether the effects are tolerable. For example, do we have the capacity to do what the budget implies we will do? Have we violated some condition or constraint, such as exceeding available working capital? If so, we must redo the budget so that it predicts financial effects based upon activities that we really think can take place. As a rule, once this has been done, let's say once a year, it is not repeated simply because the clerical process is too ponderous. This then is an official budget and, until the same process occurs a year later, we use it primarily to control costs.

This must be regarded as a disturbing state of affairs. Is there some underlying condition that says it suffices to plan once a year? Clearly, the answer is no. Financial planning should be done as often as the dynamics of the situation dictate—whenever something significant happens to clearly alter conditions.

Now, what does this all have to do with the computer? Simply this. Early in the EDP era it became clear that models could be used in a much more powerful way if their logic could be implemented by a computer. It would no longer be necessary to conclude that rebudgeting was too ponderous even though an important condition had changed significantly. The computer is the device that permits us to change in a very dramatic way the time frame with which we associate a modeling process. *It opens up the possibility of continuous budgeting.* In addition, the enormous increase in experience in financial modeling probably is leading to a profound improvement in the design of the model itself. CPAs can and should employ this planning capability in behalf of their clients.

The CPA has access to a series of financial statements expressing the financial history of a particular client. Allowing for the fact that the account structure may change to some extent from year to year, it is an easy matter for the CPA to array a series of balances for the same account over a period of years—the sort of thing a statistician would call a time series. It is now possible to take the data to a computer and treat the information with a variety of statistical programs. It is not necessary for the user to understand the underlying mathematics in order to employ these programs. The act of using these programs reveals much more about the way the values in a particular account have been changing than the primitive processes employed in the past.

A meaningful example would involve a series of values describing sales for a particular product month by month over a period of years. Statistical treatment of this series would produce a forecast of future sales with a higher degree of accuracy and with appropriate adjustments for seasonal trends and random conditions. This statistical treatment can also determine whether one account predicts the behavior of another or is dependent upon another and in what way. This leads to a series of observations about the character of the data and it is now possible to construct the model (define relationships) that I referred to earlier.

Consider this illustration. Statistical analysis reveals how sales are behaving and future sales can now be expressed as an equation in which factors which appear to affect sales are properly related. Also, assuming that a statistical relationship between sales and several significant expense accounts has been ascertained, an equation can be written to "take" us to net income. Once the profit and loss environment has been modeled, this can be put to work by making assumptions about what is going to happen—forecasting sales. The model has now taken the form of a program which is inserted into the computer. We can run the program frequently, which means that as we try assumptions and examine results we are probably disposed to alter our assumptions and examine new facts. Computer people call this "iteration" and it is a powerful dimension. By trial and error, or what is now fashionably called "what if," we can examine assumptions continuously. This is likely to lead to the consideration of a better model.

PROBABILITY AND SENSITIVITY

There is also some icing on this cake in the form of additional capabilities. Whenever you do financial planning, or any kind of planning for that matter, you must acknowledge that your forecasts are estimates. Sales may increase 10 per cent next year, but then again they may not. Labor costs may go up 6 per cent next year, but maybe they will go up 10 per cent. You think you may be able to increase certain prices but you are not sure how the market will react. In fact anyone who forecasts says: *"I am guessing and I would really be more comfortable if I only had to tell you what range my forecasts would fall in."*

The only thing that is certain about a forecast is that the specified value is not the actual one. The critical issue is not, "Will we be off the mark?" but "How far?" In the computer world the values we assign to the variables in our equations are values which can only be expressed over some range, but within that range we have some confidence. In short, it is now possible to comprehend probability and to do financial planning which recognizes that the planner himself is saying "Look, what I am doing is educated guessing."

Probability is one leg of sophistication in financial planning. Sensitivity is the other. Sensitivity is the capability built into our model to recognize that in complicated processes involving many variables each has a different degree of influence on the final result and the degree of influence is not necessarily visible to the naked eye. If a company makes a product composed of seven parts of direct labor and three parts of material, it might assert that profits are far more sensitive to fluctuation in the price of labor than the price of material. This would seem to be obvious. Sensitivity calculations, however, would recognize the degree of confidence that we have in predicting the future cost of labor and materials. They would reflect the effect, the sensitivity, on profits of stable labor costs and unstable or uncertain material costs for example. Sensitivity measures materiality.

The structure of a new world in financial planning has been outlined; it may sound sophisticated. It does require new know-how. It does not, however, require depth or credentials as a mathematician, an extensive understanding of statistical techniques, an understanding of how a particular computer works or even the manner in which it is programmed.

A good deal of what is involved here is the process of knitting together programs that already exist and of being able to interpret data after the model has been run and tentative conclusions have been reached.

Thus far we have concentrated on a model that produces future financial statements. We know, however, that specific values on the financial statements depend upon what happens over some period of time as we operate various segments of the business activity. For example, the future value of a parts inventory depends upon the way in which we manage that inventory. The future value of accounts receivable is more than the function of a low level of sales. It also depends on credit-granting policy and the management of accounts. There are a wide variety of situations for which models can be designed. Accordingly, lack of imagination, ingenuity and energy are the only important constraints preventing one from using the computer to forecast the level of a specific account by building and operating a model of the subsystem that affects the value of that account.

I would add that there is practically no such thing as a business model that does not have a financial ramification. Can the accountant say that he is not interested in a model that represents the way in which orders are scheduled in a factory when such a model predicts the back order condition and inventory levels as well as the speed with which orders turn into sales?

It all boils down to this. A business is a set of co-ordinated activities. The accounting system measures and reports the financial effect of all of these activities. One can program a representation of these financial relationships and also can program representations of many of the underlying processes that have an effect on the financial statements. In theory one can construct a model that is representative of the entire firm. However, this is no mean task.

There are some collateral values in all of this model building. The kind of account analysis that I advocated in the earlier discussion of statistical evaluation is, perhaps, a tool of some value to the planning of an audit engagement. Once the auditor can determine account sensitivity with a precision that he could never achieve before, he can organize his engagement plan and the related allocation of effort by himself and his staff by ranking the accounts based on their influence. It is also possible that the emerging forecasting art foreshadows the possibility that the value of significant accounts can be predicted in advance and an important effect will bear on an audit when the accountant observes significant differences between the actual value of an account and its predicted value.

A very significant increase in the power of the budgeting process can be obtained if one does nothing more than program the procedures already in place.

WILL CPAS RESPOND?

I have tried to provide an understanding of the forces currently operating to widen and deepen the impact of the computer on CPAs. The subject cannot be left without examining the question of our concern over this changing environment and whether or not we are disposed to adapt to it. I could have concluded innocuously by saying "Here are my observations; draw your own conclusions," but that would seem cowardly, particularly in the context of my feeling that a significant response is imperative.

The accountant has a serious problem. The evidence seems to indicate that he is unconcerned. He is behaving as if the computer is having no effect on him. This attitude is not surprising since it is impossible to discern day-to-day developments involving the computer that have bread and butter significance to the CPA; nothing strikes him as a threat, nothing is compelling him to join or to fight. No doubt this is because the forces in motion are asserting themselves gradually and furtively.

Why are accountants so unconcerned? First, because the effects are not conspicuous. Second professional groups—perhaps any group with a vested interest—make slow adjustment to profound structural changes. Third, the field of information science as we know it has attracted a lot of people who five years ago might have found it difficult to locate a niche in business. These mathematicians and scientists have so far played a greater role in shaping information science than have accountants. In the aggregate they are a powerful group intellectually. Are they better fitted to the requirements of the computer game than accountants? Perhaps there is some support for this view arising from the comments made recently by academicians that there isn't a sufficient flow of top-flight students into accounting programs.

The principal reason for thinking that accountants may be occupying a changing position is the growing awareness that although accounting systems were the first formal information systems and are probably the most highly developed, they have now become subsets of a larger information process. In a report rendered by the Committee on Information Systems of the American Accounting Association, it was observed that a major development in the information function is "the formalization of information processes in many parts of the organization" and that now "the accounting information system is that operation of the formal information system concerned with the measurement of production, income, wealth and other economic events." The same report also observes, "It is clear that the accountant has ceased to be the information broker standing between the source of information and the user."

What can we do to obtain greater interest and a desire on the part of CPAs to play a more important role? I've reached some rather fatalistic conclusions. If accountants decline to some lesser role than they now play, would it pose a problem in our society? If the decline is the consequence of being displaced by others who do certain things better, such a shift is not prejudicial to the total business community. This might be a distinct possibility. Accordingly, the whole question of the accountant's adaptation to radical change in the information environment precipitated by the use of computers, and now by the management sciences as well, is something that CPAs have to work out themselves. They will have to consider the consequences and then conclude whether it is preferable to let the situation unfold, unmolested by any action on their part, or whether the profession should come together, reach a conclusion and, if they find it necessary, develop a program.

HOW DO ELECTRONIC COMPUTERS AFFECT ACCOUNTING AND AUDITING TECHNIQUES?

by Max S. Simpson

The business world of today is characterized by a state of innovation and change unsurpassed in history. This is not surprising when one considers the technological revolution that has taken place in the last 20 years. While man is striving to reach the moon and beyond in space, he is to no lesser extent attempting to apply technical and scientific advancements to optimize the complex art of managing a business in a highly competitive marketplace. One of the major contributing factors in attaining this objective is the electronic computer and associated scientific devices.

What has been the impact of the computer on business management? The answer to this question is difficult and not easily visible at first glance. To say that the computer impact has been extensive is not sufficient. The possibility exists that in the decades ahead history will show that the computer, as a management tool for decision making and control, was the catalyst in revolutionizing business concepts as they are known today. An indication of this premise can be seen in examining the far-reaching effects of the computer on accounting and auditing techniques.

Long-established accounting theory has not been altered by the computer impact, rather, the effect has been in the area of the changed implementation practices of this theory. Specifically, these machines have provided an environment where not only has labor saving justified their existence, but it has also become possible to service larger geographical areas out of a centralized location and to generate more detailed, accurate in-

---

Reprinted by permission of the publisher from *Financial Executive,* February 1966, pp. 38-45.

formation for business management purposes. Further, standardization of accounting procedures and of accounting classification has been stimulated by the centralization of the accounting function, and accelerated processing of data has substantially shortened the accounting cycle.

COMPUTER EVOLUTION

The emergence of these activities has occurred during the past 10 years. From the computer standpoint, this decade was marked by an evolutionary machine development which saw significant advances in higher processing speeds, greater and more flexible storage capacity, and the emergence of communications capability. For little or no increase in equipment costs, speeds and capacities are increasing at a geometric rate as computer improvements continue to be generated. The computers available today can even process various major programs concurrently on a time-shared basis in a communications-oriented data-processing environment.

Along with the development of improved computers, tremendous strides have been taken in knowledge of how to exploit the speeds, versatility and capacities of the modern computers.

Concurrently with computer improvements, significant advances were taking place in the development of related scientific devices: that is, a large array of communications equipment and computer input/output devices without which a modern computer cannot function. In the communications area, telephone and telegraph lines and microwave circuits are used for the transmission of business data, and the use of satellites is in the foreseeable future. In addition, there are about 50 different types of computer input/output devices ranging from such ordinary equipment as punch-card readers and conventional printers to some highly sophisticated and scientific instruments, such as remote console devices, cathode ray tube terminals, and audio-response devices.

Now computer-communication-oriented concepts for the processing of the business and scientific information flow are a practical and highly desirable objective. The most sohpisticated examples of this type of processing are generally associated with real-time systems where there is instantaneous response to any physical transaction at the time of occurrence. An example of this in the commercial area is seen in the more advanced current airline reservation systems, in the scientific area in the control of missiles and in space exploration activities.

ADVANCES IN SYSTEMS INTEGRATION

The accountant and the auditor should be familiar with the current developments in the area of systems integration. Certain companies have attempted with varying degrees of success to integrate the data flow from an initial point-of-sale inquiry to the sending of the material ordered by the customer. For example, one of the leading manufacturers of electrical equipment in the United States has in operation an integrated nationwide message switching and order-processing center, which for certain of its product lines permits automatic triggering from sales inquiry to sales order to shipment of material along with the necessary recording of inventory changes and issuance of re-stocking orders. Also, standard accounting applications such as invoicing, accounts receivable and sales statistics are automatically spun off from this integrated system. In this example, everything we need to know about a customer's order is generated by the system whether it be concerned with aspects of marketing, distribution, inventory or accounting—all without human intervention. The extension of this conceptual approach may be further characterized by a company having the capability of updating all records on an as-occur basis, culminating theoretically in an ability to project control statements even to profit and loss on an as-required basis. While this concept is somewhat esoteric in nature and may not be obtainable or economical within the near future, a conceptual direction definitely has been started.

The centralization of the accounting function even in a decentralized company environment has been prompted by cost and control advantages. The computer as a management tool permits large-volume accounting applications to be maintained and processed at a centralized location. Accounting application examples include payroll, accounts receivable, accounts payable, credit accountability, fixed assets and associated summary and analytical evaluation reports. With the inherent records being maintained and processed in this manner, operating divisions are relieved of the administration of these arduous tasks and are permitted to concentrate their energies on other pertinent areas of responsibility. The bringing together of these accounting applications facilitates the standardization and integration of accounting applications.

The computer impact on standardization and integration of accounting applications is already discernible. The standardization provided to a large American steel company by a single wage payroll system affords uniform interpretation of labor contracts with standardized audit procedures regardless of the number of processing locations. The increased control, accuracy and monetary savings of this approach have been confirmed.

An interesting example of accounting application integration is being-implemented by a large banking organization in the United States involving the consolidation of payroll, personnel records, expense distribution and work measurement standards. Not only can an employee be properly selected for a job but he can also be paid, evaluated and have his benefits controlled from a composite data base.

Also, through adoption of a uniform chart of accounts, monthly closings processed in a communications-oriented data-processing system can provide for the preparation of financial statements at a much earlier date than was formerly possible. The management benefits involved are significant in providing more timely, accurate information for over-all planning and decision making.

MANAGEMENT CONSIDERATIONS

Such business intelligence systems will go far beyond the limits of classical accounting procedures to process and analyze a broad range of information—both financial and other decision-making data—that are needed by management to run the business. The ultimate achievement would be a system that not only encompasses all information handling requirements but processes each piece of information instantaneously.

Management would be notified on an "exception" basis of any irregular behavior of business performance requiring immediate action. The environmental aspects would depict a management "control center" where, through the use of graphic displays, pertinent information could be recalled from the computer system and exhibited in chart form for management decision making.

As an accompanying development, operations research techniques would be employed to permit the structuring of composite company profit plans in the form of a "profit model" whereby management could evaluate alternative profit forecasts prior to final selection of the most appropriate profit plan.

A progressive example of current activity in this area is the Financial Executives Institute Research Project, "Impact of Computers on Management and Organization." The project's main objective is to present for general management the constructive uses of computer utilization. Emphasis is being directed toward computer system definition—present and planned, influence of the computer on decision making, management's part in today's and tomorrow's system, and the influence of the computer on organization.

CHANGING ROLE OF THE ACCOUNTANT

The underlying significance for the accountant in this changing business environment is his emergence in a new role. Traditionally the accountant has dealt with historical facts. The accountant of tomorrow, however, will have the ability to deal with current information at time of occurrence, and with computer-generated projections, so that his services to management can be infinitely greater than was possible with the old tools. The accountant must not only accept and understand the new techniques, he also must take the lead in designing systems which fully exploit the computer and its related sciences. His task then will be adapting to a new profession rather than continuing an old one.

AUDIT CONTROLS

Insofar as the auditor is concerned, it can be stated that his basic objectives and responsibilities are not altered by the installation of a computer system. The nature of the "control" problem for a computer system is different from other systems, however, and this not only requires new audit techniques but also substitutes new areas of control that must be examined. Since the computer offers a system that replaces manual activities, the auditor will now be more concerned with testing the controls over the system than with controls designed to prevent human error. Although valid for all computer systems, these requirements are intensified in a real-time or on-line data-processing environment.

The American Institute of Certified Public Accountants has recognized the necessity for exploring in depth the computer impact on accounting and auditing techniques. Recently a project has been initiated to develop an applied research and education program in computer technology. Particular attention is being directed toward the capabilities of information processing systems as they relate to accounting, auditing, tax work and management sciences. The research findings will be used in organizing an expanded educational program to service the needs of the Certified Public Accountant on the last developments of computer technology.

Another perspective of the computer impact on auditing, however, is represented by the use of the computer to conduct various comparisons and tests involved in an audit in a faster and more economical manner than manual methods which would otherwise be employed by the auditor. In this context, reference is made to the use of the computer to facilitate an audit, rather than to problems posed the auditor by the existence of a computerized accounting system. The computer has provided for the auditor centralized control and information accuracy previously not available.

For electronic data processing systems, it is common to designate three areas of control with which the auditor must be concerned.

1. Controls over the movement of data into and out of the computer operations, commonly referred to as "input/output controls."
2. Administrative controls over the organization and operating procedures of the computer department itself.
3. Controls incorporated in the computer programs—that is, built into the sequence of instructions followed by the computer in processing data.

Input/output controls are usually handled by a control section which monitors all data into and out of the computer system. Specific functions would include the monitoring of source data, the processing of rejects and errors due to incorrect input data and insuring accuracy of final output reports.

Administrative controls over the computer operation include the separation of functions that is so important for effective control, such as the separation of the programming section from the operating section of the computer function (Figure 2-1, "Organization of Functions for Control of EDP Data Flow"). Other controls include the requirement that procedures and operator instructions be fully documented, with flow charts describing each application; also, that log sheets be maintained to account for all computer operating time.

Controls incorporated into computer programs are of many types. Examples of controls that may be used—such as "zero balance" checks, reasonableness checks, sequence checks, self-checking numbers and feedback controls—are generally well described in the many books and articles on the subject, such as Felix Kaufman's *Electronic Data Processing and Auditing.*

CONDUCT OF AN AUDIT

The conduct of an audit should certainly cover a thorough review and testing of the first two areas of control as described above; that is, evaluation of the input-output controls and of the administrative controls over the computer operation itself. The techniques involved in the audit of these two areas are not particularly technical and, indeed, no

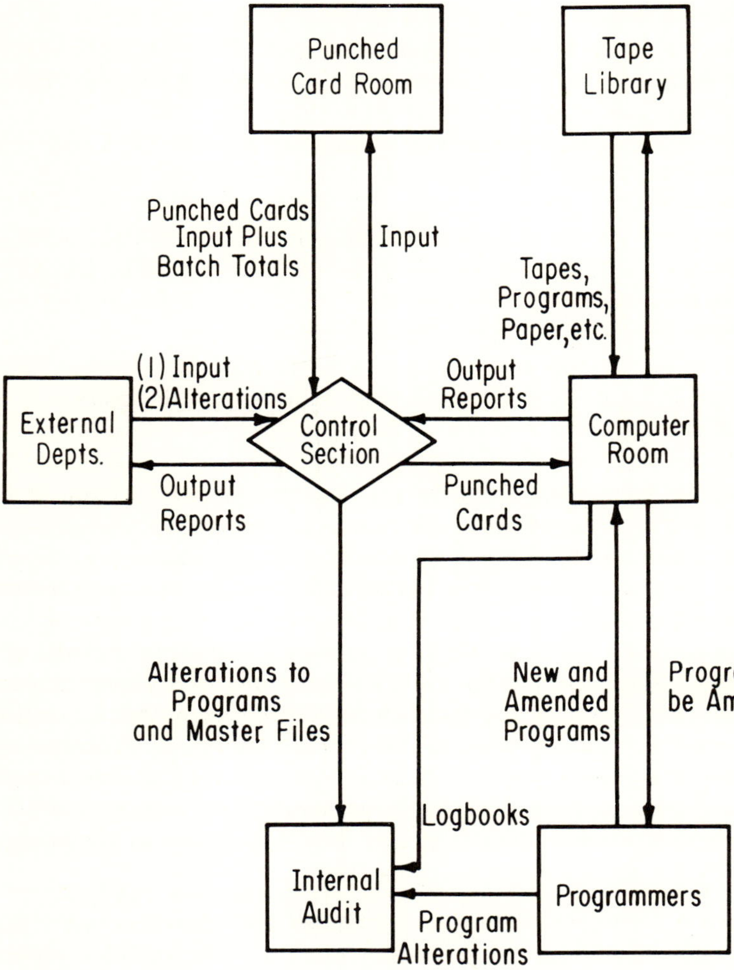

Figure 2-1. Organization of Functions for Control of EDP Data Flow. (Source: The Impact of Computers on Accounting. T.W. McRae.)

unusual training is required once the auditor has familiarized himself with the nature of these areas of control. Actual input controls can be compared against a list of those generally acceptable; organization must be reviewed for proper separation of duties; procedures employed must be written and understood.

It is in the third area—controls over actual computer programs—that the auditor generally experiences difficulty. In the past, a technique was employed which involved taking a sample of computer input and manually checking the validity of the output in terms of the pertinent input data. If the sample of output data was correct, the auditor assumes that all of the processing procedures were also correct and that they had sufficient control features.

With the growing complexity of computer programs, the greater use of exception reporting, and the trend toward integrated processing without separate printout between operations, it is necessary that the auditor now assume a direct responsibility for auditing the adequacy of the computer programs themselves. To an increasing degree, relying only upon the evaluation of an input-output sample will not represent an efficient or adequate check of the operating controls involved.

AUDIT REVIEW AND TESTS

The best time for initial audit review of computer programs is while the programs are being designed. In this manner the auditor may make suggestions for improved controls to be built into these programs—suggestions which could be extremely expensive to implement were they to be developed after the program was in operation. Some large companies, in addition to developing training programs and manuals for computer auditing, have established procedures whereby agreed-upon program documentation of all new computer accounting applications is forwarded to the internal audit department for evaluation of control requirements. Principal elements in this documentation generally consist of a flow chart showing the flow of data through the various processing steps, and a narrative description of the system, including the various control procedures over the processing within the computer.

In addition to evaluating controls incorporated in computer programs, the auditor needs techniques for testing transactions to insure that the programs, as written, are producing accurate and complete results in actual operation. The two techniques that have so far been found to be most practicable are sample testing (perhaps using the more refined statistical sampling techniques) and simulation. Indeed, statistical sampling can be aided by designing a computer program to select the proper sample.

For the auditor who has sufficient computer knowledge, probably the most desirable technique is simulation, using what are commonly referred to as "test decks." These "test decks" of punched cards or magnetic tape simulate actual transactions involved in the system's processing. They can be introduced into the system like actual transactions and are a relatively inexpensive method of testing transactions since no programming requirements are involved. The system, in effect, checks itself to insure that the necessary outputs are reliable, accurate and appropriate.

The computer also presents the auditor with a unique opportunity to use its services in performing many of the time-consuming tasks normally involved in an audit. Computer programs can be designed which will test the records maintained on magnetic tape and which will select data from a tape file and print it out for audit. Other computer programs can be designed which will perform such functions as comparison of activity between periods, measure actual versus budget figures, or material on hand versus normal stock levels.

One of the international oil companies has developed a computerized payroll audit program which prints out for the auditor all changes since the previous audit in master payroll tapes and also develops a statistical sample of those items to be given detailed audit verification. This same program also makes certain comparisons to test for such cases as salary or overtime outside of normal limits, incompatibility between base pay and income tax deductions or between base pay and employee savings deductions.

CHALLENGES AND OPPORTUNITIES

In review, ours is a changing world, changing at a technological rate that challenges comprehension. One of the prime motivators of this revolution has been the computer. The computer impact has been significant on business practices, and specifically on the accountant and auditor and the techniques utilized in the administration of their functions.

The accountant must accept the challenges posed by his changing environment. He must adapt to a new profession rather than continue an old one. He must provide management with unbiased, timely recommendations on day-to-day business activities and future predictions to optimize long-range plans and goals. If the accountant does not accept this premise or is not up to this responsibility, he runs the risk of being relegated to a restricted role as various organizations are formed to carry out these "management service" functions. Certainly these functions must be performed if the company is to wage a successful battle in the increasingly competitive world-wide marketplace.

Similarly, the auditor must recognize the full impact of the computer revolution. He must view a computer as a centralized tool of control previously not available to accomplish his objectives. A "through the computer" approach must be adopted along with the necessary knowledge involved to insure that factors of reliability, timeliness and control inherent in computer systems are realized.

Finally, the years ahead will be marked by opportunity. The accountant and the auditor have an unparalleled opportunity to exploit the utilization of the computer as the prime tool in servicing management's needs. This opportunity must be seized eagerly but with intelligence, lest we forget that the computer must supplement and complement, though not pre-empt, man's role in achieving his business objectives. As Gilbert Burck states in *The Computer Age:*

> The machines compel men to formulate their problems so much more intelligently and more thoroughly than they ever have that men can hardly be unaware of the shortcomings of their programs. . . . Nothing would make a company more vulnerable to smart competitors than to abdicate responsibility to the neat, clean, consistent judgments of a machine.

By keeping this belief basic to our professional philosophy, we can successfully respond to the changing accounting and auditing techniques demanded by the computer and other scientific devices.

EDP AND THE AUDITOR OF THE 1970'S

by John W. Wagner

In a profession as dynamic as auditing has become, it is certainly not too soon to begin speculating on the challenges EDP will present to the auditor of the 1970's. During the 1960's we have witnessed rapid technological advances in EDP, and there appears to be little doubt that the pace will accelerate. Accordingly, the purpose of this article is to indicate where the auditor currently stands in relation to EDP, and the extent to which this relationship is likely to change in the 1970's.

THE PRESENT SITUATION

At the present time, it is readily apparent that the EDP revolution has not produced the disaster for the auditing profession that so many people had expected. With few exceptions, computer systems are currently providing as many, if not more, paper records than the previous systems. The audit trail is still visible, or can usually be made visible, with relative ease. Auditing around the computer remains the rule rather

---

Reprinted by permission of the American Accounting Association from *The Accounting Review*, July 1969, pp. 600-604.

than the exception, and auditing through the computer is seldom a requirement that cannot be avoided. In fact, the profession has the situation so well in hand, one cannot help wondering how we achieved this surprising result in view of the expectations to the contrary.

Stated simply, the answer is that most of the expectations were not well founded. We intuitively felt that computers could add a whole new dimension to business management, and we assumed the possibilities would be quickly exploited. For instance, we expected highly sophisticated integrated management information systems to be developed and implemented rapidly. We expected business managers to welcome eagerly the use of completely new concepts in organizational structure, information technology, and management techniques. Faced with these expectations, we were understandably concerned with the impact these changes would have on the audit function.

As a matter of fact, few of these developments have taken place. The tremendous power of the computer has not been utilized, and the tremendous promise of the computer is still largely unfulfilled. With only a few notable exceptions, the basic change in information systems seems to have been that what was formerly done by manual or mechanical means is now being done by electronic computers. Since the underlying systems have been little affected fundamentally, the auditor has not been faced with any need for major changes in his procedures. There is small wonder then that the auditor has the situation so well in hand.

The auditor's present comfortable circumstances appear to be largely due to the fact that the development of sophisticated computer systems has lagged far behind the capabilities of the hardware. While a certain amount of systems lag seems inevitable, there are a number of unusual factors that appear to have accentuated the lag during the 1960's.

First, the 1960's are still a part of the beginning period for computer hardware. In the initial stages of any new invention, there are usually many relatively obvious ideas that can be developed rapidly. After these ideas have been exploited, improvements in the invention tend to become more complex and costly. Computer hardware has probably been benefiting from the advantages of its initial stage. Advances in hardware technology have been exceptionally rapid during the 1960's. This nonrecurring factor would, in part, justify a seeming lag in systems development.

Second, in order to sell the hardware during its initial stages of development, the manufacturers had to assume responsibility for conceiving how the hardware would be used as well as manufacturing it. Since the manufacturer's could not hope to become experts in every possible field of application, they tended simply to convert the existing systems to the computer. This tendency has been influential during most of the 1960's.

Third, most of the experts in the EDP area have received their computer training, directly or indirectly, from the manufacturers. They were either employed by the manufacturers, trained by them at a customer's computer facility, or trained by use of the manufacturers' literature. As previously noted, while the manufacturers know a great deal about the capabilities of their hardware, they are at an obvious disadvantage when trying to create sophisticated uses for it. As a result the education provided by the manufacturers tends to be hardware oriented. Graduates of this type of education know how to operate computers in detail. But unless they have previously attained expertise in some particular field of application, they are not likely to be leaders in imaginative systems development.

Fourth, during the 1960's, our EDP experts have been spread rather thinly. It takes a long time to acquire an expertise in EDP, and we are only now beginning to develop some backlog. Even so, the changes in hardware have been so rapid, that much of the EDP man's time has been spent trying to keep current with the field. As a result, very few resources have been available for creative or imaginative systems development.

Finally, sophisticated computer systems are still difficult to justify. During the 1960's, we have had sufficient problems in simply converting to computers. Attempts to implement dramatically new applications would only have added to the burdens. The benefits of new designs cannot be assured or often even measured. The costs cannot be accurately estimated, except that they will be high. In a really sophisticated system, the user is usually completely dependent on it because the application is not possible except by use of the computer. A breakdown in the computer or the system can therefore be disastrous. Consequently, the current initial stage of development has been one in which experience and confidence have been generated, but these have not as yet been translated into highly advanced systems designs.

On the basis of the foregoing, it seems rather clear that the auditor's present comfortable position relative to EDP is due more to the lack of certain types of achievement on the part of others than to his own spectacular accomplishments. No doubt, as EDP experience and insight are accumulated, the gap between hardware capability and systems design will be slowly closed. In short, many of the applications we were so fearfully anticipating in the 1960's will become realities in the 1970's—at a time when our present comfortable circumstances may have led us to believe that the computer will no longer seriously affect us.

THE FUTURE SITUATION

In a field as new and dynamic as EDP, statements about the future are, at best, imaginative guesses. But since some advanced planning is vital, the only safe choice is to confine ourselves to statements about the very broadest trends.

The major trend of the 1970's will probably be an increased emphasis on software development. The major disappointments of the 1960's have come primarily from the fact that the capabilities of the existing hardware have not been adequately utilized. The growing number of experienced software companies and consulting firms gives promise that more resources will be devoted to developing sophisticated systems during the 1970's.

By simply increasing the utilization of existing hardware capabilities, the following additional trends are suggested. There will be:

- greater integration of information systems.
- more on-line real-time systems.
- more time sharing and use of service centers.
- less need for operator intervention during processing.
- more transmission of data directly from one computer system to another.
- more use of optical scanning and less need for human conversion of input data.
- more input initially created in the form of electronic impulses, and less use of hardcopy source documents.
- more use of television display units for output, and less need for hardcopy printouts.
- more economical means of storing data in microelectronic form for long periods of time, thereby further eliminating hardcopy and its storage problems.

These trends can be expected to have a number of important effects on the audit function. Some of these effects will be detrimental and some beneficial.

AUDITING THROUGH THE COMPUTER

One of the major effects will be an increased difficulty in avoiding auditing through the computer. At present, the audit trail tends to *go to* the computer rather than through it. Input data are, in general, processed sequentially in batches with sequential files of information being accumulated after each major step. In their present status, these files stored on magnetic tapes, disks, or hardcopy printouts, provide a well documented, easily followed, sequential information trail from input to output. In short, the computer is presently being used fairly often as if it were a piece of high speed tabulating equipment, and the audit trail, which parallels the information trail, exists as an appendage relatively separable from the computer system itself.

In the future, the audit trail will cease to be a separable appendage in many more cases. Integration of information systems will make the relationship between input and output more complex. Data, whether introduced sequentially or randomly, will simultaneously update numerous files in a variety of ways. The audit trail will, therefore, become an interwoven tangle of programmed relationships. In addition, automation of computer operations by use of programmed operating systems will reduce the need for conversion of data to man-sensible form at various stages of the processing. Use of television displays and real-time access to information will reduce the need for hardcopy printouts. Consequently, while the audit trail will still exist, it will literally go through the computer.

ELECTRONIC DOCUMENTS

Another major effect will be an increased need for the auditor to accept and comprehend, as evidential material, source documents in a new form. At the source level, the auditor is presently accustomed to examining paper documents on which the data and authorization for a transaction are presented in man-sensible form. Data of this type must be converted to machine-sensible form before it can be processed by the computer system.

In the future, the need for conversion will be eliminated because the source data will be initially recorded in the form of electronic impulses. The data will be introduced into the system on the keyboard of a direct input device. Authorization will be indicated through the use of a key to unlock the device, a plastic plate, a symbolic recognition code, or a combination of these or other techniques. After being subjected to some programmed control checks, both the data and the authorization will be recorded as electronic impulses. Thus, while evidential material will be created for the auditor, it will not be in its usual common-sense paper document form.

USING THE COMPUTER IN AUDITING

Probably, the most beneficial effect the trends of the 1970's will have on the audit function concerns the use of the computer as an audit tool. There are two basic factors which will tend to cause an increasing necessity and value in the greater use of the computer by the auditor.

The first factor again involves the gradual change from paper to electronic documentation. Computer files consisting of magnetic tapes, disks, and data cells already store data in electronic form. In the future, as more input becomes electronic through the use of direct input devices, and more output is viewed by television displays, there will be even less need for paper documents. This does not mean the auditor will no longer be able to examine and test documents, but only that he will have to perform these tests in a new way. Since there will be no paper documents to test manually, he will test electronic documents electronically. In other words, the computer will be used routinely as a tool in the performance of an audit on a computer system.

The second factor promoting the use of the computer is the nature of auditing itself. In auditing, a highly reliable opinion must be rendered on the basis of a relatively small and selective set of samples. Even when the auditor scans a large file of data, he is usually looking for exceptional situations requiring more detailed analyses. Given these requirements, it is inefficient to require the computer system to produce a mass of printouts when the auditor is concerned with only a relatively few items. If, instead, the auditor would stipulate the characterisitcs of these items, the computer would do his scanning for him—in less time, in greater detail, with more extensive tests of all items, and with improved clerical accuracy.

There are several advantages to this approach. First, it does not require the client to make extensive special printouts for the exclusive use of the auditor. Equally important, it uses the computer as a powerful audit tool, and improves the quality of the audit itself. Of course, this approach is already being used to some extent, e.g., in selecting accounts for confirmation, checking extensions, and comparing physical counts of inventory to the perpetual records. But, as previously noted, there has, as yet, been no real urgency, and so developments have not been very extensive in this area. However, as more of the audit trail is irrevocably merged into the computer system, and more of the data is created and stored in electronic form, use of the computer in auditing will be increasingly necessary and profitable.

CONCLUDING COMMENTS

Even assuming the 1970's produce a rapid implementation of sophisticated information systems, there are internal and external factors that will help the auditor meet the challenge.

Externally, other responsible groups have much the same problems as auditors have. For instance, no matter how the systems of the future are designed, management will still have to maintain adequate control over them. Designers of systems may convert the information and audit trails exclusively to electronic form, but regardless of their form, the trails must remain for control purposes. In addition, the Internal Revenue Service already requires that every system "must provide the opportunity to trace any transaction back to the original source and forward to a final total." It seems clear, therefore, that the audit trail will not literally disappear, although it may appear to do so to those who do not acquire an adequate knowledge of the EDP area.

Internally, the profession has developed some momentum in dealing with the auditing aspects of EDP. We have our share of the available EDP experts, and we have several short EDP orientation courses in the professional development program. But it is quite apparent that we are just beginning to "scratch the surface" in relation to our educational needs in the EDP area. However, we have had sufficient experience to recognize that the advent of sophisticated computer systems is primarily a problem in professional development, and not a threat to our existence. If the time provided by the slow progress in developing sophisticated systems is used wisely in professional development, there is little question we can meet the challenges that EDP will present in the 1970's.

THE AUDITOR AND THE COMPUTER

by Gordon B. Davis

The certified public accountant may perform many functions related to data processing—design of data processing systems, furnishing of data processing services, consultation on system design and auditing. This article is directed solely at his function as independent auditor of organizations with computer-based data processing systems.

THE IMPACT OF THE COMPUTER ON DATA PROCESSING

The computer is one of the most important technological developments of the twentieth century. Its uses and capabilities have been described in both popular and technical publications, so that it is not neces-

---

Reprinted by permission of the publisher from *The Journal of Accountancy,* March 1968, pp. 44-47, copyright 1968 by the American Institute of Certified Public Accountants, Inc.

sary to document the importance of computers in this article. The impact of computers on public accounting can be appreciated by noting the dramatic growth in numbers of computer installations for the period 1956-1967 (Figure 2-2). Computer installation estimates from different sources vary by about 20 per cent, depending on the treatment of small computer-like equipment, but the figures show a clear trend in the use of computers. The impact of computers has been predicted for several years; the major effects have been in the last few years. Although the first commercially available computer was installed in 1951 and the first business installation was in 1954, the popular business-oriented computers can be dated from the early 1960's. Over half of the computers in place in mid-1967 had been installed in the preceding three years. The outlook was for the number of computer installations to double in the succeeding three to four years. The decreasing cost of computer equipment plus the development, now in embryonic states, of computer-sharing arrangements clearly portend computer use by an increasing number of

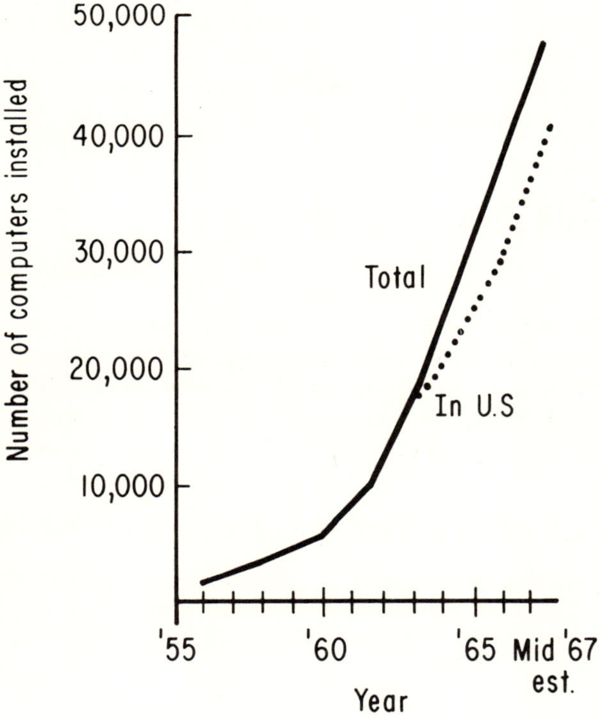

Figure 2-2. Number of Computers Installed by U.S.-Based Companies from 1956 to 1967.

organizations and an involvement with computer-based records by more and more CPA firms.

The computer has caused significant changes in business information systems, expanding both scope and operation. The first computer data processing systems tended merely to computerize existing clerical functions. Soon, however, systems embracing larger areas of the business and incorporating decision-oriented analytical techniques not practicable in clerical systems began to be implemented. Thus, although many computer data processing systems merely automate the prior manual processes, the trend is plainly toward higher level information systems. The auditor, therefore, frequently faces not only a computer but new system concepts as well.

AN OVERVIEW OF AUDITING FOR EDP SYSTEMS

The impact that computers have had on the audit process varies among clients and is dependent to a great extent on the level of complexity of the computer data processing system. A simple system may so resemble the predecessor card or manual system that the auditor has very little difficulty in adapting his audit procedure to the computerized system. A more complex computer-based system may require considerable computer expertise on the part of the auditor for understanding the system he is evaluating and for planning his audit tests.

It is logical to suppose that auditing standards, which have been established in the light of the primary objective of auditing, are independent of the personnel or machines used to process and maintain the accounting and financial records. The auditing standards must be broadly based in order to have applicability to a wide range of audit situations. However, they still relate specifically to each audit examination since they refer to an acceptable level of quality which must be maintained by the auditor in the selection and application of appropriate auditing procedures. Hence, auditing standards are also guides to procedures.

Auditing procedures are affected by the presence of a computer, especially when the system is complex. In describing these effects it will be useful to structure the discussion in terms of the major phases of an audit examination: (1) the evaluation of the system of internal control and (2) the evaluation of the records produced by the data processing system.

If he is to deal effectively with the computer, the auditor should have computer knowledge and capability at two levels: (1) a knowledge of computers and computer-based data processing sufficient to review adequately the internal control of the system he is auditing, to conduct proper tests of the system and to evaluate the quality of the records and (2) an ability to use the computer itself in the tests, if necessary or desirable. Whether or not the computer should be used in performing audit tests depends on the applicability, effectiveness and cost of the alternatives for each particular situation.

EVALUATING INTERNAL CONTROL

EDP does not lessen in any way the need for an evaluation of the system of internal control. On the contrary, it appears that increased emphasis must be given in the review of internal control to ascertain that it is effective. The need for this emphasis has been brought about by the centralization and the concentration of data processing in an EDP system and the appearance of new controls that must be evaluated.

The evaluation of internal control rests on a review of the system to obtain a knowledge of how it is purported to operate and on an accumulation of evidence which demonstrates how it actually does operate. The manner in which the auditor seeks the necessary information and records it in his working papers is largely a matter of individual preference. Techniques used for this purpose include questionnaires, checklists, flowcharts and narrative memorandums.

Having obtained information on the system, the auditor must next obtain evidence to determine the existence and effectiveness of the client's processing procedures and controls. This is done by making tests of the performance of specific control procedures. The nature and availability of evidence and the types of tests to be performed depend somewhat upon the complexity of the system design and upon the audit trail found in the electronic system being audited. In some cases, the evaluation of the operation of the data processing system may emphasize direct testing of the processing programs; in other cases, the evaluation may rely largely on tests using printed output from the computer processing runs.

EVALUATING RECORDS PRODUCED BY THE SYSTEM

In addition to evaluating the system of data processing and control, the auditor must evaluate the reasonableness of those records produced by the system which relate to the existence and proper valuation of assets, liabilities, equities and transactions. Historically, the records evaluated have consisted of printed reports, listings, documents and business papers—all of which were readable by the auditor. To the extent that such records are available in electronic systems, the auditor may use traditional auditing techniques. However, part of the output from EDP systems is very frequently in machine-readable forms such as cards, tapes and disks. Although output in this form can always be converted to readable printout, it presents the auditor with an opportunity to use the computer to analyze the records.

Computer audit programs can assist in the performance of auditing procedures such as: (1) selection of exceptional transactions and accounts for examination, (2) comparison of data for correctness and consistency, (3) checking of information obtained directly by the auditor with company records, (4) performance of arithmetic and clerical functions and (5) preparation of confirmations. In using the computer to analyze machine-readable records, the auditor may either design and develop specific computer programs for each client and application or use generalized audit routines.

THE EFFECT OF THE COMPUTER ON DATA PROCESSING CONTROLS

It is incorrect, from an audit standpoint, to view the computer as a giant calculator. The installation of a computer introduces new control elements and causes changes in the form of traditional control procedures in the data processing system. These changes in controls may be classified as:

1. New controls necessary with the automation of processing.
2. Controls which substitute for those controls in manual systems that were based on human judgment and division of duties.

The auditor needs to understand the nature of these controls in order to properly evaluate and test the computer data processing system. The changes in data processing controls due to the computer are an important reason why the auditor cannot ignore the computer in his evaluation of internal control.

New controls are necessary because of mechanization. Their purpose is to detect and control errors arising from the use of EDP equipment and EDP-processing methods. If these controls are absent, the system may be exposed to undue risk of error. If the omissions are considered to be serious, the scope of the audit procedures is influenced.

In a manual system, internal control relies upon such factors as human alertness, care, acceptance of responsibility and division of duties. Computer processing reduces the number of persons involved in data processing. Since the data processing activity is concentrated, many controls based on human judgment or division of duties are no longer available. However, for many checks, the computer program provides an alternative which substitutes for the judgment of humans engaged in processing. In most instances, the computer checks can be more extensive than those performed manually. The presence or absence in a computer-based system of controls such as those which substitute for human judgment or division of duties should influence the nature and extent of auditing procedures used in the circumstances.

The determination of the extent to which controls are embodied in the computer programs and the testing to determine if they are operative may utilize different techniques depending on the circumstances. One common method makes inferences about the program and the controls in it from an examination of inputs and outputs; the other method relies on a rather complete understanding and testing of the program itself.

It has been a common practice for an organization making changes in data processing methods to seek the help of its auditing firm in designing the changes or in reviewing proposed changes for adequacy of controls. This practice has also been followed by many organizations when implementing computer applications. The pre-implementation control review is recommended because of both the probable value of an outside review of control features and the contribution of such a review to the planning of future audit procedures.

In his review of the control features in a proposed application, the auditor can point out probable weaknesses in the controls and in provisions for audit trail and safeguarding files. Making these suggestions at the time the system is being designed will help prevent undetected errors, loss of data, loss of files and other serious conditions which affect not only the client's processing but also the ability of the auditor to conduct the audit.

A NOTE ON EMPHASIS

It has been common in the recent literature of auditing to refer to two approaches to auditing computer-based systems—"auditing around the computer" and "auditing through the computer." These terms have been avoided in this article because they tend to be misleading. "Auditing around the computer" may imply to some that the auditor can ignore the computer and work around it. This is not true. The auditor should always consider the control framework in which the computer processing is carried out. In his tests of the operation of the system, he may choose to use computer printouts as the basis for audit tests rather than to test the computer program directly. For a test of the records produced by the computer system, the auditor may have the records printed out for manual review or he may make use of a computer routine to test them in their machine-readable form. In other words, he may use computer printouts in much the same way as he would use manually prepared records, or he may utilize the computer itself in performing audit steps. Consequently, this report distinguishes between auditing a computer system without using the computer and auditing a computer system using the computer.

The question of whether or not to use the computer in audit tests usually depends on the effectiveness and cost of the computer procedure versus the effectiveness and cost of the manual alternatives. This article does not favor one method over the other. The auditor should be capable of using the computer for audit tests when its use is advisable, just as he should be capable of testing without using the computer when its use is not advisable. Generally, it is not necessary or economical to use the computer to test simple data processing systems or to test files with small numbers of records. Audit tests of advanced systems or of files with large numbers of machine-readable records are more likely to require the use of the computer.

MEETING THE CHALLENGE

Perhaps the major difficulty faced by auditing firms relative to audits of computer-based records is the staffing of audits with personnel adequately trained in computer methods. Relatively few auditors have received instruction in computer methods as part of their formal training, so the profession must provide substantial training for existing personnel in order to ensure an adequate number of auditors competent to conduct audits in an EDP environment.

If an audit involves a computer, the CPA must have sufficient competence in the methods and techniques of auditing EDP systems to enable him to conduct the audit properly. The proficiency requirement implied by this statement varies depending on the complexity of the system being audited. An audit of a company having a small, batch-oriented data processing installation requires less proficiency than an audit involving a complex, integrated computer system. Not all members of the audit team need be equally competent. In general, the audit of a computer-based system requires the auditor to possess a good basic understanding of computers and computer data processing methods. A specific understanding on the part of the auditor of computer facility organization, documentation, controls, safeguards and computer system audit techniques is also important. The approach followed by many firms is to have one or more members of the staff specialize in computer audit problems.

SUMMARY

Computers have been commercially available for over 15 years, yet the recency of the major impact can be appreciated by noting that at mid-1967 over half of all computers had been installed in the preceding three years. The number is expected to double again in the next three years. Although much has been written about the impact of computers on the auditor, many CPAs are just beginning to be affected.

This article provides an overview of the auditing of an organization using a computer for recordkeeping. The auditor may not properly ignore the computer in the audit—first, because the computer requires its own set of controls related to automated procedures and, second, because many controls normally resulting from division of duties and human review and judgment are now concentrated in the computer programs. The auditor may use the computer in carrying out audit procedures but this is frequently optional, depending on the characteristics of the system and the cost and effectiveness of this alternative. The auditor should be capable of choosing and implementing the best method for each data processing application and each particular audit test.

PART TWO

Controlling Computerized Applications

3

Organizational Considerations

Computer-based information systems offer new organizational options to top management. The organization may change in an attempt to realize operational and strategic advantages; the information flow can then be designed to support the desired organizational patterns.

The general impact of the computer on organization structure is difficult to assess. Predictions of a high degree of centralization have been premature because, perhaps, they did not anticipate the long, costly process of developing the total information systems that would be required.

Segments of the organization whose work was predominately the processing of a large volume of data have felt the impact of the computer through reductions in size and combinations with other activities.

Another trend is toward centralization of the computer activity. The superior performance of large computers, the desire to build integrated corporate data banks, and the reduced costs of long-distance data transmission are strong forces underlying this trend.

The benefits of centralized application development can be even more attractive. Development costs of advanced systems are large and highly trained personnel are scarce. The redundancy in system development tolerated a decade ago may be no longer acceptable.

Changing organizational patterns present an opportunity to strengthen internal control partly because of the increased formalization of procedures. The increased size of the centralized data processing staff also permits specialization, separation of function, and standardization *within* the activity. Such changes, difficult to secure in smaller decentralized groups, are a welcome correlate of centralization and growth.

DATA PROCESSING'S EVOLVING PLACE IN THE ORGANIZATION

by Frederick G. Withington

In the good old days data processing functions fit easily into organizations—computational functions into engineering or R&D, accounting functions into the comptroller's organization; nobody had a problem. The advent of the integrated system with time-shared and data-base-oriented management information capabilities has changed the picture, though. The old arrangements do not seem to work anymore, a variety of organizational experiments are being made, and a trend seems to be emerging. The purpose of this article is to explore the forces at work and present what appears to be the consensus about the desirable new organizational pattern.

In early 1968, Arthur D. Little, Inc., conducted a private survey of eight large, multidivisional organizations. In all eight, computers had been used for 10 years or more, and in all eight the initial pattern of computer management was completely decentralized. In the 1964-1965 period each had computers and programming groups scattered among its divisions. Each group was then entirely independent of any other, and reported only to its divisional management. Corporate-level computing resources were rare, and where they existed their sole function was to fill special data processing needs of corporate management.

Between 1964-1965 and early 1968, the eight organizations had changed as follows:

Three had completely centralized system analysis and programming. All computer personnel received their assignments from corporate headquarters, though in two of the three they were still physically located in the divisions. Computers were still dispersed through the divisions, but their procurement, operation, and management were also controlled by corporate data processing management.

Three of the organizations had centralized systems analysis and programming of standardized interdivisional programs, but still permitted divisions to develop programs for internal use. In each, about half of the corporation's computer personnel were located in the corporate staff, and about half in the divisions. In all three corporations, as time passed, one after another of the important data processing functions were being redefined as company standards or interdivisional applications, and thus

---

Reprinted by permission of the publisher from *Datamation*, vol. 15, no. 6 (June 1969), pp. 58-63.

being transferred from divisional control to corporate control. However, in each corporation both divisional and corporate management believed that there would always be unique programs required by single divisions and that some programming resources would always remain in the divisions.

Two of the eight companies remained decentralized, with all data processing personnel distributed among the divisions and reporting to divisional management. In both, however, there was more corporate influence on divisional data processing than there had been three years earlier. Corporate data processing groups had been established to "consult with and assist" the divisional data processing groups in evaluation and acquisition of advanced equipment, in solving problems and in personnel matters. In both cases, the corporate data processing group had been asked to establish improved systems of accounting codes for uniform financial reporting throughout the divisions.

In summary, all eight of the organizations started with completely decentralized computer programming and operations. Three of the eight had become completely centralized, three others were partly centralized and becoming increasingly so, and the two that remained decentralized have established centralized "consulting" groups whose influence was increasing.

As this study convincingly shows, there is a strong trend in large multidivisional organizations toward centralizing the management of the data processing resource (in smaller organizations, it would necessarily be more centralized from the start). The reasons why this is so are not difficult to perceive; there seem to be three primary ones.

DESIRE FOR STANDARDIZATION

Obviously large organizations will make some effort to standardize data processing procedures, if only to reduce wasteful duplication. But how are standards established, and how is compliance with them enforced? No one division is in a position to consider the needs or observe the performance of other divisions equitably; it is almost mandatory that a corporate staff group perform the function. It follows, however, that the corporate staff group will "meddle" in the data processing procedures of the divisions and must seek authority to enforce compliance with its standardized procedures if it cannot obtain compliance voluntarily. As the following true story suggests friction may result.

An aerospace company with five geographically separated divisions had its corporate headquarters at the site of the largest division. All five divisions had installed computers at one time or another. In two divisions the computers performed both business data processing and engineering computations, while in the other three relatively small computers performed business data processing alone.

Corporate management, as part of an attempt to revitalize the company, instituted a "profit central organization" across divisional lines to provide more responsive and explicit measurements of performance, and to increase operational flexibility. In support of this profit center organization, they developed a computer-based accounting and reporting system in which all activities and charges were reported in a uniform, detailed manner and measured against anticipated performance. Management assigned the authority for development and installation of the standardized reporting system to a corporate staff group especially established for the purpose.

At the same time, management became aware of the existence of large time-shared computers that could perform both engineering computation and data manipulation for management more responsively than the relatively simple machines the divisions had installed. Management was attracted to the time-sharing concept, and wanted to study the desirability of replacing the separate divisional computers with a large, time-shared central one available through remote input-output devices to all the profit centers in all the divisions. Since this replacement of equipment would universally affect every computer and every program, management understood that the study would be a long and complex one, best performed by an objective, central group.

In view of these two considerations, management decided to assign complete authority over the corporation's data processing functions to the corporate staff group initially established to develop the new financial reporting system. The head of this group was entitled "corporate director of data processing"; he reported directly to the executive vice president for operations. Some thought was given to making the post subordinate to the corporate comptroller, but since a primary concern was with the computing support of research and engineering activities, and also since it was anticipated that computers would be used more extensively in production and industrial applications, it was judged desirable to separate the post from any one functional affiliation.

Since the corporate headquarters were at the site of the largest division with the largest programming staff, it was convenient to transfer the staff and equipment from divisional control to that of the new director. The computers and personnel of the outlying divisions were also organizationally subordinated to the director, but for the time being they continued to respond mostly to their divisional managers.

The first difficulty arose when the corporate director began to assign the most senior system analysts from the divisions to develop new corporate-wide procedures. There were objections from the divisions these system analysts had previously served that they could not be spared from pressing divisional assignments. The manager of the central division was particularly concerned because, as he pointed out, the other four remotely located divisions continued to obtain most of the services of the data processing personnel they originally had, while his central division, by accident of physical co-location with headquarters, had lost the use of its computer personnel to the new directorate. The director had to concede the justice of this contention, and began to make up his system development teams for corporate applications using personnel from the remote divisions as well as from the central one. He also found occasion to borrow a few people from the remote divisions to apply to an important problem of the central division, thereby demonstrating that under some circumstances they could gain as well as lose by the organizational change. Each of these borrowings was accompanied by a struggle with the affected management, though, so the director did less borrowing than he had expected. He also postponed the planned study of a centralized, time-shared computer because he now perceived that the standardized programs for it would require years to develop.

The next difficulty arose when the standardized financial reporting system was ready for implementation and was presented to the divisional managers. To a man, they rejected it as inapplicable to their unique operations, too time consuming and difficult to support, and requiring a change from existing methods so radical as to be impracticable. A process of negotiation ensued in which:

The diplomatic ability of the director of data processing was tested;

The ability of his system analysts to develop a single, universally applicable coding system from a mass of divergent detailed requirements was tested; and

The determination of top management to persevere with the installation of the common profit center system was tested.

At the time this is written it is still not clear what the final result will be. It is clear, however, that the process of centralizing the data processing organization in the interests of standardizing procedures and equipment has brought with it a host of problems.

SHORTAGE OF PERSONNEL

Few organizations have as many programmers and systems analysts as they would like. For many, the shortage grows worse rather than better as they attempt increasingly ambitious computer applications. Even though new personnel are continually hired, the most experienced are likely to leave for better opportunities elsewhere. The increased technical demands of advanced systems (e.g., data communications technology, time-sharing computer systems, and the accompanying software) call for knowledge and experience not found among most companies' programmers. Companies therefore tend to find that the quality and quantity of their computer-trained personnel is an increasingly tight constraint. In order to use the personnel optimally, they find themselves compelled to bring them under central management so that they can be assigned to the most important projects of the whole company rather than just to those of divisions.

This process is exemplified by the case of a certain large electric utility holding company, which consists of many semi-autonomous local electric utilities operating under a corporate management that views its role as that of over-all financial manager for the group. The individual companies have for years been installing and using computers for engineering, accounting and customer billing functions. The corporate management appreciated that the companies were duplicating one another's data processing efforts by preparing programs many times over for such functions as customer billing, and knew that savings would result from doing them centrally. However, they felt that the healthy competition they were able to foster among the companies benefited all by improving the quality of the programs, and that, in principle, any interference in the management of the individual companies would do more harm than good.

One by one, the affiliated companies have become interested in advanced computer systems. In most cases, they are interested in time-shared computer systems with inquiry consoles in the offices where customer service and billing matters are handled. The clerks, using the inquiry consoles, can obtain complete and up-to-date information so that better service can be provided when a customer calls with a question or request for service. These time-shared computers involve more complex equipment and programs than the companies are used to. They cost more than previous computers did, and much of the experience of the companies' programmers is not applicable. Corporate management discovered to their sorrow that the price of duplication had become unreasonable, since there were no more than a handful of computer programmers and system analysts throughout the corporation who were experienced with time-shared systems.

Reluctantly, and after much study of the problem, corporate management instituted a centralized data processing authority to develop standard programs to be used throughout the company for the time-shared customer service applications, and transferred the few experts in time-shared computers to the corporate authority. As far as possible they left other applications in the hands of the affiliates, but they appreciate that once the present effort is successful other corporate-wide time-shared computer-applications will almost surely follow. Also, now that the thrust of new application development is shifted to the corporate staff, it is there that most improvement in experience and ability will occur rather than in the affiliates.

The company has instituted centralized control over their data processing, and knows it will grow, but they did not and do not want to do so. They assert that they saw no alternative, that the shortage of competent personnel forced them to standardize programs and manage the personnel resources centrally.

GROWTH OF APPLICATIONS COMPLEXITY

This problem, associated with the shortage of personnel, derives from organizations' desires to institute steadily more complex computer applications. In the case of the electric utility holding company, the shortage of personnel would not have been so severe if the company had not become convinced that time-shared systems were desirable. Such advanced systems usually incorporate data from more than one functional part of a company, and serve more than one functional part. As the applications of computers spread across the business it becomes impossible for a functionally-oriented group to deal with them, to have a balanced knowledge of the several functions, or to avoid parochial viewpoints. Only the company-wide view of corporate management is appropriate. A vivid example of the need for this view is found in an automated bakery which installed a computer for controlling production and for operating its freezer warehouse. After considerable effort the production control and warehouse operations were running well, and the team of production department people who had developed the computer programs decided to undertake more advanced applications. They felt that the next step was to tie in their production control system with the ordering of raw materials for production, so that the inventory management and production scheduling could be performed as a single process.

While the production department's team was developing its computer applications, another team within the comptroller's department developed a set of financially oriented computer programs. Starting with the payroll and conventional accounting procedures, this team, too, had progressed steadily toward more sophisticated computer applications. They had successfully programmed the purchasing and accounts receivable functions of the company, and decided that their next step, too, was the management of raw materials inventories. They felt that since they were responsible for the purchasing system and for the company's financial resources it was logical for them to control the expenditure of money for raw materials. The production people did not see it that way; they felt that the ordering and management of raw materials was a natural by-product of the physical needs of production schedules for which they were responsible.

Both parties agreed that each had to work closely with the other's programs and data, but each felt that it should be in charge of the effort because its contribution was the most important. Corporate management found this confusing, and was unable to decide in favor of either of the parties. Finally, with the advice of a team of consultants they decided to do away with both the production and the financial computer programming groups, and to merge them into a single one reporting to corporate management. This radical change was intended to eliminate the cause of the disagreement, and management hoped that the two groups would find a way to work together on the new, broader computer applications that necessarily transcended the old functional lines.

Enough large organizations have completed their change to centralized data processing to make clear the general form of the new organizations. As Dean found in a survey of 108 manufacturing organizations,[1] the trend is toward the establishment of a central data processing executive (sometimes a vice president, sometimes not—a frequent bone of contention) reporting directly to the top management of an organization. This executive is explicitly not placed within any of the functional departments of the organization, because the applications for which he will be responsible will transcend functional lines. The programming and system analysis resources of the company report directly to him; thus, perhaps for the first time, a significant line function is found reporting directly to the office of the president or the executive vice president. In many cases, large organizations also permit groups of programmers and system analysts to remain physically dispersed among the departments, partly because of the inconvenience of and resistance to wholesale moving, and partly because computer applications remain that affect only individual departments which may still be permitted to be implemented entirely within the department. However, in all cases these personnel are subject to assignment by the central authority, and if a corporate-wide project requires their services it almost invariably takes priority over a departmental project.

Most large organizations have (so far) continued to use numerous

---

[1]Neal J. Dean, "The Computer Comes of Age," *Harvard Business Review*, January-February 1968.

computers located where the work is, rather than completely centralized computing equipment at corporate headquarters. In cases where the files to be used by corporate management dictate their consolidation in one place, the computers follow; but as long as the files of information pertaining to the departments, plants and dispersed facilities are primarily updated by and used by personnel there, economics invariably indicate that the equipment should remain there, too. The reasons for this are simple: long distance data communications are expensive, there is mutual interference between large numbers of different kinds of jobs run at the same time on the same machine, and there is competition for priority of service. This does not mean, however, that the departments have any more control over the equipment than they have over the personnel. Because of standardization of programs (and often equipment), and because of the increasing difficulty of evaluating and selecting new types of equipment and programs, the specification of equipment and control of its operational use are also performed by the corporate authority. The equipment, then, is located wherever the work is; but the kind of equipment selected, the programs for it, and the way it is used are under complete central control.

EMERGING STRUCTURE

The accompanying figure depicts the approximate organization structure that seems to emerge. Naturally, peculiarities of particular organizations cause variations from this general structure; even the personal characteristics of the managers involved may do so. However, this figure is sufficiently representative to be instructive.

The corporate director of data processing reports to the executive vice president or whatever corporate executive is responsible for the organization's operations. Sometimes this is the president; sometimes it is the senior financial executive, but only in cases where the senior financial executive has broad corporate responsibility. The trend is unquestionably away from affiliating data processing with financial management. Dean's study supports this, and other impressive evidence is provided by a survey published by the Japan Computer Usage Development Institute[2] which contrasts the organizational status of computer installations in Japan with those in the United States; 157 Japanese firms were surveyed and 250 American. In 62% of the Japanese organizations, the computer operation reported directly to central management; this was

---

[2]*Computer Utilization in Japan,* published by Japan Computer Usage Development Institute, 1967.

true in only 6% of the American firms. By contrast, the finance or accounting department was responsible for computer operations in only 18% of the Japanese firms whereas 78% of the American firms assigned computer operations to the financial management function. These figures would tend to prove conclusively that there is no intrinsic association between data processing and the financial function—that the traditional association between the two in America has arisen more from habit than from intrinsic desirability.

In the United States, to a much greater degree than in any other country, the computer was preceded by less versatile data processing techniques—punched card systems, accounting machines and the like—that were used almost exclusively for accounting and financial data processing. In most organizations these were the only data processing machines in use at the time the computer was first introduced, and it

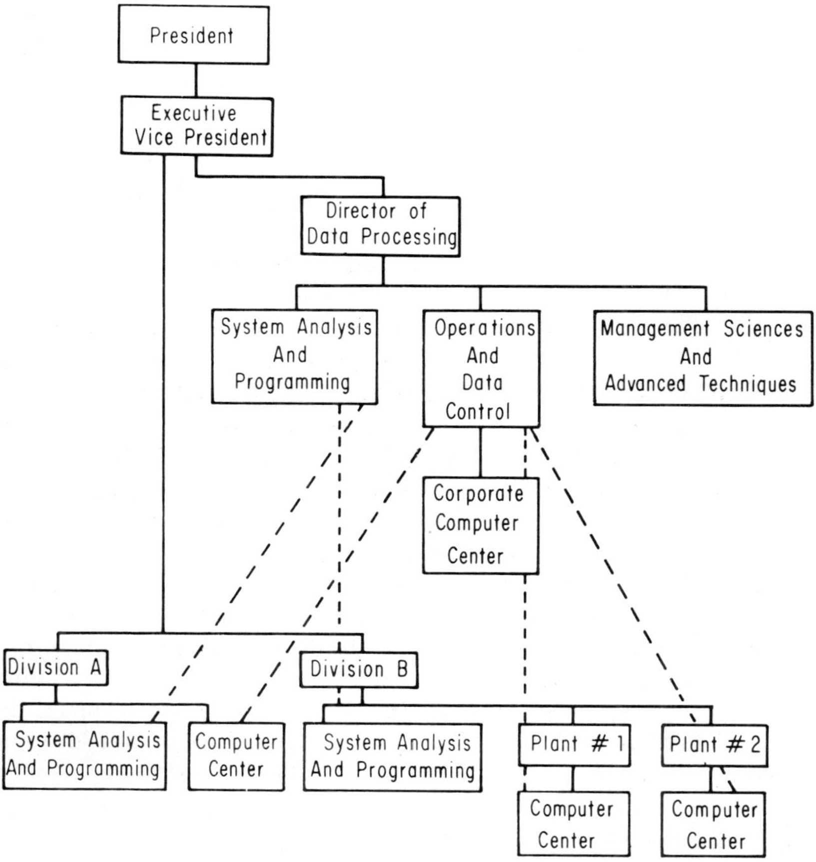

Figure 3-1.

was natural to apply the experience of the personnel in the financial organization to installing and operating the new (and, initially, apparently similar) tool. It has now become apparent that the computer tends to outgrow the inevitably somewhat parochial viewpoint of finance, and associate itself with the broader viewpoint of the central management group.

The system analysis and programming functions report to the director of data processing. Most system analysts and programmers are centralized and report directly to him. These people work on the organization's standard programs and those directly supporting corporate management. They also spend part of their time on programs designed to support individual divisions. If the staff is large, as it typically is in a large organization, system analysis and programming may well constitute two separate and co-equal organizational units rather than one as shown here. However, some organizations prefer to keep all systems analysts and programmers in a "pool" and assign them as teams; there seems to be no clear trend one way or the other.

DEVELOPMENT GROUP

Operations and data control is responsible for the operation of the corporate computer center in the usual manner, and a third group, here called "management sciences and advanced techniques," also reports to the director of data processing. It takes many names and is sometimes more than one unit, but its functions are always more or less the same. This group is responsible for the evaluation and development of hypothetical and experimental data processing techniques that might be used by the organization in the farther future. Usually, the operations research analysts of the company will be found in such a group, and the personnel engaged in the development of simulation models, optimizing techniques, and the like. As these applications become demonstrably feasible and can be selected for definite adoption, responsibility for their detailed planning and implementation moves over to the system analysis and programming group. The advanced techniques of data processing go hand in hand; the same personnel are likely to be associated with both areas.

The organization may have any number of divisions; two are shown here arbitrarily, reporting through the executive vice president to the president. Because each probably has an identity, geographic location, and product line of its own, it will have data processing applications unique to it. Each is therefore permitted to retain a system analysis and programming group to be devoted to divisional programs, or to assisting the corporate group with implementation of standard programs as the relative priorities dictate. The final authority over the assignment of these people necessarily resides in the director of data processing, but he usually finds it necessary to be responsive to the desires of divisional management.

This "tug of war" between the demands of the corporate group and the demands of divisional management for the services of the data processing personnel on division staffs is obviously a potential source of continuing difficulty, but most organizations seem to find this compromise arrangement preferable to either total concentration of the people in a single location or to total decentralization. It is often observed that a continuing competition for resources leads to a healthy, continuing re-examination of project priorities.

As indicated above, the computers are found where their work is. A single computer center is shown for division A, and for division B two computer centers located at manufacturing plants. Each of these is responsible, above all, for providing adequate service to the plant or division served. However, each is also responsible to the director for satisfactory operation of standard procedures and for maintenance of the accounting control and personnel standards established by the director. Here again is a source of friction; authority over the computer centers is divided between the "customer" directly served (the plant, or division) and the central directorate which establishes and monitors the methods of performing the work. Friction occurs, but again most large organizations seem to have found this divided authority preferable to either one extreme or the other, because experience tells them that both corporate and divisional requirements must be represented in the management of the computing centers, and experience also proves that with a spirit of cooperation on both sides such an arrangement can work well.

Centralization of data processing at the corporate level poses new problems of allocating data processing costs. When the divisions employed their own computers and programmers they paid for them, sometimes allocating the costs to still lower levels and sometimes not, but in any case having a clear measure of divisional data processing cost to evaluate against its effectiveness (assuming they took the trouble; which few ever did). When the major data processing cost is incurred at the corporate level, though, and most of the effort goes into standard programs to be used by all the divisions, how can the cost be divided fairly among the divisions? This question is not easily answered, because:

There are many variations between one extreme where the corporate group works almost entirely on divisional assignments and the other where it works entirely on central ones, so many compromises are arrived at.

Some residue of corporate cost always remains that cannot fairly be charged to any division, and the more applications are standardized the more they must be supported by corporate management. Apparently, standardizing the data processing function implies centralizing its financial support.

SIZE AFFECTS STRUCTURE

While the large organization centralizes its data processing because of the increasing complexity and breadth of applications and because of the shortage of resources, the smaller organization must look to other alternatives; there are no separate pools of programming and system analysis talent to consolidate. At best there is one relatively small group, and management may despair of the possibility that their few people will ever be able to deal competently with all the increasingly complex data processing applications they would like to attempt. The same difficulty faces the smaller research laboratory and college because the researcher requires increasingly sophisticated computing facilities, and the small research establishment is likely to have difficulty obtaining and supporting the specialized technical staff needed to acquire and support it.

For the smaller organization, a different kind of centralization of data processing seems to be emerging, though in a small way so far. Because the data processing services required by smaller organizations often have an element of commonality (e.g., computational time-sharing services for scientists, inventory record keeping and accounting for retail firms), service bureaus become a possibility. They are obviously growing fast; more than 20,000 small business organizations[3] now subscribe to the services of organizations providing computers and general programs for groups of users having common needs, and computational time-shared services also have many thousands of subscribers. These data processing services are growing rapidly, and represent an important new element of the data processing industry. It appears, then, that the small organization can join the trend to centralization of data processing by sharing the support of a central service with other users having common interests.

In summary, it is clear that the data processing activities that support the operating functions of organizations are being centralized more quickly and dramatically than the line functions of the organizations. Broadly speaking, data processing is a staff function rather than a line

---

[3]Frederic G. Withington, "The Market for a Computer Utility Industry," in *Computer and Communications—Toward a Computer Utility,* F. Gruenberger, ed., Prentice-Hall, 1968.

one, so this is perhaps logical; line functions traditionally demand more layers of management supervision and more dispersion, while staff functions, such as purchasing, contracting and personnel, lend themselves to central administration. It might have been anticipated that when shortages of data processing resources (relative to management's aspirations) began to pinch, the increased efficiency associated with centralizing a staff function would become the dominant factor.

The "good old days" of organizational simplicity are gone, then, but good riddance to them. The new complexity is a direct result of the increasing importance of the data processing function, and accompanies increasing opportunities and professional challenges. Life always becomes more complicated as you grow up.

INFORMATION TECHNOLOGY AND THE ACCOUNTING ORGANIZATION

by Sexton Adams and Doyle Z. Williams

In recent years many predictions have been made about the impact of "information technology" on the traditional accounting function. The consensus is that the accountant of the future will find himself swept into a new role. This role may be one that enhances the accountant's importance in the business organization, or it may be one in which he is subservient to a more broadly conceived organizational function.

One author recently wrote, "It is possible that future organization charts will show a 'direction of [total] management information,' whose responsibilities will include the disciplines of statistics and operations research as well as accounting and its already related activities such as budgeting, cost accounting, electronic data processing, and systems analysis. . . . This function is beginning to evolve in some companies but in a somewhat disorganized and unidentified manner."[1] For a firm to realize its maximum potential, this author suggested, there must be a systematic, integrated approach to the realignment of the accounting organization in the wake of information technology advances.

CASE HISTORY

In any case, the advent of information technology in any firm has

---

Reprinted by permission of the publisher from *Management Services*, vol. 3, no. 5 (September-October 1966), pp. 15-23.

[1]Harold W. Jasper, "Future Role of the Accountant," *Management Services*, January-February 1966, pp. 51-56.

an immediate impact on the accounting organization and ultimately on the total organization structure. The exact nature of the changes wrought by information technology is rapidly becoming more clear-cut and more readily identifiable.

This article examines the impact of information technology upon the accounting organization of a large, progressive American corporation. This company, a leader in its field, has long been an advocate of continual modernization in all phases of its operations. The empirical evidence presented here concerning the reorganization of the accounting activities of this company indicates how the introduction of information technology may affect the location of the accounting function. In addition, an examination of the development of an actual integrated processing system, with the related organizational changes, may provide some hint as to the future nature of the accounting function in large industrial enterprises.

PUNCHED CARD EQUIPMENT

This company readily accepted a mechanized data processing system in the late 1930's, when it acquired an installation of IBM punched card equipment. This installation was located in, and operated by, the accounting division and was devoted entirely to accounting operations. Acquisition of new equipment continued over the years, particularly during the period immediately following World War II, as more and more of the accounting work was mechanized. The organization chart in Figure 3-2 reflects the location of the accounting division within the organizational structure in the mid-1940's. It should be noted that the head of the accounting department reported directly to the president's office.

By the early 1950's the original investment in punched card equipment had been substantially increased. In broadening the applications of this equipment, the company concentrated on the mechanization of accounting work as a means of cost reduction. As a result, the number of accounting division employees was reduced from 263 in 1946 to 174 in the early 1950's. As a result of plantwide interest, data processing activities were gradually expanded to other departments. By mid-1953 a considerable amount of nonaccounting work was being performed on IBM equipment.

EQUIPMENT LIMITATIONS

In the mid-1950's the systems staff in the accounting division became convinced that the limit in cost reductions and improved systems

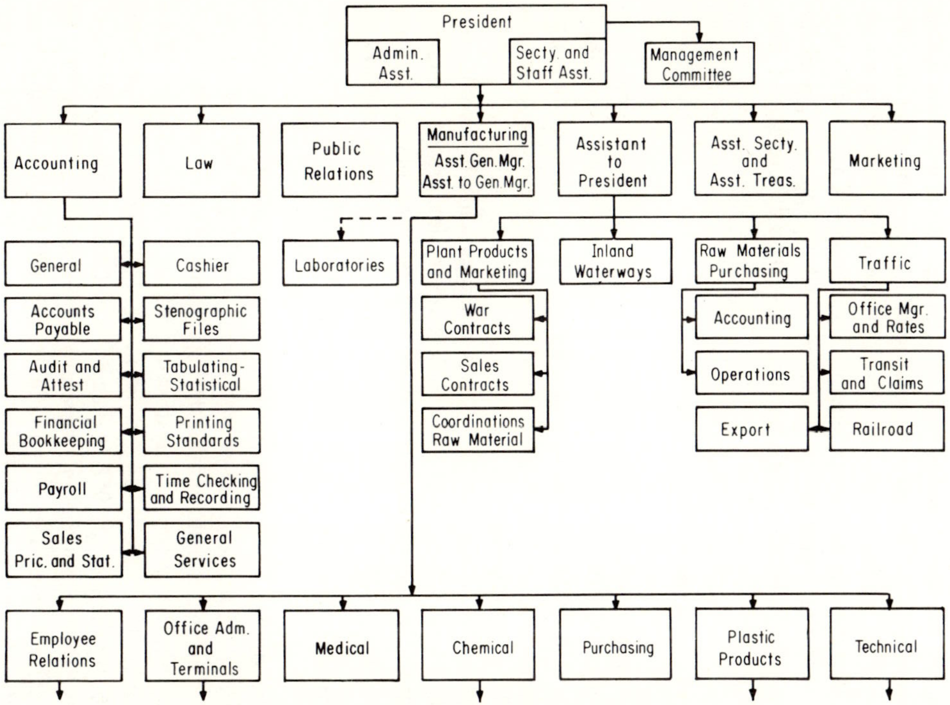

Note: To simplify this organization chart, the subordinate positions in some of the units not directly related to the accounting and computer functions have been omitted.

Figure 3-2. Organization Chart Before the Introduction of Information System.

had been reached with punched card equipment. The personnel directly involved with the data processing activity were dissatisfied with the approach that had been taken in developing the data processing system. Through a process of evolution a system of small pieces had been developed. Mechanization had taken place on a departmental basis rather than on an integrated functional basis. A study of the problem clearly indicated that maximum benefit from mechanization could come only from development of an integrated functional system crossing departmental lines. This study led to the development of a basic framework for an integrated data processing system. The report of the study also pointed out that the conventional punched card equipment lacked the speed and flexibility for fully implementing this broadly conceived integrated system.

FEASIBILITY COMMITTEE

While management was reevaluating its information system, International Business Machines Corporation was releasing information about the then new 650 electronic data processing machine. A three-man committee was appointed to look into the feasibility of this machine for the company's data processing.

This feasibility study convinced top management that computers could provide the speed and flexibility to develop the integrated functional system on an interdepartmental basis. Orders were placed for two IBM 650's and one IBM 705, which were delivered in 1955 and 1956.

SYSTEM DEVELOPMENT

After the orders were placed, the committee began to work on the development of data processing systems suited to the use of this equipment. The "Automated Information Development System" or "AIDS," that resulted from the systems analysis work of this committee is illustrated in Figure 3-3. Five of the projects, A, B, C, D and E, went into effect in 1956. By the end of 1958 Projects F and G were also operational. Originally, these applications were programmed on the IBM 705. In 1958, however, a conversion was made to the IBM 7074—a machine of much greater sophistication. The 7074 was placed in operation on two shifts a day running all seven projects.

ORGANIZATION OF EDP

Originally the computer was placed under the responsibility of the company's chief accountant. The decision, which was practically auto-

Project A—Materials and Stores

1. Storehouses issues and receipts
2. Stock level control
3. Central tool control
4. Domestic Research Co. inventory control
5. Automatic purchase ordering
6. Purchase follow-up
7. Invoice verification
8. Payable checks
9. Material distribution
10. Analyses and reports

Project B—Payroll and Personnel

1. Manpower scheduling
2. Timekeeping
3. Payroll administration
4. Payroll deductions and checks (incl. thrift, annuity, and tax reports)
5. Employee benefit plan administration
6. Service records and seniority
7. Education records
8. Personnel statistics
9. Medical records
10. Safety and training records
11. Labor distribution
12. Locker identification records
13. Retirement income computations

Project C—Fixed Assets

1. Appropriation control
2. Construction records and reports
3. Construction close-outs
4. Plant records
5. Retirements and transfers
6. Plant ledger
7. Depreciation calculation
8. Plant catalog
9. Annual reports

Project D—Financial and Cost

1. Cost distribution entries
2. Code checking and translation
3. Cost allocation
4. Voucher register
5. General ledger
6. Cost and financial reports and analysis

Project E—Secondary Reports

1. Short and off-sequence reports
2. Multi-project reports and analyses
3. Off-frequency reports

Project F—Sales and Shipping

1. Order record
2. Package inventory reports
3. Shipping schedule
4. Shipping papers
5. Bills of lading
6. Invoices
7. Sales statistics

Project G—Operations Analysis

1. Operating data
2. Inventories
3. Meter and gauge calculations
4. Laboratory data
5. Material balances
6. Miscellaneous statistics
7. Utilities and chemical distribution

Figure 3-3. Automated Information Development System Projects.

matic, was considered sound. The computer was thought of as an ultra-high-speed version of the conventional tabulating machine. Its principal advantage was thought to be more rapid and more accurate processing of the same data that had been prepared in the past.

There was another reason for locating computers in the accounting division—the chief accountants leading role in the feasibility study preceding the installation. This study was, generally speaking, chiefly concerned with drawing a comparison between the expenditures for the new equipment and the anticipated clerical cost reductions. In addition, this study indicated that maximum benefit from mechanization could come only from development of an integrated data processing system. This kind of analysis was a proper function of the financial officer, and most of the cost elements and savings were within his own field of responsibility.

COMPUTING CENTRALIZED

With the initial installation of the computers, a group was set up to handle the technical computations on the IBM 650 and 705. As time went by, it became evident that all computing should be centralized in one department and that the programming for business and technical computations should be performed by one group. Consequently, a methods development and programming department was formed for this purpose and remained under the supervision of the chief accountant as noted in Figure 3-4. Thus data processing, although now a separate section, continued to operate within the accounting division, with responsibility for operation of the computer and the maintenance of all operational programs.

As the AIDS program became more complex and as other phases of information technology developed, the placement of data processing in the accounting division was questioned. The range of computer applications far exceeded the limits of the traditionally structured accounting

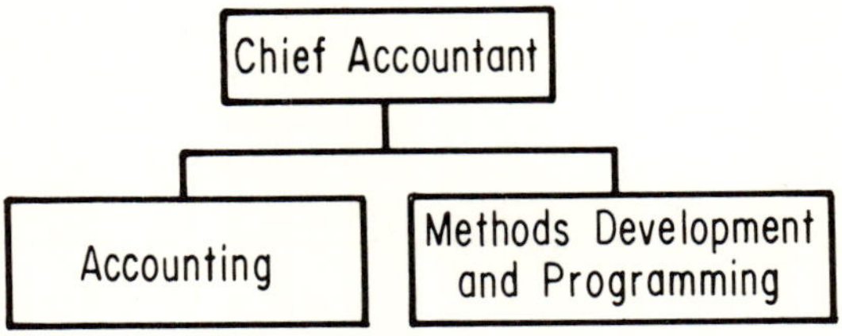

Figure 3-4. Accounting Division.

process. The growth of this management information system extended the organizational impact of electronic data processing from the machine room to other departments.

AIDS

An examination of the Automated Information Development System program provides some insight into the developments that led up to what may have been the most significant reorganization in the company's corporate history.

PROJECT A: MATERIALS AND STORES

The company's storehouse contains some 25,000 items of maintenance and operating supplies. In addition to controlling this inventory, the IBM 7074 is utilized for reordering, follow-up, checking and paying invoices on these 25,000 stock items. This not only makes the function of inventory control easier and the entire system of record keeping more accurate, but it also makes important information for decision making more easily obtainable by several levels of management. For instance, information heretofore difficult to compile is being obtained for use in value analysis, appraisal of vendor performance, reports to management, and studies of stock obsolescence.

PROJECT B: PAYROLL AND PERSONNEL

There were two major goals for the payroll and personnel project: (1) to reduce the tremendous duplication of personnel records and (2) to assist management in employee job scheduling. The first objective has been accomplished with the expected success. In general, the reduction in clerical work has greatly aided supervision and management personnel by permitting them to concentrate on their primay task—supervising. But the attainment of the second objective has proved to be of greater importance. Planning personnel in particular now can do a more effective job of forecasting construction and maintenance projects and scheduling the manpower necessary to carry out these projects. One scheduler states that thanks to this phase of the AIDS program he now receives ten times as much pertinent information as before to assist him in fulfilling his function.

PROJECT C: FIXED ASSETS

This project involved maximum mechanization of fixed asset reports and records, formerly prepared manually. Until July, 1956, when this project became operational, the company accounting records were maintained on approximately 30,000 manually posted cards. These records have now been converted to master tapes and are updated on the 7074. This tape serves as one of the subsidiary ledgers underlying the general ledger, which is maintained as part of Project D.

PROJECT D: FINANCIAL AND COST

Project D covers the general accounting, financial and cost report preparation. It involves the accumulation of a general ledger history tape and the preparation of general and subsidiary ledger entries, including the voucher register. Each of the other projects provides basic accounting data to this project for processing. Output consists of a variety of reports including labor and material cost distribution reports, material issues by classes and accounts and cost reports by processing units.

PROJECT E: SECONDARY REPORTS

This project provided for collecting and organizing data for the preparation of reports that could be conveniently produced directly in the other projects. It also provided for the collection and organization of this information and the subsequent preparation of these reports. Since its conception in July, 1956, many additional reports have been initiated. Not only has this project eliminated the manual effort formerly involved in such report preparation, but it also has provided faster, more accurate information to all levels of management.

PROJECT F: SALES AND SHIPPING

Through the use of the IBM 7074, customer data and shipping data are processed for maximum mechanization of the sales and shipping function. Two departments of the chemical operations division, the packaging and shipping department and the chemical movement department, work closely on this project. The 7074 also produces shipping papers, package inventory reports, customer invoices, sales statistical reports and the necessary accounting entries to reflect customer sales. Moreover, the program determines the most economical number of packages of various styles that should be carried, based on prior shipping experience. This program has resulted in some reduction of inventory items and also provides optimum use of floor space. Finally, the optimum scheduling of the manufacture of various products is a major function of Project F.

PROJECT G: OPERATIONS ANALYSIS

This project is designed to maximize mechanical preparation of operating, raw materials inventory and laboratory data. As a result of the operation of Project G, control of the manufacturing output is accomplished more quickly. This project also provides valuable information for the plant simulation program, for the checking of errors in measuring instruments and for use in determining the design of future chemical processing units.

INTEGRATED SYSTEM

The seven major systems provide essentially an integrated system. Each has an output that enters directly into daily plant operations. In addition to this direct output, there are various accounting entries that are fed into a financial project for the preparation of the profit and loss statement and balance sheet. These seven projects also provide a variety of statistical data. Thus, this single Automated Information Development System furnishes top and middle management personnel with valuable information to increase the profitability of operations.

ORGANIZATIONAL CHANGES

During the first stages of the AIDS program the methods development and programming department performed many of the clerical functions formerly carried out in the affected operating departments. When the AIDS Program became fully operational, there was evidence of an increased need for greater coordination and communication among the affected operating departments. Consequently, there were signs of pressure building up in such a way as to challenge the efficacy of the departments that communicated with one another through the projects of the AIDS program.

The development of the integrated information system resulted in the organizational structure presented in Figure 3-5. This corporate structure was established in 1962 and has remained basically unchanged at this writing. In comparing this organization chart with that of the mid-1940's (Figure 3-2), it is readily apparent that there has been a revolutionary change centering around the location and function of the accounting division.

ACCOUNTING DIVISION

The accounting division has been reduced in status in the organizational hierarchy and is now called the accounting department. In mid-

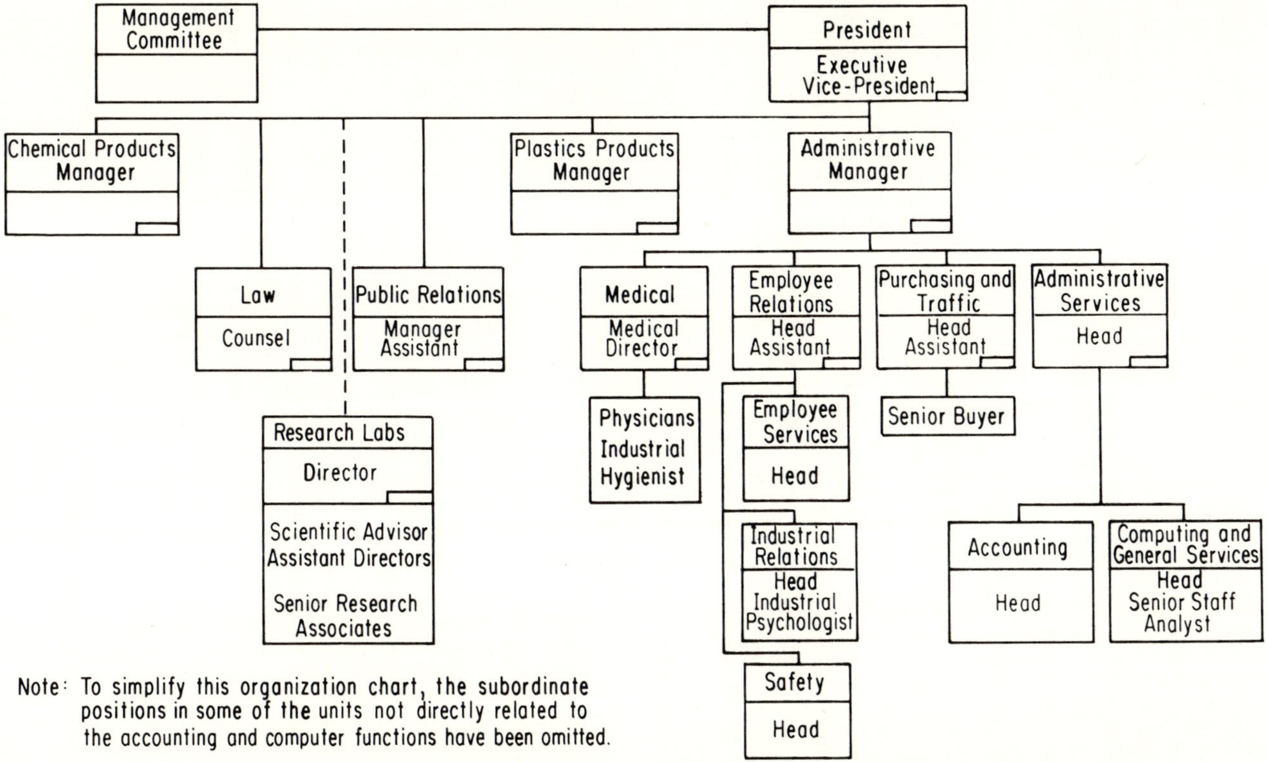

Note: To simplify this organization chart, the subordinate positions in some of the units not directly related to the accounting and computer functions have been omitted.

Figure 3-5. Organization Chart After the Introduction of Information System.

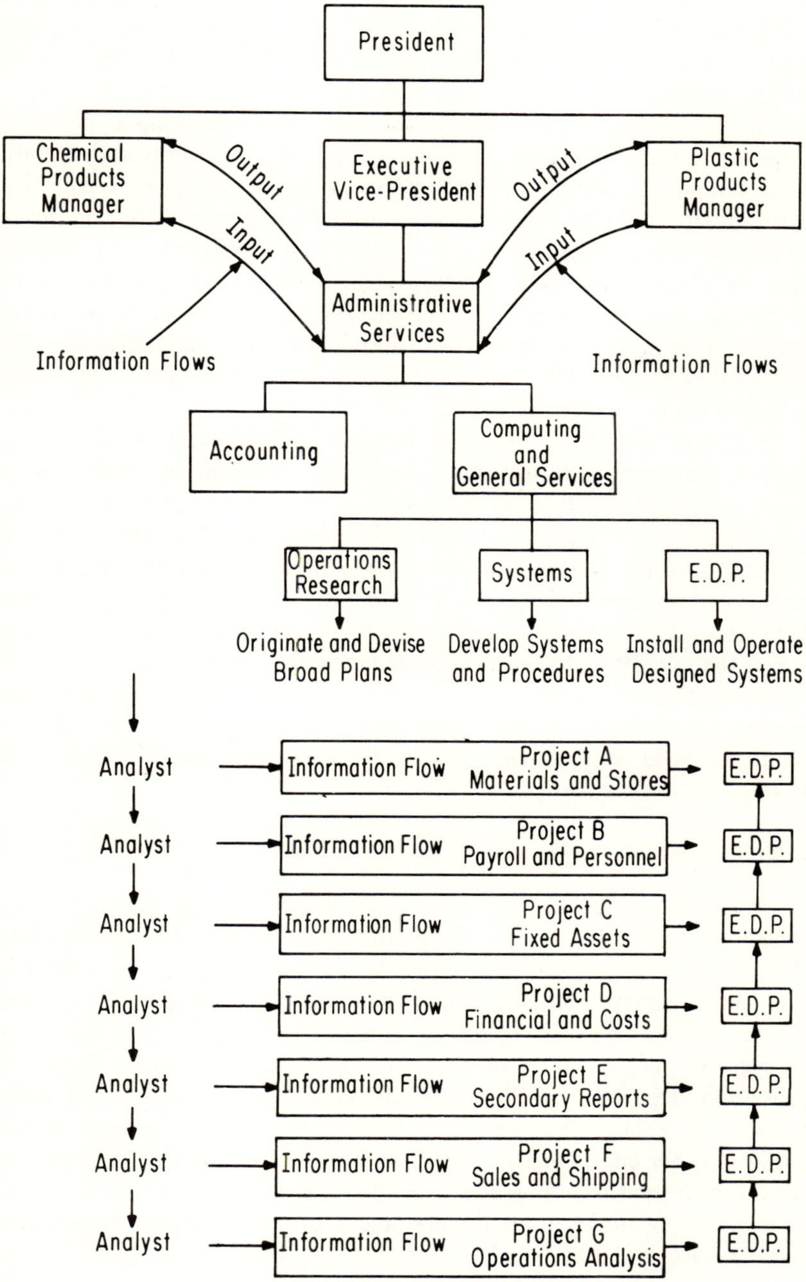

Figure 3-6. Information Flows.

1964 it included 72 people. It reports to a new division, the administrative services division. Whereas the chief accountant formerly reported directly to the president, he now has two intermediaries between himself and the president's office.

On the same organizational level with the accounting department is the computing and general services department, formerly styled methods development and programming department (Figure 3-4). The operation of the AIDS program is the primary function of the computing and general services department. For operational purposes, this department is divided into three sections—business systems, operations research and data processing. This department, like the accounting department, reports to the head of the administrative services division. The functional operation of the computing and general services department is illustrated in Figure 3-6.

The creation of the administrative services division was the primary result of the advent of information technology through the operation of the AIDS program. It developed out of a real need to plan and manage more effectively the flow of information—the lifeblood of the company. In this connection, it should be noted parenthetically that the administrative services division "charges" the other division for services rendered much as a service bureau charges its clients. In evaluating the performance of the operating divisions, top management is conscious of the cost of the information to them. As a result, the operating departments must evaluate the usefulness of information against the cost of that information as charged to their operations. Thus, information is not generated for information's sake.

CONCLUSIONS

Through a series of events over a period of time this company learned an important lesson: If maximum benefit is to be derived from data processing equipment, the computer must be utilized as something more than merely a large accounting machine. A vast quantity of information becomes available. With the reorganization that is almost always necessary to obtain and effectively utilize this information, the traditional accounting department becomes ancillary to the primary information process. Whether the nature of organizational development will be similar in other companies as they, too, reorganize for an integrated information system remains to be seen. The developments described in this paper, however, make it abundantly clear that accounting departments of the future will not be able to remain in their *status quo*.

The company discussed in this article has found it impossible to proceed without a director of management information, the administrative services director. The day has already dawned when his responsibilities include the disciplines of statistics and operations research as well as accounting and such related activities as budgeting, cost accounting, electronic data processing and systems analysis.

A CONTROL FRAMEWORK FOR ELECTRONIC SYSTEMS

by W. Thomas Porter, Jr.

Top management, once conservative in its approach to the use of electronic data processing, has begun to realize the tremendous potential of the computer. Current EDP applications are becoming bolder in their extensions to management control functions and more sophisticated in the use of management-by-exception techniques. New systems, using EDP, have been devised to promote operational efficiency and to enhance effective decision-making.

EDP also requires management to challenge traditional methods of internal control which may no longer be efficient and effective. This article discusses the types of controls in an EDP system and their relationship to the design and implementation of a management information system. The discussion is organized in three major sections: (1) organization considerations in an EDP system, (2) administrative and operating controls in electronic installations, and (3) procedural controls. Each of these control aspects will be dealt with separately; however, they are not mutually exclusive but interrelated in such a way that serious deficiencies in any one would normally preclude the successful operation of the system as a whole.

ORGANIZATIONAL CONSIDERATIONS

Although the shape that an organizational structure takes in any particular company results from a variety of influences, one principle of organization is universally applicable—the establishment of clear lines of authority and responsibility. The division of functional responsibilities should provide for a separation between the functions of initiation and authorization of a transaction, the recording of the transaction and the custody of the resultant asset. Such a division of responsibilities, in addition to safeguarding the assets, provides for the efficiencies derived from

---

Reprinted by permission of the publisher from *The Journal of Accountancy,* vol. 120, no. 4 (October 1965), pp. 56-63.

specialization, makes possible a cross-check that promotes accuracy without duplication or wasted effort, and enhances the effectiveness of a management control system.

From a control standpoint automation has had a great effect on existing organization structures. The result has been increased centralization of data processing activities and the concentration of data processing functions.

CENTRALIZATION

Before the advent of EDP systems most of the individual operating departments—shipping and receiving, production control, inventory control, marketing, budgeting, accounting—did their own clerical paperwork to a great extent. Now, to establish a "control network," we find that a separate functional and organizational entity—the data processing center—has emerged. This entity, in an attempt to tighten coordination and eliminate duplicate demands, now processes data and reports for the various operating departments as the basis for carrying on their individual operating activities.

EDP has also been characterized by a physical centralization of data processing activities. The major factors for this physical centralization are the high fixed cost of electronic equipment and improved data communications equipment. Such a centralization of data processing activities is characterized by the transmission of data from its source, which may be a remote point such as a warehouse or sales branch, to the processing point. The completed processing task is then returned in the desired format to the applicable locations. The systems are justified on the basis that the time and costs associated with processing data are reduced and, accordingly, management has more timely information on which to effectively control company operations.

CONCENTRATION

The centralization of data processing activities has resulted in the concentration of many processing steps into one department and the concentration of traditional accounting data along with operating data. This concentration is commonly referred to as integration, which may be defined as a concept of operation whereby the related elements in different data processing activities are combined into common and coordinated procedures and a logical work flow. The effect of integration is to prepare all desired and necessary managerial reports from only one recording of each business transaction with all transactions processed in a completely unified system.

NEED FOR CONTROL

The centralization of data processing into one department emphasizes the importance of proper control of the data processing center itself. As noted, one of the basic principles of internal control is the separation of the people who authorize a transaction, those who have custody of the asset acquired, and those who record the accountability for the asset. This basic separation in accounting, as well as in other functions, must be maintained in order to achieve satisfactory internal control. Although there is nothing in EDP which is inconsistent with this requirement, the means for authorization and the nature of the authorization may have changed. For example, if under automated inventory management a computer prints out a purchase order because an inventory item has fallen below a certain balance, this may on the surface appear to be elimination of a separate authorization. The authorization, however, goes first from the operating people to the people who have designed the program for consideration of factors which will permit or require a purchase.

To maintain the continued integrity of the system where the authorization and recording functions are embodied in the program itself, it is necessary to separate the systems planning and programming function, the machine-operating function, and the program maintenance and tape library function. Such a separation is important because:

1. It provides an effective cross-check of the accuracy and propriety of changes which are introduced into the system.
2. It avoids the undesirable situation in which operating personnel implement revisions without prior approval and thorough checking.
3. It eliminates access to the equipment by nonoperating personnel.

In addition, such separation of duties is desirable from an operational efficiency standpoint, since the capabilities, training and skills required in carrying out these activities differ greatly.

A typical organization setup for the EDP activity in a large organization is represented by the organization chart of a manufacturing company shown in Figure 3-7. This chart indicates the separation of systems planning and programming functions from the EDP and EAM (electronic accounting machines or tabulating equipment) operations. Within the operations function the major control aspects include the segregation of the tape library and scheduling unit, both physically and operationally, from machine room operations; and the functioning of the data acquisition and control section.

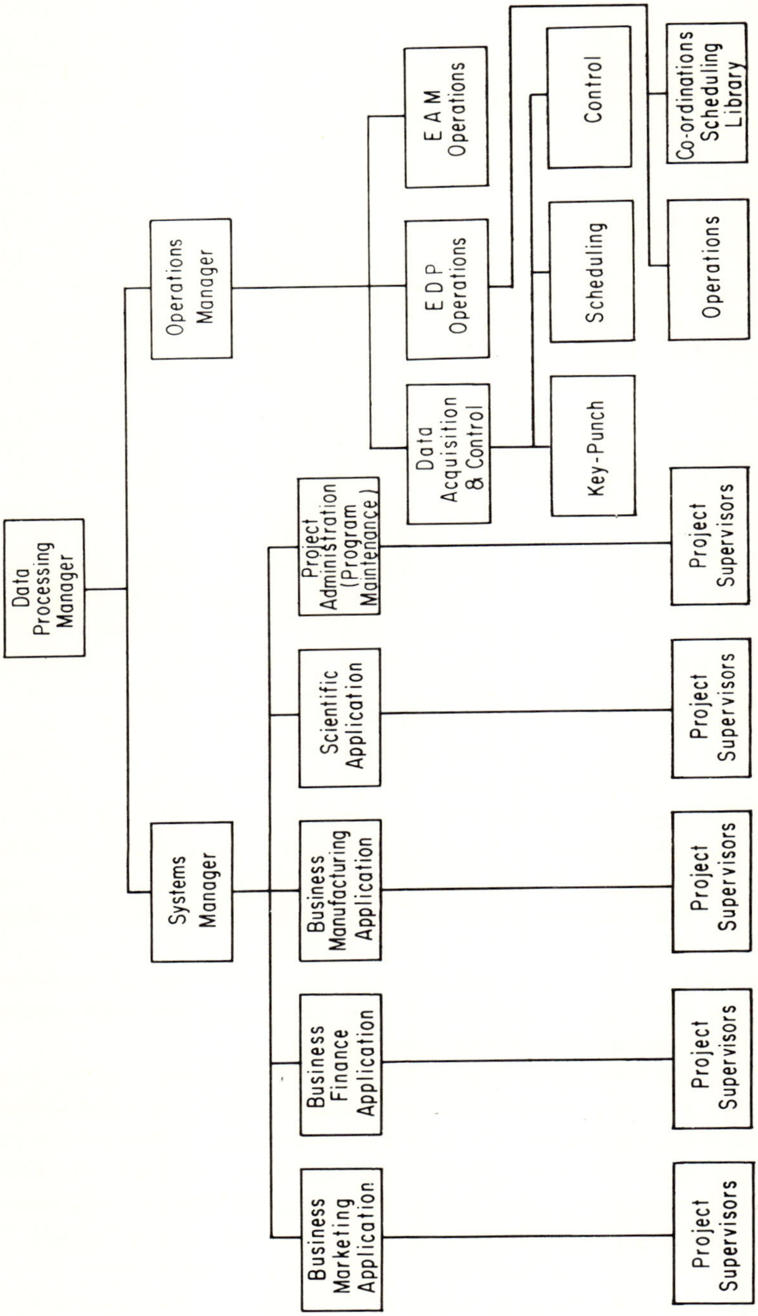
Data Processing Manager
Systems Manager
Operations Manager
Business Marketing Application
Business Finance Application
Business Manufacturing Application
Scientific Application
Project Administration (Program Maintenance)
Data Acquisition & Control
E D P Operations
E A M Operations
Project Supervisors
Project Supervisors
Project Supervisors
Project Supervisors
Project Supervisors
Key-Punch
Scheduling
Control
Operations
Co-ordinations Scheduling Library

Figure 3-7.

The tape library unit is responsible for physical control of all completed computer programs and for all magnetic tape reels and the proper release of these programs and tapes for processing purposes. Personnel employed in other units and sections do not have access to the programs and tapes, except on an authorized basis.

The data acquisition and control section is responsible for all input into the EDP center and maintains control of the data being processed until the finalized output is returned to the user. The maintenance of control is achieved by comparing previously determined totals, either by the organization using it or by the data acquisition and control section itself, with the output from computer processing. This group is also responsible for meeting predetermined schedules for all input and output data and arranges the mode of reporting back to the ultimate user. Any necessary conversion of input data to machine-readable form for electronic processing also comes under the responsibility of the data acquisition and control section.

The control normally exercised by units or departments within the EDP center, similar to the data acquisition and control section, is what may be called "procedural" control. The using organization which originates the data to be processed and which receives the output from the data processing center normally exercises the "substantive" control. In large companies—where certain data processing activities are voluminous, involve many using organizations and, in management's opinion, require extensive controls—separate control units, reporting to the controller or someone else outside the data processing department, are set up to provide much of the "substantive" control.

For example, in the company whose EDP center has been described above, a payroll control group has been established. This particular company maintains payroll records for approximately twenty thousand employees on magnetic tapes. The payroll master record consists of a "fixed" section containing permanent-type information and "variable" sections for earnings and deductions data. The fixed section includes data such as name, social security number, pay rate, budget section and year-to-date and quarter-to-date payroll totals. The variable earnings sections are used to record data for regular or normal earnings, overtime earnings, holiday pay, sick leave pay and numerous other earnings categories peculiar to the company. The variable deductions sections are used to record the twenty-five different types of payroll deductions. The payroll group:

1. Reviews all changes to the payroll record, such as pay rates, new employees hired, terminations and all changes in pay deductions.

2. Compares labor hours and dollars on reports generated from the labor collection system to total hours and dollars on reports resulting from payroll processing.
3. Reviews exception reports and takes whatever action is necessary for the particular exception. The exception report lists all the transactions which are rejected because of the programmed controls in the payroll program.

In smaller companies such an organization of the data processing activity described above may be impractical because of the multiplicity of functions performed by EDP people. For example, systems designers may also be programmers, and computer operating personnel may maintain the tape and program library. Although segregation of duties in such an installation is more difficult to achieve, the previously stated reasons for maintaining functional segregation are still valid.

ADMINISTRATIVE CONTROLS

Administrative controls in electronic systems can be associated with the formulation, documentation and implementation of operating procedures in: (1) systems design, (2) programming, and (3) computer operations.

SYSTEMS DESIGN

The complexity of electronic systems requires detailed systems design and programming. This detail must be adequately documented in order to evaluate and modify the system. In my opinion, one of the principal reasons for lack of control in EDP systems is a lack of documentation of a company's present and former methods of automatic data processing. Only with documentation can management accurately determine how much progress has been made and what remains to be done. When corners are cut in the quantity and depth of documentation serious delay occurs in modifying systems. Too much design work has to be done over again when the original designer has departed without leaving adequate documentation. The formulation and documentation of an EDP application can be broken down into three phases: data systems survey, data systems study and programming.

The data systems survey should outline the scope and objectives of application, the plan and schedule for completion, and estimated costs and benefits. An important part of the documentation of a data systems survey, and hence an important control feature, is approval by management before proceeding to the data systems study. This approval should be made as high up in management as possible. Too often situations are encountered where management personnel do not know, much less understand, what EDP is or is not doing for the company. Conversely, systems personnel are often not aware of management policies important to the design of the system.

The data systems study should include a review of current procedures. Such a review should indicate what features and controls are necessary and beneficial in the new system and what changes can be made in improving existing procedures. After review of the current system, a new one should be designed to include adequate definition and documentation of the contents of master files, input and output requirements, methods of processing and control requirements. In addition, the documentation should include a timetable of data collection, processing and reporting; estimated execution times; required equipment; and method and timing of conversion. This documentation should be reviewed, approved and signed by all the department managers concerned to assure that the EDP applications have been thoroughly investigated, documented, and agree upon before programming begins.

PROGRAMMING

Computer programming involves the preparation of flow charts, program listings and computer operating instructions. During the planning and installation of an EDP system or application, it is desirable to document all aspects of program development as explicitly as possible. Such documentation serves both as an essential tool for understanding and controlling the programs and as a permanent history of all pertinent facts related to each program.

One extremely useful document is the *program run book*. Important run book requirements on all programs include: (1) a description of the purpose of the program, (2) a complete set of flow charts, (3) an assembly listing of the program, (4) computer operating instructions, (5) program testing documentation, and (6) a sample of all reports produced by the program.

In addition to the above document, *a console run book* should be prepared for specific use by computer operating personnel in operating each program. Normally, the console run book includes: (1) a flow chart of the portion of the system of which the program is a part, (2) identification of tape units used for input and output files, (3) console switch settings, (4) a list of all program halts and required action, and (5) a description of any exceptions to standard routines and any variable data (dates, constants, and so forth) to be entered in the program.

Efficient program development requires programming standards. A *programming manual* should be set up and maintained and should contain a written record of all policies, procedures and techniques which are to be standard throughout the organization. Its existence will facilitate communication and prevent the development of duplicate or conflicting procedures. Many areas of program development lend themselves to standardization, such as program documentation procedures, tape labeling, program-testing procedures, and tape retention policies.

The dynamic nature of most business activities causes *program changes*. Program changes require well-formulated and documented procedures to prevent the manipulation of programs for special purposes, fraudulent or otherwise. Several procedures are necessary for maintaining control over program changes:

1. The nature of the proposed procedure change should be explained in written form, and formal approval for the change should be given by a responsible individual, such as the manager of the department that will be affected.

2. Procedure changes (coding) to the program should be prepared only by the systems group, not by members of the computer operating group. The change should be supported by readable documentation in flow chart form (as opposed to direct patching of the program).

3. The change should be reviewed and approved by a person who is separate from and independent of the individual designing the change.

4. After review, this material should be given to the computer operator, who should retain control of the program changes until they are posted to the program. Then the operator should process test input data, using the original program and, next, the revised program. The output from both operations should be reviewed to ascertain that only those records which should have been affected were affected, and that only the changes contemplated were actually made. Operation of the computer during the process of making changes should be under the control of the personnel ordinarily responsible for the regular operation of this equipment and not a member of the systems (programming) group.

5. Finally, all correction sheets and print-outs should be filed in the program book, thus providing a permanent record of all changes made to the program.

COMPUTER OPERATIONS

Several forms of documentation and procedure are important to achieve control in computer operations. One of the most important controls over computer operations is the record maintained for recording and analyzing time. This *utilization record* is used to record the computer operation, the equipment used, and the time involved in processing the job. The record should be analyzed and reviewed by responsible operating personnel to determine the time spent processing each job and reasons for all lost time.

Another major control in EDP operations is the *off-premises record storage program* of the company. Since magnetic tapes are small in size, compared with other media of data storage, it is generally practicable to store a duplicate set of important tapes in an area physically separated from the computer center. Thus, at least one set of tape records will be available in the event of a fire or water leakage to the tape library. A tape library evacuation procedure should also be developed and documented. The specific tapes which should be stored off-site will depend upon the particular system. At a minimum, the program tapes and master file tapes should be stored away from the computer room.

Adequate *control procedures* are also necessary in the tape and *program library* function. Strict control over access to the library must be maintained to prevent unauthorized individuals from obtaining tapes and thereby circumventing other controls which have been established. Generally, access to the library should be limited to those personnel who require use of the program and other tapes in connection with the normal operation of the system. In very large installations, where the tape files are maintained by a tape librarian, access to the files should be limited to this person.

Apart from a tape labeling system, both internal and external, and control over access to the tapes, procedures and forms must be set up to maintain effectively the tape and program library. The reels, upon receipt, should be tested to ensure that they are not defective, and then given serial numbers. They can then be assigned to the various applications by these serial numbers, thus permitting efficient scheduling through the data processing system. To achieve efficient use of tapes and to ensure control, a rigorous record system must be maintained on the filing and status of the tapes. Such a system should provide information on: (1) the physical location of any given reel, (2) the tapes available to be written on, and (3) the usage history of each tape.

Another important control in electronic systems is *console control.* The console of a data processing system is used by the operator to control the system and monitor its operation. The console is used to start and stop the system and to restart the computer when error conditions cause it to halt. The console indicates the instruction being performed and can be used to alter the mode of operation. Using the console, the operator can determine the status of internal registers and switches and can have this data printed out. In addition, the console can be used to enter data into the system manually. In many cases the electronic equipment includes a console typewriter which can be used to create a log of console activity.

Several techniques can be employed to provide effective console control:

1. Review of the console typewriter print-out. The paper in the console typewriter should be two-part: the original for operating uses, the duplicate for supervisory review. In addition, the paper should be serially numbered for accountability. On some machines a locked recording device is available, to which the operator does not have access.
2. Rotation of duties among operators.
3. Accounting for processing time. Computer manipulation by the operator through the console takes time which would significantly increase processing time on the computer run affected. An analysis of EDP equipment utilization records by responsible personnel provides a strong console control.
4. Operation of computer in "nonstop" mode. By use of a monitor system, which quickly brings into operation the proper processing program (contained in certain magnetic tape reels mounted on specific tape units), and by use of error procedures which do not halt the computer, the EDP system precludes any manual intervention by the console operator during processing.

PROCEDURAL CONTROLS

Once management has determined its plan of organization and designed administrative controls, management must develop a system which records, processes, summarizes and reports transactions in accordance with operating responsibilities and information needs of the individuals making operating decisions. Basically, such a system includes three levels: (1) the source data level, (2) the data processing level, and (3) the reporting level.

Normally, in non-EDP systems, auditors are accustomed to three basic records: the source document, the journal, and the ledger. The processing is normally performed by people; the accuracy and propriety of the processing is insured by a segregation of duties and human review and inspection of the documents and records. EDP systems have eliminated the need for some of these records or have resulted in records not available for human inspection. Alteration of the audit trail in a system is not necessarily bad, so long as the data are recorded, processed and reported with the propriety, accuracy and timeliness required by management. The timeliness factor is achieved by the tremendous speed at which EDP equipment operates; the accuracy and propriety is achieved by source data controls, machine processing controls, and output controls. The types of procedural controls can be associated with the level of processing and the objectives of controls at each level.

SOURCE DATA CONTROLS

The objectives of source data controls are:

1. To determine that all transactions have been properly recorded at the point of origin or source.
2. To determine that all transactions are transmitted from the recording point to the processing point.

In non-EDP systems these objectives are achieved largely by source document controls, such as (1) registration at the point of document entry, (2) sequential numbering with full accountability at point of document origin, and (3) grouping or "batching," with predetermined document counts or other control totals. These controls, familiar to the auditor, are largely people-oriented. In EDP systems many of these controls can be included in computer programs and can be termed computer-oriented.

In EDP systems where conventional source documents are still used, no new control problems are presented prior to processing of the data. A preaudit of the source documents by knowledgeable personnel will detect misspellings, invalid codes, unreasonable amounts and other improper data. Key verification of punched cards or punched paper tape, the use of batch and control totals, and machine or "hard-copy" listings can be employed to determine that all source documents are correctly converted to machine-readable form for subsequent EDP processing.

In EDP systems where the source document is eliminated or is in a form that does not permit human review, there are basically two solutions to ensure proper recording. First, control can be moved to the point of origin so that access to and use of the recording and transmitting equipment is properly controlled to prevent unauthorized or improper use. A second solution is to let the computer exercise the same review of the transaction that would be made of source documents by people.

Because of the characteristics of a computer, an EDP system has unusual capabilities to examine or edit each element of information processed by it. This editing process involves the ability to inspect and accept (or reject) transactions according to the validity or reasonableness of quantities, amounts, codes and other data contained in the input record. Obviously, such an ability is also relevant to a system not using automated data collection and transmission equipment. The editing ability of the computer can be used to detect errors in input preparation that have not been detected by human review and inspection.

The editing ability of the computer is achieved by installing checks in the program of instructions for the purpose of detecting errors; hence, the term "programmed checks." Although I am now talking about programmed checks to edit the propriety and accuracy input data, programmed checks are also used to achieve the control objectives at the data processing level. The type of programmed checks at this level will be discussed later.

Programmed checks to determine the validity of input or source data include: (1) Checks to determine whether a particular transaction code is active or whether an identification number is valid (existence or valid number check); (2) checks to determine the logical relationship that exists between various data fields in a record (combination checks); (3) checks to test whether data amounts have exceeded predetermined limits (limit checks); and (4) checks to determine that the input is complete (completeness checks).

PROCESSING CONTROLS

Processing controls established to ensure the accuracy of processing of input data have three objectives:

1. To detect loss or nonprocessing of data
2. To determine that arithmetic functions have been performed correctly
3. To determine that all transactions are posted to the proper record

The accuracy of the processing is dependent upon the accuracy of programming, the checks designed and built into the equipment by the manufacturer, and the programmed checks included by the user in his programs. Accurate programming depends upon the careful conception and implementation of systems design and program instructions, proper program documentation and adequate review and approval—all sound practices which were discussed earlier.

All EDP equipment manufacturers have checks built into the equipment to ensure that data is correctly read, processed, transferred within the system and recorded on output media. These checks are sometimes referred to as "hardware" controls, and include parity checks, dual read-write heads, dual circuitry and file protection rings. These hardware controls are described at length in the various publications prepared by the equipment manufacturers.

In addition to the hardware checks, data processing accuracy in an EDP system is achieved by programmed checks. Programmed checks to detect loss or nonprocessing of data include record counts, control totals and hash totals, and sequence checks. Programmed checks of arithmetic calculations include limit checks, cross-footing balance checks, proof figures, zero balancing and reverse arithmetic.

Programmed checks for proper postings may be classified as file checks and are used to achieve accuracy in file and record connections and in the changes to the files. The problem of file connections is a significant one in EDP systems because of the absence of "visible" records and because of the ease with which wrong information can be written on magnetic tapes and disks. Such checks include tape labels, identification comparisons and file maintenance routines.

OUTPUT CONTROLS

The function of output controls is to determine that the processed data do not include any unauthorized alterations by the computer operations section, that data are substantially correct or reasonable, and that all errors detected in the processing of data have been corrected.

One of the biggest controls in any system is the review of reports and output data by the originating group and the taking of whatever corrective action is necessary. This review normally consists of a search for unusual or abnormal items. The use of programmed controls described above, coupled with exception reporting, actually enhances the ability of responsible personnel to take necessary action.

The most basic output control is the comparison of control totals of data processed with totals independently obtained from prior processing or original source data. Systematic sampling of individual items processed affords another output control. The testing can be performed by the originating group, the control unit or the internal audit staff.

SUMMARY

The design of a management information system dictates that substantial amounts of time and effort be spent in the formulation of controls. Such effort is necessary to use the power of the computer most effectively and to control the cost of data processing.

PROTECT THE DATA BASE

by Frederick H. Lutter

Since the very beginning of its emergence, the corporate dp function has always been far ahead of any pursuers who wished to hold it accountable. Now may well be the first time in the 20 year history of computer users that the control effort is catching up with development.

Many persons expect that one day soon we shall uncover among our midst a fraud more scandalous then the salad oil scandal that occurred several years ago.

There is—all too often—the unprofessional petty thievery of letting a third party use idle computer equipment at night for under-the-table payments. There is the procurement and use of optical reader equipment (in Chicago) for the benefit of a service-bureau, the copying of valuable customer lists for re-rent and reusage by unauthorized persons (large encyclopedia publisher), etc. These types of frauds are still minor compared to what is theoretically possible.

To prevent fraud, there are three main control problems:

1. Database protection.
2. Program security.
3. Application audit-trails.

Where all three of these interrelated areas are not controlled, the opportunities for fraud are many. The programmer can alter and modify his programs. He can create dummy records in the database. And the lack of audit-trails makes it difficult to discover and trace these misdeeds.

RESPONSIBILITY

For database protection, a senior person should be made responsible for its integrity. He must see to it that the database (or master files) contains all live records, nothing but live records, and that the data contained in these records are the latest available and up-to-date. No records can be added, no records can be deleted, no fixed or categorical fields altered without his knowledge. He is solely responsible for file maintenance.

The importance of this procedure is apparent in payroll, stock certificates, bookkeeping, accounts payable, and other areas. From a systems point of view, it requires a basic separation of file maintenance, separate

---

Reprinted by permission of the publisher from *Administrative Management*, vol. 31, no. 11 (November 1970), p. 10.

from regular transactions against existing records—even though the state of the programming art and computer power seem to favor combining the two functions.

For purposes of program security, no primary language programs should be kept in the operations room. After programs have been declared operational, no program alteration should be permitted without specific authorization. All modifications duly authorized should be made in the primary language.

Records should be kept of all authorized program alterations and the resulting computer program listing. These should be audited from time to time.

Application audit-trails is quite a large subject, but in general, strong balancing and cross-footing controls should be maintained from input preparation to computer printout. This makes it difficult at least to slip in a few hours of overtime, and extra payroll records, or an extra account payable. But, audit-trail procedures must allow the reconstruction at any time of any master record taken at random. Conversely it must be possible to trace any transaction, action document or management report in detail back to the corresponding master record—as it existed at a specific time.

4

Verification and Control of Data in Computerized Environments

Regardless of the size or sophistication of its equipment or the size or prestige of its staff, the actual value of a data processing organization is no greater than the value of the information which it provides for management's use. The timeliness of that information is critical, but even more critical is the need for accuracy. The fundamental importance of accurate data in any information system is succinctly described by the oft repeated phrase GIGO—garbage in, garbage out.

The tasks of verifying and controlling data generally involve the activities of properly capturing source data, accurately transcribing nonmachine-readable data into machine-readable data, and guarding against any subsequent loss or distortion as the data is subjected to the many different manipulations, summaries, and transformations performed upon it during the course of normal processing operations. A variety of techniques, some manual and some computerized, are employed to insure the accuracy of the data used and thus enhance the value of the information produced for use by management.

The manual operation of key verifying may be used in conjunction with an editing program which checks for probable errors, such as missing fields or amounts which fall outside expected value ranges. The use of label records for tape and disk files, combined with carefully organized procedures for the file libraries, can prevent file confusion and accidental destruction of current files.

Well defined and carefully planned procedures for controlling the quality of data are generally indications of properly administered data processing organizations. Effective error control makes possible more reliable output and lowers total costs by reducing expensive reruns and data correction procedures.

USE OF CONTROLS IN EDP ACCOUNTING

by Joseph V. Miccio

There are several questions to be answered about data processing controls. What are the objectives of controls? Who is responsible for them, how do we control the source data, how do we assure everyone that computer programs are reliable, how do we control the actual processing, how do we check the output and how do we satisfy other interested groups, such as public accountants, federal tax authorities, etc., that information given to them is correct? Let us take these points one at a time.

OBJECTIVE

First of all, the major objective of control is to insure that only valid data is accepted and processed and that no invalid data is introduced during processing. Controls should prevent loss of information or incorrect processing of data. Loss of information might result from loss of a field in a record, loss of a whole record, loss of a reel of tape in a multi-reel file, or even loss of an entire file. Controls should also ensure the accuracy of file results.

KEEPING THE AUDIT TRAIL ALIVE

An important function of controls is the provision for audit trail. With data processing, audit trails can become lost in the collection and summarization of data. There are several ways to keep the audit trail alive in data processing, and they all involve essentially the same concept: keeping a detail file of the transactions as they occur. The detail file might be kept by printing daily proof listings of each day's transactions. It might be kept by printing a transactions journal showing opening balance, detailed transactions and closing balance for each active account over a short period of time. Or it might be kept by assembling all transactions on a journal tape. This tape could then be the input for an audit program which would extract the transactions for selected accounts and print them in such a way that the accountant or auditor could trace the status of an account, transaction by transaction.

Are controls economically feasible? To answer this question, we must balance the incremental cost of controls against the risk of loss

---

Reprinted by permission of the publisher from *Financial Executive*, August 1967, pp. 50-54.

that could result from the lack of controls. The cost resulting from lack of controls, which might consist of rerun time, a dissatisfied customer, an out-of-stock condition in inventory and many other intangibles, is difficult to measure. The incremental cost of controls is not difficult to measure, though some of it is involved in other functions and is, therefore, not essentially an out-of-pocket cost. I think most data processing people would be willing to pay the cost of controls just to avoid reruns.

DIVIDED RESPONSIBILITY

The responsibility for controls should be divided. If the responsibility is laid entirely upon the data processing department, not only is there greater risk of error and possibility of fraud, but some errors can become self-perpetuating due to lack of feedback. In general, the responsibility should be divided into four parts. The operating department should be responsible for the accuracy of the input and should be provided by the data processing department with those items necessary to check the accuracy of the input data, such as error lists and batch proof totals. The data processing department should be responsible for processing from keypunching through printing of the reports even when the keypunching or data preparation is done in other departments. The user or the final recipient of the report should be responsible for the output. The systems and programming sections should be responsible for the reliability of the systems and program.

Let us review more specifically each of these four responsibilities. First of all, how should input data be controlled? The procedures for the recording of the source input documents can have a great deal to do with the accuracy and the ability of the data processing department to control these documents. Although this is a step that is somewhat removed from the data processing department, document design and recording procedures nevertheless have a very great effect on the accuracy and costs of data processing, particularly keypunching.

The operating department creating the source data should be responsible for providing batch controls. Simple adding machine tape of the hours contained in a batch of time cards or the dollars in a batch of invoices can save much grief later on. The computer, of course, should then calculate a total of the detailed transactions for matching against these batch controls.

Various edit controls are designed to catch keypunch errors or possible transcription errors in the preparation of source documents. The editing is done by the computer on first entry of detailed transactions into the system. One approach is in editing to match the details against the master file to insure the accuracy of account numbers, payroll numbers or names, with exceptions being printed out in an error list. Other things would be:

- Testing numeric fields against absolute or reasonable limits which they are not allowed to exceed;
- Checking against format to see that a numeric field is all numeric or does not contain blanks;
- Checking that a field which is expected to contain information does contain the information;
- Checking logical relationships in the data; for example, a man whose job code represents a maintenance function would only be able to charge to indirect labor;
- Using a *check digit,* whereby the digits in an account number, including the check number, must add up in some predetermined manner to a predetermined figure. With the use of such check digits, it is usually not necessary to match details against the master file merely for the purpose of checking the accuracy of account numbers.

REWORK IS EXPENSIVE

The next area of responsibility is program reliability. This pertains to the systems and programming function whether it is a separate department or part of the data processing department. Proper systems design is of paramount importance to control. It is the responsibility of systems design to specify the use of batch totals, the use of a journal tape to keep audit trails, the use of edit programs, and most of the other things that I have already talked about.

Following good systems design, of course, must be good programming. In connection with both of these functions, I would like to state as an aside that senior talent is cost effective in these areas. Competent people may be expensive, but mistakes and problems and rework are more expensive.

Another step to insure program reliability is good documentation. More and more data processing departments are realizing the importance of documentation. We see better documentation these days than used to be the case.

After the program is written and documented, it should be tested first against test data and then against live data. Sometimes the live data test can be a parallel run, although the changes in system design are quite frequently so radical that a parallel test is impossible. However, just running a batch of live data not parallel with anything can be useful in pointing up exceptional conditions that were not considered in the test data or perhaps not even provided for in the systems design.

Before the program is implemented, preferably early in the design stage, the systems design should be reviewed by the accountant. The systems department and the entire computer operations can be in serious trouble if it is discovered after several production runs that the auditor does not approve, for example, of the method of round off. The auditor might suggest exception tests and reasonableness tests which will help to pick up serious errors in design or errors in data preparation.

After the program is implemented and running and everyone is satisfied with results, the problem of future changes to the program arise. Changes to the program should be controlled; they should not be made without documentation and review by the systems manager and the data processing manager. These reviews are necessary to insure that the changes do what they are supposed to do and do not have unforeseen effects.

In addition, the program itself should contain controls in order to assure that proper tapes are used and that records are not lost. These would include controls for:

- Tape labels.
- Record counts which are checked from program to program as a file passes through the system.
- Hash totals for the same purpose.
- Redundant identifiers, such as an alpha code corresponding to the last name of an account.
- Memory protection and file protection to prevent valuable information from being wiped out in error.
- Suspense accounts for the accumulation of the amounts of error records which are discarded from the system.

Suspense accounts help in balancing the data and point out the errors to be corrected.

RESTRICTED AREA

The next control area is the computer room or processing shop, which comes under the aegis of the data processing operations manager. There are several control possibilities in this area. The first is to restrict access to the computer room. Programmers, analysts and outsiders should submit jobs on a job request form and should not be allowed to enter the computer room unless they receive the permission of the data processing operations manager. A good programmer will not resent this; it gives him more freedom to continue with his work. In any event, a programmer is too expensive to be acting as an operator. It is usually necessary for a programmer to attend the initial runs of a new system, although some computer operating systems are set up with memory and tape dumps so that the programmer does not need to attend even the initial runs.

Another important point is that of operator intervention. If a program does not run through to the end of the job or if it required that the operator take action of any kind, this information should be logged either manually in an operator log or on the console typewriter. Programs should be written in such a way that operator intervention is minimized and, when it does occur, that logging is required.

The importance of control over tape or disc libraries cannot be overemphasized. Anyone who has had a master file or an important transaction file wiped out realizes the importance of having a tape library set up with logging of tapes in and out. There are other advantages of tape libraries: we can keep tape histories and get information on life of tapes and be able to forecast tape usage so that supplies can be purchased enough in advance to prevent exhaustion of the tape supply.

Backup and rerun procedures come under the control of the data processing department. Backup procedures require knowing what compatible equipment is available, making an arrangement with the user of that equipment and setting up procedures so that the operation can be run on the alternate equipment. Rerun procedures are related to the tape library policy to prevent rerun unless there are backup files for the rerun. It is necessary to insure that father and grandfather generations of master files be kept, that the detail files be kept on hand for a fixed amount of time (usually at least one and preferably two accounting cycles). It is also necessary to make provision for storing copies of master files and program tapes in a remote location from the computer room. This is called vital records control and provides protection against fire and other eventualities. Proper vital record control can result in reduction of insurance premium if insurance is carried against computer room damage.

The user is responsible for checking the output. In some cases, this is merely a test to determine if the figures are reasonable. In other cases, the user can check against other related totals to see that the totals bear a proper relationship. The user should control exceptions, such as where a report flags numbers that are outside some predetermined range. It is up to the user to check the exceptions to see if they are reasonable. The user can also perform statistical analysis of the output data to insure that it is correct.

WHO IS INTERESTED IN CONTROLS?

In addition to the people who have direct responsibility for controls, there are other groups that are interested in them. The corporate controller is usually, by corporate charter and by law, directly responsible for the accuracy of the company's financial reports. Any data processing operation involving the accounting function of the business is of interest to the controller. And both the internal and external auditors naturally have an interest in data processing controls.

There are many outside agencies interested in controls: the federal and local tax authorities are interested in the accuracy of the financial reporting of the corporation, as may be military procurement agencies if government contracts are involved. Unions and many other regulatory bodies may also be involved.

The accountant will frequently want to determine the controls in the EDP system, appraise their accuracy, and check their operation. A preaudit by the internal auditors or the accounting department can be a great benefit to all levels of management, but particularly to those designing and programming the system. It is easier to make changes before and during the design of the system than to make them afterwards. With the concentration of the data processing function in EDP equipment, auditors will usually find it necessary to make audit tests of the processing by the equipment. On many occasions they will wish to use the EDP equipment to perform some of their audit tests. Since it is in the best interest of all concerned that any system errors be detected, it is vitally necessary that the data processing department cooperate with the accountants in establishing such procedures. The data processing department can save considerable effort by enlisting the assistance of the accounting and auditing departments in the early stages of systems design. The accountants and auditors can ensure that the results of the data processing effort will reflect good accounting practices if they give as much assistance as possible throughout the design effort.

THE INTERACTION OF CLERICAL AND PUNCHING PROCESSES IN DATA INPUT

by W. L. Charlton

In evaluating the cost efficiency of large scale data preparation, the two

---

Reprinted by permission of the publisher from *The Computer Bulletin,* October 1970, pp. 345-346.

processes of clerical work and punching (or encoding) interact and must be considered together. There can be no standard formula to this but it is vital to identify any pressures seeking to maintain or even increase departmental autonomy to the detriment of the overall cost efficiency. There are applications where the separation of clerical process from punching is obscured or even eliminated by the use of keyboard equipment producing both typed source documents and punched tape (etc.) in one action. Other specialized systems (OCR, mark sense, etc.) also have this merit of forcing common control disciplines.

Nevertheless the majority of EDP departments are faced with the need to process large batches of hand produced documents at a central point and to do this a clear preference is shown for blind punch action in which speed of character by character punching is the criterion.

PUNCH/VERIFY

Blind punching is usually followed by punch verification which is a purely internal punch control and which can be developed in isolation to a high degree of accuracy. This allows the clerical processes necessary to prepare or amend input to develop separately, competing, as it were, against a hypothetically perfect system. The natural result of this competition is for clerical management to apply more stringent controls, compounding the total problem by splitting it into two self-contained areas, resulting in a highly redundant system in which the common aim is forgotten.

Sometimes one suspects that the use of punch/verify systems originally stemmed from this separatism, but in truth there are very real advantages in blind punching based on the economics of throughput speed. This has nothing to do with equipment response. It is purely a product of character punching in which input accuracy remains unchecked and therefore the punch operator cannot stop to check back and correct clerical errors, thereby completely breaking the work flow. Some loss of computer time in input validation and correction is thereby made inevitable but it may be a small price to pay for advanced input control on large throughput volumes.

The input control must allow for some punch errors passing through verification. This type of error can frequently be detected by record logic checks. These may be applied with great ingenuity and skill to the code content of input records but it is in the apparently simple quantity or amount controls where costly duplication of effort is most frequent and where the original cost benefits may be completely lost. One common form of input to blind punching is made up of individual documents (possibly listed line by line) on each of which there is one amount item without any breakdown.

BATCH CONTROL

The standard accounting solution is to pre-list and total using a small add-lister and subsequently when the input is run, pick up control differences and (dependent on the system) either pass the batch and report the error or treat the batch as invalid and hold for amendment.

The average batch size must first be considered. Assuming 1,200 documents of 20 characters each, the content is 24,000 characters and the probability of pre-list or punch error in one batch is very great. Some types of error may be identifiable to individual records but if one assumes 5 pure amount errors in the batch, equally spaced, the control clerk will not find the last error until he has called back 1,000 lines. On the other hand if the batch was split into 12 sub-batches of 100 items, 7 would pass, 5 would fail and the control clerk would only need to call back 5 x 50 per cent x 100 = 250 lines representing a reduction of 750 lines (or 75 per cent of workload). When considering this it should be remembered that an accurate call-back needs two staff; and using the particular example above a realistic average would be 10 lines per minute resulting in a workload saving of 2-1/2 clerical hours by sub-batching one run.

In these comparisons it is assumed that the error is in the sub-batch content itself and that call back is between the input list and the pre-list. To ensure that no sub-batch is omitted some batch control over the content is required. A sub-batch count is generally preferable because if batch control by overall total is preferred the main benefits of sub-batching only apply if the number of sub-batches themselves are restricted.

DOCUMENT CONTROL

If on the other hand batch control by count is applied there is no practical restriction on the number of sub-batches, and the greater the number, the more accurate the error identification. If carried to extreme, every document could in effect conform to sub-batch logic by simply punch/verifying the amount fields twice. This would need to be done once at the beginning and once at the end of each record to avoid a misread being memorized by the operator and re-punched. A system thus evolves in which the amount fields are keyed four times (punch/verify twice) and the code fields keyed twice (punch/verify once) and the computer produces the only detail input list.

Departmental considerations aside, in pure economics this could be valid because the extra amount of punching is really taking the place of pre-listing (frequently itself called back) which is a more expensive process, and error identification is 'on the dot'. Another common form of accounting document is designed to carry a total and an agreed analysis of that total. Such a document is a natural sub-batch in itself, particularly as the clerical entry of the detail is often small enough to be completed at sight.

COUNT PHILOSOPHY

The common factor is that in both cases the document or line amount content is cross-checked during punching, and clerical control uses a count only. Unfortunately as it stands there is only one batch count and if this reports in error, the system reintroduces the need to call back the full run.

One solution is to preprint, stamp or hand enter sequential numbers on the documents which are punched so that missing or duplicated numbers may be referenced on print-out. More simply, the documents (or line entries) could be made up in groups of, say, 10, with group reference numbers. These would be coded and punched and by splitting the count this way, attention could be drawn to short or over count in any one group. The number of documents in a group should be defined for control purposes only and not be subject to variance enforced by otherwise logical data requirements.

ACCEPTANCE PROBLEMS

It is generally very difficult to gain acceptance for 'amount' documents to enter EDP systems without a cumbersome trail of pre-lists, although strangely, bulk 'quantity' documents are often handled this way. There is, of course, no difference, but even if it is argued that amounts need an extra check this can still sensibly be regarded as a punch discipline. Warning must be sounded that before eliminating pre-list disciplines, input programs must be well proven as far as the agreement of amounts to cross-check entry and the document counts are concerned (one can assume that other errors fall into an existing acceptable control pattern including file total reconciliation). During the proving process pre-listing is virtually essential whether regarded as parallel running or not. Unfortunately once instituted this type of control is difficult to remove.

SUMMARY

No one can dispute that the success of any commercial installation will be measured in the long run in terms of economics and that the major factor in this is the correct use of the computer in terms of output information. Nevertheless before system design, before document design and certainly before considering the many competing claims or statistics on punch equipment and conversion process in general, there should be a complete understanding and effective disciplining of clerical/punch control interaction, overriding departmental politics and reactionary attitudes.

In stating these points I am aware that these problems are not exactly unknown in computer management. There are two sides to most cases and in some instances this paper may be regarded with disinterest (if nothing worse). For any computer specialist who feels this way, it may be a sobering experience to try walking round his house looking at it from outside.

ERROR CONTROL IN EDP SYSTEMS

by Norman D. Peterson

This article is concerned with methods of machine detection and correction of errors in data attributable to both human and machine sources. The data that is naturally of greatest concern is that which is submitted to the system for the first time. The initial submission of data may occur as current transactions, or as files inherited from a previous, perhaps less disciplined system.

ERROR HANDLING PROCEDURES

Error handling procedures in electronic data processing (EDP) systems may be introduced by considering the steps of the typical system, illustrated in Figure 4-1. Data preparation consists of creating source documents, and converting them to machine-readable form by keypunch, portapunch, mark-sensing, optical character reading or other means. In keypunching, the cards are usually subjected to key-verification where the punched cards are passed through a second machine while an operator goes through the same motions as in the original punching.

Reprinted by permission of the publisher from *Management Accounting*, November 1970, pp. 34-36.

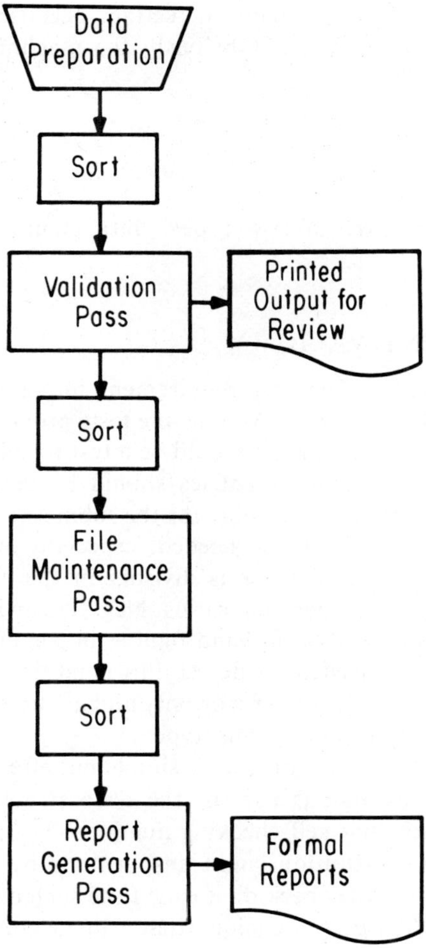

Figure 4-1. Typical System for Data Processing.

Next, or after an intervening sort, the cards are read into the computer or a traditional card tabulating machine. In this phase the data is subjected to error tests, at whatever level of sophistication the equipment may permit, and a printed output is produced for review. This output may be limited to detected errors or it may be a proof list of the complete input. The latter is visually proofread against the original source documents.

After rejecting disallowed data, the remaining data is passed forward to successive phases of computer processing. Subsequent errors may be detected either by machine processing or by visual detection. Maximum use should be made of machine detection, because of the computer's speed and superior reliability. Obviously the machine is not subject to fatigue or lapses in memory.

ERROR CRITERIA

Error criteria are of two types, data element validity and file validity.

DATA ELEMENT VALIDITY

Self-Consistency. The first requirement imposed on recorded data is that it be self-consistent. Among the tests programmed to assure the satisfaction of this requirement, would be a test for blank entries. Where these are not allowed, blank entries should be detected and called to the attention of persons responsible for the submission of data. Likewise a test for zero values may be needed, especially when they are to be used in performing extensions or as divisors in the computation of unit prices, percentages or operating ratios. Negative quantities also may not be realistic, as with balance-on-hand figures in an inventory application and a test may be needed to detect this condition. If certain fields are known to consist of only numeric or only alphabetic information, a simple test will reveal errors of this type.

A procedure for introducing a simple but effective consistency test is to include a check digit as part of the code structure of certain data elements, thus yielding self-checking numbers. The purpose of this technique is to detect substitutions and transpositions by requiring the computer to recalculate the check digit each time such data is read and used.

Probability Limits. A technique that can be applied to many data elements is to establish limiting magnitudes beyond which the data will be reported for review. Thus, in an employee file, ages less than 12 years or more than 75 are probably errors. Note that broadening the limits will reduce the number of false alarms but will catch a smaller number of true errors.

Authority Lists and Internal Tables. Another control device is to set-up an exhaustive table of all allowable codes for certain data elements. Tables of this kind are then kept up-to-date within computer memory, and individual codes are checked against them.

Contextual Consistency. Often error detection can be strengthened by considering data fields, not only singly, but also in combinations. Sometimes the acceptable values for one field will depend upon the values of one or more fields.

FILE VALIDITY

Computer Set-Up. Error control should include proper data-submission and operator procedures. It is also important to keep human intervention to a minimum and where possible to use control totals.

In the typical processing run, a number of options are built into the programs. These may offer choices between weekly, quarterly, and year-end processing, or between white-collar and blue-collar payroll. Sometimes the selection of desired option is made by the operator by the use of switches or keyboard. A better procedure is to use control cards which are prepared in advance by clerical personnel. Still better, when it is possible, is to program the machine to infer the options from the characteristics of the data submitted. In any event, the computer should print out hard-copy documentation of the choices made, so there need be no doubt afterward.

Batch control totals should be submitted to the data processing installation along with the source documents that are to be converted to machine readable form. Submission may be done by adding-machine tape or on transmittal forms, themselves designed for easy conversion. The control totals should at least include record counts, but might well include totals of all numeric entries.

These control figures are then input with the data, aggregated as appropriate and passed from run to run by internal end-of-file labels. Once the data has been read into the computer for the first time, control totals for alphabetic data may also be established by first converting individual letters to numeric equivalents according to some reasonable convention.

Between successive phases, record counts and other control figures are verified by machine comparison, thus eliminating risks of human error. If discrepancies occur, the process is terminated to allow investigation, and, most likely, re-running. In any event, clearly labeled control figures and messages are printed out at the end of each phase.

Sequence Checks. In sequential processing, it is desired that each file be in sort according to certain specified fields or sort keys. The verification of this sequence each time a record is read is perhaps the "universal test" in data processing, in that it can, and perhaps should be, included in every run. "Step downs" will detect unsuccessful sorts or perhaps incorrectly identified files. Further, sequence tests can detect missing records if these are to be numbered consecutively or duplicate records if these are disallowed.

File Maintenance. Whenever a transaction file is processed against another file to up-date the latter, the two input files should be compared against each other for logical discrepancies.[1] If no matching occurs when a transaction is intended to modify or delete an existing record, this should be reported as an error. If a transaction is intended to institute a new record, a record already present with the identifying code likewise indicates an error.

In modifying an existing record, a transaction can carry either a replacement value or a value to be added to the record. For numeric data, the latter practice is generally preferred since this will allow transactions over a period of time to be summarized arithmetically and reported for verification against old and new values.

A further precaution sometimes used for file up-dating is to require each transaction to contain a special code or password that assures that the person submitting data has the authority to make the kind of change specified.

File Retention. To give protection against loss or damage of files, each updated file is generally retained until its second or third successor is generated. By such retention, it will be possible to recreate a lost file.

Reasonable retention periods should be established for source documents, not only to allow the recreation of transactions but also to facilitate any investigation that may be necessitated when errors are encountered.

RESPONSE TO ERROR CONDITIONS

Sequence and control-total errors require that processing be aborted. But for other errors, it is generally preferred that processing continue without interruptions, and that offending transactions be noted and suspended until the next processing cycle. However, before logging out such a transaction, the program should process it through all remaining error tests. The same record should not have to be rejected again when resubmitted with corrections.

As an alternative, the errors can be counted and processing aborted when the count exceeds some predetermined level. This level may be made dependent on elapsed time. Especially as the end of a run is approached and most of the time has already been invested.

As other alternatives, the system can accept transactions with known errors (when they will not have any serious effect), or cause the computer to make corrections on a "best guess" basis. In any event, known and suspected errors should be printed out and routed to the responsible persons with adequate identification of the nature of the error

---

[1]"A Standard Pattern for Sequential File Maintenance," *Computer Group Repository,* Item #R-69-139, Institute of Electrical & Electronics Engineers.

in each instance as well as full particulars as to machine-made corrections so that they can be over-ridden if desired. The errors might be reported in the order of occurrence, or perhaps grouped according to type.

Highly important, but often neglected, is the fact that every kind of error should be capable of direct correction by the user himself. This means that the user should not be dependent upon any programmer or computer specialist even when errors of an exotic nature are encountered. To this end, machine-generated lists of erroneous transactions must include adequate descriptions of the errors, and comprehensive adjustment documents and procedures must be programmed into the system.

THE TRANSACTION VALIDATION PASS

It is the judgment of many data processing specialists that as many data validation functions as possible should be consolidated into one program. Two advantages of such a practice come immediately to mind: First, changes in the design of the system are made more easily since the complex logic typical of error detection is limited to one program where the inter-relationships are more apparent. Second, by placing this program as early as possible in the series of programs, errors can be detected before their effects become more diffuse and more difficult to correct.

However, it can be debated whether the primary sort of transactions should occur before or after the validation pass. Sorting prior to this pass will facilitate the detection of missing data where multiple records have been created for the same transaction. However, in machine generating transcripts of the input, comparison with original batches is easier if the original sequence is retained.

In designing a validation pass, it will often be possible also to include edit features, such as changes in format and machine insertion of codes. The latter may be necessary for sorting or for other processing requirements where it is not practical or necessary to require their inclusion in the submitted data.

THE AUDIT TRAIL

An audit trail is generally provided by assigning a consecutive identification number to each document at its point of origin, and cross-referencing related records by this means. The utility of an audit trail in researching and correcting both visually-detected and machine-detected errors is as follows:

1. Documentation is provided from which any transaction can be reconstructed and its processing continued, should that transaction be misplaced or destroyed at some point in the procedure.
2. A method is provided for tracing transactions from original source document to printed output, from final output back to the original source, and through any intermediate stages of the procedure.

ACCEPTANCE TESTING

The proof of any data system lies in its use. For this reason, no system should be installed without a comprehensive acceptance test.[2]

Too often, acceptance tests are limited to so-called normal data. The test would be more significant if a full range of errors and exceptions were deliberately introduced into the system to verify the manner in which they are detected and handled. Test data should be designed to include as wide a variety of combinations as possible.

Because data processing involves a man-machine system and the human element must be included in the operational test, the effectiveness of written procedures, forms design, computer output, and user training must be verified. In particular, the ability of user personnel to submit correction transactions successfully, and verify their execution, must be confirmed by actual use of the computer and appropriate user and operator procedures.

CONCLUSION

Design of effective error controls in an EDP system is an exacting assignment, but must not be neglected if serious operational troubles are to be avoided. It is also suggested that the users of any EDP system participate actively in the design of the system and the controls associated with it. In addition, it should be remembered that an EDP system is in reality a man-machine system, and should be designed as such. The user should be given the means of making corrections to machine-readable files without dependence on computer specialists for *ad hoc* changes. Both machine elements and human elements should be evaluated by a realistic acceptance test.

---

[2]"A Guide to Acceptance Testing of Computer Software," ***Business and Economic Dimensions,*** June 1970, pp. 5-11.

THE CHECK DIGIT

by Brian Rothery

In the battleground where input devices are sold, there is probably more nonsense thrown about on data verification than on any other subject in the computer trade. Most of it is centered on the check digit.

Briefly, this is a code used in an arithmetic system involving remaindering, which is added to digits to come up with a figure between one and ten. This figure is appended to the field—that is, attached to the right hand side as an extra digit. During future transcription, if any digit in the field is wrongly entered, or dropped, or gets switched with another, the computer in recalculating the check will come up with a different result to the one already entered, thereupon rejecting the document involved.

There are many input devices being sold through heavy emphases on their ability to project data with check digits and batch totals. The first impressions one gets is that the check digit will be magically appended to all of the data in the output record, usually paper tape, thereby guaranteeing its subsequent validity. Let us assume that this is done in the following manner.

A machine operator writes up an invoice on an accounting machine. Her machine has a paper tape attachment, which as she keys in the invoice data, paces her, capturing her input. At the end of the record, she presses a key, bringing the modulus 11 check digit circuitry into action. It scans her line of data, establishes the check digit to match the particular combination of digits and characters and adds it to the end of the row of punches in the paper tape.

FURTHER CHECK BY COMPUTER

Later the tape is read by a computer which again checks the check digit to ensure that it is the same. It is impossible for it not to be the same, unless the holes punched on the paper tape in the first place have somehow moved. Painfully obvious as this may be, it is no more than the straightforward results of speculation on check digit advertising and sales. The trouble is that this sort of check digit gives invalid data as much protection as valid data. The error takes place, of course, as the clerk keys in the information.

Reprinted by permission of the publisher from *Data Processing Magazine*, June 1967, pp. 58-59.

If, however, we look closer at the claims of the check digit, we notice, in the small print, that it will verify check digits already on the source documents. It begins to make sense—operator keys in data followed by check digit, machine adds across the data to arrive at the same check digit. The only problem is to get the check digit onto the original document in the first case. Send it out on invoices so that it comes back in on orders, the paper tape people say, but that is absolutely impossible, unless we know exactly what the customer is going to order.

At last we become aware that the check digit can only be appended to the customer number, and only if our customer is good enough to use the number as shown on our bills to him, the last digit of which, unknown to him, is a check digit. All we can check for then with this equipment is that no digits have been switched or changed in our customer number. Which brings us to the question, why bother? This can be done just as well in the computer, at no delay if we store our error output, with other errors, during the Edit Run, on an exception file.

IMPORTANCE OF CHECK DIGIT

What then can we say that will summarize the position of the check digit? We can say that it is useful for control fields—that is, those fields we access by and sort on, customer number, employee number, etc. We can go further and say that it really matters only with certain control fields, not all. With control fields, the keys by which we find and access records, it is essential that they be correct if we are to find the correct record. If they are incorrect through juxtaposition or other errors in transcription, we will (1) not find the record, and (2) find and process the wrong record.

It is the second case that the check digit tries to protect us against. We fear that we may bill the wrong customer, switch customer bills, or switch pay checks to employees. Remembering the trouble it takes to get customers to use codes that we need, with or without check digits, we then ask what does the check digit give us that is worth this trouble.

If we switch bills to customers, the one that gets the biggest will soon tell us; if we switch employee pay checks, we will hear from one of them even sooner. We achieve better customer relations perhaps if we can avoid the first case; but it already appears that it is impossible to get all of our customers to cooperate with us and our check digits.

There is one job where the check digit is very useful—indeed, absolutely ideal. The job is stores, and the reason why it suits stores is that stores has a certain peculiarity. It is that, being a management by exception system that operates on inanimate bins rather than people, we are not aware of a switch when we make one. Let us say that the digits of a large requisition get switched so that the quantity is deducted from the wrong bin on the master file. Bolts went out to the production line, from the bolt bin, but nuts were deducted from the "Nut" master record.

The reduction caused the stock of nuts on file to drop below reorder level, raising an indent and an order. Nuts that are not needed are ordered, while bolts, very much needed, are not ordered. The situation comes to light when someone notices the level of the bolt bin, probably after the next requisition. By then there could be a stock out situation, resulting in a production hold up. Check digits guard against this.

OPTICAL SCANNING USE

One of the most novel uses of the check digit can be seen in the IBM 1287 optical scanner. The writer enters his control field followed by the check digit. If one of his characters is not clear, the machine looks at the check digit, carries out its arithmetic on the legible characters, and subtracts the result from the result that would give the check digit to establish the character in doubt. It then rebuilds this character.

It can be seen then, that check digits, if they are to be of any use, must be on the original documents appended to control fields, or any other fixed fields. If they are to become a part of such numbers—material code for stores say—how is this to be done? It is done just prior to the original computer conversion job, before the master or ledger cards are punched up and converted to magnetic files.

All of the material codes, in a long list, are punched up and run through the computer on a special check digit calculation run. Check digits appropriate to each material code are calculated, and printed out as part of that code, in tables of material codes. These tables, or lists of new material codes, are sent to stores where they are used to enter the check digit, the extra digit to be added to the material code, onto the master records. It is by no means an overwhelming job, but well worth the investment.

COMMENTS ON THE STRUCTURAL CHECK OF INPUT DATA IN A COMPUTER SYSTEM

by Joseph A. Greco

Reprinted by permission of the publisher from *The Journal of Accountancy*, June 1968, pp. 46-52, copyright 1968 by the American Institute of Certified Public Accountants, Inc.

Both accountants and information processing specialists recognize the importance of designing proper control over input data in computerized information processing systems. Many internal control features have been built into existing computer programs and the search for new internal control techniques continues.

SOME COMMON PROGRAM CHECKS OF INPUT DATA

In computerized systems, part of the task of verifying the accuracy of the system's input is assigned to the computer, and input checks are incorporated in computer program design. Some of the common programmed checks of input data are the composition check, the limit check, the coding check and the combination check.

COMPOSITION CHECK

The composition check verifies the completeness of data; based upon the transaction code, the input is analyzed to assure that all required information has been reported. By way of illustration, in reporting a sales transaction, the required information might include the part number of the product sold, the quantity sold, the customer account number and the salesman's code. If such is the case, each sales transaction would be scanned by the computer and the presence of these required variables verified.

LIMIT CHECK

The limit check is employed to test the reasonableness of the data. In processing payroll, the reasonableness test might be employed to ascertain that no employee paid on a weekly basis is paid for more than 72 hours (assuming company policy to limit hours worked to 12 hours per day, 6 days per week).

CODING CHECK

The coding check tests the validity of codes used in recording input. Accordingly, a self-checking feature is built into the code itself. A basic coding structure is developed (such as the use of the social security numbér for identifying employees in recording transactions); then a formula is employed to calculate a check digit based on the existing coding structure. In reporting transactions, the modified code (including the check digit) is used to report transactions. When such transactions are entered into the computer, the formula originally used to calculate the check digit is employed to check the validity of the individual code (see Figure 4-2).

COMBINATION CHECK

The combination check tests the interdependence of data. If a company deals in two product lines—one of industrial nature while the other is consumer-oriented—and it sells the products to two unique sets of customers (industrial firms and wholesalers), it could identify these characteristics in its customer and product codes. Then, when processing sales transactions, the product-customer relationship could be tested to ascertain that it represents a logical product-customer combination.

LIMITATIONS OF PROGRAM CHECKS

The employment of these program checks does not provide a fail-safe verification of input data in computer-based systems.

The composition check verifies the presence of the necessary variables but not the accuracy of the individual items. The limit check while protecting against gross errors still allows errors within the limit. If a weekly employee works 45 hours and his time is recorded at 54 hours, the error will not be detected by a limit check. The coding check will verify that the code used is a valid code, not the correct code. If a manager, in preparing a salary increase authorization for himself, erroneously records an employee's identification number on the form rather than his own number, the computer will give the salary increase to the employee instead of to the manager. The combination check, while verifying that only industrial products are billed as sales to industrial customers, will not verify that the correct industrial product is billed.

STRUCTURAL CHECK OF COMPUTER INPUT

The use of a structural check of accounting input data has been recently advanced as a candidate for improvement of control of input data by Professor David Li in an article entitled "A Structural Check

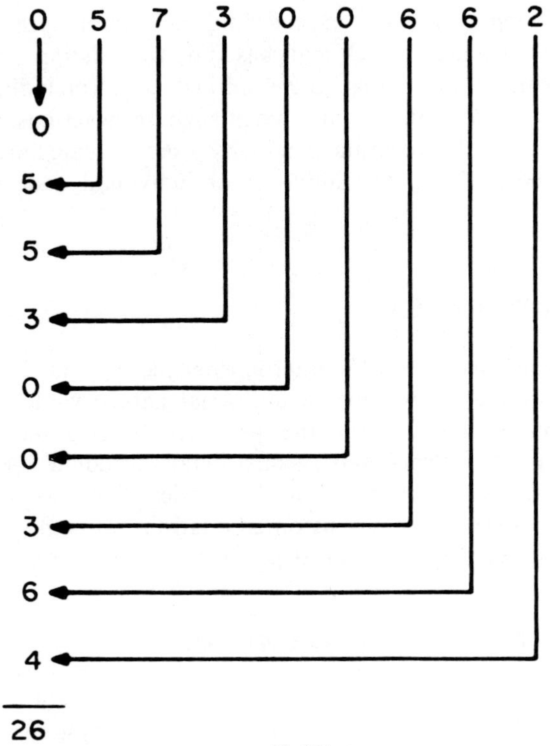

10-6=4

1. *Formula:* Starting with the left most integer of the basic code, multiply the first integer by two. (If the result of a multiplication is greater than ten, the value is equal to the sum of the two resulting integers.) To this result add the next integer, multiply the next integer by two and add the result; continue applying these alternate procedures to the remaining integers. Subtract the units integer of the result from ten and designate this value as the check digit.

2. *Example:*
   A. Basic code: 057-30-0662
   B. Application of check-digit formula:

i. 0 X 2 = 0, add 0
ii. add 5
iii. 7 X 2 = 14, 1 + 4 = 5, add 5
iv. add 3
v. 0 X 2 = 0, add 0
vi. add 0
vii. 6 X 2 = 12, 1 + 2 = 3, add 3
viii. add 6
ix. 2 X 2 = 4, add 4
x. Total result
xi. subtract unit integer of result (6) from 10 giving check digit 4

Figure 4-2. Illustration of the Calculation of a Check Digit.

of Accounting Input Data in a Computer System."[3] The structural check is defined as a ". . . variation of the combination check,"[4] and is employed to test ". . . the logical relationship of debit and credit accounts of each transaction transmitted to the computer for processing."[5] Accordingly, Professor Li develops his check based upon an analysis of the chart of accounts. In the example set forth, he empl ys a chart of accounts consisting of 25 account numbers. Noting that there are 600 unique transaction combinations (multiple debit and/or credit entries are disallowed in the system), Dr. Li goes on to demonstrate that the number of logical transaction combinations is much less. He limits the number of acceptable transaction combinations to 26.

The list of acceptable transaction combinations is incorporated in the computer program to process accounting data; the debit and credit account numbers of each transaction transmitted for processing are jointly tested against the acceptable transaction combinations and only those transactions with account coding corresponding to those contained in the computer program are accepted for processing. All other transactions are rejected by the computer as unacceptable.

THE BASIS OF DETERMINING LOGICAL TRANSACTION COMBINATIONS

In discussing the design of transaction combinations, Professor Li stated that ". . . to take full advantage of the structural check, the chart of transaction combinations should be made compact rather than exhaustive. . . ."[6] Some of the typical transaction combinations provided for are:

Transaction Title	*Debit/Credit Accounts*
Remittances	Cash/Accounts Receivable
Cash Sales	Cash/Revenue From Sales
Sales on Account	Accounts Receivable/Revenue From Sales
Purchases	Inventories/Accounts Payable

In limiting the number of transaction combinations, illogical combinations of valid account codes are rejected and purged from the system.

---

[3]David F. Li, "A Structural Check of Accounting Input Data in a Computer System," *JofA*, June 1967, p. 54.

[4]*Ibid.*

[5]*Ibid.*, p. 55.

[6]*Ibid.*, p. 54.

Accordingly, a transaction coded as a debit to Depreciation Expense and a credit to Cash would be rejected, because such an illogical combination would not be listed as an acceptable transaction combination. Without the structural check, even if account codes included a check digit, the transaction would be accepted, provided the correct Depreciation Expense and Cash account codes were recorded. Here lies the principal advantage for the employment of a structural check of accounting input data.

EVALUATION OF THE STRUCTURAL CHECK OF ACCOUNTING INPUT DATA

The use of the combination or structural check of input data, implemented in a sophisticated integrated information processing system, has potential as an internal control technique. However, its implementation in the context proposed by Professor Li, based upon a test of the relationship of the debit and credit account numbers used to record business transactions for computer processing, is inappropriate. The use of the structural check in connection with account coding of business transactions would necessitate a negation of the advance made by the development of special journals used in recording accounting information.

The use of special journals has enabled accountants to eliminate the task of assigning and recording a debit and credit account number to each journal entry used to record the common repetitive transactions of the business. By recording the amount of the transaction in the appropriate column of the special journal, the debit and credit account numbers are automatically assigned to the transaction. As an example, in posting the amount of a receipt from a customer on account in the cash receipts journal, a debit to cash and a credit to accounts receivable is automatically assigned to the transaction.

In computerized accounting systems, the method employed to provide an efficient means of recording common repetitive transactions is the transaction code. When preparing data for computer input, a unique transaction code is used to identify such a transaction (e.g., a cash receipt from a customer on account). While processing the data, the computer program, on the basis of the transaction code, would automatically assign the appropriate debit and credit account numbers to the transaction. Therefore, a system designed to provide a structural check based upon the chart of accounts would require the elimination of transaction coding and its replacement by debit and credit account coding. Since transaction codes are more compact than a code based on a double account number, transaction coding is more efficient in terms of coding, data conversion and minimum error potential.

INTEGRATED VS. NONINTEGRATED EDP

The development of integrated information processing systems and their underlying concept of single information flow reinforces the desirability of maintaining the transaction code concept. Integrated data processing concepts differ substantially from conventional sequential (batch) processing concepts.

The development of economically feasible random access storage devices added a new dimension to data processing designs and concepts.[7]

Prior to the advent of random access storage, business data processing was designed on the basis of the sequential (batch) processing concept. The computer was employed on a functional basis to process data for a particular task such as payroll, customer accounting or inventory control. Each of these systems was independently designed with the only possible interrelationship that of the sharing of common input data. Employing the sequential processing concept, the data sets for the systems were arranged in a significant sequential order (such as employee number in the case of payroll), and then transactions affecting the data set were accumulated into batches for daily, weekly or monthly processing—depending upon the economics of the situation. In processing the batch, the transactions were first sorted into the same sequence as the data set and were then processed. If the same transactions affected another data set, they would be re-sorted into a new sequence corresponding to the sequence of that data set (see Figure 4-3).

RANDOM ACCESS PROCESSING

Random access storage devices have been designed to store large data sets in a manner which allows for the rapid direct access of any record in the data set without the necessity for searching sequentially through the whole set.

With this random access capability, the single information flow concept arose.[8] This concept advocates the storage of all the firm's data sets on random access storage devices, and the processing of a transaction by introducing it into the computer once and, simultaneously, recording its effect on all data sets affected by its occurrence. This concept became feasible because, with all the data sets on random access processing, the record in each data set affected by the transaction can be directly

---

[7]Victor J. Dankis, "Random Access Equipment—Its Effect Upon Accounting," *NAA Bulletin,* 1962.

[8]A.F. Moravee, "Basic Concepts for Planning Advanced EDP Systems," *Management Services,* May-June 1965, p. 52.

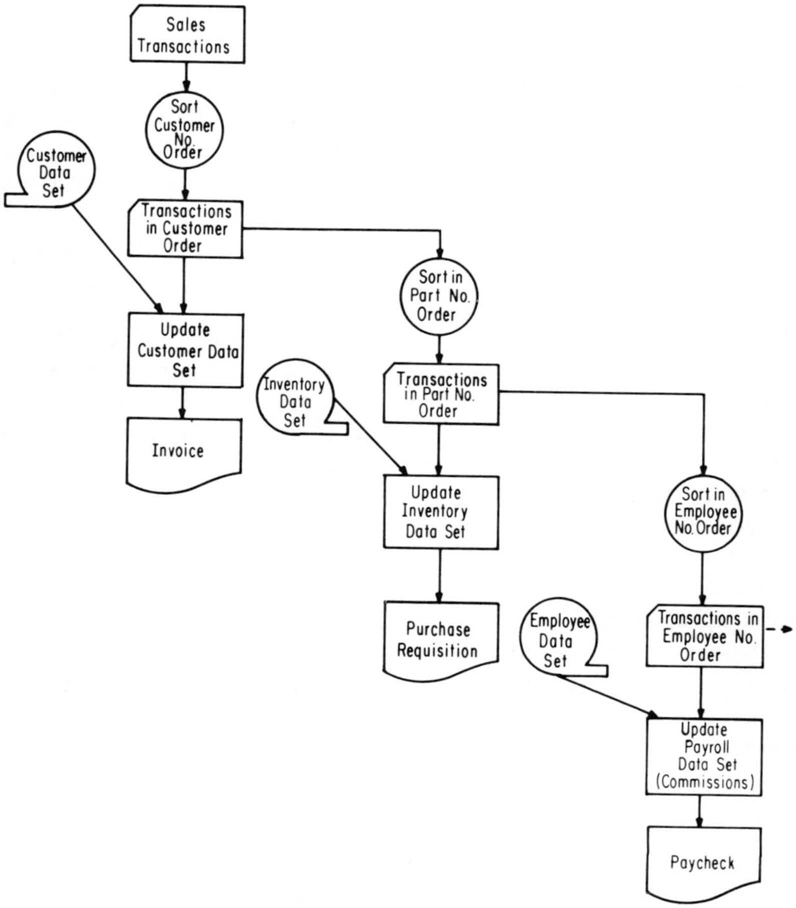

Figure 4-3. Illustration of Sequential (Batch) Processing; Processing Effect of a Sales Transaction on Customer, Inventory and Payroll (Commissions) Data Set.

retrieved, brought into the computer and the effect of the transaction recorded there (see Figure 4-4).

TRANSACTION CODES IN AN INTEGRATED SYSTEM

In the environment of integrated data processing based upon the single information flow concept, the concept of a transaction becomes critical and the uniqueness of transactions must be determined with reference to a much expanded universe.

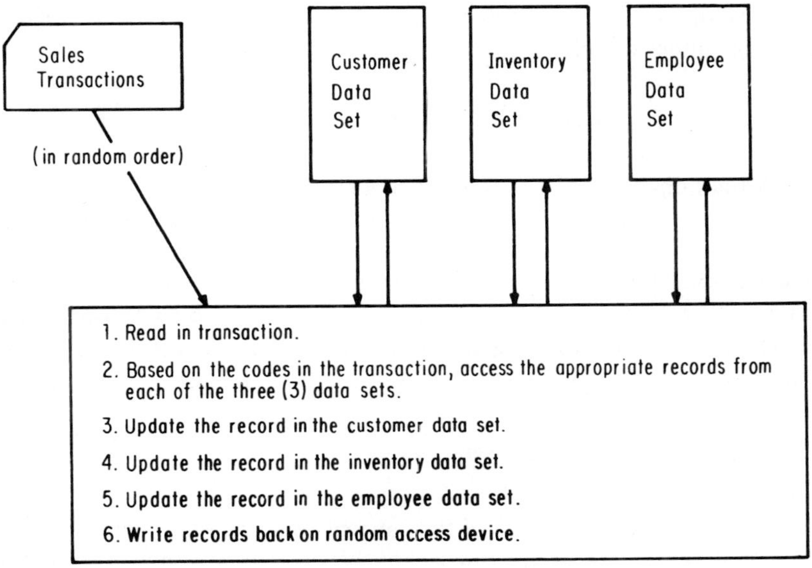

Figure 4-4. Illustration of Random Access Processing; Processing Effect of a Sales Transaction on Customer, Inventory and Payroll (Commissions) Data Set.

As an example, in a computerized system that is not integrated, the shipment of merchandise to a customer is recorded as a debit to accounts receivable and a credit to sales, regardless of the circumstances under which the shipment is made. In an integrated system where a shipment in addition to affecting sales and accounts receivables also affects inventory balances, the uniqueness of transactions might have to be redefined. Assuming in such a situation the policy of backordering shipments when out of stock and the maintenance of a record of backorders in the inventory data set, the shipment of merchandise has to be defined as two transactions rather than one. One transaction would be the shipment of merchandise that was not backordered. Such a transaction would affect sales, accounts receivable and inventory on hand. The second transaction, the shipment of a backordered sale, would affect the same records and would also have to be recorded as a reduction or elimination of the quantity backordered.

Because of the efficiency of the single information flow concept in reducing duplication in input data and in the computer time used to bring data into its computer, the thrust in development of new information systems is and will be toward integrated data processing systems. A structural check based upon account coding would be in conflict with this development. As a consequence, this use of the structural check would be undesirable.

BEHAVIORAL CONSIDERATIONS

A final objection to the concept of a structural check of logical combinations of debit and credit account numbers is based upon behavioral considerations. In working with a system employing such a check, personnel responsible for coding will soon adopt the list of acceptable transaction combinations as the list of transaction codes used to classify input to the system. This will negate the structural check and lead to *de facto* transaction coding that is inefficient.

AN ALTERNATIVE ILLUSTRATION

Although the application of the concept of a structural check to account coding is undesirable, the use of this concept in sophisticated integrated information processing systems would improve the internal control of the system.

In fact, under the single flow concept, since all data sets related to the transaction being processed are accessed at one time, many more opportunities for employing the structural check present themselves. One hypothetical application of the structural check concept that comes to mind is in an information processing system for a manufacturing plant operated on a job order basis.

Such a system implies the integration of inventory control, production control and scheduling, cost accounting and payroll. This example will also assume random access storage of the appropriate data sets and input terminals (to the computer) on the factory floor. In such a system, one of the key transactions is the use of direct labor resources in the production process. In recording these transactions, the concept of a structural check will be employed to verify the accuracy of the input (see Figure 4-5).

IMPLEMENTING THE STRUCTURAL CHECK

The structural check will be implemented on the basis of the interrelationships of the sequenced operations specified in the Job Order Operation and Routing Record prepared by the industrial engineering organization of the plant. This record lists in appropriate sequence and describes each operation that has to be performed for the particular job

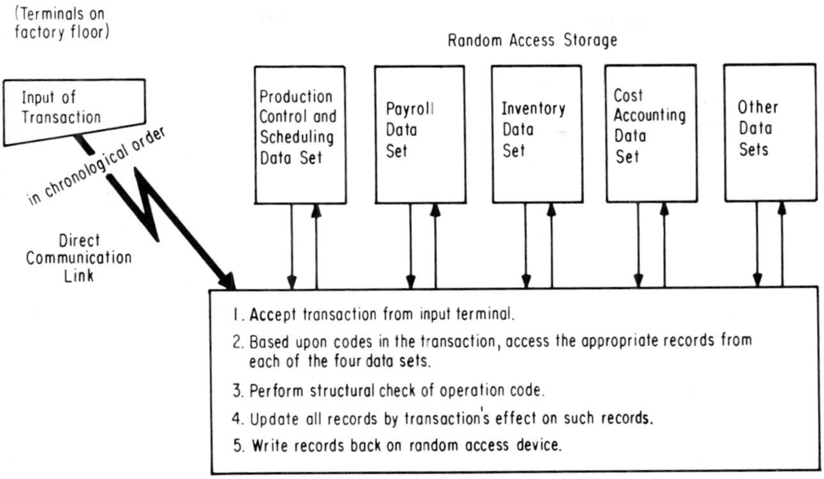

Figure 4-5. Illustration of Random Access Processing: Direct Labor Usage Transaction—Using a Structural Check of the Operation Code.

in process. To facilitate the structural check and to provide the basis of the scheduling and expediting systems, this record will be stored in the random access storage of the computer.

As each employee records his labor time at the input terminal on the factory floor, he would enter his employee number, the job order number and the operation number he is about to perform. When this information is received by the computer, the records in the data sets affected by this transaction are accessed and brought into the computer, and a number of structural checks are performed.

First, the computer would test the Job Order Operation and Routing Record for the job and ascertain that the operation to be performed is listed in that record.

Second, the computer would ascertain that the operations sequenced prior to the operation currently being performed have been completed. (This check assumes that the system will record operations as they are completed in the record.)

Finally, the relationship between the employee's job classification and cost center of employment, on the one hand, and the operation being performed, on the other hand, would be tested to ascertain that this particular combination is a logical transaction combination.

In such a system, if we assume that time is recorded internally by the computer's clock, that each employee is furnished with a badge with his employee number that is readable by the input devices, and that a similar badge or card is prepared for each job entering into production, the amount of variable data that the employee enters is reduced to the operation code. And this one item of variable data will be verified by the structural checks described earlier.

Of course, flexibility would have to be provided for deviations that conflict with the structural checks; since such deviations would be of an isolated nature, the system could provide for structural checks being overridden on the authority of the direct laborer's immediate supervisor.

Once the operation code is verified by the structural checks, the transaction can be used to update the inventory, production control, cost accounting and payroll data sets.

CONCLUSION

The use of the structural check as proposed in the above hypothetical example is more appropriate than its use in an account coding context. A structural check based upon account coding does not provide for an efficient method of recording common repetitive transactions. Because it negates the use of transaction codes, it is not in harmony with the single information flow concept (the basis of integrated data processing systems). Finally, because of behavioral considerations, its implementation in practice would be perverted and the acceptable logical transaction combinations would degenerate into a transaction code that is inefficient and unwieldy.

The structural check, however, if employed imaginatively in an integrated data processing system (which provides more opportunities for its use), is a powerful tool in controlling the accuracy of the systems input. Such use is not in conflict with the transaction code concept and does not increase the amount of input that has to be entered into the system; rather, this use of the structural check is employed to verify the remaining variables that are subject to error.

NEW GENERATION EDP CONTROL CONSIDERATIONS

by Robert F. Moloney

Fast-response data processing systems, generally referred to as "real time" or "on-line systems," have made rapid progress over the past sev-

---

Reprinted by permission of the publisher from *Management Services,* March-April 1968, pp. 15-22, copyright 1968 by the American Institute of Certified Public Accountants, Inc.

eral years. Much of this progress can be attributed to the introduction of third generation computer equipment and supporting software capable of handling the complexities inherent in these systems.

The traditional control concepts, painstakingly built up over the past decade for batch-type operations, are no longer adequate. The use of communication facilities operating in an on-line mode, duplex equipment configurations, multiprocessing and multiprogramming necessitates the development of additional control techniques if these systems are to process all data accurately and efficiently.

The purpose of this article is to discuss some of these new control requirements which systems analysts, programmers and auditors should be considering in the design of any real time system. These controls are considered in this article in four categories: on line controls, data protection controls, diagnostic controls and emergency procedures.

ON-LINE CONTROLS

The use of communication lines to transmit data in systems of this type requires the use of an on-line terminal device by which messages are transmitted to or received from a computer. The most important consideration when operating in this mode is to ensure that the data being transmitted are received and properly processed. It is always possible for messages to be lost or garbled or perhaps for a line or terminal device to go out of order during transmission. To prevent this from happening the system should provide program routines to check on messages sent through the system. These routines should provide for at least the following:

MESSAGE IDENTIFICATION HANDLING PROCEDURES TO ENSURE THAT EACH MESSAGE IS PROPERLY HANDLED

Every message received at the data center should be identified by a message header showing such information as message number, terminal, date and action code. This information is necessary for the initializer routine to route the message to the proper program for processing. If a message with an incorrect header is received, it should be routed to a control group for corrective action or rejected with a request to the originating terminal for retransmission of the entire message.

MESSAGE TRANSMISSION CONTROLS TO DETERMINE THAT ALL MESSAGES TRANSMITTED OVER THE LINES ARE RECEIVED

This is done by assigning each message a number, usually within a block, and subsequently verifying the sequence of the message numbers received. Unaccounted-for numbers are considered exceptions to be investigated. Another control is the confirmation by the computer or terminal of all messages received.

One such system used a combination of these two methods. Each location was assigned sequential numbers 000 through 999. As an item was transmitted to the computer, it was assigned a message number, which was stored internally by the computer. Periodically a routine checking of these numbers would produce a report of out-of-sequence numbers and those remaining unused. These were forwarded to each originating location, which checked them against a log maintained for that purpose. Lost messages were retransmitted. Additionally, every message received by the computer was confirmed. This told the operator downline that it had been received by the processor and enabled him to verify the accuracy of the data.

REROUTING PROCEDURES TO HANDLE MESSAGES SENT TO DOWNLINE STATIONS WHICH ARE NOT OPERATING

When this happens it is necessary to provide routines to reroute the message to another terminal or store the message internally in the computer until such time as the down terminal restarts operation. The procedures for dealing with this type of operation are sometimes called "willful intercept." (The action to be taken when the computer breaks down is not discussed here since this topic will be covered under the category of emergency conditions.)

CHECK CHARACTERS TO DETECT TRANSMISSION ERRORS

Two data verification procedures generally used to check the accuracy of transmitted data are the character and message parity checks. The character parity check, with which most accountants are familiar, verifies the accuracy of each character transmitted. The message parity check is a check digit compiled at the originating terminal, based upon the number of bits in the message sent, which is tacked on to the end of that message. The receiving terminal, similarly, compiles a check digit based on the number of bits received, and both check digits are compared. If they agree, a "transmission correctly received" signal is sent to the terminal or processor. If the communication lines have introduced errors, the system should provide for an alert signal to the terminal notifying it of the error or, preferably, for the automatic retransmission of the entire message.[9] In the latter case, if the error condition still exists the terminal should be alerted.

DATA PROTECTION CONTROLS

The on-line capability inherent in a real time system creates a problem of data protection. Information stored in the files may be made available to terminal operators at their request. This raises the question as to what procedures are necessary to prevent data from being accidentally destroyed or used by unauthorized personnel. The question is especially critical when the information involved is highly confidential or the system operates in a time sharing mode. The problem becomes even more complex in a multiprogrammed system: What assurance is there that program segments read into core storage will not be accidentally loaded over data currently being processed?

For purposes of this discussion data protection includes those measures incorporated in the system to prevent concurrent updating of stored files, unauthorized use of stored files and accidental destruction of data in core storage during processing by the computer. Applicable control considerations are discussed in the following three sections.

CONCURRENT UPDATING

The normal types of errors which can occur during the transmission of data over the communication lines do not pose serious problems as the majority of these can be discovered through the use of a strong edit routine and the incorporation of the on line controls previously discussed. But what about the problem of concurrent updating, as when two transactions in a multiprogrammed system attempt to update the same file simultaneously. For instance, transactions A and B retrieve the same file and update it. If the updated version of the file resulting from transaction A is stored first, it will be lost when transaction B is stored. What is needed is a procedure which permits only one transaction to update a

---

[9] For a more thorough discussion of this topic refer to IBM Corporation, "Message Control System Concepts," Reference C20-1609, p. 5.

file at a time. In the IBM system software package this is referred to as "exclusive control."

"Exclusive control" can be achieved by requiring each transaction to "request" permission of the supervisory program to update a file. If the file is available, the supervisory program grants the request and the transaction updates it. During this time no other transaction is permitted access to this file.

DATA SECURITY

The prevention of unauthorized access to stored data can generally be accomplished by the use of lockwords, authority lists and dedicated communication lines. Lockwords, sometimes referred to as "keywords" or "passwords," consist of several characters in a data file which the input transaction or inquiry must match in order to gain access to the file. The use of this device to control file references may be further refined by supplying several lockwords. For instance, one set of characters may permit the file to be retrieved for reading purposes only (read-protect), and still another set may permit both reading and writing.

When using lockwords, consideration should be given to the type of terminal used. If the lockword appears on each document printed by the terminal, it may defeat its own purpose since it becomes relatively easy to compromise it. There are devices available from which the lockword can be entered into the system in a non-print mode. This type of terminal should be used where feasible.

AUTHORITY LISTS

Authority lists are another form of protection. In this instance, the lockword is used to identify the person transmitting from the remote location. After the initial identification has been established, reference is made to an authority list which indicates which type of data the sender is authorized to receive. As with lockwords, the authority list may classify references to the files as read only or both read and write.

The previous discussion regarding the use of these two techniques does not exclude the use of other approaches to accomplish the same ends. For instance, "if an inquiry is received from a remote station. . . . . asking for confidential data, the computer might break the connection and then redial it, after checking to see that the station is authorized to receive the data."[10] The extent to which these controls are used will depend on the type of system and the nature of the stored data.

When lockwords and authority lists are not used, terminals may be identified by means of dedicated communication lines. This generally implies the use of only one terminal on the line. Where terminals are attached to a party line or a similar network, answerback would be used in lieu of a dedicated communication line. With answerback a signal is sent to the terminal, and the latter responds within a prescribed amount of time with its code identification. Because this system can be compromised, it is not recommended where the security of stored data is of major importance.

The first two methods discussed should successfully exclude unauthorized personnel from the stored data files. However, even the best coding system can be broken if an individual can work on it. What procedure, then, can be incorporated in a system of this nature to prevent an unauthorized individual from transmitting data to the processor in an attempt to decode the lockword and gain access to the system? A monitoring routine could be established which would count the number of unsuccessful attempts to enter the system and after a certain number had been reached, say, three times in succession, a message might be printed out at the data station with instructions to call the downline station for an explanation. The point to be made here is this: If the data are important enough to require the use of lockwords and authority lists in the system, it is important to ensure that these controls are effectively accomplishing their assignments.

BOUNDARY REGISTERS

MEMORY PROTECTION

In a multi-programmed system, a number of different data elements will be in core storage at the same time. These will consist of the control program, a portion of which will permanently reside in core; a number of operational programs, and various queues of messages awaiting processing or in the process of being handled by the computer. Because of the possibility of a programming or a machine error, an operational program could address portions of core storage outside the limits of its own

---

[10]Canning Publications, Inc., *EDP Analyzer,* vol. 4, no. 3 (March 1966), p. 12.

coding, work areas or other applicable areas. The result could be the alteration or modification of another program; the destruction of data on tape, disk or drum; or perhaps the creation of a series of endless loops. To keep this from happening the system should provide for some form of memory protection.

One technique currently employed is the use of boundary registers. This requires additional equipment in the form of an upper and lower boundary register. In the simplest form of this system the boundary registers are loaded with the upper and lower core storage addresses of the program when it is loaded into the processor. If during the course of the program the address portion of the instruction exceeds the boundaries indicated in the registers, an interrupt occurs, and control is passed to the supervisor program for appropriate action.[11]

The IBM and the Spectra 70 use storage and protection keys. Core storage in these systems is broken up into blocks. Each block has a four-bit storage key assigned to it. The program status word for each program has a four-bit protection key. Before any program references a block of core storage for the purpose of writing data, the storage key and the protection key must be matched; otherwise the operation is aborted, and control is passed to the supervisory program.

It is easy to see that there are a number of different approaches, depending on the equipment used, to provide memory protection. Since this topic has been thoroughly discussed in various EDP publications,[12] it will not be discussed further in this article.

DIAGNOSTIC CONTROLS

One of the characteristics of a real time system is that it must operate without stopping for fixed periods of time. The duration of time will depend upon the equipment configuration. A duplexed system can be designed to operate 24 hours a day, whereas a simplex system operates for only part of the day. Suppose, however, that there is a malfunction of some component part or that a programming error occurs while the system is operating. Should the processing halt, as was usually the case with second generation equipment, or should it continue processing after branching to some routine to handle the problem? The general rule is to keep the system operating if there is some way of circumventing the

---

[11]For a more thorough discussion of this topic, refer to William H. Desmonde, *Real-Time Data Processing Systems, Introductory Concepts,* Englewood Cliffs, N.J.: Prentice-Hall, Inc., 1964, chap. 4.

[12]See especially Canning Publications, Inc., *EDP Analyzer,* pp. 10-12.

trouble. To accomplish this objective, it is necessary to build into the system some way of detecting and isolating error conditions so that appropriate action can be taken. This can be done through the use of diagnostic programs.

"Diagnostic programs are a tool used to test computers, isolate component malfunctions, and improve overall computer system operations."[13] We are interested only in those on-line routines which detect the fact that errors are happening and isolate, where possible, the cause of the error.[14] Once the error has been isolated it is up to the supervisory program to determine what action is necessary. According to Martin,[15] one of six actions can be taken:

1. Re-execute the faulty instruction and continue processing.
2. Restart the program in question.
3. Transfer to an exception routine characteristic of the program in question.
4. Initiate switchover.
5. Initiate closedown.
6. Halt.

Each of these alternatives will be discussed in the section on emergency procedures which succeeds this section.

The number and types of diagnostic programs in a particular system will depend on the design of the system and its equipment configuration.

For purposes of illustration, the following is an example of how these programs might work:

Consider a real time system communicating with a number of remote terminals. Suddenly a terminal breaks down. When this happens, a diagnostic program checks the communication network and establishes that there is a problem. Another diagnostic program checks each line until the down terminal is isolated. Once the error has been isolated, control is returned to the supervisory program, which might close down this line until repairs are made and route all interim messages to an adjoining terminal for manual handling.

It is always possible, of course, that errors may occur which will not be detected by such routines. The only protection against invalid data created by such errors is to have adequate file reconstruction procedures.

---

[13]James Martin, *Programming Real Time Systems*, Englewood Cliffs, N.J.: Prentice-Hall, Inc., 1965, p. 125.

[14]Although there will be a number of off-line routines peculiar to real time systems, we are not interested in them for purposes of this discussion, since they do not affect the system while it is operating and are generally used only by the systems engineer.

[15]Martin, *Programming Real Time Systems*, p. 224.

EMERGENCY PROCEDURES

Once an error or malfunction has been isolated, it is up to the supervisory program to take appropriate action. As was stated previously, it has a number of choices. The first three of these—re-execute the faulty instruction, restart the program or transfer control to an exception routine—do not present any unique problems. They have been satisfactorily tested in the traditional batch processing systems, and similar procedures can be incorporated into real time systems. The last three alternatives—initiate switchover, close down part of the system or halt—are unique problems and require careful consideration if the system is to provide for all contingencies.

Failures that can cause a system to switch computers or close down a part of the system are generally due to hardware malfunctions. When a system is able to switch its operation from one computer to another, as is possible in a duplexed system, without changing its method of processing data, we say a "switchover" has occurred. On the other hand, if an equipment malfunction occurs in the system which requires the system to close down some part of the operation and modify its method of processing data to circumvent the error, we say it is functioning in a "fallback" mode. Whenever either of these conditions arises it is necessary to provide procedures to ensure that they are efficiently handled.

Switchover, as stated previously, assumes the use of duplex computers so that if the operating computer breaks down its supporting unit will take over processing. When the change from one unit to another takes place, whether it is automatic or manual, the machine operator should be informed via the console or printer what action he is required to take, if any, and the reason why the change was made. For an automatic switchover to take place, the on line computer should initiate action. However, if the malfunction is serious, this may not always be possible. To ensure that a changeover is effected when such a malfunction occurs, the standby computer should periodically check its counterpart. If it detects a malfunction, it should initiate the switchover. Whenever this transition takes place, a message notifying terminal operators of this fact should be sent downline.

During the transition it is vitally important that transactions not be lost. Messages that have not actually entered the system present no problems since these will be noted as missing when the sequence check (discussed under on line controls) is made. The problem lies with those that have entered the system and are awaiting processing on input, work, or output queues. This problem may be resolved by recording the message sequence number after a record has been updated rather than as each message enters the system, or perhaps both actions might be recorded and subsequently compared to each other. Another method is to post the message sequence number to the file as it is updated. In the event of a switchover the comparison of the transaction and file message number will prevent a file from being updated twice. It may or may not prevent messages from being lost depending on the system design.

GRACEFUL DEGRADATION

Fallback or "graceful degradation," as it is sometimes called, occurs in a non-duplexed system when a part of the equipment configuration breaks down but the lossof the particular piece(s) is not serious enough to shut down the entire system. When this happens, the machine operator should be informed by the control program as to the current status of the system and what action he should take. In some instances terminal operators should also be informed. Procedures should be available to advise supervisory personnel what clerical action is necessary to support the system until it recovers and, finally, what action is necessary to restore the system to the condition that existed before the fallback occurred.

The results may be catastrophic when a real time system halts. If the halt is due to a complete breakdown of a major component the only thing to do is repair it as rapidly as possible. Procedures should be available for supervisors so that they may take necessary emergency action and guide clerical personnel in work which must be done while the system is down and initially after it recovers.

It is imperative that restart procedures be incorporated in the system. The restart is based on a complete checkpoint record written on a peripheral device such as a disk file. The checkpoint record, provision for which should be incorporated in the system, is a complete record of all messages, counters, logs and status indicators in the system at that time. When a restart is necessary, the checkpoint record is used to restore the system to its condition at the time the checkpoint record was written. Each terminal is advised of the restart and the number of the last message properly received from the terminal at the time of the checkpoint. Subsequent messages are retransmitted, and the system is again operational.

If the halt occurs because of a system overload the problem is not as serious. System overloads can occur when a number of messages are read into core and subsequently it is discovered that there are not enough available core blocks to complete all the work the computer has started. This problem can occur in a multiprogrammed system using random input. There must be some emergency procedures in the system to handle this dilemma.

It is possible to prevent this from happening, except in rare instances, by anticipating when the level of core blocks available for processing data in the computer is reaching a danger point. When this level has been reached, the computer should shut down and refuse to accept any more input. This means the computer must be able to control the volume to input during peak periods. This control is exercised in a system utilizing "polling" techniques by not "polling" the transmitting locations until the overload is ended. Another method that may be used is for the processor to send a signal either requesting the operator to reenter the message into the system or locking the terminal pending further notice from the computer.

If the overload does occur, however, the system should be able to handle the problem by first determining the application programs temporarily in core which are not currently being used and making their applicable blocks available for the further processing of data. If this doesn't solve the problem, the system may have to destroy messages in the system, preferably on a last-in basis, and request the applicable terminals to repeat the messages.

CONCLUSION

Real time systems are here to stay. If systems analysts, programmers and auditors are to design and review these complex applications, it is necessary that they understand what a real time system is and, more important, the controls necessary to ensure that the desired results are produced. An understanding of the traditional controls is not sufficient when operating in a real time environment. Although these controls, such as matching and batching or validity and limit checks, are just as necessary to the effective operation of a real time system as to a batch system, the nature of the real time system has necessitated additional controls to ensure that the system operates as desired.

This article discusses many of those control considerations. It is not intended as an all-inclusive statement of control requirements in real time applications, since these will be dictated by such factors as system design specifications, the equipment used, security requirements and many other factors. It merely summarizes some of the more common control considerations basic to a well designed real time system.

CONTROLLING DATA TRANSMISSION ERRORS

by Dixon R. Dale

Error control procedures assure that messages transmitted over a noisy communications channel will be received exactly as they were sent. To implement these procedures, a sending station comprised of a modem and some type of business machine or terminal equipment is equipped to generate redundant information. These extra bits are combined with the actual message data and transmitted over the link.

Redundancy is a feature of all natural languages. Y.u ere r7lying on tke enherend redUntansi ow t__e engelsc langwage tu cowwekt th*s sentinse. In somewhat similar fashion binary checks of various kinds add sufficient redundancy to messages to allow the receiver to detect and correct errors.

For most applications, three basic ways of coping with transmission errors are available:

- ignore the errors
- detect errors and retransmit the data
- employ forward error correction (FEC) methods

Ignoring errors is sensible in applications which include substantial amounts of English language text or other types of messages with sufficient inherent redundancy.

The other techniques both involve the transmission of extra or redundant bits which the receiving terminal employs to check for errors in the information bits. With detection/retransmission procedures, the redundant bits only serve as a reference for errors. If an error is sensed, a request is made for the sending terminal to retransmit the message portion discovered to be in error. With FEC however, the redundant bits take part in the realtime detection and correction of errors at the receiving terminal; here no feedback signaling or retransmission takes place. Although less redundant information is required for detection/retransmission techniques than for the same degree of protection with FEC techniques, FEC permits uninterrupted transmission of a continuous data stream. It also offsets other undesirable effects of the detection/retransmission method. Regardless of which scheme is employed, some errors will ultimately evade the detection process.

The effort is to reduce the residual bit or block error rate to an acceptably low level in the most economical way. Most errors occur in clusters or bursts and as random events. Burst errors can sometimes be corrected by codes designed for detection alone.

Reprinted by permission of the publisher from *Data Dynamics*, July 1971, pp. 18-22.

DETECTION/RETRANSMISSION PROCEDURES

Detection/retransmission procedures generally involve partitioning or blocking the bits into groups; the redundant bits in a given block relate only to the information bits of the same block. If an error in a received block is detected, an automatic request for repetition (ARQ) is generated at the receiving station output and transmitted back to the data source over a reverse channel. In the simplest type of ARQ-control encoded message blocks are sent one at a time, making a decision to repeat the transmission whenever errors are detected.

Block codes generally transform a group of k information bits from the data source into a larger group of n bits by inserting *n minus k* redundant bits into that block. The redundant bits, the difference between n and k, check only the information bits in the block. In the more complex convolutional codes, the *n minus k* extra bits check positions in more than one preceeding block. Thus, for every k bits entering the encoder from the source, n bits are sent to the channel for transmission. Almost any desired degree of protection against errors can be obtained by making n sufficiently larger than k. However a point can be reached where efficiency falls sharply due to the large difference between n and k.

Almost all the important block codes used for error detection and correction are parity check codes. The redundant bits are determined by computation using modulo-2 arithmetic, in which only two results of an addition or subtraction are possible, regardless of the number of bits being added. Modulo-2 arithmetic obeys all the rules of standard arithmetic with a few exceptions and there is never any carrying. The rules for modulo-2 arithmetic necessary for binary codes are:

$$0 + 0 = 0,\ 1 + 0 = 1,\ 0 + 1 = 1, \text{ and } 1 + 1 = 0.$$

In general for modulo-2 additions, an odd number of ones sums to one, while an even number of ones sums to zero.

Each parity bit in a code word is formed by taking the simple modulo-2 sum of various information bit positions in the code word. The simplest kind of parity check code makes use of a single parity bit to check all information bit positions of a code word (a one-dimensional parity check code). With this code, the encoder sets the parity bit for every block so that the number of ones in every code word must be even (an even parity convention) or must be odd (an odd parity convention). Then if an odd number of bit errors occur during transmission, the decoder can immediately detect the occurrence of the error and take appropriate measures.

One-dimensional parity check codes are in wide-spread use in business machine applications. In these instances, each data block ususally corresponds to one character which is checked by its own parity bit. If the bits of each character are assumed to be vertically positioned, then the parity check is known as a vertical redundancy check (VRC). For horizontally oriented arrangements, the same one-dimensional scheme is known as a horizontal redundancy check (HRC). The horizontal and vertical array of bits can be visualized by ordering the characters into rows and the bit positions into columns. The combination of two different parity check schemes to yield two-dimensional parity is known as iterative coding.

Other versions of parity check schemes are sometimes used in which the information bits of a block are checked diagonally. Since the one-bit parity check cannot detect an even number of bits in error, it is most effective in applications where a channel is predominantly characterized by random, single bit errors. In such cases, the probability of a single bit error would be substantially larger, say ten times, than the probability of two or more bit errors in a code word.

Although there has been a proliferation of methods to encode characters into bit sequences for data transmission and computer storage, the American National Standards Institute (ANSI) has standardized the seven bit code known as USASCII. This code permits 2^7 or 128 different alphanumeric symbols to be represented, thus accommodating upper and lower case and a full range of control characters.

ANSI has also recommended the combined horizontal and vertical parity check scheme for the USASCII code, shown in Figure 4-6. Here M is a variable depending on the application, and the seven information bits of each data block (row) correspond to one USASCII character.

Two other types of block coding techniques are frequently used to detect transmission errors. One is based on the so-called polynomial or cyclic types of codes. With these codes, a block of information bits from the data source forms a binary number which is divided by another suitably chosen predetermined binary number. The binary remainder forms the parity checking bits. These are appended to the information bits and transmitted over the communication link as one block.

The receiving station performs an identical binary division operation on the sequence of received information bits. If the computed remainder matches the actually received parity bit sequence, it is assumed that no error occurred. This scheme is sometimes referred to as a cyclic redundancy check (CRC). Two of the most important of the class of cyclic codes are the Hamming and Bose-Chaudhuri (BCH) which have many variations.

M-out-of-N codes, or constant ratio codes, form another class not based on parity checking principles. Each transmitted character is en-

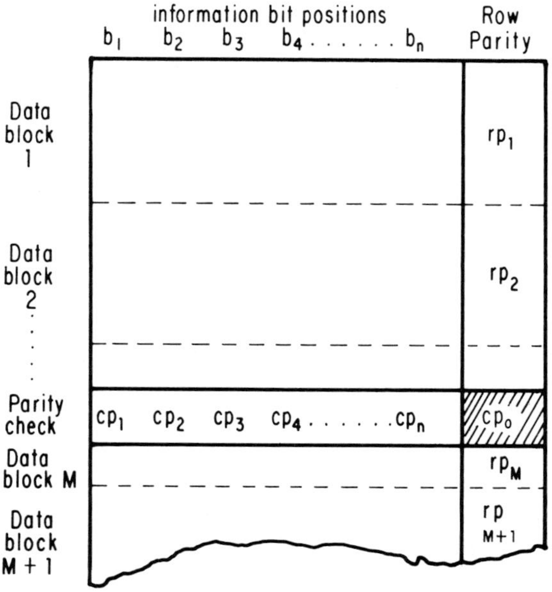

Figure 4-6. Generalized Scheme of Two-Dimensional Parity Checks (rp = row parity, cp = column parity).

coded to always contain the same number of zeroes and ones. Transmission errors will be detected as long as offsetting error patterns, in which a one is switched to a zero and a zero is switched to a one, do not occur. It is not possible to correct all errors with this type of coding. Various types of control procedures are employed which send a control signal back from the receiver to the transmitter. These rely primarily upon ARQ generation at the receiving decoder.

ARQ IMPLEMENTATION

ARQ implementation involves transmission of one block at a time, with the receiver sending back either a positive acknowledgment (ACK) or a negative acknowledgment (NAK) over the reverse channel. A copy of the encoded block is preserved in the buffer at the transmitter until an ACK or NAK control signal is received.

If a NAK is received back at the transmitter, the message block in the buffer is retransmitted over the channel and the buffer contents are still preserved awaiting the receipt of the next control message. The size of the buffer required is determined by the length of the largest block which must be stored. This buffer can either be a subsystem within the transmitter or an integral portion of the terminal equipment. If the data source is a tape unit, for example, the tape itself can provide the buffering, obviating additional channel buffering.

In this scheme the forward channel must remain idle for the time taken to decode the received message block, and to generate and transmit the proper control signal. This overhead is particularly costly when block transmission times are approximately equal to the idle time. Usually, the ACK/NAK-after-each-block scheme will apply where the message blocks are long enough to minimize the effects of this interblock overhead time due to idling.

A means of reducing the interblock overhead is to overlap data and control signal times by transmitting additional message blocks over the forward channel while acknowledgment signals are being fed back to the transmitter. As long as no block errors are detected, the overhead due to interblock times will effectively be nil. When a NAK is received at the transmitter, the block detected in error and the one currently being encoded, plus all blocks in between, must be retransmitted. Therefore, the size of the buffer storage must depend on the transmission delay between transmitter and receiver; it must be at least two data blocks long in any case. The efficiency of this method is greatest when the probability of detecting a block error is low. The disadvantage is the necessity to buffer all blocks which are in transit when an error is detected.

This technique is actually a NAK-interrupt-only scheme, since it keeps sending more blocks as long as no NAK is received. It is only necessary, therefore, to transmit NAK information over the reverse channel. A two level control signal can readily carry out this scheme at relatively high efficiency.

The NAK interrupt scheme can only be used when the reverse channel is functionally independent of the forward channel. Private, 4-wire telephone channels often use 2-wires for the forward-channel and 2-wires for an independent reverse channel, and are well suited for the NAK-interrupt-only type of ARQ scheme. A dial-line telephone channel is usually a 2-wire circuit, capable of transmitting in only one direction at a time. If a dial-line channel must be reversed to send control signals, then the forward and reverse channels are not functionally independent and the NAK-interrupt technique may not be used. In some cases a lower speed reverse channel can be multiplexed onto a 2-wire system and remain functionally independent. However this reverse channel is not compatible with a large number of existing terminals.

Adaptive ARQ involves dynamic variation of the block lengths in an attempt to keep the channel efficiency as high as possible at all times. The receiver is equipped to monitor the rate of requests for repetition as well as for channel noise characteristics. This information is fed back to a threshold decision device in the transmitter. When the ARQ rate and the noise reach a significant level so as to activate the threshold decision device, the transmitter alters the block length. Whenever the threshold is crossed and the block length changed, the transmitter must inform the receiver. This decision feedback process forces short blocks to be transmitted during noisy periods and long blocks to be sent when the ARQ rate and the noise characteristics indicate relatively good channel conditions. The increased complexity of the circuitry required for the adaptive ARQ as opposed to the fixed ARQ, limits its advantages.

Odd-even record counting is another variation of ARQ. It is a detection/retransmission approach where NAK signals are generated by the receiver whenever an error is detected in a received block. The receiver send an ACK *0* control signal for all even numbered blocks of a transmission in which no errors have been detected. A different control signal, ACK *1* is transmitted for all odd numbered blocks in which no errors are detected. This odd-even record count arrangement protects against complete loss of a block between transmitter and receiver, possible error in the control signal itself, and other situations not covered by the other basic ARQ methods.

FORWARD ERROR CORRECTION

In forward error correction (FEC) a sufficient amount of redundancy is incorporated into a code to allow for automatic correction as well as detection at the receiver. No reverse channel is required. For example, two-dimensional parity checks are capable of detecting and correcting errors within any row or column having a single erroneous bit. There is a very close relationship between a code's capability for detecting errors and correcting them. In FEC links it is the power of correction which is primary. The advantages are that with FEC a continuous data stream may be readily accommodated without the need for a reverse channel. The tradeoff disadvantages are closely related to the increased equipment and coding complexity needed to achieve a given error rate, and to time delays associated with FEC shift registers.

But where reverse channels are not available or where channel propagation times are not critical FEC can prove to be the most reliable recourse.

Convolutional codes are generally preferred for FEC applications. In convolutional encoding, information bits are fed directly out to the communication channel and are continuously interleaved with outputs from a parity check generator which performs certain binary additions upon the most recently received k information bits. The rules for the specific arithmetical operations depend upon the code being imple-

TECHNIQUES FOR ERROR DETECTION AND CORRECTION CODING

BIT STREAM FLOW

00000011 01000001 11010100 01000001 01000100 10000010 11101101 10110100 01110111 11010010 ··········

• **USASCII. One dimensional parity check.** This horizontal convention consists of the 7 information bits in an USASCII character, followed by a single bit parity check bit. This bit indicates the modulo-2 sum of the information bits in the character, corresponding to an even parity convention. If an odd bit convention were employed instead, all parity check bits would be changed.

00010010 01000001 11010100 01000001 01000100 10000010 00101000 11101101 10110100 01110111 ··········

• **USASCII. Two dimensional parity check.** In addition to the single parity check bit for each USASCII character, an entire 8-bit parity check character is inserted after every M USASCII characters, in this example M = 5. Each of the first seven bits in this special word respectively equal the modulo-2 sums or the corresponding information bits positions in the preceding five code words. The 8th bit checks the seven parity check bits in the special word.

01111 10110 10101 01100 00011 11010 11001 00000 01100 01111 11001 00011 00011 10110 00000 ·····

• **Simple 5,3 Block code.** Each encoded block consists of 3 information bits and 2 trailing parity check bits. The 4th bit equals the modulo-2 sum of bits 1, 2, and 3; the 5th bit equals the modulo-2 sum of bits 1 and 2.

1001011 1010101 1001011 1001100 0000000 1010101 1100110 1010101 ··································

• **7,4 Hamming Code.** Each encoded block contains 4 information bits and 3 parity check bits. The 1st, 2nd, and 4th bit positions in each code word are reserved for parity checking. The 1st parity check bit equals the modulo-2 sum of bits 3, 5, and 7. The 2nd parity check bit equals the modulo-2 sum of bits 3, 6, and 7. The 4th parity check bit equals the modulo-2 sum of bits 5, 6, and 7. This particular code can be used to detect all single and double errors, any two bits, in a 7-bit block.

································ 000111011011011011011010101011000110110 ································

Simple ½ rate convolutional encoder

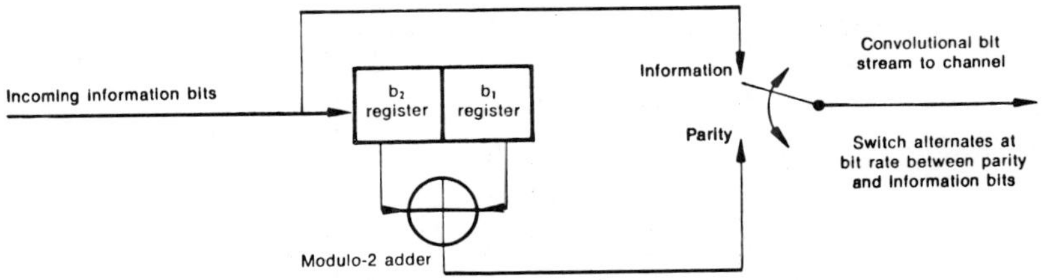

• **Output of simple 1/2 rate convolutional encoder.** Each parity bit is the modulo-2 sum of the immediately preceding and immediately following information bits. There is no block structure and the propagation of parity checks and interleaving of them in the bit stream is continuous.

Figure 4-7.

mented. Convolutional codes are non-block codes, the length depends on the capacity of the shift register stages which are usually hard-wired into the decoder. The total number of bits in this sequence used as the basis for parity computations is also referred to as the constraint length of the code. The convolutional codes can be operated at half-rate where $n = 2k$, thus giving a new check bit for each information bit to be fed out of the encoder.

Their non-block structure makes them easier to decode than block structured codes; block synchronization and framing are not required. Information bits and parity bits are continuously transmitted over the channel in an interleaved manner. The parity bits are computed by taking modulo-2 sums on various information bits for a period generally extending over more than one data character from the terminal.

Two basic types of decoding are most widely employed for convolutional codes—threshold decoding and sequential decoding. Threshold decoding is a simpler concept which works effectively with short codes where it is necessary to correct a few errors. The scheme involves a majority count of the parity check bits associated with a particular information bit. Sequential decoding was developed primarily for convolutional codes. Digits are decoded in sequence, each is tested to determine whether it is a binary *0* or *1*. Whenever a decision about its value can be made with certainty or at least a sufficient degree of confidence, a digit is read out of the decoder. Decoding is probabilistic and depends on the lengthy sequence of bits just received. Sequential decoding is more powerful but requires more complex circuitry since longer constraint lengths are generally used and successive decoding decisions are highly interdependent.

Character rows	Bit positions 1	2	3	4	5	6	7	Vertical parity check bits
1	0	1	0	0	0	0	0	1
2	0	0	1	0	0	0	1	0
3	1	0	0	0	0	0	1	0
4	0	1	1	0	1	0	1	1
5	1	0	0	0	0	0	1	0
6	1	1	0	0	0	0	0	0
Horizontal character check bits	1	0	0	0	1	0	0	0 Check bit on the column of parity check bits

Row 4, position 2*

Figure 4-8. A message of six data characters in USASCII code showing both horizontal and vertical parity check bits. There is one bit in error; use the parity checking principle to locate it (even convention).

There have been thirteen years of refinement and sequential decoding has improved to the point where it is likely to become the standard technique for convolutional decoding for future FEC applications.

5

The Importance of Standards and Documentation

Adequate control and auditing of computer applications require adequate standards and documentation. This theme, which is introduced in this section, recurs in each subsequent chapter.

The lack of standards and documentation eliminates the formal expression of many control and auditing aspects of the application design and may substantially reduce the likelihood that the completed task will meet all requirements satisfactorily.

Standards and documentation are also vital ingredients in attempts to separate clearly functions within the information processing activity and to control changes in design, programming, and operations.

Attitudes toward documentation are changing. Increasingly, improved documentation is viewed as a natural outcome of a carefully planned and coordinated systems development process. This is particularly true of large, integrated applications where documentation can represent much of the work product of each phase of development, as well as the blueprint for subsequent phases.

In larger organizations there is growing recognition of the role of standards and documentation in improving productivity in programming and operations. Those who do not invest in standards development and good documentation may in the long run pay far more in terms of high costs for systems maintenance, weakened controls, and a shorter useful life of completed systems.

COMPUTER SYSTEM STANDARDS FOR A LARGE ORGANIZATION

by W. Barkley Fritz

With the continuing rapid evolution of the computer field, the need for standards has been apparent for some time. Although national and international computer standardization activities have been under way for about a decade, until recently it has been difficult for a large organization using computers to properly interface these developments and fully exploit the advantages of the "right" standards.

In a large organization, the development of a consensus as to what specific standards should exist requires a considerable amount of communication and interchange of ideas among various groups with somewhat diverse requirements and goals. By associating the reasons for standards with the actual standard, the on-going standardization program can be sold to the individual members of the organization and be highly successful in spite of a variety of problems.

By any measure, the Westinghouse Electric Corp. is among the largest industrial organizations in the world. Its diversity of products, its unique over-all engineering orientation and its success as a major factor in a wide variety of fields provide an organizational environment particularly suited to highly effective use of modern computer technology.

As a user of the Univac I in the early 1950's, Westinghouse was one of the first industrial organizations to use digital computers successfully as an integral part of its operations. That usage has expanded rapidly over the years and today this organization relies heavily on a wide variety of computational equipment. Westinghouse ranks as one of the major industrial customers of several U.S. computer manufacturers.

The effective use of this ever-expanding computer power did not just happen. Behind this use has been extensive planning to search out and

---

Reprinted by permission of the publisher from *Datamation,* vol. 15, no. 2 (February 1969), pp. 39-42.

implement new and profitable application areas.[1,2] Also because of the pace of the fast changing computer technology, it has been necessary to develop an environment for rapid equipment change in order to efficiently implement major new technical developments.[3]

A major factor in this effective computer use and rapid exploitation of new technology has been the development of corporate standards. It is the subject of computer standards—including our corporate *standards policy, areas* for standardization, *procedures* for development, and the *benefits* of such standardization—that is discussed in this article.

From the entire spectrum of the national and international standardization program, those specific areas that are most critical to an industrial organization are outlined. Specific corporate computer standards of the Westinghouse Electric Corp. are listed with some indication of the motivation that led to the standards adopted. The closing emphasis is on the changing nature of standards resulting from the dynamic nature of the computer industry and the economic advantages of the kind of program presented in the paper.

As recently as 1966, the Westinghouse Electric Corp. was moving in the direction of a single "super" computer to handle the workload of the major divisions of the corporation. This concept is no longer considered feasible for the following reasons:

1. The continuing extremely *rapid growth* in total Westinghouse computer requirements.
2. The *limitations* of existing state-of-the-art *hardware* and *software* to implement such a plan.
3. The Westinghouse divisional *profit center organizational structure* that is not especially appropriate for a single "super" system, because it would constrict the profit center manager.
4. The over-all *risk* involved in the "all eggs in one basket" concept, too great a risk to take for an organization so highly dependent on computers.

---

[1]R.C. Cheek, "Concurrent Processing and Program Priorities at the Westinghouse Tele-Computer Center," *Proceedings of IFIP Congress 65*, pp. 541-542.

[2]R.C. Cheek, J.F. Dudas, and C.E. Skidmore, "Message Switching as a Subsidiary Function of Centralized Information Processing," *Proceedings of IFIP Congress 65*, pp. 517-518.

[3]W.B. Fritz, "Computer Changes at the Westinghouse Defense and Space Center," *Proceedings of the FJCC-1967*, pp. 581-586.

Replacing this "super" computer concept is a computer-direction that supports both strong centralized systems and effective decentralized division-based equipment. What is involved in the familiar "check and balance" concept, i.e., each division uses in-house equipment when this is justified from an economic point of view, but uses central computer or time-sharing facilities when this is desirable. Usually each operating unit or profit center does not take one path or the other, but uses in-house equipment for a portion of its computer load, and also uses a Teletype or batch type terminal to time-sharing or corporate tele-computer center facilities for another portion. Economics, turnaround, load conditions, nature of the load with respect to corporate involvement with the information and other factors determine where the application is run. However, in a very real sense, the use of Teletype or line-at-a-time data communications brings the capability of the time-sharing computer or the corporate tele-computer center directly to the remote user, thus minimizing any real difference between the two approaches. At the present time there are in excess of 500 Teletype and about 20 line-at-a-time terminals within the corporation.

Consistent with this policy on computer direction is the policy to make use of multiple vendors with competitive hardware. Such a policy is dependent upon the fact that various suppliers introduce new competitive equipment at different times. Such announcements followed up by successful software and hardware deliveries provide a means for a continual reduction in the cost per unit of computation. In addition, such a policy results in an excellent opportunity to obtain better contract conditions and improved delivery, thus making it possible to exploit new developments in the field rapidly and with limited risk.

This multiple supplier policy (both serial and parallel) requires standards in a variety of areas and essentially provides the motivation for the development and implementation of corporate computer system standards that are independent of any single supplier. Thus, Westinghouse does not have standards for their own sake, but as a necessary means of supporting corporate policy.

Another type of organization might be willing, and even find it desirable, to live with one supplier, adopt that supplier's software and hardware as it exists, and not be concerned with other equipment now or in the future. Such an organization has thus dictated for itself the "standards" of that supplier and thereby runs the risk that fast-paced changes in computer technology will cause them to become locked in to obsolescent computer equipment or to an expensive transition to the next generation of the same supplier.

Westinghouse policy has been established to prevent a lock-in to any single supplier or generation of equipment. Computer standards and guidelines are thus a necessary requirement to implement a more fundamental policy—that is, an ability to use a variety of suppliers and to be able to change to the newer, more effective, lower price per unit computation equipment as dictated by the requirements of the dynamic economy in which the corporation operates.

AREAS FOR STANDARDIZATION

To implement this policy and to control our development of information systems, it is necessary to adopt and use standards—the right standards. The national and international standardization activities provide an over-all outline of the areas where standards are being developed and thereby serve as a guide to appropriate areas for corporate standards. Based on the USASI, IFIP and ISO[4] activities, the following areas are suitable for organization standards:

1. Optical character recognition (OCR)
2. Codes and input/output
3. Data transmission
4. Common programming languages
5. Vocabulary
6. Problem definition and analysis
7. Magnetic ink character recognition (MICR)
8. Data elements
9. Program documentation

At the USA level, some standards have been adopted in essentially all of the above areas including, ·for example, the following: a code for information interchange, perforated tape, punched cards, magnetic tape, vocabulary, flowchart symbols, MICR, COBOL and FORTRAN. ALGOL and certain data elements are in the pipeline of the standardization process.

It is almost obvious that if a national or international standard exists in a particular area, then any large organization should adopt that standard or at least be working toward its adoption. The assumption is that the standard is a good standard and that it will be generally adopted.

---

[4]USASI (The United States of America Standards Institute), formerly known as the American Standards Association (ASA), has changed its name to American National Standards Institute (ANSI). IFIP is the International Federation for Information Processing. ISO is the International Organization for Standardization.

However, corporate adoption of even the "wrong" standard is usually better in the long run than inconsistent use of various nonstandards.

It is this requirement for national and international "communication" and an effective "working together" capability that led to effective USASI, IFIP, and ISO standards activity in the first place. Corporate entities and other large organizations have many of these same requirements and can benefit from such broader effort; however, each organization must evaluate and implement standards in such a way as to support its own objectives.

As the title of this paper implies, standardization is a developmental process, an on-going process. The standardization progress of the Westinghouse Electric Corp., including a brief listing of our corporate computer standards, is provided later following a discussion of the procedures involved in the standardization process.

PROCEDURES FOR DEVELOPING A CONSENSUS

The development of standards at the national or international level is extremely time-consuming and, in general, because of the length of time it takes to get agreement, somewhat of a frustrating experience. Standards, in the context of a large, diversified industrial corporation with essentially autonomous division profit centers, present a similar problem. Guidelines and good practices must be "sold" to those who must comply. Each division must agree that adoption of a particular standard is "good" for his operation. The advantages of corporate standards must be understood by each level of management in terms of why adherence to the standard is desirable for his operation.

The adoption of a new standard usually requires change from existing local conventions. Change, in general, has some cost associated with it. In some cases, the cost of change can be quite high. The advantage of that change must therefore have a greater value than the cost of making the change. Personnel must be available to make the change. Because of schedule requirements, local operating functions may bypass a corporate standard. Standards thus in a practical way may be regarded as a "direction to go" or a guideline rather than a rigid edict. Local management, in order to meet other objectives, must have the authority not to adhere, when the "not adhering" has greater advantages such as higher immediate profits or an ability to meet a committed schedule. However, the longer-term consequences of not adhering to the standards must also be recognized. The *direction* indicated by the standard *must* be accepted by all levels and the "deviation" recognized for what it is, a temporary expedient.

A problem with standards is that they are not rigid. An argument against their adoption is that the standard will probably be changed "someday." The fact that the standard may be changed, however, is no reason not to adopt the standard as a self-consistent mode of operation, thereby simplifying change to that new standard when and if the change takes place. Standards thus provide a basis for getting to new standards.

A major influence in the development of standards is the environment in which the operation exists. Of course, the major input in a large organization is the need of the various units to communicate effectively with one another. This need for a standard and the requirement that the parts of the organization be sold on the fact that the standard adopted is the "best standard" requires a consensus—that is, a general agreement as to the desirability of using this single way of doing things.

But the units of the organization, and the organization as a whole, must deal with the outside world and this is where the trade associations and the national and international groups carry heavy weight. Economics dictate that organizational standards not be in conflict with the national and international standard, assuming, of course, that the standard is sufficiently well defined and accepted. However, local practice and the corporate standard must come first, at least in the chronological sense. The large organization cannot sit back and wait until "*the* standard" is agreed to at the international level. The requirement for an in-house standard, before the fact, that is hopefully not inconsistent with later national and international efforts almost forces the organization to work closely with the various industry and government standardization bodies in order to contribute to the direction that will be taken and take advantage of the knowledge gained as to the direction in which "things are going." As indicated in the previous section, Westinghouse, by being fairly active in USASI activities, has been able to move in directions consistent with the direction later taken by USASI. Of course USASI is being influenced by ISO and IFIP activities.

Another factor involved in the standardization activity in the computer field is the role played by the one dominant supplier, IBM. The role of the "de facto" standard cannot be overlooked as one attempts to reach a consensus. Although, as I have mentioned, Westinghouse uses equipment made by nearly all of the major suppliers in the USA, the influence of IBM on Westinghouse as a user and on the other computer equipment suppliers to Westinghouse is considerable. The 80-column punched card and the one-half-inch magnetic tape represent two areas where Westinghouse and most other computer users had standards long before formal acceptance of these "de facto" standards by a standards body.

A formal means for getting standards agreement within an organization is difficult to define. Certainly formal seminars, meetings, committees, policy letters, standards manuals, and related activities and documentation can, and do, all play a part. Indeed even agreement by a "duly appointed committee," while desirable, is not the complete answer. As most of you know, large American corporations are not generally "dictated to" by committees, even inside committees. The *existence of* a complete standards manual does not assure *adherence to* standards. Essentially, standards represent what is being done, rather than dictate what is to be done. Standards represent a direction, and in the traditional sense provide a means of measuring performance toward achievement of the organization's objectives.

In another sense, standard performance generally will not be the best possible performance, however it will be a "standard" to which any variation from standard can be compared. If a truly better way is developed, then this new approach should be made the basis of a new standard. The economic benefits of the change can then be evaluated in terms of the cost to make the change. The existence of, and adherence to, standards are thus not to be a means of limiting progress, but a means of evaluating, controlling and promoting progress.

WESTINGHOUSE STANDARDS

Before concluding, I would like to give an indication of Westinghouse progress to date; I shall list briefly those areas where effective Westinghouse corporate computer center standards now exist.

1. FORTRAN and COBOL are the standard programming languages. The specifications of these languages are as defined by USASI.
2. Standard equipment selection procedures and guidelines have been adopted. Corporate approval procedures are consistent throughout the corporation.
3. The standard character set in Westinghouse is that of USASCII. The character sets used by FORTRAN and COBOL are both subsets of this code which has been implemented by different bit configurations by various computer and communication equipment suppliers. Hopefully the suppliers will eventually adapt a single code representation; however, in the meantime automatic hardware and software conversion can be used.
4. The USA Standard Flowchart Symbols as published by USASI are standard.

5. For purposes of standardized written and oral communications, the USA Standard Vocabulary for Information Processing has been adopted as a base.
6. In the area of data elements, standard machine formats have been adopted for the following: date, time, individual and business designation, location, and phone number.
7. The USASI tape labeling standard has been adopted.
8. Standard formats for data files are defined.
9. A standard library of subroutines has been adopted and is being maintained on most computational equipment operational within the corporation.
10. Standard program documentation procedures have been developed and implemented.
11. The ACM Guidelines on "Professional Conduct in Information Processing" have been adopted as a means of providing a standard in this area.

At the present time 1 and 2 are published corporate standards. The others indicate the corporate direction and as such are documented at the corporate computer center by means of a loose leaf document entitled "The Tele-Computer Center Standards and Facilities Manual." This document has proven to be extremely valuable not only in serving as a general guide in the training of new personnel but also as a reference for experienced personnel. In addition, good practices and conventions are defined and included with the manual. Emphasis is on modular programming.

An adjunct to Westinghouse standards are its standard hiring practices for personnel in the computer and management-systems area. Adherence to educational requirements and a specified level of performance on a standard battery of tests also help provide a basis for the effective interchange of personnel within the divisions and staff function activities. This commonality of approach gives the corporation a depth of backup for key positions that makes it possible to find qualified candidates from within for openings created by the establishment of new divisions and expanded computer system activities.

CONCLUSION

An organization-wide set of computer system standards provides support to the achievement of the organization's prime objective. In the computer systems area that goal might be stated as providing the best possible computer operation at the lowest possible cost.

Experience at Westinghouse in the use of COBOL and FORTRAN has simplified programmer training and increased programmer productivity. With respect to the training phase, our experience has shown that the new inexperienced employee begins to become productive during the first month of his employment period following some 40 hours of on-the-job training. Both languages are well documented themselves and are essentially self-documenting for ease in program maintenance. Each provides a fair amount of machine independence and each provides a useful base for program exchange between different groups having the same or very similar applications.

The existence of standard data elements, file structures, tape labeling, and related standards helps reduce redundant effort, simplify the preparation of new programs, reduce the program maintenance effort and ease the program debugging problem. Because of the variety of factors which influence performance it is difficult to prove, but not difficult to demonstrate, that effective standards provide at least a 20% increase in overall productivity. Westinghouse being a profit-minded organization has converted this increased productivity to increased profit.

In conclusion, an effective standards program provides a means for the best possible on-going utilization of men and machines to effectively solve the problems for which modern computers were designed.

DOCUMENTATION FOR APPLICATION PROGRAMMING

by William L. Harper

Third-generation computers and sophisticated input/output devices have increased the scope and complexity of the manufacturer's software (supervisor and utility) systems. This has made the interfacing of application programs more difficult, and certain aspects of programming, e.g., multiprogramming/multiprocessing, access and linkage, program modularity, file organization, and man/machine interactions more exacting. With the advent of some of the higher level languages, e.g., COBOL, the "English" language, it was hoped that such languages would be "self-documenting". However, this has not been the case. Computer manufacturers have developed precise rules for syntactical logical manipulations but their documentation stops there. The guidelines, concepts, and methods for developing applications documentation have been left to the users

---

Reprinted by permission of the publisher from *Modern Data,* September 1969, pp. 54-62.

and, as a result, this has become the "achilles' heel" of an EDP system.

Even the methods of updating documentation have not been effectively exploited. OCR equipment and CRT visual display units can be highly effective means of automating documentation updating, and are becoming increasingly popular as data input and visual inspection devices for EDP systems. If a program is to accomplish one function and then be discarded, documentation is not too important. But if the program is of long life, then documentation and methods of updating must be viewed as equally important as the software and hardware.

Application programming documentation can be generally defined as consisting of: (1) a narrative description of software objectives derived from requirements studies, (2) a graphic presentation in the form of general and detailed flowcharts, (3) symbolic and technical descriptions to include the coding language and machine listing of the program, data specifications, formats, etc., and (4) an operational description in the form of reference manuals, summaries, and abstracts. These four items constitute a summary of the programming tasks and other documentation by-products that comprise complete documentation for an application program or system (see Figure 5-1).

NEED FOR GOOD DOCUMENTATION

Poorly documented programs may not have immediate adverse effects on software performance, since the originating programmer can usually compensate for inadequate documentation. But the effects of poor documentation subsequently come to the surface when modification is necessary and the original programmer(s) is no longer available, or has forgotten program details. Without adequate and controlled documentation, the task of converting to newer hardware or higher levels or programming languages becomes increasingly difficult and costly. In addition, when matching hardware characteristics to software requirements, documentation on such variables as the appropriate peripheral devices and speeds, the volume of data to be processed, and the core capacity and speed of the computer must be accurately determined. Although these factors are usually ruled on in the systems design study plan, it may be difficult to assess their true dimensions until documentation on data and programming requirements has been developed. Unless managers are technically qualified to assess methods and needs for data processing, they must, in actual fact, delegate these important decisions to subordinate EDP personnel. Such decisions may be the result of compromises reached in conferences, or studies prepared in a joint effort by systems analysts and programmers. While delegation of authority and consultation with subordinates on such matters should not be

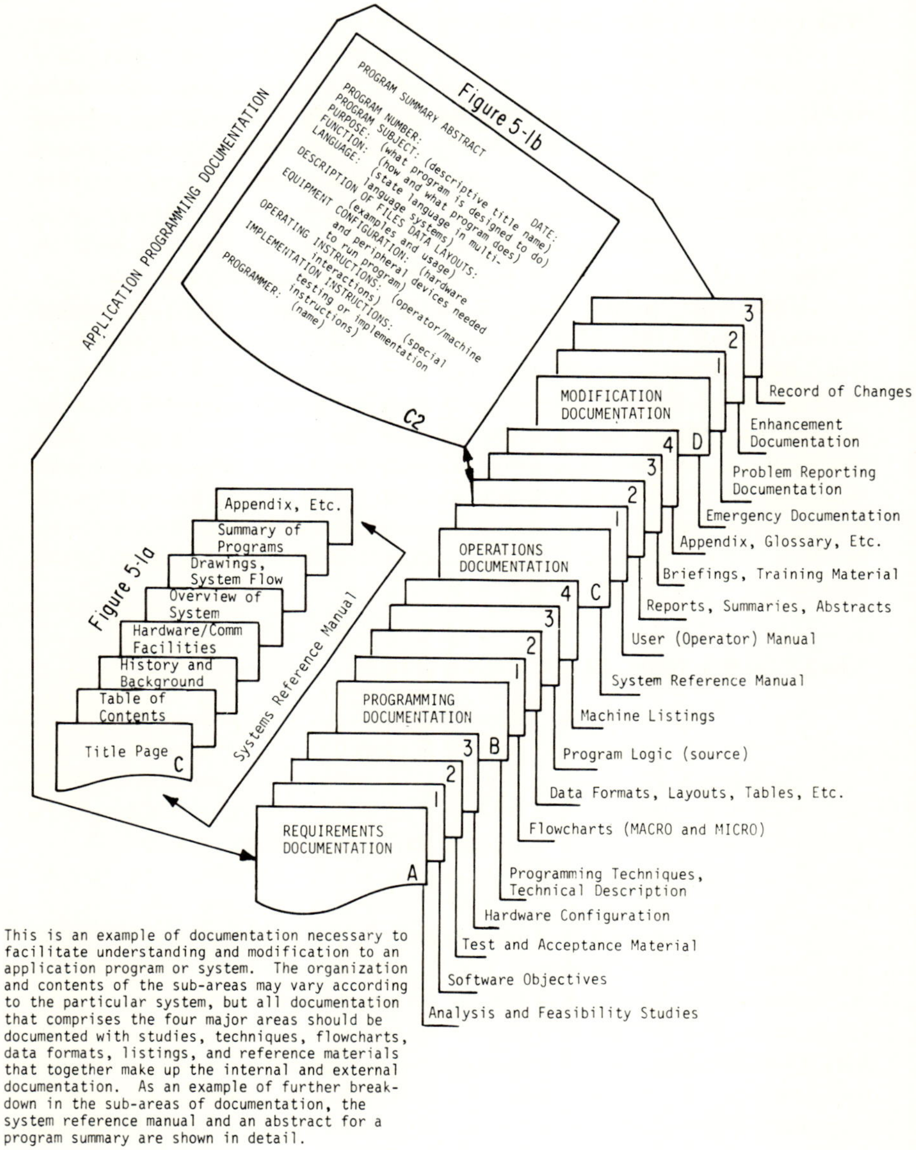

Figure 5-1.

discouraged, programming and EDP managers must have adequate documentation to interpret correctly the information, advice, and opinions of systems analysts and programmers.

DOCUMENTATION WRITERS

A system's size will determine the volume, but not the methods and standards of documentation. The size of the programming task should not effect such things as the scope and type of documentation, the need for standardized flowcharts and coding forms, and the various controls that are necessary for maintenance and management.

Because software documentation is a laborious and relatively unexciting chore, most programmers are reluctant to document their work sufficiently. Therefore much of the administrative and time-consuming task of preparing documentation should be the responsibility of software documentation writers. Documentation writers need not possess a degree or extensive programming experience, although college training and some programming experience is helpful. However, they must demonstrate good English usage and the ability to write logically and functionally.

A documentation writer should be assigned as a team member to the programming project at its inception. The programmers would be responsible for describing the logic, flowcharts, input/output formats, data files, etc., to be used for "internal" documentation, i.e., for use by other programmers. The documentation writers could assist in this technical documentation, but they would be primarily responsible for compiling, formating, and organizing material for "external" documentation, e.g., the operator reference manuals, narrative summaries, and abstracts needed by management and operations personnel to develop and maintain the system. As a rule of thumb, a programmer should not spend more than twenty percent of his time writing external documentation. To burden the programmers with this type of documentation is a misuse of their talent and reflects an inefficiently manned organization.

AREAS OF APPLICATION DOCUMENTATION

There are two levels of application program development: initial programming, to develop an application program or system; and modification programming, brought about because of advances in the state of the art, discovered errors, or changes in requirements. The four basic areas of application documentation are requirements, programming, operations, and modifications. These areas are discussed in the order of their development and as they relate to the maintenance of an application program or system (see Figure 5-1).

REQUIREMENTS DOCUMENTATION

This encompasses documentation necessary for the programming analysis and objectives of an application program or system (or modification thereto), and testing requirements (see A and D in Figure 5-1). This documentation is usually derived from (or it may include) a systems study and design plan. It consists of the originator's narrative requirements for a programming task. An automated system study and design plan normally consists of detailed studies of the present business or system, and includes information on equipment, software, personnel requirements, and communications facilities (lines, terminal gear and devices—if applicable), as well as environmental factors that make up and affect a data processing system. Unless the requirement is sufficiently detailed and clearly stated, all desirable features of an application program may not be known at the outset, and confusion and duplication of efforts may occur in the initial stages of program development. Documentation procedures specifying the material for testing and the validation necessary for program acceptance should be part of the requirements documentation, but may be listed under separate cover and made available subsequent to, or concurrent with, final program development. This documentation should be developed by the originator of the initial programming requirement, or persons other than the programmers who will develop the software. For the most part, only new systems or major modifications to an existing system, need a test and acceptance document. There are two sub-areas of requirements documentation: software and test and acceptance.

SOFTWARE REQUIREMENTS

This includes detailed programming analysis and should contain essential information that describes the scope and software objectives, as well as general operational or hardware requirements. This documentation is used in assessing the programming features and routines for developing flowcharts and for subsequent coding. A comprehensive analysis study of an application program requirement is an essential prerequisite in determining programming concepts and techniques. After carefully reviewing the overall software objective, the various functional programming features can be identified and programming tasks can be assigned to individual programmers in order of their significance and complexity.

TEST AND ACCEPTANCE REQUIREMENTS

These are detailed descriptions of what the software must accomplish to be accepted by user personnel. This documentation should define end results for operational specifications and the procedural steps to be taken in testing a major program or system. The test should be accomplished off-line; examples of test material necessary to test all features of the program or system, with keypunch instructions, should be part of the test document. However, the true validity of the software cannot be ascertained until it has been run on-line in a dynamic or real-time environment. The procedures should identify each operational function so that user personnel can test all areas of software logic. A predetermined quantity of testing material specific to the designated equipment configuration should be specified and in place prior to testing.

The testing of a program or system should be a joint effort. Team members should consist of a combination of computer operators, systems analysts, programmers, and the originator or representative of the programming requirement. Test and acceptance documentation should not be written by the programmers who developed the program, although they may be consulted.

The nature of the EDP system will dictate the material and number of personnel involved. In a real-time communications environment, sufficient test material (dummy message data) should be prepared to validate:

- message recognition by unique identification and precedence;
- message recovery during computer failure;
- temporary low precedence withdrawal during peak load conditions for subsequent re-entry;
- message accountability; and
- other switching and processing software features necessary to protect and deliver message to users.

In conventional batch processing systems, sufficient test data should be prepared to validate:

- branches and transfer of control;
- data and file formats, record layouts, tables, etc.;
- input/output timing and processing areas;
- modular interface areas.

PROGRAMMING DOCUMENTATION

This documentation includes programming techniques, evaluation of the functions the equipment is to perform, general (macro) and detailed (micro) flowcharts, symbolic source code and machine listings, and any data structure that is needed for the program to perform a desired function (See B in Figure 5-1). Such documentation can be referred to as an internal documentation because it concerns the action and interactions of software and hardware.

After the programming analysis has been completed and all programming objectives outlined, changes should be frozen until the program is operational, otherwise, target dates for completion may not be met. Although some undocumented changes to clean up logic construction in a conventional batch processing system may take place without affecting the overall system, in large real-time systems, undocumented and uncommunicated changes to a routine may cause endless trouble during test and acceptance. Some of the reasons programming documentation becomes more imperative in real-time systems than in batch processing systems include: (1) programs that interface and run concurrently and share the same storage and input/output devices; (2) critical timing, priority interrupts and switching controls; (3) complicated linkage and overlay techniques; and (4) a greater degree of unpredictable and uncontrolled data input.

PROGRAM TECHNICAL DESCRIPTIONS

This documentation provides the technical descriptions, programming techniques, and terminology for programmer-to-programmer communication. It should be a concise explanation of how the program is designed and its purpose. Maximum use of descriptive "English" comments in the symbolic source coding is recommended. (In some cases, this may negate the necessity for detailed [micro] flowcharts.) The program technical description is used primarily for program maintenance and modification and should be programmer-oriented. Because original programmers often become unavailable, these descriptions constitute perhaps the most important area of software documentation. Many programmers are involved in the logic development of a large application program or system, and logic is developed independently, routine-by-routine. Since there is no "perfect" or exact method that dictates a program's logic construction, each routine shows varying degrees of logic development and programmer independence. Without a technical description of each routine or program, it would be difficult and costly to recode or modify the original software.

PROGRAM FLOWCHARTS

These are graphic symbols and symbolic notations depicting data flow, processing steps, and the sequence of computer operation. Flowchart symbols as defined by the United States of America Standard

Institute (USASI) should be used. However, a situation may arise requiring a different or modified symbol(s) to depict a unique processing or input/output function. For large and complicated programs, a macro flowchart should be drawn up to present a general overview of the application program or system. The purpose of the macro flowchart is to depict the major input/output functions, subroutines, and major processing steps of the system. From the macro flowchart, detailed micro flowcharts should be drawn to describe the separate input/output, arithmetic, and logic operations involved in data processing. For ease and effectiveness of programming, actual coding should follow the logic layout of the micro flowcharts.

PROGRAM LISTINGS

This ties all the "bits and pieces" of the logic structure together and becomes the by-product of all inputs. It is a detailed list of the symbolic codes, logical instructions, and narrative comments (to explain what the coding does) shown in their respective processing sequences as they appear in the program. A listing serves as an indispensable tool for debugging, modifying, and understanding a program. Each time a substantial change is made, a new listing should be obtained by reassembling or recompiling, rather than by "patching" the object code.

OPERATIONS DOCUMENTATION

This documentation is used for day-to-day systems management, operations, and training. It should contain detailed descriptions and operational terms which give a *narrative* explanation of the functional and operational interactions of a program or system because the terminology used by programmers often has a nebulous meaning to managers and operating personnel. A system comprises hardware, software, and documentation (this last factor being the human interface element) and, unless it is clearly illuminated, the other factors may not function at all. Operations documentation, therefore, consists of narrative summaries and reports; material for operator use, training, and system briefings; and systems reference manuals and abstracts for management (see Figure 5-1b). Such documentation can be referred to as external documentation because it concerns the man-machine relationship relative to the applications of the system's software and hardware operational features. There should be a minimum of two reference manuals for each unique application system.

USER'S (OPERATOR'S) MANUAL

This reference manual should be sufficiently comprehensive to explain the interactions of the operator and computer, and the various functional aspects of the computer and peripheral equipment. The manual should describe outputs and inputs derived from the system, tell how and when operator inputs should be introduced, give examples of console type-ins and type-outs, and explain the use of combinations of input/output devices, including data sets, moderms, etc. Procedures for emergency restart/recovery after computer failure, details an orderly shut-down, initializing and loading techniques, and instruction on how to run various related jobs, i.e., keypunch, tape library, etc., should be included in the operator's manual. The type of EDP system will determine the contents. For example, a real-time communications system involved in message processing, switching, and statistical accountability would require more material on communications (type-in/type-outs) between operator and Central Processing Unit than a conventional batch processing system.

SYSTEMS REFERENCE MANUAL

The purpose of this manual is to provide various levels of management with an explanation of operational and functional features. It should consist of general overview of the entire system, and should identify and explain the purpose and the significant details of each important routine (see Figure 5-1a). While the size and complexity of the system will again dictate the type and amount of information contained in the manual it should be narrative and generally nontechnical, and not operator-oriented or as detailed as the user's manual. A glossary of acronyms, abbreviations, and terms should be made part of both manuals.

MODIFICATIONS DOCUMENTATION

Modification consists of proposals for changes or corrections to an existing program or system (see D in Figure 5-1). Regardless of the experience of programmers or how much study and care is devoted to application programs, coding errors will exist, and there will always be a need for modification. No amount of planning can foresee all possible combinations or circumstances that a system may encounter. Modifications are necessary because of logic or hardware errors that do not show up during acceptance testing, or which are brought about to accommodate more sophisticated operational concepts.

Changes to application programs should be carefully approved by the system's custodians, and an efficient method should be devised to incorporate these changes with minimal disturbance to the on-line system. Because of the difficulty of making modifications, only *essential* changes should be made to the on-line program. "Good-to-have," but not really necessary changes, i.e., modifications to clean up sloppy logic or to modify internal processing that does not contribute appreciably to the system's performance, should be saved for future routine re-assembly or re-compilation. It also follows that each modification must be studied and properly documented as outlined under requirements, programming, and operations documentation. A record should be maintained to show what program or routine was changed, who changed it, who authorized the change, the date of change, etc. Normally, the need for modification to application programs falls in three categories:

ENHANCEMENT PROPOSAL DOCUMENTATION

This is a request to change an error-free program and normally comes from a user, EDP manager, operator, or programmer who has discovered a new operational concept or programming technique that he believes will improve data processing efficiency. Requests for changes may be minor, requiring only a few simple logic changes, or they may be very complicated, involving a major modification to the overall application system. All proposals should be in the form of narrative descriptions, giving complete details of the proposed change. If the proposal is from a programmer, it should be aimed at convincing management of its superiority over the existing program, routine, or feature. If the request is from the user or management, it should be detailed enough to preclude unnecessary coding, and clear enough to insure that programmers will know exactly what the change is expected to accomplish. Because of the manhours (and money) involved, major enhancement proposals should be given the same scrutiny as proposals for equipment and other major expenditures.

PROBLEM REPORTING DOCUMENTATION

This explains the details of a problem or abnormality (other than an operator-induced error) that arises during on-line operation. Problem documentation should include printouts, console "pictures," operator information, and analyses of environmental conditions, such as loss of air conditioning or power surges that exist at the time of the computer halt or I/O device malfunction.

EMERGENCY PROGRAMMING DOCUMENTATION

In many systems, owing to the nature of the data processing environment, it becomes necessary to "patch or fix" a program on-line when the condition cannot await the normal program development and documentation processes. In most cases where emergency programming action is instituted on-the-spot, the requirement to have the documentation available before, or while, the emergency is attended to is impractical. Correction of a software problem that impedes data movement is paramount and documentation becomes secondary. After the problem has been corrected, however, complete documentation of the type suggested under *Programming and Operations* should be prepared. All previously developed documentation concerning the altered program(s) should be updated within a reasonable period. When the on-line program or system is re-assembled or re-compiled, the emergency programming documentation may be discarded, providing all affected documentation is updated.

In large real-time communications environments, there are many data processing variables (i.e., multiprogramming, multiprocessing, critical timing, switching, etc.) that may necessitate frequent correction. An extreme case would be a multiprogramming, multiprocessing system developed and maintained by different programming groups operating semi-independently and not subject to the same controls and management. Particularly when the programs process the same data, share the same core and I/O and, in some cases, interface with each other, software problems are inevitable and frequent on-line fixes are required.

Consider two programming groups —A and B— working under separate management controls but sharing hardware resources and processing the same data. Group A finds it necessary to modify a program online. The program interfaces with a program developed by Group B. Dictated by the urgency of the problem, a change is made at an odd hour of the day by a programmer called to the computer center to correct the problem. The change is not recorded, nor is it communicated verbally to Group B. A few days later, Group B runs into problems it finds difficult to isolate. Because of the precise bit configuration and logic required to interface the two programs correctly, Group B's programmers eventually begin looking for a particular bit configuration in Group A's program, but are unable to find it. The time and effort lost in attempting to overcome the effects of this kind of inadequate documentation are legend.

These situations arise most often immediately after implementing a major modification to a complex real-time system. It has been my experience in such environment, where frequent changes were performed by independent programming groups, that inadequate problem reporting documentation often necessitates "fixes to a fix," and usually results in causing many subsequent problems that are difficult to isolate and correct. It would be difficult to overstress the serious consequences of making urgent modifications without taking the time to document them adequately, regardless of how inconsequential they may first appear.

EXTENSIONS TO APPLICATION DOCUMENTATION

Thus far, we have discussed only those aspects of documentation necessary to develop and maintain application programs. Also necessary, however, is some method of conveniently saving past and current programs for instant recall and use. The following two extension areas of application documentation will minimize program duplication and facilitate the development and maintenance of subsequent programs.

PROGRAM DOCUMENTATION LIBRARY

As programs are developed, a method of cataloging and condensing the large bulk of narrative (external) and technical (internal) documentation into a more convenient method of storage for subsequent recall and use should be established to minimize program duplication. This could be achieved by archiving current documentation on magnetic tape or disk packs or by microfilming. Programs subject to frequent recalls are best stored on magnetic tape or disk packs for four reasons: First, the entire application program can be "written out" to tape or disk from main storage or from an external storage device; second, as each "stand-alone" program is developed, the documentation material is available either on punched cards and/or in narrative form (which can be keypunched or input via an optical character reader); third, tape or disk equipment would be readily available; fourth, approximately 40,000,000 bytes (alphanumeric characters) or 480,000 punched cards (240 boxes) can be stored on a 2,400-foot magnetic tape. Disk packs can contain up to 30 million bytes per pack. Thus, one magnetic tape or disk pack can contain a "mountain" of documentation.

This library of programs would serve as both a historical record and as a useful tool in developing subsequent programs. When a request for a new program is received, a catalog search could reveal a routine or program with similar operational features. Magnetic tapes or disks could be searched off-line, and the desired features or programs printed for review and comparison. Various features and programming logic could be extracted, or an entire program modified to fit the user's request, thereby saving much programming time in developing the program logic. In its original form, application documentation would soon become too time-consuming to search manually for desired programming features, and would become too bulky to retain "on-the-shelf."

The method of cataloging and indexing would be the key to the program library. Each feature, routine, or program of an entire application system should be indexed by subject, that is, each stand-alone feature or routine of a major program, or each stand-alone program of an application system should be associated with an abstract stating its purpose and function. These would not be "canned" ready-to-use programs: changes or even major modifications would usually be required. But a considerable amount of time would be saved by not having to re-invent completely each new system.

Of course, to implement such a library would require some "in-house" imagination and considerable planning. Procedures for cataloging and indexing would have to be devised and a program would have to be written to enable searching the tapes or disks for the desired programs. This could be a stored program with updating performed via type-ins from console or card inputs, or a card deck could be updated manually. Perhaps the most convenient and fastest method of updating would involve utilizing a cathode ray tube visual display unit. Selected portions of the catalog could be viewed and deletions or insertions made by keyboard. The CRT display unit would also serve as a useful tool in randomly retrieving, reviewing, and modifying stored documents, i.e., program summaries, abstracts, and other reference material. A master catalog listing of all routines and programs printed from the stored catalog or from the card deck could be circulated to all programming sections, or retained in the reference documentation library for review.

REFERENCE LIBRARY

This should be a must for any programming system. The central library should be where all programming documentation, vendor's documents, and reference manuals are deposited. Only those reference manuals, brochures, newsletters, and other documentation applicable to the particular hardware and software configuration should be on file. (For many EDP systems, it may be more practical to combine the program documentation library and the reference library into one Central Reference Documentation library. See Figure 5-2 for a graphic outline of the functional aspects of this library.) For larger software systems, a qualified librarian should be employed to organize and maintain the reference library. In smaller systems, a clerk can be trained for this job.

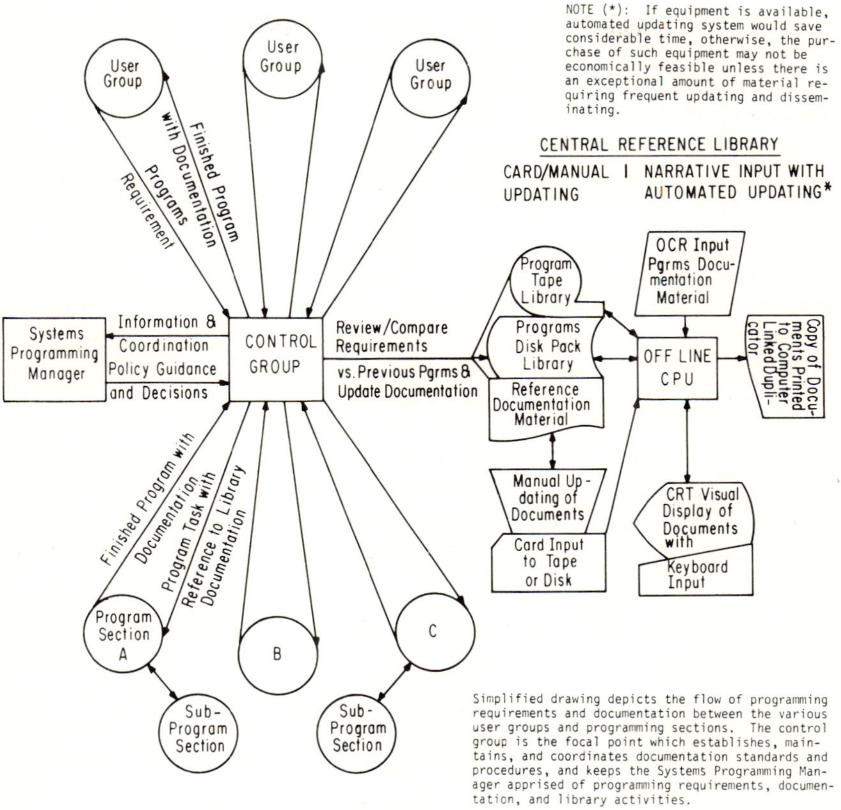

Figure 5-2.

As a program or application system is developed, the programming analysis studies (software objectives), flowcharts, program listings, user (operator) and system reference manuals, card decks (source and test), and the test and acceptance documents should be placed on file in the reference library. Individual programming sections may establish separate reference files for their own programs or those they are responsible for, and these files may include the vendor's manuals for the equipment that the programs are run on. If a program library is not established, and the reference library is to be the focal point for all reference and documentation material, then a catalog system similar to the one discussed for the program library should be established for indexing and cross referencing.

An external numbering system should be devised to identify each stand-alone program. This numbering system would be for library administrative and control purposes and could take on several forms. For example: a program could be assigned a series of numbers to represent the date, month, and year that a program was implemented, e.g., 082869—where 08 is the month, 28 is the day, and 69 is the year. The unique number could also represent the equipment configuration which is required to run the program. Example—AAAAAABBBBNTU, where AAAAAA represents the processor, BBBB is the direct access device, and N is a numeric to represent the number of tape units (TU). Of course, the number would vary depending on the nomenclature of the equipment. These are just two examples of a numbering system which would facilitate logging and locating programs. The number, along with the subject of the program, could be assigned by the librarian at the start of the development of the program or, preferably, after the program is developed and ready for implementation.

Copies of reference books and trade journals should also be retained in the library. Making this material known to EDP personnel would require a comprehensive library catalog. Such a catalog should list programming documentation and vendor's manuals by subject matter, and books and journals by title, author, publisher, and date of publication.

DOCUMENTATION MANAGEMENT AND PROGRAM CONTROL

To provide effective control and management for application programs documentation, it is essential that a control group be established to supervise documentation development and maintenance, to evaluate and act as the "clearing house" for all programming requirements, and to monitor program implementation. The concepts discussed thus far in this article cannot be effectively implemented without such a group to direct library activities and all aspects of program documentation. This group should be the focal point where all documentation from the various programming sections is routed for review. All programming requests should also be routed to the control group for comparison with previously developed programs (see Figure 5-2). When a "match" is found, a task/memo sheet referencing the library documentation is attached to the programming request and sent back to the programming section. The programming section could then check out the reference material, and/or print that portion of the documentation or program desired from the program's library tape or disk. The programming section would then use this documentation, coupled with the originator's requirement, to prepare programming analysis studies and other software objectives for program development.

The control group would also serve as liaison between the departments requesting computer services and the programming sections.

Before a programming task is released to a programming section, the control group would insure that adequate requirement documentation is available. Any questions arising concerning the programming requirement would be referred to the control group rather than to the originator of the requirements. The control group could also keep track of available resources (core, processor time, etc.) and coordinate test acceptance and program implementation. When a program is modified, the control group would be responsible for updating the reference documentation stored on the program's machine records or on file in the central reference library, and communicating these changes to all appropriate programming sections. It would remain the responsibility of each affected programming section to update any separate reference documentation on file in their own files.

One centralized control group intimately familiar with systems and documentation principles would be in a better position to monitor the overall system and guard against duplication than several decentralized control groups located in each major programming section. In large systems, several individuals could make up this central group, which would supervise the documentation writer/analysts, the program library, and the central reference library (a documentation writer/analyst working with the various programming sections would serve as the link between the control group and the programming sections). In smaller systems, one or two personnel may be sufficient.

Finally, to insure that the control group does not become a bottleneck and delay programming projects, its functions should be clearly defined, namely: to evaluate programming requirements; to establish standards and guidelines; to control procedures for documentation development, library organization, and management; and to coordinate documentation between the various sections involved in the development and maintenance of programs for an EDP system.

CONCLUSION

Harold V. Semling, Washington Editor for *Modern Data,* quoted Mr. L. H. Woodward of NASA's Ames Research Center as saying "analysis and documentation of the time-shared/multiprogrammed interactive system performance is badly needed" *("NASA Views Its EDP Needs," Modern Data,* Sept. 1968). Mr. Woodward's remarks are just as relevant to batch processing or real-time communications programming as they are to a time-shared multiprogramming environment. Because of the absence of recognized methods and concepts for organizing and developing documentation, this subject has not kept pace with the software state of the art. Perphaps one of the reasons for this was touched upon by Ronald D. Jones in the January 1969 issue of *Modern Data.* In his article, *"Information Systems in Operations Analysis,"* Mr. Jones stated that "the temptation to postpone the problem of thinking by immersion in the busy work of data collection seems to afflict us all." Not enough thought has been devoted to the importance of adequate documentation. We tend to lose ourselves in our own immediate environments, and fail to consider the long-range effects of our present efforts.

The wave of the future in EDP is the direction of time-sharing and real-time communications multiprogramming/multiprocessing, with OCRs and CRTs emerging as the principal data input and visual display units. These units are fast and efficient, and there are no better tools for updating and reviewing documentation, whether it be in narrative or consist of the actual logic structure of an application program. With the rapidly spiraling increase of data processing systems, unless application documentation and methods of updating are viewed as equally important as the software and hardware, the computer will not only be "I/O bound," but it will become increasingly "documentation bound." The methods and concepts that have been suggested do not supply all of the answers. However, I believe that the majority of them, modified with some "in-house" imagination, will be beneficial to any EDP system.

EDP DOCUMENTATION: TEN WAYS

by F. Stuart Magie, Jr.

Most data processing people agree that documentation of individual programs as well as entire systems is a necessary requirement. But what type of documentation should an EDP installation have? Here are ten points to help you develop effective documentation.

1. Each processing system should have a *system flow diagram:* a complete diagram of the system from data control clerk through each computer operation and back to the data control clerk. This flow chart, in order to be meaningful to the particular installation, should be created in a standard manner that is adopted by that particular installation. One easy-to-follow format is illustrated in the following chart.
2. A *general narrative* of the complete data processing system

---

Reprinted by permission of the publisher from *Administrative Management,* vol. 30, no. 6 (June 1969), pp. 62-64.

Diagram below shows standard production flow techniques that should be employed by systems analysts and programmers when finalizing production flow documentation. *Three numerical blocks given in processing flow are respectively: system number, program number, estimated average run time.

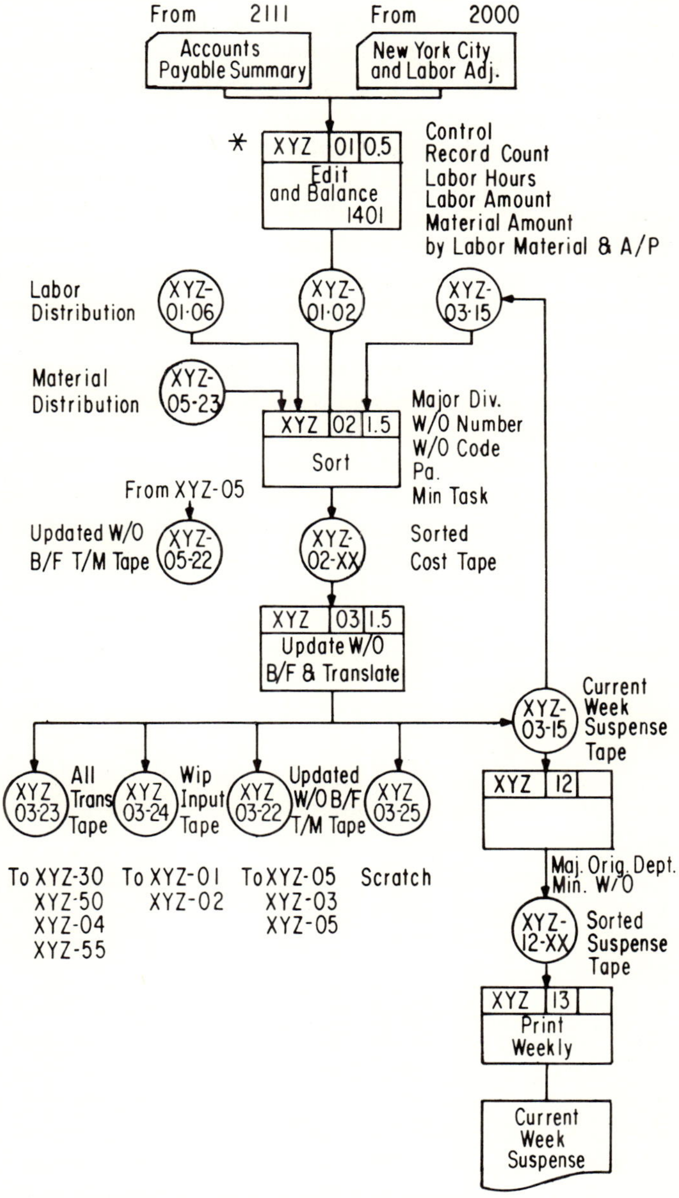

Figure 5-3. Data Processing Flow Chart.

should be created and should include a "picture" of the total system from the user through the data control clerk and computer operations back to the user. It should include such things as input/output schedules, number of computer operations, methods for balancing and clerical procedures, etc.

3. A *detailed program abstract* should be found in the form of a narrative or program abstract written for each computer operation. The abstract should describe in detail that particular operation. A standard method for writing abstracts should be established for the installation in order to simplify the effort analysts and programmers to read abstracts and thereby know what is to be found within the program. It has been my experience that the abstract should start by defining the name and number of the system, followed by the name and number of the particular program within the system. Next should be a short description of the objective (or the problem solved by) this particular program step. After the objective there is a description of all input files. The next section of the abstract will contain a description of all output files. This section also refers to any output reports produced by this particular computer step. After the output files have been fully described, the last section of the abstract should indicate the problems that must be solved by the computer program. This description, whether done with matrix tables or in narrative fashion should communicate enough detail for the programmer to create and construct the proper logic to build the necessary program.
4. There should be a *detailed program logic narrative,* which can be best systematized by requiring all programmers to write a narrative describing their program, after it is implemented into production. In order to enforce this rule, a program is not accepted without the logic narrative.
5. A *current program listing* of the present production program must be retained as documentation for the program. This listing will be produced by the final assembly and filed with the other documentation.
6. In order for the programmer to positively assure that the program functions are as per specifications, *test data* must be created. Usually "static" test data are created by the programmer and "systems" test data supplied by the user or by the analyst. The test data that most thoroughly "checks" the program should be maintained on file. This includes not only card decks, but a listing of the test data and the results. Whenever a change is made to the program, the test data can be rerun and thereby

prove if the new version of the program is correct.

7. The *record layout* of all files must be included either with the abstract or filed by themselves with each program within a system. Also, samples of the printed output and input should be filed. In this section of the file, one other piece of documentation must be kept and that is keypunch operator punch instructions.
8. Clear *computer operator instructions* must be created for the operator to follow when running each program. Two copies are usually made: one filed in the documentation book and the other is forwarded to the computer operations department with the program.
9. Any other documentation should be kept as *miscellaneous documentation* and filed. These may be memos and letters from and to the user or customer of this particular system.
10. *Clerical instructions* may be written if the system requires any manual handling prior to keypunching, or requires clerical handling after computer operation.

LIBRARY

As can be seen, control of documentation can become very cumbersome. Some EDP installations have created a documentation library. These libraries have complete files for sort and object decks. In a large installation, it becomes necessary to assign one or two people to act as source documentation librarians, their job being that of maintaining all documentation and keeping track of who has withdrawn the documentation. This practice is also a fine starting point for programming trainees.

In most cases, it is necessary to require the programmer and analyst to update documentation when a program is being modified or changed. If the installation can afford a librarian, he or she should be given the responsibility of seeing that documentation is updated and changed when modifications are implemented.

6

Breakdowns in Control

Although some breakdowns in computer security and control have been widely circulated, and possibly exaggerated, even more instances may have gone unpublicized. Many may not have been recognized yet.

Protection against the intrusion of outsiders bent on sabotage and destruction may be obtained through physical and procedural safeguards.

Protection against employees whose aim is theft or damage is more difficult for they have access to files and equipment as well as to specialized knowledge. Perhaps the most common breakdown is caused by well-intentioned employees making common human errors.

The concentration of information in the computer center and the organization's dependence on the computer have made breakdowns in control a most serious issue.

The publicized instances of breakdowns serve a constructive purpose in stimulating increased attention at three levels: prevention, detection, and recovery.

COMPUTER SECURITY: THE CORPORATE ACHILLES HEEL

by Albert L. C. Chu

In a fraction of the time it takes to read this article, a disgruntled employe or an innocent-looking saboteur from outside, armed with a

---

magnet the size of a quarter, could quietly wipe out thousands of reels of magnetic tape that may contain vital corporate data and probably cost millions of dollars to collect.

This is exactly what happened to a West Coast electronics manufacturer last year, where accountants and auditors are still trying frantically to reconstruct the files from original source documents. Had there been no original data to fall back on, the company would have been doomed.

The crime is but one of the many hazards surrounding today's computer installations. Many companies and institutions have already learned a bitter lesson.

An 18-year-old Cincinnati youth used long distance telephone to tap the lines of a time sharing firm in Louisville, Ky., and extracted data from its ledgers as well as records of its customers. He had bypassed almost all the security programs before he was apprehended.

An employe of the Encyclopaedia Britannica was able to walk off with a tape in his briefcase, containing a customer list. He used a service bureau to duplicate the list for sale.

A data processing manager was able to steal $81,000 from a brokerage house by making program changes that caused payments to be made to his fraudulent account.

A customer at a Boston bank printed his MICR account number on a batch of blank deposit slips. He then left the slips in the bank lobby and watched other customers deposit money in his account.

Many other disasters can result from ordinary human errors. Take the classic computer fire at the Pentagon basement in 1959. A 300-watt bulb overheated a fire-resistant ceiling and touched off a blaze that engulfed both the tape library and the adjacent computer room.

A rookie operator at a large New England manufacturing firm bypassed a safety device to speed up the updating of the customer file. In the process he lost two-thirds of each of the two copies of the file. An experienced operator accidentally discovered the mishap just in time to save the third copy, and the company.

A Florida city auditor recently revealed a loss of an audit trail occurred during conversion of the accounting system to computer. As a result, the city wasn't really sure who owed the city how much, nor how much the city owed others.

A large bank in New York once noticed data mysteriously dropped from magnetic tapes. A security firm later found the culprit as a magnetic door holder designed to hold the door to the computer room open during emergency.

It was recently reported that at the Internal Revenue Service's Austin, Tex. processing center, several reels of tape containing 1969 income tax return records were erased by energy emitted from the radar of a nearby airport.

Computer centers have also become targets of bombing and mob action by radical students, as evidenced by the destruction of the Army Mathematics Research Center at the Univ. of Wisconsin, and the damages at the computer center of Sir George Williams Univ. in Montreal.

SDS members who ransacked a Dow Chemical computer center in Midland, Mich. last year, also expertly scrambled 10,000 reels of tape containing valuable research data.

MANAGEMENT UNDER FIRE

While natural or human-engineered disasters could happen despite all reasonable precautions, many victims to date point their fingers to company or institution management for its failure to recognize the potential hazards to which computer installations are vulnerable, and to adopt adequate protective measures.

Various security experts in the computer field share the opinion that most of today's computer installations do not have a formal, well-organized security program; and that most of the traditional security programs can be broken.

This failure to face up to the security problem and to take proper action may become a costly one for many business executives. According to Roy N. Freed, a Boston attorney who has conducted many studies in the computer fraud menace, company stockholders have filed suits against corporate officers for failure to take proper precaution to protect company information. It is reasonable to project, he says, that similar actions could be taken where computerized data is involved.

"Corporate officers have a legal obligation to their company to exercise the same care in the performing of their duties that a reasonably prudent man would devote to his own affairs," Freed states. "They may be held liable to any corporate loss as a result of their failure to take proper care of the data, and may be obligated to reimburse the company for such losses."

There are, however, indications that more and more business executives who were complacent in the belief that "it can't happen to me," are becoming aware of the ugly reality that they, too, can become prime targets of saboteurs, crackpots, vandals, and dissident students, not to mention internal thieves. More and more companies are appointing security monitors from their EDP staffs to centralize security matters.

Trade organizations such as the American Management Assn. and the Bank Administration Institute, and research firms such as the Advanced Management Research, Inc., find their seminars on computer security overcrowded by data processing managers and security officers from business, industries and government.

What constitutes computer security? According to Richard F. Cross, security officer for the Bank of New York, it involves "an interface of physical, personnel and procedural security, audit controls and insurance." Each of these five broad segments, he says, "must be considered and applied to achieve maximum protection for the computer center at minimum cost to the institution."

Physical security considerations should include location and layout of the computer center, control over access and exit, the protection of the center against fire, flooding and power failures, the protection of data files from malicious destruction and theft, and the security of the personnel.

"Many companies invited trouble because they regard their computer centers as showcases of their corporate facilities," states Louis Scoma Jr., president of Data Processing Security, Inc. of Park Ridge, Ill. "They do not realize the computer center is actually the nerve center of their companies, vital to the organizations' daily operations. How many banks put their vaults in the front window? How many financial institutions let visitors wander through the safe deposit box area?"

While no two computer installations have exactly the same requirements for physical security, Scoma recommends certain guidelines. A computer center should be located at a site where employees can get to work conveniently and safely, especially those working second and third shifts. Within a building, the center should be located out of the main traffic flow, out of public view, and behind substantial walls.

The light damage suffered by the Univ. of Kansas computer center after a bomb exploded outside the machine room proves the prudence of access control. According to university officials, after several bomb threats, the back door of the center was permanently locked and only those persons with legitimate purposes were allowed in the computer room. Otherwise, they believe, the bomb could have been brought into the machine room and blown the computer into scraps.

"We should go out of our way to make it difficult for one to enter a computer room," Scoma adds. "The programmers, systems analysts, and customers should not be allowed in the computer room without proper authorization."

Data Processing Security, Inc. has developed an electronically controlled double-door entry system for access control in computer centers. Once a person enters the first door into the buffer zone, the door locks behind him while he is subjected to an electronic search by concealed probes for magnets and other 'illegals.' If a magnet is detected, the system 'freezes' the second door and automatically alerts the security guard. The second door can only be opened with a special badge-key issued to authorized employes. If the person doesn't have a badge, or if a wrong key is used, he is trapped in the buffer zone and has to call the guard via a voice communications system. At any time the guard could view the buffer zone through a closed-circuit television camera (see Figure 6-l).

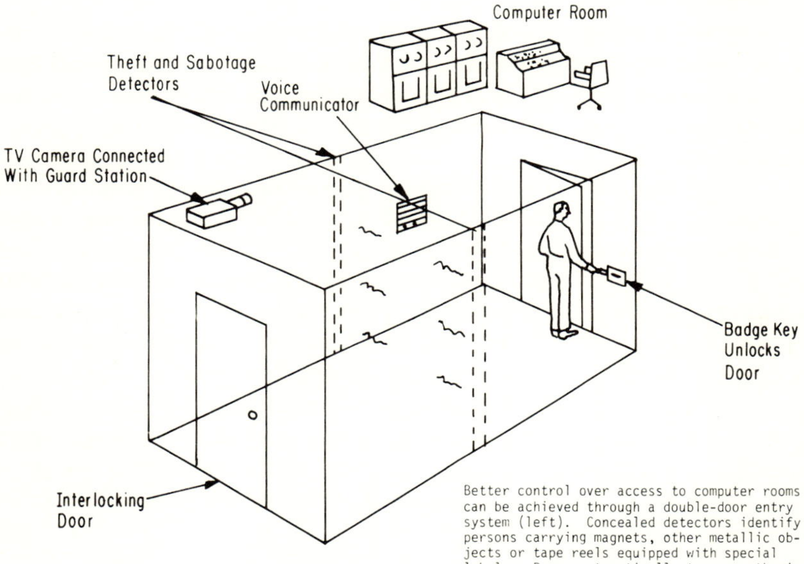

Better control over access to computer rooms can be achieved through a double-door entry system (left). Concealed detectors identify persons carrying magnets, other metallic objects or tape reels equipped with special labels. Doors automatically trap unauthorized persons.

Figure 6-1. A Double-Door Entry Control System.

The operation of the computer center depends heavily on closely controlled temperature and humidity, as well as the continued supply of electric power. Therefore, the air conditioning unit should have sufficient power to do the job, and should be regularly maintained. An additional safeguard would be to arrange for air conditioning equipment serving other parts of the building to be diverted to the computer room in case of emergency. Protection against power blackout or brownout can be achieved by using two different power sources, but by far the best protection against power failures is the in-house stand-by power supply unit.

YOUR NEIGHBOR'S KEEPER

Protection against fire involves fire prevention practices and the installation of a fire detection and extinguishing system. The center should be built of fireproof materials throughout, including partitions, floor, ceiling racks, and even the paint. Good housekeeping practices must be maintained, which means no waste paper or carbons on the floor. Some computer centers prohibit smoking inside the computer room in order to keep dirt off the tapes and to reduce fire hazards. Smoke and temperature deviation detectors are a must.

Fire protection should also include a careful assessment of the condition of the building in which the computer center is located. Scoma cites a case where a computer installation located on the second floor of a building with perfect fire protection devices found its floor collapsed when the office underneath caught fire.

Sprinklers are the most commonly used fire extinguishing system, but it is not the most efficient one since the water that dampens fire can also damage computer equipment and supplies. The carbon dioxide (CO^2) type of fire extinguishing system offers a satisfactory alternative, such as the one installed at the Chase Manhattan Bank's New York City headquarters. Engineered by Walter Kidde & Co., Inc., Belleville, N.J., the system uses a battery of remotely located cylinders containing the liquid gas. When actuated by smoke detectors, the gas discharges and builds up an inert atmosphere in the immediate surrounding area and extinguishes the fire without damaging equipment or data files. Employes could go back to work five minutes after the fire is put out and the ventilation system is restarted.

Another fire fighting system has been developed by the Ansul Co. of Marinette, Wis., using Halon extinguishing agents which are discharged in the form of a colorless, odorless and non-toxic gas. Since Halon agents do not work by diluting oxygen, they are well suited for areas where humans are present.

The Guaranty Bank and Trust Co. of Worcester, Mass., adopts another approach to fire fighting. A system installed by Security Control Systems, Auburn, Mass., detects fire, smoke and excessive temperatures and humidity fluctuations, and causes a monitoring and reporting device to call up four pre-selected phone numbers for help.

Data files, whether in punched card, magnetic tape or magnetic disc form, whether records or programs, are key elements of any data processing facility and may represent the lifeline of the company. They should be zealously protected from tampering and destruction by outsiders and employes.

The fact that data recorded on computerized media is not readily recognizable by humans further amplifies the need for adequate, unfailing protection; for the loss or tampering of data may not be discovered until the data is needed, or until the damage is done. Imagine what would happen if the labels on several reels of tape were switched.

Robert V. Jacobson, president of the Waltham, Mass.-based consulting firm Bradford Assocs., and a recognized expert in data files safety, offers the following guidelines for the protection of data files:

> Current files should never be released for processing without backup copies;
>
> Backup files should be put under the control of a group independent of the computer operations staff;
>
> Input data should be checked by independent editing processes;
>
> Input data from on-line terminals should be recorded on an independent transactions file;
>
> Programs should be subjected to rigorous testing before they become operational, and should be supported by backup copies.

"There is no magic or mystery about file security," Jacobson says. "It can only come from a systematic analysis of the requirements of a specific situation, institution of needed protective measures and continuing supervision of operations to assure compliance and to spot promptly changing circumstances which require new measures. The well-placed 'stitch in time' can save the prudent manager many more than nine."

One of the most common practices in data file security is to back up the current file with a "father generation" file and a "grandfather generation" file; another would be to store copy of all vital records at an off-site location, so that even a complete destruction of the computer center will not threaten the existence of the company.

A software package called Panvalet, developed by Pansophic Systems of Lombard, Ill., is a direct access library system for programs, designed to improve operating procedures and to provide backup security for all source and object programs. The package systemizes the storage (on disc or data cell), retrieval, updating and maintenance of all programs; automatically creates complete and current program backup; and prevents program tampering.

To protect magnetic tapes or discs from theft, Data Processing Security, Inc. has developed a patent-pending tape reel label. Permanently attached to the tape reel, the label will send off a warning signal when it is carried—even inside a briefcase—past a magnetic detector.

Automated tape storage and delivery systems, such as those developed by Supreme Equipment and Systems Corp. and Advanced Digital Systems, Inc. store tapes in enclosed metal modules that are protective against fire and magnetism. Upon signal from the operator, the Supreme system delivers tapes to an opening via conveyor, while the ADS system delivers each tape via a shuttle to the tape drive or printer where it is needed. A minicomputer is used to maintain tape scheduling and to handle the bookkeeping chores for the entire tape library.

The breakdown of procedural control can probably be credited for a majority of the computer mishaps that have hit corporations. Joseph J. Wasserman, president of Computer Audit Systems, Inc., East Orange, N.J., puts the blame for this control problem on management. "Many companies mistakenly think procedural controls are dispensable under computer environment because 'the computer doesn't make mistakes,' and therefore overlook the need for effective controls," he points out. "While the computers don't make mistakes, the people who program and operate them often do."

THE COMPUTER DUPER

It is ironic that the computer, while permitting new and superior control techniques, also allows more powerful and sophisticated means of perpetrating embezzlement and frauds. Brandt Allen, assistant professor at the Harvard Business School, finds that computer-based frauds are most often committed by manipulating input data, by developing improper computer programs, or by making fraudulent program changes.

A programmer at a Minneapolis bank, for instance, was able to put a "patch" on the demand deposit accounting program he developed to make it ignore overdrafts on his own checking account.

In another embezzlement case, a vice president of a brokerage house stole more than $250,000 over a five-year period by coming in the office at off hours and during the weekend, and punching fraudulent input cards.

The flow of data in a company's information processing system is often full of loopholes, and can be utilized to commit frauds. Thus a systems analyst in a large Canadian department store placed orders for expensive appliances, intercepted the documents during the process and changed the prices to nominal figures. The scheme was discovered, only after the cycle was completed, by a systems consultant called in to review the adequacy of the internal control procedures.

How widespread these computer-based frauds are is anyone's speculation. Most companies are reluctant to publicize such incidents because no one involved could gain from the resultant prosecution or publicity.

One reason why frauds can easily be committed in a computer environment is the concentration of data, Allen asserts, "Frequently all of the basic records and supporting detail, as well as the transaction data and even the processing programs themselves are in one central location. Fraud attempts that in an earlier day may have been too difficult because the necessary records were located in too many different offices, now may be possible," he says.

Wasserman points his finger to the violation of a basic control principle by most computer installations: the separation of responsibilities. "In today's data processing environment, a person often performs functions that were previously separated among several business units. Unless there are proper control procedures, knowledgeable but unscrupulous employes can manipulate programs for their own benefits, and incompetent employees can cause lasting damage by making errors." He charges that most computer-based frauds reported to date can be traced to improper separation of programming and operation.

Wasserman, whose firm specializes in computer audit software and consulting services, as well as auditor training programs, emphasizes the internal auditor's role in the development of a computer security system. "It is the auditor's responsibility to ensure that computer systems are auditable when they are operational, and they should be continuously on the alert for possible effects of a proposed system on the internal controls, and to develop all consequent audit requirements accordingly."

He believes that auditors should learn more about using the computer as a tool to audit computer systems, and that they should not get involved in the enforcement of the system, but merely serve as devil's advocate to evaluate the system on behalf of the top management.

Some security breaches at computer centers can be attributed to the attitude of the personnel, who are basically profession-oriented rather than company-oriented, as indicated by Allen. "Most firms have found it difficult to instill in their computer operators and programmers the same degree of concern over cards and tapes that conventional accounting clerks held over ledgers and journals," he says.

HELLO, GOODBYE!

Some companies found their employes stay just long enough to learn trade secrets before they leave to work for a competitor. Software houses are particularly vulnerable. In order to help prevent this situation, Arthur Pritchard, president of Financial Timesharing Services of San Francisco, suggests that a strict legal agreement that would protect the company's rights to trade secrets be signed by all employees associated with or having access to a specific program, and re-signed every time a major supplement is made to the program. A model agreement, called Proprietary Program Protection Plan which is being offered free by the firm, stipulates that the signee cannot use information he obtains from the company to help a competitor develop hardware or software products within 12 months after his employment is terminated with the company.

Some dishonesty problems are results of imprudent hiring practices. During the past few years, there has been such a shortage of EDP personnel that many companies hired people without making sufficient background investigations or even requiring employment references, a procedure they would normally take even for the employment of persons not involved with sensitive data. As a result, an individual with questionable qualifications or character, and even the ill-intentioned, could find their way into the inner circle of a company, and become entrusted with vital corporate data. To correct this situation, pre-employment security checking for all EDP personnel should be strictly enforced.

The increasing popularity of time sharing systems among large corporations and service bureaus, which often link the central processor with a large number of on-line terminals located at remote points, has given rise to even more potential security breaches. Not only is access to terminals difficult to control, but data transmitted over communication lines could be subjected to wiretapping and a number of other hazards, such as "piggy-back entry" where the intruder intercepts and compromises communications between a terminal and the processor; and "between-line entry" when the intruder talks to the processor while a legitimate user is inactive but still holding the lines open. The intruder could even cancel the user's sign-off signal and continue operation in his name. A knowledgeable person could enter program changes from a terminal and play havoc with the system.

TIME SHARING'S SHARE OF PROBLEMS

The need for security safeguards in a time sharing environment varies, depending on the location of the terminals and the sensitivity of the data involved. When all terminals are located in offices with access control, and many employes are allowed to use them, simple passwords as provided with most standard systems are often sufficient. When sensitive data is involved, a more complicated setup, such as one using a security profile, user identification or badge key, would be necessary. The computer can also be programmed to record all unauthorized requests for information, and to disconnect the terminal from the system upon such request.

To protect data transmission from wiretapping, a simple cryptographic transformation is usually sufficient because it would make it so costly to steal the information as to discourage most potential spies.

Continental Airlines' Sonic 360 reservations system illustrates some basic precautions that could be taken to protect a time sharing system. The system uses duplex 360/65 CPU's, one maintained on-line full time while the other is used for backup and off-line processing. A total of 550 on-line terminals are located in reservation centers, airports and remote ticket offices. To ensure that only authorized personnel could enter data from the terminals, each terminal is assigned an address, and each ticket agent is given an agent number and a duty code. The authorization information is stored in the system's Agent's Assembly Area (AAA). When an agent comes on duty, he signs in with his number and duty code and waits for an OK from the AAA. When he leaves the terminal, he has to sign off.

The cost of EDP insurance coverage is substantial, due to the high concentration of value in a relatively small area, and to EDP equipment's high susceptability to damage. An annual premium for the coverage of $1 million against equipment damage and loss, and $500,000 each against media loss, extra expense and business interruption, would be approximately $7,000.

Adequate security safeguards in the computer room, however, could help bring down the premium rates. According to Gordon M. Paine, assistant secretary responsible for EDP insurance programs at St. Paul Fire and Marine Insurance Co., safety features such as Halon or CO^2 fire extinguishing system, smoke detectors, no smoking provision in computer room, gas masks and backup air-conditioning units would help reduce insurance cost. On the other hand, the absence of certain basic safety measures would increase premium rates.

"Actually, security protection should always be the prime concern of any EDP installation, and an insurance program just serves as additional protection," Paine says. "I would advise anyone who is establishing a computer center for the first time to consult with his architect or insurance agent on the safety aspect, so that adequate safety features could be included in the facility. It is always cheaper to provide such features the first time around than adding them later on," he adds.

There is no question that top management is ultimately responsible for the security of the computer facility, as well as the rest of the company. But on a day-to-day basis, who should be charged with the overall security responsibility, given the situation that the data processing manager who should be aware of all the hazards involved is often preoccupied with applications, and that the security officer is most probably not trained to detect some of the invisible hazards that surround a computer?

Scoma, who is a former EDP manager, suggests that the EDP manager be charged with initially developing security standards, while the security officer be responsible for the enforcement of the measures. Wasserman agrees, but adds: "No one group should bear complete responsibility for protecting the computer system. The need for controls should be instilled in the entire organization, starting with top management and extending to all personnel."

WHAT PRICE SECURITY?

Prof. Allen points out the value of an internal security group composed of skilled computer-security specialists. Independent of the EDP line management, the group would design, implement and monitor the various control procedures, check for failure and sabotage attempts, plan for emergency backup, and conduct periodic tests of the system. But he emphasizes that any system can be as good as it is continuously enforced:

"One way a general manager can effectively secure his company is to take off his white coat and put on a black hat and play the role of an imaginary defrauder. See how you can break the system," he says.

But how much security is enough? First of all, there is no such thing as a 100 percent secured installation. The consideration should be based on a cost-benefit concept, and is a trade-off among the value of the data, the inconvenience created by the security measures, and the cost for such protection.

"Security is like the seat belt," says Dr. William F. Brown, director of Avco Computer Services, who conducts a data and file security seminar for Advanced Management Research, "It is a nuisance and it doesn't guarantee there will be no accident. But when an accident does occur, you will find it much cheaper. It may save you money, your job, or even your company."

USING THE COMPUTER TO STEAL

by Harvey S. Gellman

I am not a gambler, yet I am willing to bet any computer user that his computer installation is vulnerable to theft and other abuse. I am

---

Reprinted with permission from *Computers and Automation,* April 1971, copyright 1971 by and published by Berkley Enterprises, Incorporated, 815 Washington St., Newtonville, Mass. 02160.

confident that I would win my bet almost every time. Does this sound farfetched? It is not.

There are plenty of examples to show that most computer installations today have inadequate controls to protect them against theft or damage to programs or data. Here are two examples:

> Between 1959 and 1963, the manager of data processing for a stockbroker embezzled over $80,000 from the company by having cheques made payable to fictitious payees. The inadvertent return of a cheque revealed the thefts.

> A group of enterprising individuals in an investment firm embezzled customer funds and then told the customers that a service agency had processed their accounts incorrectly. Because the public is ready to believe a cry of "computer error," considerable time elapsed before the raid was discovered.

This last example reminds me of the story about the man who looked at wildly incorrect results printed by a computer and said, "You know, it would have taken forty mathematicians working for three years to produce a mistake like this."

The typical computer centre offers an open invitation to the thief or vandal. My objectives are to describe the problem, show how serious it is, and suggest an approach for solving it. I will deal with damage to computer systems as well as fraud, because the action I will recommend will provide protection against both of these hazards.

WHAT IS THE PROBLEM?

The problem can be stated simply: most computer centres do not have adequate data security. This means the computer systems are not protected against destruction or unauthorized access or manipulation.

The list of potential hazards includes: (1) accidental or malicious damage to computer programs or data stored in computer systems; and (2) theft of assets or private information.

Even though these hazards relate to computer installations, they are rarely the fault of the computer. A computer will have breakdowns, but these are usually repairable. The main hazards are due to people who fail to use proper operating and control procedures.

With computer systems, one employee can perform functions that were previously assigned to several business units. Unless there are proper controls, knowledgeable but unscrupulous employees can manipulate programs for their own benefit, and incompetent employees can cause damage by making errors.

WHAT ARE THE RISKS?

The risks can be high. An organization can lose large amounts of money, vital information without which it cannot function, or secret information that may be of value to competitors. Unless an organization takes adequate steps to protect its computer systems from destruction, malfunction or manipulation, it can be badly hurt. In one organization, for example, a disgruntled member of the computer room staff used a small magnet and erased information on nearly every reel of magnetic tape that contained the company's files and programs.

WHO SUFFERS?

Who suffers most from these hazards—large or small organizations? I believe that all are almost equally vulnerable. The large organization's spectacular losses involving large sums of money get more publicity, but many incidents occur in small companies which feel the effects just as much as large ones. Small companies find it difficult to implement effective controls because the knowledge of how to manipulate the computer system may be concentrated in only one person.

No organization is safe. University computer systems have been used by unauthorized people who have tapped telephone lines and broken the code.

The Human Resources Administration, a New York antipoverty agency, lost about $2 million during the first nine months of 1968 through phony Youth Corps payroll cheques processed by a computer at the rate of 100 a week. A policeman discovered a batch of the cheques when investigating an illegally parked, overdue rented car.

It is therefore clear that all organizations are vulnerable and their losses or damages can have serious effects on their customers and their employees.

WHO ARE THE CULPRITS?

Who does the stealing or the damage? The list includes:

1. Computer centre personnel who are authorized to have access to computer equipment or files (machine operators, programmers, librarians, repairmen, etc.)

2. People who create or handle incoming or outgoing data.
3. Outsiders who wish to penetrate the system.

Here are some examples:

- A manager of claims in a government-sponsored medical aid scheme introduced false doctor claims and directed the payment cheques to an office he had rented in a fictitious name.
- Programmers have stolen information from a payroll system for use in union bargaining.
- Programmers have stolen information from a payroll system and sold it to a life insurance company agent.
- Programmers and operators have sold name and address lists.
- At a large Canadian department store, a systems analyst placed orders for expensive appliances and coded them as "special pricing orders." Using his knowledge of the system information flow and procedures, he intercepted the documents as they reached the "special pricing orders" desk. He changed the list price to a nominal price of six or seven dollars and then put the forged documents back into the regular stream. The appliances were delivered to him and he paid his account promptly. The practice was discovered by systems consultants called in to review the adequacy of the system's internal control procedures.

It is important to recognize that an inspired bungler can sometimes do more damage than a thief or vandal. If a computer centre does not have proper procedures and controls, then a programmer or machine operator can make serious mistakes. For example, he could erase a magnetic tape file containing several years' historical data.

WHY IS THE PROBLEM STILL UNSOLVED?

We have enough examples of inadequate data security to show that serious abuse is possible and that this problem deserves the attention of executives. Why then have most organizations not yet solved the problem? Stringent controls in non-computer systems are traditional, so why do managers fail to establish similar controls for computers? Especially when we all know that to err is human, but to really foul things up requires a computer.

Several reasons come to mind. The first is that in the early days, computer systems were developed haphazardly. People were happy when their computer programs finally appeared to work correctly; they had little patience with the problems of data security.

A second reason for lack of security is that some executives think that computer programs are complex and therefore difficult to manipulate. They do not realize that a skilled programmer can quickly alter computer programs to suit himself, do his stealing, then return the programs to their original state.

A third reason for lack of control is that senior executives who are responsible for their organization's computer systems have more pressing problems to worry about. They worry about the steady stream of complaints from users who get inadequate service from the computer centre. They also worry about their own lack of understanding and control of the data processing activities and simply abdicate responsibility to their data processing manager.

Perhaps a fourth reason senior executives ignore the problem is because their expenditures for computer systems usually total less than 1% of sales. They should be more concerned, because the effect of computers on their company's performance can be significant. Just as I was willing to bet that most computer centres are vulnerable to theft and other abuse, I am equally willing to bet that most senior executives do not know how much money is being wasted, how much profit is being produced and what weaknesses exist in their computer systems.

The fifth reason is that many presidents do not realize how vulnerable their organizations are. A few months ago, for instance, there was a fire in the office building occupied by a large Canadian corporation. The computer centre floor escaped damage. When newspaper reporters asked the company president what would have happened if the computer centre had been damaged by the fire, the president stated that it would have had virtually no effect on the company. That company's systems personnel were astonished by their president's statement, because they knew that if the fire had reached the computer centre, the accounts receivable and other vital records would have been destroyed.

The fact that many managers have the false impression that their auditors will protect them is a sixth reason for lack of data security. I submit that the auditor cannot protect them unless his knowledge of computer systems approaches that of the skilled programmer who sets out to modify data or programs without being detected. Is it realistic to expect auditors to have this kind of specialized skill, in addition to their other necessary skills?

Finally, many other people remain unworried about the data security problem. They think that computer fraud or destruction occurs so rarely that they can safely ignore the problem. But these occurrences are not that rare. Many cases are hushed up. I will show later that the problem is probably growing more serious.

The unworried people seem to believe that these cases occur in fiction rather than in real life:

> Those of you who saw the movie "Hot Millions" a few years ago may recall the key event one night when Peter Ustinov saw the cleaning lady hit the computer with her fist. The door on top of the computer opened and she was able to heat her teapot on the hot electronic equipment. Ustinov then used her method to unlock the computer and introduce false information into the computer's storage units. He thereby arranged to have dozens of cheques for large amounts paid out to his fictitious companies all over Europe. In real life, events may be less amusing:
>
> - A vice-president of a stockbrokerage firm embezzled about $250,000 by personally creating punched cards to transfer credits to his own account from the company's interest revenue account.
> - A few months ago, five men, including a bank vice-president, were charged with defrauding two banks of more than $1 million by using a computer. Deposit slips for cash deposits were made out when the embezzlers were actually depositing cheques. Since cash deposits are recorded for immediate credit, cheques subsequently drawn appeared to be covered by the false cash deposits. If the deposits had been correctly made as cheque deposits, the computer would not have credited the money to the account immediately, so that when withdrawals were made the computer would have indicated insufficient funds available, with an uncollectable cheque on deposit. Ordinarily, a teller or branch manager would notice cheques deposited as cash and refuse to accept them. In this case, an assistant branch manager (one of the thieves) accepted the cheques. The scheme was uncovered by accident when a bank messenger failed to deliver a bundle of cheque deposits to the clearing house, leaving $440,000 worth of cheque withdrawals uncovered.

THE PROBLEM IS GETTING WORSE

Managers should be more concerned about data security because the problem will get worse unless something is done about it.

The importance of data security is growing because:

1. The growth in size and complexity of computer systems makes errors harder to detect.
2. Computer systems eliminate many of the paper records.
3. There is a growing reliance by managers on computers, not just for financial data, but also for marketing, production, engineering and forecasting information.
4. There is a continuing shortage of skilled systems personnel and

this leads to the hiring of unqualified people who are incapable of designing adequate controls.

DATA SECURITY IN TIME-SHARING SYSTEMS

The advent of time-sharing computer systems has also made the data security problem more difficult. In time-sharing systems, each user can have an electric typewriter, or a TV-tube terminal connected by telephone lines to a remote computer.

Such systems involve large, complex sets of computer program instructions. These programs are prepared by people—none of whom is perfect. The complexity of these programs makes it extremely difficult for the designer to eliminate loopholes or "security trapdoors." A computer expert can penetrate such systems.

Professor E. L. Glaser of Case Western Reserve University in Cleveland, is such a skilled, experimental penetrator. After learning the standard operating procedures for the system and then thinking about it for a few hours, he has been able to break into a system after five minutes at a terminal.

In one system that Professor Glaser tested, the security system was considered to be good, but he discovered one "trapdoor" in a relatively short time. He wrote a simple program which went through every file in the system, found the owners' names and passwords, extracted all passwords and stored them in a new file after scrambling them so they could not be recognized. He was then able to read any file at any later time.

In another case, Professor Glaser tested the security measures of a new commercial time-sharing system. The security measures were again considered to be good, but again he found a number of "trapdoors". Within five minutes at a remote terminal he was able to "crash" the whole system, bringing it to a complete halt.

Another newly recognized hazard is that signals are transmitted from a computer installation unless the computer room is shielded. In one test, a truck equipped with sensitive receiving equipment, as well as processing and printing facilities, was parked near an unshielded computer centre. A high-speed printer driven by these signals produced the same output as was printed in the centre.

When you think of the possibilities, both in the movies and in real life, perhaps you will agree with me that those managers who are not worried about their data security are deluding themselves.

SOME MANAGERS ARE GETTING WORRIED

During the past year, I have found that some executives are becoming concerned about some aspects of the problem. One indication of this concern is the fact that a new data security service introduced in Toronto six months ago is selling very well. This service provides safe, off-site storage of magnetic tapes, disks, punched cards and other documents.

Perhaps people have been buying this protection because they have read about bomb scares and the increasing level of violence in our society. Because some people consider computers a potential threat to individual freedom, there have been a few attempts to destroy them. An example, right here in Canada, was the destruction of the computer centre by militant students at Sir George Williams University in Montreal.

Some managers are becoming more conscious of the need to protect their computer systems. Perhaps eventually it will be as difficult to get into a computer room as into a safety deposit vault or a high security military area.

WHAT CAN MANAGERS DO?

First, the manager must recognize that his most powerful weapon against fraud or damage is control. An adequate set of controls will not be achieved unless the manager takes the following steps:

1. A study of the data security needs of his organization, measurement of the risks, and the cost of disruptions or losses;
2. A determination of how well the existing data security system meets these needs;
3. The development and implementation of a data security system that covers security of computer programs and data.

The manager might use his own computer personnel to develop this data security system, but it is probably unrealistic to expect these people to rigorously check their own work for security weaknesses. A fresh look should be taken by computer experts. These experts will, in most cases, have to be outside consultants if a comprehensive and objective appraisal and an effective design are to be obtained.

The study should be authorized by the chief executive. This exertion of influence by the chief executive is essential. He cannot afford to abdicate his responsibility to his data processing manager.

All responsible executives have an obligation to their companies to ensure that an adequate data security system is implemented. They should ask themselves the following questions:

1. Do we maintain computer files which, if lost, could stall our day-to-day operations and involve a loss of a substantial amount of money?
2. Could someone alter one of our computer programs without detection?
3. Could someone alter our financial records without detection?
4. Could someone enter our computer room and damage the system?
5. Do we know the estimated cost of recreating our current computer data files if they were destroyed?
6. Do we have a periodic independent review of our data security function by computer experts?

The manager's answers to these questions will help him determine the severity of his data security problem. In most cases, I am sure he will find that his company is more vulnerable than he expected.

CONCLUSION

No security system is perfect, but at a relatively low cost, companies can provide considerable protection for their computer systems. For example, an effective packaged program to provide system and program security has recently come on the market. The acceptance of this inexpensive and easy-to-use "software package" has been excellent and it has been selling very well.

The examples I have given provide a warning of things to come—unless senior executives take faster and firmer steps to control what is happening and what could happen to their computer systems. Solutions are available, but the problems will not be solved until the chief executive and other senior executives direct their attention and initiative to this potentially serious situation.

SABOTAGE, ACCIDENTS, AND FRAUD CAUSE WOES FOR COMPUTER CENTERS

by A. Richard Immel

One crisp winter weekend in 1970 five members of an antiwar group

---

Reprinted with permission of *The Wall Street Journal,* March 22, 1971.

called Beaver 55 broke into Dow Chemical Corporation's Midland, Michigan data research computer center and ransacked the place.

"Tapes and cards were thrown all over the floor," a Dow Chemical official recalls, "but damage appeared to be slight." That is, until someone in the clean-up crew discovered a small, circular magnet about the size of a quarter in the debris. The following Monday, when the computer tapes were checked out, the manager of the center discovered to his horror that the data on 1,000 of the tapes had been erased by such magnets. Cost to reconstruct it: $100,000.

Computer center operators are finding out the hard way that the Dow incident wasn't an isolated occurrence. Last year millions of dollars worth of computer equipment and data were damaged and destroyed by sabotage alone. Add to that increasing instances of computer misuse—such as for fraud and embezzlement—and serious accidental disruptions, and it becomes clear why some observers see troubles ahead in the computer age.

BUTTONING UP THE COMPUTERS

The growing specter of deliberate and accidental assaults on computers has spawned a new kind of consulting firm that tells companies how to button up their computer operations to avoid embarrassing—and usually costly—incidents. Within the past two years, about a dozen of these computer-policing concerns have appeared, offering everything from a simple security checkup to the complete rebuilding of a company's computer center.

Lou Scoma, an Illinois computer-security expert who heads two-year-old Data Processing Security Inc., sees a wide-open market for his services. He projects revenue of $4 million this year, up from $300,000 in 1970, and expects to draw heavily from the 90% of the nation's 70,000 computer centers that he considers to have inadequate security.

Joe Wasserman, another pioneer in the field, says: "Computer security in general stinks. Computer centers tend to be either completely secure or completely insecure." He says most of the secure ones are companies dealing with classified government work—"and that's a pretty small number." Mr. Wasserman expects his New Jersey firm, Computer Audit-Systems Inc., to do five times the business it did last year.

Many companies, of course, have long had their own security experts who were responsible for protecting company property and trade secrets. In recent times sabotage by antiwar groups or other members of the "anticomputer culture" has become a major concern of such security departments. A number of security executives employed by western

U.S. companies with large stakes in research and development have formed a group called Research Security Associates, which meets quarterly to swap information on sabotage threats and techniques and the people thought to be responsible for them. But security experts admit this type of watchfulness is only partly effective. "The biggest problem with the anticomputer culture is that it isn't organized. You can't develop data on them," complains one security man.

FROM SHOPLIFTING TO BOMBS

It isn't just war-related industries that are being threatened. "Seven years ago we were worried about shoplifting and employee theft," says the security chief for a national grocery chain. "Now it's bomb threats and computers." Bewildered executives of one West Coast clothing manufacturer got eight bomb threats against their computer last year.

Sometimes the danger comes from within. A computer employee at one company was given two weeks' notice before he was laid off. The man promptly removed all the labels on 1,500 reels of tape, costing the company thousands of dollars in labor to reidentify the data. "The people I talk to are beginning to realize that things can happen to them that just don't make sense," says one consultant.

As Dow Chemical found out, the technology of computer disruption is ridiculously simple and widely known. Last June a Chicago underground newspaper called Seed published explicit directions on how to wreck computers and erase tapes.

The advice didn't stop with breaking and entering. The article counseled would-be saboteurs to join the institutions they want to sabotage as computer operators and programmers and work from within.

INADVERTENT BUT DAMAGING

Instructions similar to those in Seed have appeared in a number of other underground publications as well.

In some cases the disruption can be inadvertent, but it's no less damaging. One West Coast data processing manager lost his job when a group of Boy Scouts touring the computer center happened to have some magnets with them that erased most of the company's records stored on tapes. In another case a repairman stuck his magnetic flashlight to the nearest support—which happened to be a data storage drum. The result: 80,000 scrambled customer credit records.

A less dramatic but potentially costly security problem is theft or embezzlement by computer personnel. Last summer, for example,

Encyclopaedia Britannica accused three operators on the night shift of copying nearly three million names from the company's "most valued" customer list and selling them to a direct-mail advertiser. Britannica has sued the employees for $4 million, claiming $3 million of the amount in actual damages.

Security experts say many companies probably are losing large sums each year without even realizing it. Brandt Allen, an associate professor in the University of Virginia graduate school of business, says the airlines industry alone may be losing as much as $1 million annually due to manipulation of ticket-sale records on computers. Stories also are beginning to surface about bank officials and back-office employees of brokerage houses stealing large amounts through computer misuse, and experts say these may be only the tip of the iceberg.

Consultants argue that most business executives have a false sense of security because of the complexity of their computer systems. Mr. Allen observes that the complexity actually makes fraud schemes easier to pull off for someone with the know-how—while at the same time the complexity makes misuse harder to detect. The trend toward centralization of record-keeping eliminates many of the bookkeeping procedures that used to act as a double-check, he says. "The result is to bring all the eggs together in one basket, which makes it very easy to change things. There are no erasures, no adjusting entries, no telltale marks. It's done cleanly, and an operator only needs access for a minute—or even just a few seconds."

What bothers many is the simplicity of the fraud and embezzlement schemes that have come to light so far. "One can't help but wonder what the really clever people are doing," says Mr. Allen.

The same thoughts are haunting some members of the accounting profession. Jerome Farmer, chairman of a computer committee of the American Institute of Certified Public Accountants, concedes that manipulation of computerized records could escape the attention of auditors. But he says accountants are working to come up with techniques to overcome the problem.

STEALING BY TELEPHONE

One potentially vulnerable type of computer is the "time-sharing" unit used by many customers. It's possible to steal data from such a computer by telephone.

Last summer, for example, the FBI charged a teenager with stealing information from a time-sharing computer system in Louisville by long-distance phone. After obtaining account and password numbers of system customers, the youth allegedly tapped into the computer by calling in from Cincinnati. According to the FBI report, he had nearly worked out a program to permanently bypass the center's security safeguards when a mistake tipped his hand.

Two weeks ago, in a similar case, Information Systems Design, an Oakland, California computer service firm, filed a $6 million civil damage suit against University Computing Co. of Dallas, charging two University Computing employees with stealing computer programs by long-distance telephone. The civil suit followed a criminal charge of grand theft against one of the pair. The suspect has pleaded innocent.

NO MORE FISHBOWLS

For those seeking ways to guard against sabotage or other damage to computer systems, one obvious step is to improve the guarding of data processing installations. Many companies and institutions have been so proud of their big, expensive computers that they have put them on public display, enclosing them in "fishbowl" glass cages and including them on guided tours. But many firms now are quietly cutting back or discontinuing such tours, and the old glass walls are giving way to reinforced concrete.

Companies also are being more circumspect about acknowledging that they even use computers and about advertising their location. In San Francisco, for example, several big banks have removed all bank identification from the buildings that houses their computer centers. And in Chicago a large retail concern has changed its computer printouts to make them look typewritten. "When it comes to data processing operations, we would prefer that people didn't even know we had computers," a spokesman is quoted anonymously in a trade journal.

Those companies that seek outside help in improving the security of their computer systems find that prices start relatively low, but they can quickly escalate to astronomical levels. Mr. Scoma of Data Processing Security will put a team of consultants to work running through a 172-point checklist and preparing a survey report for $3,000 to $5,000. The report points out security weaknesses, estimates the cost to reconstruct lost or destroyed data and recommends procedures and equipment to plug any gaps.

STEEPLY RISING COSTS

The plugging is the expensive part. Mr. Scoma offers a package that includes a double-door "buffer" system with electric locks, magnet sensors and closed-circuit television to control access to computer centers. The cost: $25,000. Backup power systems, which can be critical where computers can't be permitted to shut down during a power failure, may run anywhere from $50,000 for a simple generator to upwards of $1 million for the systems used by airlines for their computerized ticket reservations.

Some consultants say at least part of the blame for the vulnerability of computers lies with computer manufacturers that have failed to build security measures into their systems. A spokesman for IBM, the nation's largest computer maker, refuses to talk about the matter, protesting that "we don't feel that publicizing (the security problem) is in our best interest." But Honeywell, Inc., which bills itself as second only to IBM in computer sales, concedes that more could be done.

John Weil, who heads Honeywell's advanced systems and technology unit, says the industry has tended to neglect the security problem in its haste to develop basic computer technology. But he says Honeywell, for one, now is working on protective equipment and techniques, though he says they will have to be built into its systems from the ground up. "I think it will take the next generation of equipment to introduce these things into the basic equipment," he says—and that is several years away at least.

A CONTINGENCY PLAN FOR CATASTROPHE

by D. Van Tassel

Every computer system is vulnerable to disaster, accident, and sabotage as well as plain mismanagement. As a result, like other unpleasant realities, security measures such as entry controls, fire alarms, and off-site storage sites should be considered in advance of need. Considering the large investment business and universities usually have in their computer center some catastrophe security measures are a must. Put another way, if your organization could continue to function for days or weeks after a sudden disaster to the computer complex it is probable that much of the computer center is not needed. In a more typical situation, when the computer center goes down all company work is affected and in some situations all work stops.

Disasters—fire, flood, riot, environmental problems, hardware and

---

Reprinted by permission of the publisher from *Datamation,* vol. 17, no. 13 July 1, 1971, pp. 30-33.

software failures, and sabotage—can and do happen. Yet all too often management ignores this possibility and the security and protection that was given journals and ledgers in precomputer days is not given computer files. If management decides that the possibility of disaster to the computer center is not serious enough to warrant taking precautions, this may be a sound management decision. The important thing is that management should face the problem and decide what, if anything, should be done.

There have been several major disasters in computer centers in recent years. One of the most spectacular took place on July 3, 1959 in the Pentagon computer center. Most people would expect this to be one of the safest and best protected computer sites, but at that time it obviously wasn't.

At 10 o'clock in the morning there was a need for some tapes from the vault. This was the first trip to the tape vault for the day. When the clerk opened the vault door, flames shot out. An electrician had left a 300-watt bulb burning on a "fireproof" ceiling. The fire this caused had smoldered all night and the minute the vault door was opened oxygen hit the smoldering particles and in seconds a sheet of flame and smoke blocked all visibility in the room. Before the fire was over 19 firemen had to be treated for smoke inhalation and the entire computer area was destroyed. All tapes were lost, but programs were saved because they were stored in fireproof cabinets.

After the fire, it was discovered that the supposedly fireproof ceiling was only fire resistant. Several other things were also wrong. The master switch was located where it was difficult to reach, instead of being near an outside door. During the fire, no one could get to it to shut off the power. Consequently, the firemen were pouring water on electrical gear which was still running.

Needless to say, all this has changed. Since that day all military computer center managers are supposed to establish accessible routes and exits. Master power switches capable of turning off all power are strategically located near an outside door. All rooms are equipped with smoke detectors as well as fire alarms that are hooked directly to the base fire station. Rooms, including floors, are insulated with fire-proof material. Good housekeeping of trash and maintenance work is required. Fire prevention inspections are encouraged by the fire department.

A different type of disaster took place when Dow Chemical's computer center at Midland, Michigan was invaded by war protestors on Nov. 8, 1969. No employees were in the center at the time. A thousand tapes were damaged and cards and manuals were thrown around. Damage was said to be $100,000.

A similar, albeit more spectacular and widely publicized, case took place in Montreal, Canada at Sir George Williams Univ. On Jan. 29, 1969 students set fire to the computer center causing $2 million damage to computer equipment. An IBM 1620 and a CDC 3300 were destroyed. In addition all magnetic tapes, programs, and cards were thrown out the ninth floor window and destroyed. In this case besides the equipment, which can be easily although expensively replaced, the administrative and research files and programs were also destroyed.

Dissatisfied employees sometimes believe the risk of punishment is more than offset by the urgency of bringing to the employer's attention their own plight. In precomputer days there were several cases of plug boards being destroyed or stolen. In a recent case an edp employee used magnets to destroy every file possible. Extensive damage was done in a very short time. In fact, at last report, the auditors were not sure whether the company could reconstruct enough information to stay in business.

The important thing to notice in these incidents is that dissatisfied persons are learning what to destroy. Not too long ago in Los Angeles someone took a couple of shots at a computer. This was naive. If the culprit had aimed his shots at the tape storage room he would have done considerably more damage. All it takes is one elementary course on computers to learn what to damage.

Companies with large computer files are particularly vulnerable. The manager of a major U.S. airlines recently assessed the value of their current seat reservation system. When asked what would happen if a dissatisfied employee fouled up the computer system for at least a day, his pessimistic but realistic response was: "First it is entirely possible for many members of our computing staff as well as software or hardware problems to do this to our reservation system. And it could cost us as high as a million dollars of revenue a day during the down period."

Catastrophe normally connotes finality or total disaster. Instead, management should consider a catastrophe as any event that significantly disrupts the normal order of the system. As this definition implies, there are hierarchies or levels of catastrophies. A catastrophe may run the spectrum from a temporary shutdown of the system caused by a power failure, software problem, equipment malfunction or a self-inflicted wound by an improperly trained or misoriented employee, to the more critical conditions brought by flood, riot, fire, earthquake, tornado, or the complete loss of electric power for a prolonged period, as was experienced in New York in early 1965.

Since the level of catastrophe can range from the trivial to total, it is best to develop levels of response. When there is no contingency plan, there is a tendency to treat all processing interruptions the same—usually with panic.

The response to an interruption in processing will normally depend on its duration. Generally there are three approaches to a processing interruption. If the interruption is too brief to have any significant effect on operations, nothing is done. The second type of interruption is of longer duration and management usually reschedules work so that critical applications are given priority when operations resume. Either extra operating hours or off-premise computer time is scheduled to allow delayed work to be processed. The third type of interruption is a major disaster—flood, fire, vandalism, etc. In this case operations are shifted as soon as possible to a back-up computer site so that essential computer functions can still operate.

It is not always clear what level of response should be taken. Power failure, software trouble, or hardware problems can range from the trivial to the serious and still not be obvious at the inception. Also emergencies are more likely to occur on weekends or night shifts than the short day shifts.

To avoid waiting too long for a "trivial" software bug or hardware problem to be fixed the contingency plan should indicate what immediate actions have to be taken, including who to notify and how to get corrective action started. Such a strategy might include an immediate call to the data processing manager, a call to the computer engineer, and notification of the back-up site that time may be needed.

Establishment of wait periods will avoid the situation of the computer going down Friday night and staying down all weekend. The idea of the wait period is that after a certain length of down time (say four hours), no matter what the reason, certain responses are necessary. The allowable wait period will depend on the amount of down time which can be accepted without the need for action. In a heavily used center a small down time period is serious while a computer center that normally runs only 12 to 16 hours a day will not be seriously affected by an eight hour loss.

On-line systems can usually tolerate little down time. A back-up system available at all times is too expensive for most users. But installations with one system for on-line processing and another for batch processing can switch the batch processor on-line if necessary for back up.

Time-sharing companies are an obvious place where interruptions can be quite expensive, since no revenue is coming in while the computer is down and long periods of down time will lose customers. The dollar cost of one day delay in clearing transit checks can be calculated fairly accurately by a bank. If a wholesaler is unable to process incoming orders promptly customer dissatisfaction will cause loss of business. Because of the rather large loss possible under these circumstances, it is best for such installations to appoint one person responsible for the computer center processing should an emergency arise.

This disaster or emergency monitor, instead of the data processing manager, should have full responsibility for developing emergency guidelines. He should be responsible for deciding when an emergency situation exists. His responsibilities should also include location of a back-up site, scheduling necessary personnel, off-site file maintenance, and software availability.

The day-to-day maintenance of off-site files can be left up to the computer librarian. But the decision of which files and how often to store files off-site must be made by those responsible for the files. Because the actual user should share in the decision and cost of maintaining back up files at another storage site, it is not fair to make the disaster monitor carry the whole decision.

Today it is actually easier and cheaper to maintain a duplicate file at another site than in the days before computers, or in the edp card days. Today all types of computer files including source programs can be copied in minutes on magnetic tape and cheaply stored.

Some installations rely on on-premise libraries to protect computer files but this overlooks at least two catastrophe possibilities: (1) total disaster, and (2) that it is not at all uncommon for the source program and documentation to be lying on some programmer's desk.

It is generally possible to provide for some system back-up in case of disaster to the computer system in the normal maintenance contract with equipment vendors. Since it is much easier to negotiate before signing the contract than afterwards, this factor should always be considered before signing a hardware contract.

On-call maintenance support will generally satisfy the requirements of most batch type systems. Large scale, real-time, and time-sharing installations will require around-the-clock on-site engineering support. In addition, redundancy of system usually will be necessary.

If the installation is depending on off-site back-up it is not too wise to make preliminary agreements and then forget about them. Instead, a periodic check should be made to see if the agreement still holds. One manager who had made arrangements for back-up with another installation was surprised when he found that the installation he was depending on had changed hardware three months earlier without notifying him. Another manager discovered that the computer center which previously had guaranteed him eight hours a day if necessary, had increased their work load so much that no time was available.

It is doubtful that any back-up computer could handle the full load of most installations since normally the back-up computer has a work load of its own. Instead limited essential processing is the most that is hoped for.

Software catastrophe is the most common headache for management. Software errors often look like hardware errors at first glance. Since the majority of errors are in the software, the necessity of thorough testing cannot be overemphasized.

Software error can cause an installation to have to turn to outside computer help in a hurry. In business applications output for one file is often input for the next job. Thus troubles can multiply rapidly.

Along with maintaining operational software (programs) at a back-up site there is also the job of supplying the software for the system. If the back-up site hardware is compatible with present software there is no reason why a copy of the system software cannot be sent to the off-site storage location as an added protection in case of total disaster.

If management feels that a back-up site is necessary, then an attempted run at the back-up site should be tried. Not only must the hardware be compatible but so must the software. Whether your software or the back-up site's software is used, problems can develop. The back-up site's software may be incompatible. On the other hand if company owned software is used both computers must have identical memory size and peripherals, and logical addresses must be the same. If your company has two computer sites this problem can be overcome by company control of software and hardware. Some state installations (California State Colleges, California Water Resources) have acquired identical computers and maintained identical software to guarantee compatibility of both software and hardware.

If a computer center is not fortunate enough to have such tight control over the back-up site the only conclusive proof of compatibility of software and hardware is to successfully run production programs. This will give an opportunity to test out the back-up maintenance of files, operator instructions, program documentation, and programs. Only programs and files stored at the off-site location should be used for the test run. A test run also will point out problems of alternate input media, handling source documents at the alternate facility, available working space, and storage space.

The possibility of temporary manual processing should not be overlooked. If it is impossible to resume computer processing for a week it normally would be better to revert to manual processing than no processing at all and possibly closing the business down.

Even if a periodic test cannot be made of the off-site computer preparation there should be an occasional audit of duplication and storage of off-site files. Checks should be made to see that original procedures are still being followed, new files have been added, and obsolete files returned to the center.

Improperly trained or motivated people can be the cause of a disaster in a computer center. Prevention of this situation is part of the overall security program. During an emergency situation overtime hours will usually be needed. In addition critical people may be unavailable. Both these situations should be considered in advance and conditional approval of overtime established. There should be some freedom in using people in positions that they do not normally work. The use of rotating duties for personnel will help provide trained people during critical periods.

If a company's total assets are computer hardware and software then it may be obvious that it should be insured. But if the computer center is just part of a business it is easy to overlook insuring the critical parts of the computer center. Computer hardware often represents a large investment and is usually insured if owned, but the value of the information is more often overlooked.

Not only should the actual information be insured, but also the value of the supporting software. Such insurance is now offered by some insurance companies. The cost of reconstructing destroyed files, the loss of revenue, and the cost of carrying on normal business while files are being reconstructed should all be considered when buying computer center insurance.

There have been several recent examples of disasters involving computer centers. The most widely reported one was the bombing of the Univ. of Wisconsin Army Mathematics Research Center last August. Several computers were damaged, but more damage took place from the Hurricane Celia when it sped through Corpus Christi, Texas at speeds of 162 mph earlier in the month of August.

Two facts become evident from these two examples. Protection against a well-planned bombing or a 162-mph hurricane is almost impossible. But damage can be lessened by simple precautions such as back-up files, auxiliary power sources, fire protection measures, and site location.

Users without back-up files were ruined by the hurricane. Site location was important. Computers surrounded by glass showcases suffered greatly. After the hurricane users with auxiliary power sources were the first to start running again. Other users with back-up sources in other cities were able to start work sooner than those who had to wait for machine replacement or repair.

The greater the preparation, the less the risk. Such a small thing as keeping off-premise back-up files can mean the difference between a total disaster and just a major set-back. Each computer installation must decide on the necessary precautions to take, balancing the resulting expense against the chances they are willing to take.

PART THREE

Auditing Computerized Applications

7

Evaluation of Internal Control

The American Institute of Certified Public Accountants defines internal control as follows:

> Internal control comprises a plan of organization and all of the coordinate methods and measures adopted within a business to safeguard its assets, check the accuracy and reliability of its accounting data, promote operational efficiency, and encourage adherence to prescribed managerial policies.[1]

The introduction of computerized record keeping increases the importance of the evaluation of internal control.

EDP techniques frequently bring about centralization and a greater integration of processing steps into fewer departments, thereby eliminating some of the safeguards previously associated with separation of duties performed by employees at different points in the organizational structure. This increased concentration can be prevented from weakening the internal control if sufficient effort is made to develop adequate new approaches. Computer programs and new system controls can replace previous individual and departmental responsibilities. The data processing department itself can be properly organized to insure that no one individual within the department can affect any of the systems controls.

The auditor must obtain knowledge of how the client's system is supposed to operate. He may do this through questionnaires, checklists, examination of flowcharts, and narrative memoranda. The auditor's re-

[1] *Auditing Standards and Procedures,* New York: American Institute of Certified Public Accountants, 1963, p. 27.

sponsibility then is to obtain evidence which verifies the existence and effectiveness of the client's procedures and controls.

EVALUATING INTERNAL CONTROLS IN EDP SYSTEMS

by W. Thomas Porter

The evaluation of the system of internal control is a point of departure in auditing. Such an evaluation serves as a gauge of the quality of the system. It also gives the auditor the foundation upon which he will construct his examination and build his conclusions. The importance and increased emphasis on the evaluation of internal control are clearly revealed by a review of auditing literature. R.K. Mautz and H.A. Sharaf wrote:

> Because the extent and effectiveness of internal control is so important in audit programming and performance, a prudent practitioner will tend to give this phase of the examination a full measure of emphasis. At best, internal control is a rather amorphous subject and difficult to comprehend and reduce to satisfactory work paper notes. Yet no part of the examination is more important than his review and evaluation of internal control. Also, there is no area in which he can be of more real assistance to his client than by scrupulously examining and reporting on the client's control procedures.[1]

Although internal control does not lend itself to any simple set of rules by which it can be evaluated, it has historically been evaluated by the auditor through:

I. Observation, inquiries, and review of manuals and charts to determine whether:
   1. The formal and informal organization of the company clearly establishes and specifically prescribes a functional segregation of duties between people responsible for
      (a) Authorization of the transaction
      (b) Recording and processing of the transaction

Reprinted by permission of the publisher from *The Journal of Accountancy*, August 1964, pp. 34-40, copyright 1964 by the American Institute of Certified Public Accountants, Inc.

[1]R.K. Mautz and H.A. Sharaf, *The Philosophy of Auditing*, Madison, Wis.: American Accounting Association, 1961, p. 146.

(c) Custody of the assets involved in the transaction

2. The financial and accounting procedures are sufficient to assure that

   (a) Transactions are reviewed sufficiently to establish the propriety and accuracy of their recording.

   (b) Data processing flow permits detection and correction of errors in operating and financial data and reduces such errors to the level permitted by management.

   (c) Reports are required and prepared to reflect the responsibility for the authorization, performance, and review of financial and accounting transactions.

II. The selection of actual transactions to determine whether the purported policies, procedures and controls are operating as described

The effect of electronic data processing on the evaluation of the system of internal control largely centers on point II above, the testing of the system. In any system, EDP or otherwise, a review of the organizational aspects, procedural controls, and administrative practices is necessary to establish the extent of the audit examination and to make constructive suggestions about improving the system. But obviously, EDP affects the nature of such a review. The importance of systems development and programming practices and documentation, input-output controls, programmed controls, tape library procedures, and computer operating controls require the auditor to observe different activities, ask different questions, and review different manuals and documents than he would in his review of a non-EDP system.

TESTING THE SYSTEM

Conventionally, the auditor has selected actual accounting transactions that have been previously processed by the client to test the system. Typically, this approach calls for the tracing of a "representative" number of transactions from the recording of the source documents through whatever intermediate records might exist to the output reports or records produced. Such an approach is taken without any regard to the manner in which the output was actually developed. It is based on the logic that if the source data or system input can be proven correct and if the results of the system accurately reflect these source data, then the output must be correct and the manner in which the system processed the data is inconsequential.

In an EDP-dominated situation, such an approach has been called the "around the computer" approach to testing the system. This approach is the one which, in the majority of EDP installations, has been taken by auditors. Auditors have been using this "around the computer" approach because:

1. It is a familiar method.
2. It does not require technical knowledge of the EDP equipment.
3. The relatively unchanged audit trail conditions encountered in the EDP installations have not required a different approach.

An often unstated but perhaps more significant reason for the auditor's use of the "around the computer" approach is the auditor's unwillingness to come to grips with EDP.

The other approach to the testing of the system is the "through the computer" approach, which follows the concept that, if the controls and procedures incorporated in computer programs are effective and if a proper control of computer operations is employed, then proper processing of proven and acceptable input is bound to result in acceptable output. Such an approach is entirely dependent upon the consistency of processing operations found in computer operations.

In addition to an over-all review of the EDP system, this approach obviously requires an explicit knowledge of input and master file record layout, a fairly comprehensive knowledge of computer operations and built-in and programmed controls, and a thorough understanding of the development and use of "test decks."

TEST DECKS

In my opinion, often the conventional audit approach of testing the system by selecting actual transactions previously processed by the client is incomplete and inexact. In some cases, the transactions selected do not include the unusual ones requiring exception handling. In addition, the auditor, even with "representative" tests, can never be certain that the individuals carrying out the system actually do what they say they do or are supposed to do.

But with the advent of electronic systems, the operations research concepts of "models" and "simulation" appear applicable in the auditor's testing approach. The "model" is the client's computer program.

> . . . complete and accurate in all respects, not subject to the deviations caused by human idiosyncrasies or human temptation . . .containing in very specific language the exact instructions as to what the machine is to do. You can tell just what happened to a transaction[2]

---

[2]A.B. Toan, Jr., "The Auditor and EDP," *JofA*, June 1960, p. 44.

"Simulation" can be performed by the auditor by experimenting and testing the procedural model. The auditor can feed it all sorts of good and bad transactions to see how the EDP system reacts. These simulated transactions are commonly referred to as "test decks." The test deck is developed by preparing machine-readable data (i.e., punched cards, magnetic tape) designed to simulate every feasible type of transaction and to test specific program controls. These transactions are processed using the existing computer program, and the results of the computer processing are compared with predetermined results. Obviously, the purpose of the test deck technique is to determine for the auditor exactly how a specific processing system will react to particular types of transactions.

> In effect, the auditor allows the automatic data processing system to audit itself by merely presenting the system with a set of test problems or situations which the system cannot distinguish from normal processing activity, and then ascertaining how these tests cases are handled. Since no . . . programming is required to implement a test of this type, the procedure is a relatively inexpensive one from the standpoint of operating costs, and the results obtained are both effectively presented and irrefutable.[3]

While it is true that the computer operating costs to process test decks are rather minimal, it is also true that the development of test decks can be a complex and time-consuming project, and the auditor should be cognizant of the problems involved.

Before discussing the development of test decks, it is important to make two points clear. First, some writers fail to differentiate between test decks and computer audit programs and, as a result, such writing discusses the use of "test programs" in auditing. Test decks, as defined above, are used to evaluate the *quality* of the data processing *system* in use. Computer audit programs are used to determine the *quality* of *information* generated by the system. Such programs, to be sure, can perform detailed tests and computations. They are more often designed to elicit, from current master files, exception reports or sample selections based on criteria specified and programmed by the auditor. Such information is then used by the auditor in his evaluation of the evidence supporting the reasonableness and adequacy of disclosure of the accounts descriptions, balances, and footnotes in the financial statements under

---

[3]Department of the United States Air Force, *Guide for Auditing Automatic Data Processing Systems,* Washington, D.C.: U.S. Government Printing Office, 1961, pp. 8-14 and 8-15.

examination. Secondly, some writers and speakers have often mentioned another technique of auditing computer records—the review of computer programs. There are several reasons why this method is not very satisfactory:

1. It requires a higher level of programming skill than that required to write the original program. To go through a program which may contain thousands of instructions, complex logic, and numerous switches is an exceedingly difficult job. Even if the auditing profession had enough persons competent to make such an evaluation, it would be too costly.
2. It would not guarantee that the program reviewed is the most current version. Because of the numerous minor changes made over a period of time in the ordinary course of computer operations, the auditor would have to repeat the detailed review periodically, or control program changes, neither of which is very practical.
3. It would not guarantee that the program reviewed is the regular production program being used by the client. The auditor must have assurance that the program he is evaluating is the one which is being used to process transactions and produce financial information.

In my opinion, the only practical answer to evaluating the performance of a computer is utilization of test decks, not reviews of programs. However, a review of the client's documentation used to develop the applicable program is desirable in developing the test deck. Such documents include flow charts, block diagrams, input and output media, exception reports, and narrative descriptions of the procedures and controls in the system.

A review of these documents must be sufficient to give the auditor a complete knowledge of the procedural controls, both manual and programmed, in the EDP system so that the transactions included in the test-deck check the existence and effectiveness of these controls.

In addition, this review must enable the auditor to determine whether the client's controls are adequate or necessary to achieve the client's control objectives.

In developing and using the successful test deck, there are several important factors which the auditor must take into consideration:

1. He must decide upon the exact point in the system where the test data are to be entered.
2. He must determine the types of transactions to be included in the test deck.

3. He must obtain the master records to process against the test transactions and to compute the predetermined results for comparison with the output resulting from the test processing.
4. He must carefully consider the effects that the processing of the test transactions will have on the results of the system produced under normal operating conditions.
5. He must obtain the client's regular processing programs and assure himself that the program is used to process the test data.
6. He must make whatever arrangements are necessary to get the test data prepared and processed and to get the output in the desired form.

WHERE THE TESTS ARE TO BE ENTERED IN THE SYSTEM

Before developing the test deck, the auditor must first decide the point at which he wishes to enter the test data. If the operations and controls in the preparation of input are to be included in the test, the test-deck data must be fed into the input portion of the system as basic source documentation. If only computer operations are being tested, the data may be introduced into the computer operations in the form of punched cards or magnetic tape records.

DETERMINING THE TYPES OF TRANSACTIONS

The inherent advantage of the test deck over the selection of actual transactions is that the auditor may include every type—normal or abnormal—of conceivable transaction in his tests with relative ease. And theoretically, a sample of one for each type of transaction is as statistically sound as a large number because of the uniformity involved in the processing of data.

There are several methods which may be used to construct a simulated transaction deck, all of which require a review of systems and program documentation to gain a complete knowledge of the procedural controls in the EDP system. Although the auditor can prepare entirely imaginary transactions, it may be expedient to select transactions from the client's actual data or from the test data used by the client's programmer to check out the computer program. For example, the programmer's test deck was used in developing the auditor's test deck to evaluate payroll processing in a large manufacturer. Many of the programmer's tests were applicable from an audit standpoint and were readily included in the auditor's test deck. The review of the client's test data also uncovered some outdated tests and areas in the program which were not tested at all. The client's data processing management felt such a review was highly informative and beneficial to operations.

Selection of the client's input data or test data usually will not include all the possible variables, and additional transactions must be created. The determination of possible variables to be tested may be made by analyzing the input record layout. By analyzing the fields of data included on the input record, all combinations of data can be determined. In this connection, several observations should be made:

1. It is not necessary that all possible combinations within all fields be set out as separate problems. Distinction should be made between variables which merely represent identification data (i.e., account numbers, social security numbers) and those which involve alternate handling. In the case of the former, only a limited number of possibilities need to be included to test the identification routines in the program. To illustrate, Figure 7-1 shows the fields and their description for a rate change input card used in a payroll system of the large manufacturer mentioned earlier. The transaction will change an employee's hourly rate and pay code. The transaction is program edited for validity of dates, alpha name, old pay code and rate and whether the new rate is equal to the old rate. In addition, any new rate greater than $10 is expected. The tests included in the test deck for this transaction were:
    a. Valid rate change with all other fields valid
    b. Rate change greater than $10
    c. Valid rate change, old rate wrong
    d. Valid rate change, old rate equal to new rate
    e. Valid rate change, alpha name wrong

Card Field	*Description*
4-12	Social security number
13-14	Transaction code (03)
16	Division
18-22	New hourly rate
24-29	Rate change date
30	New payroll code
31-34	First four characters of last name (alpha name)
48-52	Old hourly rate
75	Old payroll code

Figure 7-1. Rate Change Card Format.

To test sequence checking and identification comparison routines, a card with a valid transaction number or employee number and containing valid information could be placed out of sequence in the test deck. Additional tests for sequence checking and identification comparison would not be necessary.

2. It is necessary to include at least two of each type of variable requiring alternative handling in order to test the existence and effectiveness of programmed controls. For example, in the above illustration, all rates equal to or less than $10 are handled by one processing routine; all rates greater than $10 are handled by an exception routine.
3. The tests should include transactions which determine the processing and handling of the following general conditions:
   a. Out of sequence conditions
   b. Out of limits conditions
   c. Routines arising from a major decision point where alternative processing takes place as a result of the comparison of transaction records with master records; i.e., where the transaction identification number can be greater, equal to, or less than the identification number on the master record
   d. Units of measure differences
   e. Incomplete or missing input information
   f. Wrong tape files
   g. Numeric characters in fields where alphabetic characters belong and vice versa
   h. Characters in certain fields which exceed prescribed length (an overflow condition)
   i. Illogical conditions in fields where programmed consistency checks test the logical relationship in the same fields
   j. Conditions where transaction codes or amounts do not match the codes or amounts established in tables stored in internal memory

Obviously all these conditions cannot be tested with each type of transaction, but the majority of them, if not all, may be tested in processing all transactions included in the test deck.

One of the problems involved in developing a test deck is the difficulty of reviewing its substantive aspects. Apart from a detailed review, which is impractical and time consuming for the audit manager or partner, it is very difficult for the reviewer to get a general idea as to the scope and "rightness" of a test deck. For audit review purposes, it may be useful to construct a matrix during the development of the test data which would indicate the types of conditions tested by each transaction. Such a matrix is shown in Figure 7-2. Another device which is helpful in review and which is necessary for the audit workpapers is a transaction listing of the test deck. Such a listing indicates, in code sequence, the information punched or recorded on the transaction input record. This information can be sorted and listed by tabulating equipment. The listing should include a narrative description of the type of test, the objective, and what output will result from the test.

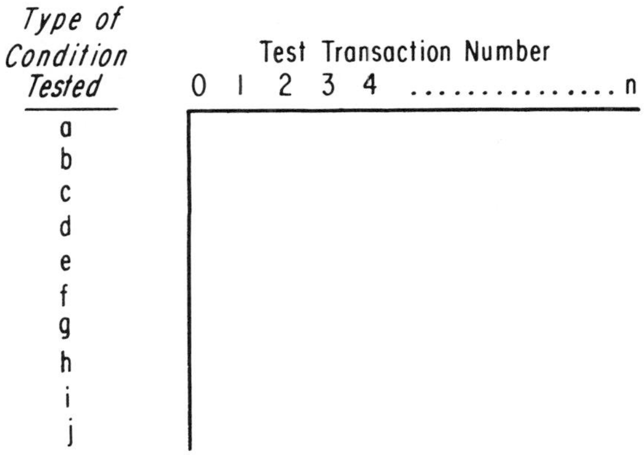

Figure 7-2.

OBTAINING THE MASTER RECORDS

The auditor must obtain the master records in machine-readable form against which the test transactions are to be processed and in visible form to compute the predetermined results for comparison with output resulting from the test deck processing.

With sequential processing, there is usually not much of a problem in obtaining the master records in machine-readable form since the master file is not written over or destroyed in processing the test transactions. There is a problem in random processing since the master records maintained on random access equipment are written over or destroyed by processing transactions. To protect the client's master records, the test deck can be run immediately after the random access file "dump."[4] After the "dump," the master records are on both the random access master files and on magnetic tape. The test data can then be processed against

[4]A file "dump" refers to the transfer or writing of the contents of the random access files on magnetic tapes, at realistic intervals, to provide the ability to reconstruct the file in the event the original file is accidentally damaged or destroyed.

the tape files as discussed above. In such a situation, the client's computer would have to be altered slightly to have the computer "read" and "write" tape rather than "read" and "write" random access files. In situations where the auditor must or wishes to run his test transactions between the "dump" cycles, the random access files may be protected by physically locking the files to prevent writing on them and altering the program so that the "write random access file" instruction becomes "write tape."

In some installations such as the large manufacturer referred to previously, test master records are used, against which the test data are processed by the company's programmers in testing the system. These masters, although comparatively few in number, represent actual masters. The advantage of these test masters is the case with which they can be used and changed to reflect certain conditions necessary for testing, and the case with which they can be printed out for visible review. For example, the manufacturer uses twenty-four test master records, in punched card form, as a test model payroll master file. These twenty-four records are used instead of the 20,000 employee master record file to avoid time in selecting and printing actual master records. The use of test masters is based on the premise that the computer cannot tell the difference between the processing of a test master record and an actual master record. A variation of the use of client's test master records is the creation, by the auditor, of "dummy" master records for use in testing the system. Such was the case in the test of an automated labor recording system in this large manufacturer.[5]

Although actual master records may be readily obtained in machine-readable form in many systems, it is difficult to get the same records in printed form without advance planning. One method is to time the tests so they are processed with the output master file used to prepare a printed report such as the accounts receivable aged trial balance or an inventory report. Another method is to have an inquiry program prepared which will print out selected master records from the master file to be used in processing the test transactions. Most installations have the ability to inquire into any file, and the auditor may, with a little planning, have his file-searching needs met by a routine procedure.

THE NEED TO CAREFULLY CONSIDER THE EFFECTS TEST TRANSACTIONS WILL HAVE ON THE RESULTS OF THE SYSTEM

Obviously, the auditor does not want to have his test transactions

---

[5] R.M. Benjamin, "Auditing Automatic Source Recording," *The Quarterly*, Touche, Ross, Bailey & Smart, September 1963.

affect the results produced under normal operating conditions. Accordingly, he must carefully consider what effects the processing of the test data will have on the results of the system. For example, the output tape resulting from the processing of test data should be clearly labeled so as to prevent improper use and subsequent incorrect processing of operating data.

Any tests that are processed along with actual transactions must be carefully controlled so as to preclude undesired results from taking place. For example, in a test to determine that the open order file was reviewed periodically for unusual items in a medium-sized steel manufacturer, a valid order was transmitted by the auditor from a sales branch location and the shipping copy was destroyed. This order had to be controlled by the auditor to prevent shipping of the order and to insure subsequent removal from the open order file.

OBTAINING AND CONTROLLING THE CLIENT'S REGULAR PROCESSING PROGRAM

One of the important procedures of testing a company's EDP system is obtaining assurance that the program being tested is the one the company actually uses to process data. Basically there are two ways in which this can be achieved:

1. If the data processing organizational and administrative controls are adequate, the program can be requested, on a surprise basis, from the program librarian and duplicated for the auditor's control and use in processing test data. As a further measure, the auditor may request that test data previously processed with the auditor's copy of the program be processed with the client's operating program and then compare the end results. This method has the added advantage of checking any computer operator intervention.
2. The auditor may request, on a surprise basis, that the operating program be left in the computer at the completion of processing operating data so that he may process his test data with it. This method has an advantage over the method above in that it usually ensures a correct version of the program. In many installations and particularly in earlier stages of conversion, program changes are made frequently. These continuing program changes may make it quite difficult for the auditor to review and check all significant changes in order to be satisfied with the operations performed by the program.

As a general rule, the auditor should observe the running of the test data with the computer program. In many installations, this may not be practical because of the "grave-yard shift" scheduling of test data processing. The adequacy of the controls in the EDP department, however, should be the dictating factor here rather than the time of day, or night.

ARRANGING TO GET TEST DATA PREPARED AND PROCESSED

In addition to obtaining master records and the client's regular processing program, the auditor must carefully design test data, obtain the necessary key punching equipment and/or personnel, and obtain computer time from authorized personnel in order to get the test data prepared and processed, and to get the output in the desired form. Most of these arrangements are procedural and involve advanced planning with systems and computer operations people.

The design of test data is not procedural in nature but is something that the auditor will find worthy of his careful consideration. Essentially the test deck should be so designed as to limit the amount of work required of the auditor to review the results of the test. The use of special codings or distinctive names which allow invalid test transactions to be easily identified, sorted out of valid tests, and listed on separate output listings are devices which can be employed to make the auditor's job of interpreting and evaluating the test results more simple and less time consuming.

In some installations where the audit trail has been drastically altered, it is pure nonsense to argue for alternative methods of testing and evaluating the system. The only practical approach is auditing "through the computer" with the use of a well-conceived test deck. In some installations where the audit trail has not been altered with the use of EDP equipment, the "around the computer" approach may seem to be a valid alternative. But even in these electronic systems, the benefits accruing to the auditor using the "through the computer" approach appear to outweigh the problems and additional considerations involved in using such an approach. These benefits are:

1. Better knowledge of the client's system of procedures and controls—many computer installations are integrated management information systems providing operating, as well as financial, information. A review and evaluation of such a system will necessarily provide the auditor with a more complete understanding of the client's "total" system of data processing and controls than normally obtained by auditing "around the computer."

2. Better letters of recommendations—a detailed review of the computer system along with the design and use of effective tests will enable the auditor to evaluate the client's input-output controls, built-in machine controls, programmed controls, and operating controls. Such an evaluation will result in more informative and constructive letters of recommendations and, hence, increased service to clients.
3. More representative tests—through the use of well-designed test decks, the auditor is able to evaluate the system's ability to handle all types of transactions, both normal and abnormal. The kind of transactions included in the test deck is limited only by the auditor's imagination, rather than by the practical limitations of time and cost involved in obtaining the same types of transactions from a sample of actual transactions. This point is emphasized by an audit manager in writing about the use of the computer in the audit testing of an automated labor recording system: ". . .The number of unusual conditions which were tested with a few simple prearranged plans would have required thousands upon thousands of transaction selections had random sampling or any other conventional testing procedures been used."[6]
4. Continuous auditing more readily achieved—one of the objectives of auditing in recent years has been the smoothing of the work flow in an annual audit examination. This has been achieved to some extent by spreading the examination between the "interim" period and the "year-end" period. Since the test deck is designed around a series of business transactions that do not change in nature from day to day, its usefulness can survive minor and perhaps major changes in the computer program. As a result, the auditor can make more frequent tests and obtain "readings" of the client's activities at different operating periods during the year without expending more time, if as much, than previously spent in testing the system.

The use of EDP equipment in no way lessens the auditor's requirement for evaluating the system of internal control; in my opinion, it makes the evaluation increasingly important to the audit examination and to the concept of service to the client. The auditor must recognize the importance of electronic procedures and the significance of the work performed within the EDP equipment. Accordingly, he must resist the temptation of assuming that, if the input to the machine system is adequately reviewed and controlled and the output can be checked back

---

[6]*Ibid.*, p. 11.

to source documents, he can then be unconcerned with what went on within the machine system itself.

At present, rarely will exclusive use of either of the two approaches discussed above be applicable to an electronic accounting system. The unusually large volume of data handled by EDP systems makes the "around the computer" approach impractical except in unusual circumstances. On the other hand, the inconsistency of processing found in all but the most sophisticated "total" systems renders the "through the computer" approach ineffective except in equally unusual circumstances. Experience has shown that the most effective method of auditing electronic systems will generally be some combination of these two approaches. Accordingly, the auditor can still use conventional techniques in evaluating and testing the system of internal control to some extent. But to a large extent, a fresh approach to the problem combined with the effective use of the computer is necessary.

AUDITING THE ADVANCED COMPUTER SYSTEMS

by Robert E. Bates

How can the auditor establish a program for reviewing a complete and complex system of the magnitude being developed today? First, perhaps an outline of a typical functional organization, drawn from my own experience, would be beneficial in visualizing an audit approach.

Work on new systems starts with a small group consisting of four or five persons representing top management. This group is known as Applied Systems Design and has the responsibility of defining total system needs and the system design philosophy for developing management information systems. At a system and subsystem level, this group defines the general objectives of the system and the functions it performs. This information is combined into a gross functional specification, which is released to an applied system development division.

Included in the applied system development division are the system analyst and programming people who are responsible for the detail design, development, and implementation of the system. They pursue a more detailed study of the system and program requirements and combine this collection of data into a system notebook.

The study is carried out in phases, which when documented in detail becomes a part of a total system notebook. The study will include the

---

Reprinted by permission of the publisher from *Management Accounting,* June 1970, pp. 34-37.

writing of system functional and design specifications, program functional and design specifications, and system and program acceptance test specifications as well as program coding and testing.

Upon conclusion of satisfactory testing of the programs and total system, and evidence of satisfactory documentation, a program review and release document is written. A history is also maintained depicting all important activity that affects the program. The main category is program changes, but every phase of program planning, development, conversion, testing, implementation and post-release activity is documented as well.

The structure of the elements which make up the total set of document types is shown in Figure 7-3. The elements shown at the left of the illustration are the major elements of the system and are arranged vertically in order of their preparation as a project proceeds. Extending horizontally from each major element block are separate blocks which indicate the individual parts of each of the major elements. Some elements are separately produced and released documents; their subsections are shown in dashed boxes. The others are independent elements produced and used during programming and for storage by the program library after release.

The responsibility for auditing should be structured to cover all functional areas of the applied systems development division from upper management, through operational management, to actual development by operating people complete with direct communication to the management design group. The audit responsibilities should be concentrated on all facets of design and development through conversion of existing files, through testing, and the implementation stage of all management information systems. Keeping in mind that the gross functional specification dictates the will of management, the audit becomes a useful objective tool in determining whether system objectives are met adequately and with sufficient controls to ensure satisfactory performance for management.

In the post-implementation world, continuing audits are necessary to cover input procedures from remote locations, daily operational procedures in various geographical areas, and maintenance effort on existing systems.

If an after-the-fact audit were to indicate control weaknesses, the effort required to make the necessary changes could be tremendous. A real-time system cannot afford to have "bugs" or errors once it is put into operation. Testing of a real-time system should demand the highest standards possible to minimize any possibility of a machine shutdown or, what is sometimes worse, misleading output information.

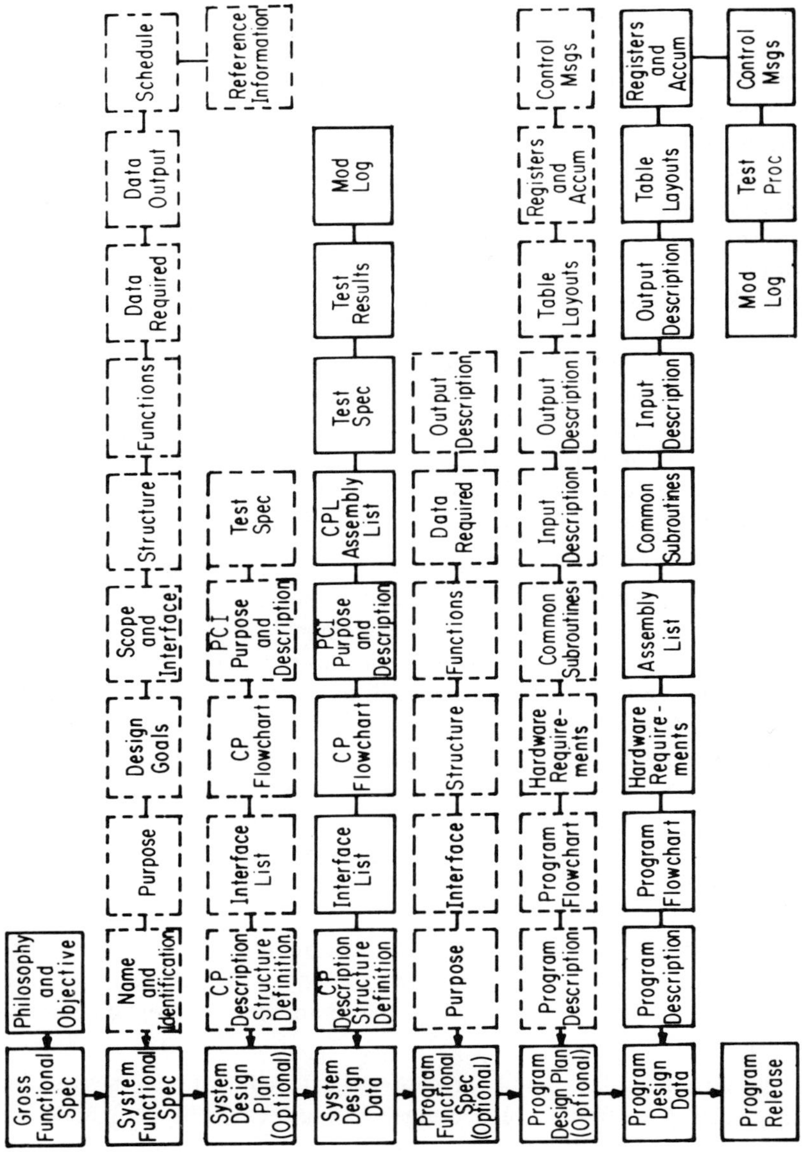

Figure 7-3. Documentation System Structure.

Historically, auditors have functioned on an after the fact basis, that is, the audit activity took place after a program or system was released and performing. This has certain practicality in a second generation computer environment where batch processing and manual intervention is the mode of operation, and where it is not too difficult to make modifications to existing programs. However, in so-called advanced systems, comprising on-line processing, integrated data flow and parallel processing under complete computer programmed control, it is imperative that auditing to include programmed controls be performed in parallel with design and development.

AUDITOR'S TASK

What might be some of the typical audit routines that should be considered, and what are some of the changes in audit environment characterized by a real-time integrated system?

1. Logically, we should review the gross functional specification with the goal of understanding objectives and policies established, and ensuring that no functional areas have been inadvertently omitted from the scope of the project.
2. As the system study progresses at the system/programming level, the system functional and design specifications should be reviewed for completeness and adherence to the gross functional specification plan, policies, and customer requirements. At this point, thought should be given to the audit or management controls being considered in the system and system interface considerations.
3. The next system design level is the more detailed program functional and design specification. At this point, sufficient detail should be available to allow for program coding. Further review should be made to evaluate these specifications for completeness and adherence to the gross functional specification, the system functional and design specifications, and again to customer requirements. The auditor should also expect to be active in the development of data management controls—or those techniques which regulate the handling of data and data files, as well as audit trail considerations.
4. Next should come an evaluation of the program acceptance test specification. This, the auditor can anticipate, will involve him in assisting the system/programmer in development of test standards, various levels of testing, and actual test conditions.

5. He should evaluate the actual system acceptance test to ensure a high level of confidence and reliability of the system.
6. Next, should be an evaluation of the completeness of the User's Manual containing all information pertinent to the program to ensure an adequate audit trail for future reference.
7. Certainly the auditor's responsibility does not end with the implementation of a program. Of equal responsibility is an evaluation of the operating techniques for controlling file space, documentations, hardware and software malfunctions, and recovery methods. He will also be interested in distribution functions and controls over handling of classified or company proprietary information.
8. Finally the auditor should be concerned with the procedures for inputting data, both at remote and centralized stations. We can see the use of remote input stations will create new problems in standardization and control techniques.

Auditing, as we know, is a continuing effort. No system remains static. Even though a thorough review is made during the development process, the auditor should follow up periodically with audits triggered either by program changes or, more simply, an interval of time.

CHANGES IN AUDIT ENVIRONMENT

We will doubtless see many changes in the audit environment brought about by new system concepts and advance processing techniques. Following are some of the items to be checked during systems development:

1. We will doubtless see a change in the visible audit trail. That is, the means to trace a transaction from creation through to final ledger posting. Much has been written about audit trail considerations, and we have much to learn as our systems take form concerning what is necessary and what is required to meet adequate control.
2. We may have no source documents, just recordings via transaction recorders. If source documents do exist, they may be scattered over wide geographical areas.
3. There may be no printed listing of transactions or file printout.
4. If files are updated in real-time, perhaps there will be no retention of past generations of records.
5. With data communications, transactions are transmitted rapidly to the data processing center with consequent problems dealing

with correction of mistakes, voiding of transactions, and proof of receipt.

6. With multiprogramming, the computer will be working on several jobs concurrently, and we will want to establish that one job cannot damage the data pertaining to another job.
7. The use of remote input-output terminals may present many control problems such as:
   a. Identification procedures for identifying both the terminal and the operator and for checking requests against authority lists. Personnel turnover necessitates constant training and necessitates changes of identification codes and perhaps procedures.
   b. Unauthorized access to the system may exist; control may be bypassed, accidentally or deliberately, and damage done.
   c. Control totals may not always be used for verification of quantity figures.
8. The control group function (found in batch systems) may be eliminated, due to data transmission, but someone must handle error rejects and control the entry of corrections and adjustments.
9. When equipment failures occur, the fallback and recovery procedures are more complex than with batch systems, and there is a greater chance for transactions to be missing or duplicated.
10. The system will use complex control programs, which in themselves can inject errors into data or programs. For this reason they should be thoroughly tested before a system is made operational. These factors and many more result in a more complex audit environment than has been true with batch-type EDP systems, and as the systems grow in complexity, more and more factors will prove to be pertinent.

TESTING

Based on the knowledge we have of the processing techniques involved in future data processing environments, we can see that testing procedures will involve several phases of testing (see Figure 7-4). System testing will not be limited to the checkout of the various application programs. It will extend also to the necessary checkout of certain control programs and their ability to function in a multiprogrammed manner.

The proportion of program errors found in each phase of testing will vary greatly. The majority of program errors will be found in Phase I where they are easy to locate. For this reason, testing should be as thorough as possible because the later errors are detected, the more trouble they can be to locate and correct.

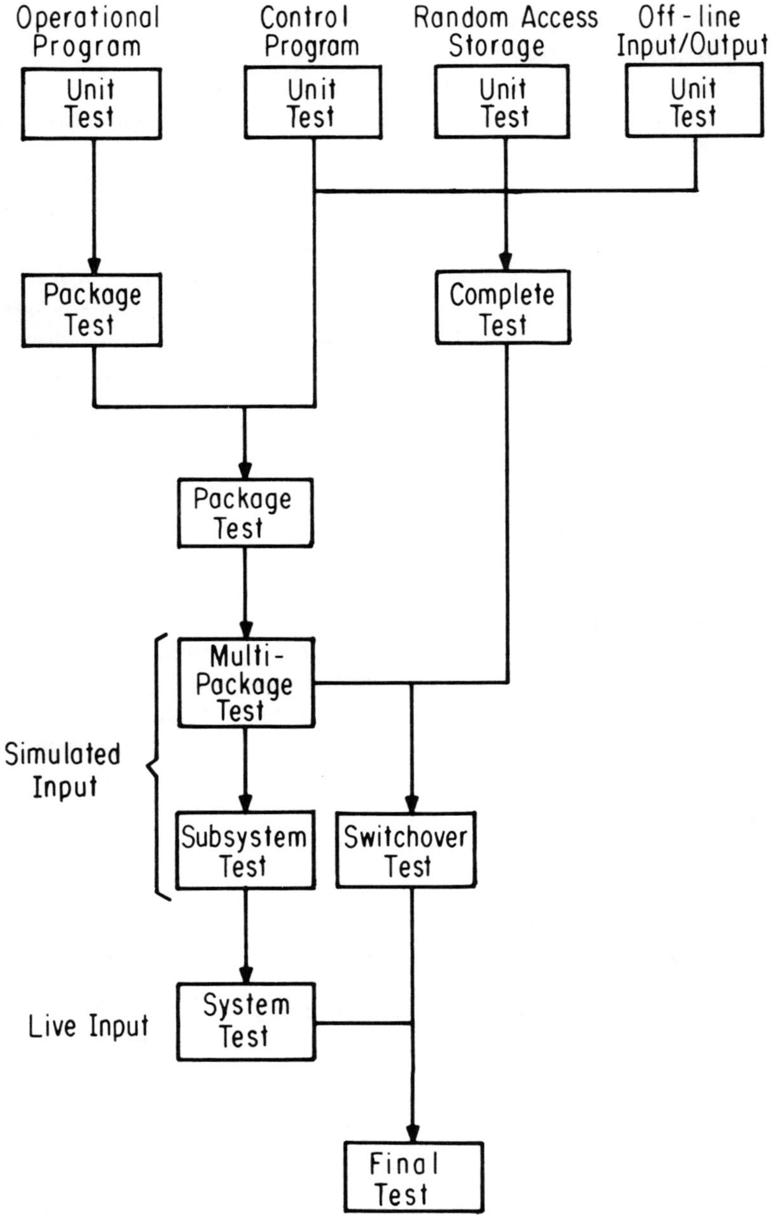

Figure 7-4. System Test Schematic.

PHASE I

The simulated testing of each individual program or program segment as an individual entity. This would include simulated test transactions representative of both valid and invalid conditions to test the ability of the program to edit and perform the intended functions of the program. All these program segments, having been found to work satisfactorily as individual units, must be tested to assure they will work correctly together.

PHASE II

Phase II would involve the testing of a number of related programs or program segments as a single package. This phase would likely bring into operation the use of certain control programs, assuming these programs have been tested and proven reliable.

We should remember that all the program segments needed for a package are not normally written by the same programmer and consequently may suffer from misunderstandings, overlooked relationship, or other logical inconsistencies. Also, it may be that not all the program segments needed to form a package are covered by one program specification; in which case, misunderstandings can occur between specifications and program levels. New errors, not discovered in Phase I, will arise in this phase, and be more difficult to locate and correct.

PHASE III

This Phase would involve multiple package testing. This would consist of testing groups of packages that have passed single package testing and are now ready to run concurrently for the first time in a multiprogrammed manner.

The input is still simulated, but the entries are fed into the system in groups representing a mixture of input types. Such an example might be in a personnel/payroll system which may include a package system for processing payroll, wage and salary information, skills inventory, and employee data. In a single package test, we would be testing each part of the system separately with test transactions characteristic of that package. In a multiple package test, our input would be of a heterogeneous mixture that would satisfy all conditions of the multiple package system.

PHASE IV

Errors arising in this phase will be still more difficult to locate in most cases than in prior tests. Dependent on established testing procedures, we should want to make sure we utilize all types of storage devices. If we utilize tape, drum, and disc type storage in normal processing, then we would want to process test data through these devices to simulate normal operating conditions.

PHASE V

The Application Programs, having reached the final system testing stage, are now required to cope with input generated at the terminals, which are linked to the central processing site, and presumably debugged from an equipment standpoint. During this final testing stage, the transaction input from the terminals should provide entries in a mix, a sequence, and a format and content that closely resemble operating conditions to flush out any error cases not detected during prior simulated tests. At the conclusion of this final system testing, a system should emerge capable of operating in a sufficiently reliable manner to permit conversion and productive operations.

PHASE VI

Through the testing in prior phases, it is virtually certain that errors will occur when the system first becomes operational. For this reason, the auditor should follow up on the system's performance until he can be reasonably sure all is going well.

CONCLUSION

In summary, it is the audit responsibility to make certain that management controls are built into all systems effort to ensure the integrity of the system and resultant confidence of management personnel at all levels.

Our experience seems to show that three basic principles should be observed:

1. It is important that the auditor be called in on the development and installation of new systems at an early stage so that any suggestions he has can be considered before changes become too costly.
2. There must be understanding and willing cooperation between the auditors and system/programming personnel.
3. The auditor should be willing to consider the acceptance of new types of controls to replace those outmoded by EDP.

EVALUATING INTERNAL CONTROL IN EDP AUDITS

by Richard C. John and Thomas J. Nissen

"I could steal a company blind in three months and leave its books looking balanced" boasts a data processing specialist. His method would be electronic embezzlement using the company's own computer. A manager of a brokerage firm did use his company's computer to siphon off $250,000 during an eight-year period. He programmed the computer to transfer money from a company account to two customers' accounts—his own and his wife's. The computer was further programmed to show that the money had been used to purchase stock for the two accounts. He then sold the stock and pocketed the cash.[7]

An enterprising employee at another firm instructed its computer to write checks to fictitious persons over a four-year period and send them to his home address. His scheme was uncovered only when the post office accidentally returned one of the checks to the firm and the clerk who received it became suspicious!

These examples of defalcations dramatize the need for adequate internal controls and continual monitoring of EDP systems.

> Internal control comprises the plan of organization and all of the co-ordinate methods and measures adopted within a business to safeguard its assets, check the accuracy and reliability of its accounting data, promote operational efficiency, and encourage adherence to prescribed managerial policies. This definition . . . recognizes that a "system" of internal control extends beyond those matters which relate directly to the functions of the accounting and financial departments.[8]

Weaknesses in internal control provide opportunities for defalcations to go undetected. Although an audit usually is not designed to detect fraud, every auditor is charged with reviewing internal control. To evaluate internal control in the EDP area, the auditor must have some skilled understanding of EDP.

Reprinted by permission of the publisher from *The Journal of Accountancy,* February 1970, pp. 31-38, copyright 1970 by the American Institute of Certified Public Accountants, Inc.

[7]Alan Adelson, "Crooked Operators Use Computers to Embezzle Money From Companies," *Wall Street Journal,* April 5, 1968, p. 1.

[8]*Auditing Standards and Procedures,* Statement on Auditing Procedure No. 33, committee on auditing procedure of the American Institute of Certified Public Accountants, New York, 1963, p. 27.

The importance of internal control in auditing is stated in the second standard of field work:

> There is to be a proper study and evaluation of the existing internal control as a basis for reliance thereon and for the determination of the resultant extent of the tests to which auditing procedures are to be restricted.[9]

Since this standard demands that *all* internal control to be evaluated, review of internal control must include a review of internal control in the EDP function.

This article is concerned with the specifics of an auditor's competence as he complies with the second standard of field work in an EDP situation.

EVALUATING INTERNAL CONTROL IN THE EDP FUNCTION

Whether the audit is of a computer system or of a manual system, internal control is evaluated in terms of the same criteria—i.e., the controls must provide reasonable assurance that information is correctly processed and complete. To assure himself concerning the EDP function, the auditor should evaluate three major areas of internal control: (1) organizational, (2) administrative and (3) procedural.

ORGANIZATIONAL CONTROLS

Organization has always been important in the structure of internal controls. Because of the greater concentration of data processing duties in the EDP system, organization becomes even more important. Although the attest function does not require it, most clients expect their auditors to recognize opportunities for improving utilization of the computer and to make constructive suggestions as a by-product of their audit. Organizational controls fall into two areas: the placement of the EDP function within the organization and the division of duties within the EDP group.

Within the organization, the EDP group should be functionally independent in its relationship to other operating departments. To be effective from a control standpoint, this independence should include a separation of responsibilities which results in a system of checks and con-

---

[9] *Ibid.*, p. 16.

trols throughout the organization. However, controls must be flexible enough so that the EDP group retains its service nature to all other functions within the organization. Where possible, data processing should be a separate functional area. Such an organizational setup enhances control by preventing domination of the equipment by one user such as accounting or manufacturing.

The other major group of organizational controls concerns division of duties within the data processing group. Frequently the functions of systems design and programming are combined in one sub-group. This group generally is responsible for systems design, systems development, and programming. To avoid undue concentration in one person or group, design and development should be separated from programming if at all possible.

For the same reason, the group responsible for operation of the equipment should be separated from the functions of programming and systems design and development. In smaller applications, this operating group may also have control over data files and records in process, as well as control over data flowing into and out of the data processing area. In larger applications a librarian, who acts as a storekeeper, should have physical control over all data files and records not actually being used.

Organizational controls are the basic framework of a successfully functioning information system. Proper division of duties within the EDP department means dividing duties among the available personnel to minimize opportunities for manipulation. These controls are part of a sound organizational structure in which administrative and procedural controls can function effectively.

ADMINISTRATIVE CONTROLS

After reviewing the placement of EDP within the organization and the division of duties within the data processing department, the auditor should review administrative and procedural controls. The administrative areas of major interest to the auditor are program documentation and program testing.

Program Documentation. Documentation is an important aspect of internal control; it helps assure consistency in operations, particularly during personnel changes. Ideally, the company should be using its own manual of programming standards which details documentation requirements.

> Documentation of programs should follow a summary-to-detail pattern somewhat as follows:

Program specification summary.

General system flowcharts.

Supplemental narratives, and decision tables (as required).

Block diagrams of computer logic.

Record descriptions: input, output, storage areas.

Program listings of coding, and program decks.

Detailed operating instructions.[10]

Proper documentation primarily serves the purposes of management, but from an audit standpoint, it is an invaluable part of the review of internal control. Details of record formats, layouts, code structures, system flowcharts, etc., assist the auditor in developing meaningful tests of the system—expecially if he intends to audit through the computer.

During his review of the documentation, the auditor must recognize those program features which perform data editing functions. Editing functions test the data for reasonableness against known possible error conditions. The computer can be a tremendous aid to management (and a strong point in internal control) by quickly and accurately performing routine edit functions. Wherever possible, such checks should be built into the program by the system designer. Edit checks are discussed with other processing controls in a later section.

Program Testing. The second aspect of administrative control is the program testing procedures applied to new programs by the client. The auditor should determine that such procedures are indeed performed and, if so, review the procedures in use.

> Some of the essential characteristics of thorough testing procedures are as follows:
>
> Mock data designed to violate the edits and other controls of the system.
>
> A large dose of "live" transaction data as an assurance check on the comprehensiveness of the mock data.
>
> "Controlled answer" violations of the system, with proper follow-up of variations from the controlled answer.
>
> Tests of more than one cycle of the same program to verify its updating capability.

---

[10]Michael R. Moore, "EDP Audits; A Systems Approach," *The Arthur Young Journal* (Winter 1968), p. 10.

> "String tests" of the entire system to verify program compatibility from input, through processing programs to reporting.[11]

Program modification procedure is an important aspect of program testing. In theory, the procedure should be the same as for new programs—i.e., documentation and testing. However, in practice, program revision suffers from a lack of enthusiasm among personnel as to application of sound modification procedures. Good modification procedures are well worth the effort involved; the auditor should direct management's attention to their absence.

PROCEDURAL CONTROLS

The third area of internal control to be investigated in the EDP function is procedural controls. These controls include source data or input controls, processing controls, and output controls.

Input is the weakest link in the chain of processing events. Controls can be designed into computer programs to check for various errors. Routines can be established between and within the various departments to detect errors. However, if at the point of origin of the transaction an error is made in recording the data, it may easily pass undetected through the system. In EDP systems, the conventional control techniques to reduce the possibility of error in the initial recording of the data are extremely important.

Once data have been recorded by an initiating department, they will be transferred through other departments for processing. To ensure that all the data leaving Department A arrive in Department B, there must be control over the movement of data. One widely used control is a batch control.

A batch may include all the transactions for some period of time or it may be a fixed number of items. In using the technique a total of the critical data in the batch is obtained, usually by the use of an adding machine, prior to its submission to the data processing department. The originating department and the receiving department each keep an independent log of the totals. The auditor can make a comparison of those logs for specific time periods.

As mentioned in the discussion of program documentation, the auditor must be concerned with data editing functions designed into the EDP programs. Because of the speed and consistency of the computer,

---

[11]*Ibid.*, p. 11.

well-designed programmed edits can perform a continuous internal audit of all data entering the computer. Edit checks are used to detect data which are inaccurate, unreasonable or incomplete. They include checks for reasonableness of data, e.g., a check to assure that a disbursement does not exceed some specified limit. Common edit routines include: limit checks, validity checks, sign checks, field checks, historical comparisons and logical relationships.

Michael R. Moore points out that "comprehensive edits are of great value to a batch processing system. They are absolutely essential in a real-time environment, in which records are updated immediately upon input from remote locations and are available for information inquiry after updating."[12] Well-designed edits filter out "garbage" and only valid data flow through to the reports.

In addition to these procedural controls, which are of especial importance in EDP situations, other necessary controls include such things as transaction counts and visual checking. Since auditors are familiar with these and they are not peculiar to computer installations, these methods are not discussed in this article.

Another area of procedural control is control over operations in the data-processing department. Good internal control reduces the possibility of unauthorized manipulation of data. Access to the computer must be limited. An organization with good controls limits access to the computer room to only those employees concerned with operation of the equipment. Another area of strict control is programs. Once written, object programs should be accessible only to equipment operators; source programs should not be accessible to them. This control makes very difficult the unauthorized modification of programs by the equipment operator.

These procedures and controls are designed to reduce the possibility of operator intervention in the day-to-day processing. Manipulation of records requires a working knowledge of the programs, sufficient time at the console, and motivation. Important elements of this kind of control, for which the auditor should be looking, include:

1. Organizational division of functions as outlined earlier.
2. Effective scheduling techniques and standards for operations such as halt logs and controlled console printouts.
3. Written instructions covering each job.
4. A log of computer running time with appropriate control.
5. Control over movement of data—especially of rejection and return of bad batches of data.

---

[12] *Ibid.*, p. 10.

These elements of control should be included in any well-designed set of EDP procedures.

Output controls are established as final checks on the accuracy and propriety of the information processed. Output control methods include control totals, sampling and prenumbering.

Control totals of processed information are compared to input control totals. These can be batch totals of the number of records processed or totals of some other significant figures in the batch. This comparison of totals is the fundamental control feature in a batch processing system.

The use of prenumbered forms is helpful in maintaining output control. Prenumbered output documents can be accounted for in the same manner as input documents. The number of payroll check forms, for example, can easily be checked against the number of input records. Through the use of sampling, auditors can check output by tracing randomly selected transactions from source documents through the processing system to the output destination.

SUMMARY OF EDP CONTROLS

A well-designed EDP system should incorporate all of the controls mentioned earlier. It should have firm organizational controls with appropriate division of duties within the EDP function. The EDP group should be located within the organization in a way which balances independence, control and service. The programs should be documented, tested and retested upon modification. Procedural controls should exist which edit the data entering the system and assure that they are correctly processed. A well-controlled computer installation will help management attain its objectives. In addition, management should be able to rely on it as an essential element in the company's overall system of controls.

AUDITOR'S NEEDED SKILLS

The auditor must have enough expertise in EDP to review, understand and evaluate the three broad areas of organizational, administrative and procedural controls. He needs this expertise to enable him to prepare meaningful tests of the controls in the system. To perform such an evaluation, the auditor must have some fairly technical knowledge of EDP including some understanding of equipment, programs, operations and the types of controls needed in each. Unfortunately, a 1965 survey showed that 39 per cent of staff auditors had neither a general understanding of how computers function, nor the ability to read and interpret flowcharts and block diagrams.[13]

AUDIT TESTS OF INTERNAL CONTROL AND EDP AUDIT TRAILS

After the auditor has studied the system and determined what controls the client purportedly has in effect, he must design tests of transactions to determine if these controls are in operation and if they are providing the checks that they were intended to provide.

Of primary concern in the design of tests is the changing nature of the audit trail. In an EDP system, source documents and visible historical records can more easily be altered or eliminated. In a non-EDP data system the audit trail consists of the journals, ledgers, workpapers and other documents which permit the auditor to trace transactions backward or forward through the system. In an EDP system the form, content and accessibility of records frequently is such that the auditor is unable to follow a single transaction completely through the system.

Typical changes in the EDP audit trail are cited by Gordon B. Davis:[14]

1. Source documents, once transcribed onto a machine-readable input medium, are no longer used in the processing cycle. They may be filed in a manner which makes subsequent access difficult.
2. In some systems, traditional source documents may be eliminated by the use of direct input devices.
3. Ledger summaries may be replaced by master files which do not show the amounts leading up to the summarized values.
4. The data processing cycle does not necessarily provide a transaction listing or journal. To provide such a listing may require a special action, with significant additional cost.
5. It is sometimes unnecessary to prepare frequent printed output of historical records. Files can be maintained on computer media and reports prepared only for exceptions.
6. Files maintained on a magnetic medium cannot be read except by use of the computer and a computer program.

---

[13]Wayne S. Bontell, *Auditing With the Computer,* Los Angeles: University of California Press, 1965, p. 164-169.

[14]Gordon B. Davis, *Auditing and EDP,* New York: American Institute of Certified Public Accountants, 1968.

7. The sequence of records and processing activities is difficult to observe because much of the data and many of the activities are contained within the computer system.

This changing audit trail is a growing challenge to the auditor. Records once easy to read are becoming visible only to the computer. Source documents are being eliminated. Printed listings are being replaced by totals; to do otherwise unnecessarily slows the equipment. As managements develop EDP systems to their fullest potentials, auditors will be less and less able to rely on traditional audit trails.

AUDITING THE COMPUTER

There has been a good deal of discussion of the relative merits of auditing around the computer vs. auditing through the computer, without defining either phrase. "Auditing around the computer" usually has meant little, if any, evaluation of internal controls in computer operations and programs. Instead, emphasis has been placed on tracing selected input to output and vice versa. On the other hand, "auditing through the computer" has involved analysis of internal controls within the EDP function and has utilized the computer to test the programs.

In his book, *Auditing and EDP,* Professor Davis emphasizes that when auditing *around* the computer, the auditor should evaluate and test internal control within the EDP function. He suggests interviews with data processing personnel, use of an EDP questionnaire and thorough review of the general system and controls. Presumably, such an audit would include a flow chart analysis of the system.

AUDITING AROUND THE COMPUTER

Auditing around the computer assumes that a test comparing selected audited input with output will prove the reliability of the internal controls in effect within the system. Auditing around the computer has the advantage of minimizing the interference with the client's day-to-day processing operations and presents no risk of tampering with "live data." The around-the-computer approach works well if the system is on a batch processing basis, if transactions are initially recorded manually and if the audit trail is characterized by extensive printouts. However, as the EDP system becomes more advanced, this auditing method becomes more cumbersome and costly.

If the client's EDP system is to develop to its fullest potential, auditors and management must be able to accept the reliability of the computer. Extensive printouts slow the system to the pace of its slowest component—the printer. In a study cosponsored by the American Institute of CPAs, the authors noted ". . . the CPA must realize that he cannot expect computerized systems to be modified to provide output that only he needs in order that he may perform his audit in the traditional way. . . ."[15] An auditor who insists on following a paper trail must justify the cost of the additional time and effort required to prepare a report for his use alone.

In auditing around the computer, the auditor cannot ignore the computer. He must make a thorough evaluation of the organizational, administrative and procedural controls in the EDP department even though he tests around the computer. Thus, evaluation requires a knowledge of EDP on the part of the auditor, if he is to comply with the second standard of field work.

AUDITING THROUGH THE COMPUTER

The alternative to auditing around the computer is to audit through it. In auditing through the computer, the computer is used to obtain information about the operation of the programs and about controls built into the machine itself. There are three audit approaches: using test decks, using "packaged" programs or using unique programs for each client.

Test-Deck Audit Approach. The most used and currently the most economical method of auditing through the computer is the test deck. In this approach, simulated problems or data using the client's programs and equipment are processed under the auditor's control. Test data are introduced in whatever form is appropriate for the particular system. The term "test deck" implies the use of punched cards. However, other media may be used, such as magnetic tape, magnetic ink, or optical characters.

The auditor must design his test in a manner that will assure him that the system of controls is functioning properly. Both valid and invalid conditions are included in the test deck. The auditor "should concentrate on developing invalid data and control violations. The error input should relate directly to the specific system controls which are critical to his objective of being assured that he can rely on the system as an information source. He will probably want to attempt to violate all the designed quality checks in the edit program."[16]

---

[15] Robert Roy II, and MacNeill, James H., *Horizons for a Profession,* New York: American Institute of Certified Public Accountants, 1967.

[16] Moore, "EDP Audits," p. 13.

The test conditions might include:

1. Out-of-balance batches of input
2. Normal transactions
3. Invalid data such as (a) alpha data where numeric should be, (b) invalid dates or account numbers, (c) incomplete data or (d) data larger than the field size
4. Edit routine violations
5. Out-of-sequence processing
6. Processing with the wrong file.

To develop an adequate test deck the auditor must completely understand the system and its control features. His understanding should include knowledge of the controls discussed earlier in the sections on organizational, administrative and procedural controls. Of course, knowledge of these controls is also necessary to audit effectively around the computer.

Auditing through the computer has other problems not encountered in auditing around the computer. Frequently, a through-the-computer approach means that the auditor will be merging his test data in with the client's processing of "live" data. If so, the auditor must identify his test data so that they may later be "reversed out" of the live data. For example, if the auditor tests a program which updates master records, he might use:

1. Current master records or
2. Special audit records maintained in the current master file or
3. Obsolete master records or copies of current master records or
4. Simulated master records in a separate test file.[17]

In the first two methods, the auditor's test data are merged into the client's live data on the master records; in the last two, the master records used are dead. If the auditor chooses one of the first two, he must be careful not to distort or destroy real data. However, these methods don't require a special computer run for the audit and are therefore less expensive. Under methods 3 and 4, no data are live, but a separate computer run is required. To use either method, the auditor must justify either the live data risks or the costs of an additional run.

A big advantage of the test-deck approach is that program changes are of little concern to the auditor, if the revised programs continue to produce acceptable output from the test data. Once a test deck is devel-

---

[17]Davis, *Auditing and EDP,* p. 164.

oped, it can be run and evaluated frequently. On the other hand, a test deck is costly to develop and can be used on only one client's system.

The successful run of test data through an existing program assures the auditor that the tested controls exist in the program. That is all it will do. The question of whether the tested program was in use during the entire period is a separate question, one not unique to EDP systems. This question is answered through analysis of organizational, administrative and procedural controls.

"Packaged" Audit Programs. To date, the use of packaged computer audit programs has been very limited. These programs are standardized programs developed to audit one segment of the client's records, such as the securities account; or, they are generalized sets of audit routines, such as Haskins and Sells' Auditape system. The Securities Account Program is intended for use in auditing securities of every client having an EDP system; the program should not have to be rewritten for each client. Similarly, Auditape is presumed to be applicable to all clients having EDP systems. These packaged computer programs assume that audit procedures in computerized systems change very little from client to client. They assume transferability of audit program among various EDP installations.

As a practical matter today, differences in equipment and software sometimes make extensive use of packaged audit programs impractical. Equipment differences may prevent the immediate applicability of a packaged program to an individual client's system. A test deck or an approach using the client's programs is usually less costly. However, the trend in equipment manufacture is toward more uniformity in design. Packaged programs, therefore, will likely be much more attractive in the future.

Using Computer Programs in Conducting the Audit. Using computer programs in conducting his audit requires the auditor to have a higher level of EDP knowledge than either auditing around the computer or the test-deck approach through the computer. This is probably why auditors seldom use them. However, the auditor could work with a programmer to write his audit programs. He might use client personnel to write programs, or use his firm's management services personnel. Some would suggest that the auditor should write the program himself. But there are very few auditors who can also program.

Using the client's personnel to write the program is the most economical, from the client's viewpoint. Some of the programs required for the audit may be already prepared by the client—such as programs for inventory turnover and obsolescence. To use the client's programs, the auditor must be capable of technically evaluating the programs to determine that they meet his requirements.

Using management services personnel to develop audit programs has the advantage of independence, but is more costly than using the client's personnel. If the auditing firm has a programmer available, he must learn the client's programming conventions and become familiar with the equipment and system involved—all at a cost to the client. Often, a practical alternative is to use MS people to review programs prepared by the client's personnel.

AUDIT CHALLENGES IN ON-LINE AND REAL-TIME SYSTEMS

As managements become increasingly reliant on the computer, computer systems are becoming more and more complex. Today's most advanced systems, of which there are relatively few, are known as "on-line," "real-time" and "integrated."

On-line refers to peripheral equipment connected directly to the central processing unit. Data are recorded at remote input terminals and are processed immediately by the computer. Transactions are processed when recorded instead of accumulated in batches. On-line processing generally requires a random access file storage unit.

Likewise, real-time systems usually require random access storage. Real-time refers to the time required for the system to respond to an inquirer. If the response is soon enough to affect current decision-making, the system is said to be real-time. A fine example of an on-line and real-time system is the computerized ticket reservation system used by some airlines.

All seats for upcoming flights constitute an inventory in random access computer storage. At any given moment, each seat is either sold, unsold or reserved pending sale. Every ticket selling point has an on-line connection to the computer inventory. The selling points make inquiries to the computer concerning unsold space available for sale. They also generate input data, which is immediately recorded, concerning sales, cancellations and reservations. This on-line input is processed immediately, making the inventory completely up to date at all times. The real-time updating is necessary to provide adequate answers to inquiries about seat availability.

In most systems, records are maintained functionally, such as purchasing records, accounts payable records and sales records. An integrated system recognizes that these various sets of records are interrelated. In an integrated system, one comprehensive set of records replaces the various functional sets. In an integrated system, the recording of a single transaction usually initiates several actions. For example, the recording of a sales order which has items identified by quantity and stock number might automatically result in: (1) reducing finished goods inventory, (2) pricing the order, (3) preparing the billing, (4) updating receivables, (5) updating sales analysis, (6) costing the order and (7) updating cost of sales.

This example suggests future data processing systems. Single inputs will initiate a number of data processing activities. Such systems will be considerably more difficult to understand and test from an audit standpoint. To understand such systems, the auditor must acquire a sound conceptual knowledge of computer capabilities. As these advanced systems come into general use, he must possess sufficient technical competence to perform a satisfactory audit.

CONCLUSION

The central problem faced by auditors of EDP installations is the greater or lesser omission of the traditional audit trail. Insistence upon maintaining conventional audit trails would only inhibit the development of EDP. Therefore, the professional must develop procedures and techniques by which his audit can be satisfactorily performed. "The auditor must recognize the full impact of the computer revolution. He must view the computer as a centralized tool of control previously not available to accomplish his objectives. A 'through the computer' (audit) approach must be adopted . . . to insure that factors of reliability, timeliness, and control inherent in computer systems are realized."[18]

If the auditor has enough expertise to audit through the computer, he can use the machine to assist him in performing the audit. An advantage of auditing with the computer is that the auditor is able to review the complete universe of the client's records. And, by delegating routine tasks to the computer, the auditor can devote more time to areas requiring his professional judgment. He thereby secures better evidence to support his opinion.

Professor Davis points out that all auditors should have at least a general understanding of the following topics and an in-depth understanding of them if they are responsible for computer audits:

1. EDP equipment and its capabilities
2. Characteristics of computer-based systems
3. Fundamentals of computer programming
4. Computer center operations

---

[18]Max S. Simpson, "How Do Electronic Computers Affect Accounting and Auditing Techniques?" *Financial Executive,* vol. 34 (February 1966).

5. Organization and management of the data processing function
6. EDP documentation
7. Controls in EDP systems
8. Auditing techniques not using the computer
9. Auditing techniques using the computer.[19]

The problem facing the auditing profession is not whether the CPA is capable of auditing a system with a computer; given adequate training he could most certainly handle it. With the constant expansion of the use of computer systems, public accounting firms will have to make some important decisions regarding their audit approach. In complex EDP systems, where the traditional audit trail has virtually disappeared, it is most economical to audit through the computer. An on-line real-time integrated system is extremely complex and a through-the-computer audit approach is essential. As the degree of complexity of the EDP system increases, so does the level of competence required by the auditor.

To meet the problem of competence, each firm performing EDP audits should have a few computer audit specialists. They should have a level of understanding of EDP which will enable them to manage the audit of an EDP system. To become specialists, they should be given the necessary training in data processing through university instruction, vendors' courses in systems and programming, firm or professional seminars, AICPA professional development courses, or on-the-job experience in an EDP installation for several months. A CPA with this training is capable of performing an audit which completely meets the second standard of field work.

Over the years accounting firms of all sizes have developed various specialists in their organization—inventory specialists, industry specialists, SEC specialists, etc. The specialist approach reduces the need for detailed technical knowledge on the part of every auditor. While every staff auditor should be able to evaluate and flowchart an EDP system, he needs, on the job, only enough EDP knowledge to follow instructions and to earn the client's respect. Therefore, EDP specialists are a logical development in the profession.

CPAs must meet the challenge of the computer with people adequately trained in EDP. A high level of technical knowledge is required to evaluate and test internal control in an EDP system. Evaluation of program controls and equipment controls are especially technical; organization and procedural controls are less technical but do require a general understanding of EDP. To obtain information on the system,

---

[19]Davis, *Auditing and EDP.*

the auditor must be able to discuss the system intelligently with the client. Once the auditor understands the system, he must be qualified to develop meaningful test data. Again, a high level of technical knowledge is required. Designing and using test decks, converting clients' programs to audit use, and the use of generalized audit programs require a technical knowledge of EDP. As EDP systems become more advanced, the level of competence required to evaluate and test them will likewise increase.

Because EDP auditing is a highly specialized subject, a public accounting firm cannot afford to develop a high level of competence in *every* staff person. Therefore, as with taxes, EDP audit specialists are a logical development. The firm which expects to comply with the second standard of field work in performing EDP audits must have auditors technically competent to evaluate and thoroughly test these systems.

INTERNAL CONTROL AND THE AUDIT OF REAL-TIME DIGITAL SYSTEMS

by Franz E. Ross

There are currently a few score real-time digital systems in operation, but hundreds more are planned and on order for installation during the next few years. While the average CPA is not likely to encounter a real-time digital system at the present, many CPAs will be asked for counsel and guidance in the planning and installation of such systems during the next few years. Moreover, it is not unlikely that in the foreseeable future some of the key economic functions of our society may be accomplished by real-time digital systems. Thus, it behooves the CPA to acquaint himself with the special problems of control and audit of such systems and to look at some of the possible solutions.

A real-time digital system may be defined as one or more digital computers and other devices used to participate in, control or monitor a business, industrial or scientific process while this process is actually taking place. In other words, the computer, input/output units and other devices have become part of a live process. The digital system must be ready with its results when they are needed for the process, and must be available for new transactions as they occur.

Reprinted by permission of the publisher from *The Journal of Accountancy*, April 1965, pp. 46-55, copyright 1965 by the American Institute of Certified Public Accountants, Inc.

Typical examples are real-time demand deposit systems, production control systems, and various control, warning and communications-switching systems in the area of national defense. The spread and status of real-time systems in various industries have been described recently in *Management Services*,[20] another AICPA publication.

Basically, such real-time systems have this one characteristic in common: transactions or intermediate stages in a process are flashed—as they occur—to a central computer installation for processing or recording, through a terminal or sensors or some other input device. This is often done via a communications network. At the central computer site is a device which handles many input sources that simultaneously try to obtain the attention of the computer. It assembles the input messages and feeds them to the computer in an orderly fashion. The computer then processes these messages. It may obtain results and feed them back to the live process so as to influence its subsequent course, or it may update information stored in the files so that the stored data represent up-to-the-minute complete and correct information available for inquiry. The system has to be capable of processing the input within the time allowed, as the penalties of not keeping pace may range from loss of revenues, in business systems, to wholesale disaster and death, in such defense systems as BMEWS (Ballistic Missile Early Warning System).

Thus, a typical real-time system includes, but is not limited to, terminals or other input/output devices, a communications control unit or real-time channel, a processor, and, almost invariably, large, random-access files or auxiliary storage. Recent equipment developments have emphasized designs oriented to carry out real-time functions, and have greatly simplified the systems design, preparation for, and implementation of, real-time digital systems.

The majority of real-time digital systems will consist of small-and medium-sized systems which process transactions sequentially, in the order of input, without pre-emption of system facilities by priority transactions. However, regardless of size and complexity, these systems are characterized by at least some of the following features:

(1) Short reaction time. Participation in or control or monitoring of the live process is effected by a series of individual transactions, measurements or status reports which are brought into the real-time system for processing. Response to each event, such as a savings account status inquiry, usually has to be within seconds. In industrial process control or scientific or national defense real-time systems, measurements may not require individual response, but critical data must be selected and

---

[20]Richard E. Sprague, "On Line-Real Time Systems—1964," *Management Services*, May-June 1964, p. 40.

analyzed and appropriate action taken within a few thousandths of a second. Thus, in almost all real-time computer systems, economy of time is a prime consideration in design.

(2) Peaks and queueing. In many real-time systems it is well known that a fairly high percentage of the periodical transactions occurs over a relatively short, predictable span of time—the peak period. Moreover, at any time, due to simultaneous input from many parts of the system, a temporary and random peak can occur. The system must be so planned that it can handle such peak loads in acceptable time. Queues of transactions and output messages result from input from various sources vying simultaneously for central processor attention and from output waiting to be moved out of the system. Therefore, there must be some prearranged priorities or some general rules such as first in, first out.

(3) Heterogeneous input. In most real-time applications, different types of transactions flow through the system, each of which has to be processed according to different rules. In an on-line savings system, for instance, deposits, withdrawals, mortgage payments and Christmas Club payments would each be processed by a separate transaction routine. In view of the usually tight schedule, it is, of course, desirable to have as many of the frequently used program routines as possible held in the main computer storage: bringing in routines from auxiliary storage as they are needed is usually time-consuming.

(4) Control program. Owing to the tight time schedule and the resultant priorities, it may be necessary for the data processing equipment to process different sets of data with different program routines at the same time. These routines may have to be brought into main memory from auxiliary storage. Many operating decisions must be made; e.g., whether to move output into some communications lines or free them for accepting input. The schedules of data to be processed, program routines to be used, and operating decisions necessary are made by the supervisory or control program, which links up the individual program routines to be used under the changing conditions. This control program also deals with the interaction among program routines which use the same account balances, constants, machine registers, etc.

Thus, in a system with priority transactions, the control program may move a set of data into the system, which processes it until receipt of data of higher priority requires interruption. The earlier data and the partially completed program routine may then remain in memory (or even be temporarily moved out to auxiliary storage) until the high-priority items have been dispatched and control is returned to the partially run program for completion of processing. In such a case the sequence of instructions actually carried out by the equipment can be determined only if all inputs received and their relative timings are exactly known.

It thus does not necessarily follow that two transactions of the same category will always be processed in the same manner in a real-time system.

(5) Continuity of operation. One of the prime differences between a real-time system and a system processing historical data is that the real-time system must be available for processing whenever transactions occur. This availability is accomplished mainly through the reliability of the equipment and through careful systems design, which relies on back-up equipment or back-up procedures when the equipment is inoperable.

(a) Reliability of the equipment. This is a subject which, because of defense and space projects, has received considerable popular attention. For clarification, the main principles are these: The reliability measurements which are significant to the user of an electronic data processing machine are the average time the machine will stay in operation until it breaks down (mean time to failure), and the average time for repair from the time of breakdown until it is again fully operable (mean time to repair). If these measurements are known for individual machines, the measurements for a system can be obtained by calculation or simulation.

Although these measures sound quite simple, they are very complicated and have many ramifications which are not obvious; thus, for the layman, they are practically impossible to evaluate and to compare.

At the present time, there are no recognized industry-wide standards for computing these reliability measures. Thus, for instance, a manufacturer may or may not include preventive maintenance time in the mean time to failure, or he may or may not include diagnosing the failure and/or final checkout after repair in the mean time to repair.

Another problem is that these measures are defined in terms of operability and breakdown, but in real life things are not always so clear-cut: The electronic equipment may not just break down; its operation may become interlaced with more and more frequent errors, which, although they may be detected by hardware and systems checks, slowly bog down operations. The point at which the user throws up his hands in despair and requests unscheduled maintenance depends on the nature of the use of the equipment and on the temperament of the user. Thus, the basis of these measures—the point in time when the equipment actually fails and requires unscheduled maintenance—is often not exactly determinable.

Moreover, these reliability measures are far more encompassing than measurements which merely calibrate hardware performance: They measure also how close the points of service (where maintenance engineers are available) are to the customer locations, the quality of equipment servicing, and various aspects of systems design and programming. For instance, it is obvious that the quality of preventive maintenance will strongly influence how long the equipment remains operable before breakdown, and that the availability of spare parts and the training of maintenance engineers are contributing factors to the speed of effecting equipment repairs.

(b) Back-up equipment and procedures. In order that the real-time system survives to accomplish its intended function even after one or several critical machines have failed, intelligent system designers will consider the backing up of critical pieces of equipment with other hardware capable of carrying out the same functions. The alternative to backing up one or more operating machines with stand-by, functionally similar units is to fall back upon some devices with lower capability or a configuration which cannot handle a peak transaction rate without delays, or to eliminate or defer certain less essential functions, or to carry them out by nonautomatic methods. All these methods of doing something less than the total job in the case of equipment failure are referred to as degraded modes of operation.

The purpose of all these techniques is, of course, to design a system which can somehow continue its most essential functions under all but the rarest and most improbable catastrophic failures. To what extent this purpose is being accomplished can be realistically measured by comparing the exposure to, and effects of, equipment failure, or other possible causes of systems interruption, of the automatic real-time system and of the prior manual or semiautomatic system.

The resultant system is a complex of machines with various stand-by units, switch-over devices, and a highly organized set of emergency techniques and fall-back procedures. Thus a real-time digital system often requires custom-built connections and special devices.

(6) Systems integration, testing and implementation. If the real-time system is not a standard configuration, considerable testing of the interconnections and relative timings by the manufacturer, known as "systems integration," is necessary prior to installation. The final checkout of the equipment really occurs, however, during the testing of the real-time programs.

Program testing of a real-time programming system is lengthy and complicated: A real-time system cannot afford to have "bugs" or errors once it is put into operation, for such program or machine errors could shut down the system or create useless or, what is sometimes worse, misleading output. On the other hand, to completely test out all paths in a real-time program is, timewise, often impossible. It has been estimated that a certain airline reservations real-time system contains 250,000,000 possible paths through which an input may pass to produce a response.

Thus, test data have to be well chosen to test out the system without causing undue delay. Special machine programs may have to be written to assist with the testing and implementation (putting into operation) of the real-time system. All programs need testing.

Implementation of the real-time system and program testing in the real-time environment are carried on simultaneously. Implementation, however, also requires organization of many other matters without which the system cannot properly perform: co-ordination of servicing arrangements with communications common carriers and equipment manufacturers, training of all operating personnel, availability of needed supplies, planning and testing of emergency procedures, and many others. Failure to complete necessary preparations may delay cutover significantly.

(8) Off-Line processing. In most real-time systems, a large part of all processing is still devoted to batch processing, which usually amounts to an after-the-fact processing of historical data. This batch or other off-line processing requirement is due to other, non-real-time, applications being run on the same system, and to the many non-real-time functions such as file maintenance runs, reconciliation of detail and control, and others which are essential to keep the real-time system in operation.

TECHNIQUES OF CONTROL AND AUDIT

It is essential that there exist a group organizationally separate from the computer installation—a group which is knowledgeable about EDP and understands the operation of the real-time system. Its members should independently monitor the operation of the system and verify that the system is efficiently used and adequately controlled and that the planned controls are actually in operation. This need goes deeper than the normal requirement of organizational independence of control and audit personnel: No group within a business should have a monopoly on some specialized knowledge which would enable them to avoid supervision and restraint.

The real-time system makes transaction detail and summary information centrally available on a current basis for computer analysis. This capability means that the "control by exception" technique can be broadened to a management review of exceptional transactions in time to intervene, and not merely after the fact. It also implies use of the computer as the main tool of control rather than imposition of extraneous controls, which might make it impossible to keep up with real-time events.

There have been several years of argument as to how much the auditor has to know about EDP. This problem has really been a "front" for a deeper and more serious problem: Should the auditor audit the total EDP system or should he "audit around it" by just examining and correlating the original input and final output of the system? There will be real-time systems where it is no longer possible to match inputs and outputs and where an auditable sample of correctly processed transactions does not constitute full assurance that under the many possible sets of conditions the same transactions will always be correctly processed. Thus, the only way the auditor can gain the necessary confidence in the operation of the system and its results is by having a basic understanding of how the system operates, how results are produced, and what controls and other safeguards have been instituted and are actually utilized.

The problem of audit trail is no different in a real-time system than in any other EDP system which has large-scale random-access storage and has, thus, the capability of processing transactions in the order of occurrence rather than by batch. This problem and its solutions have been very adequately described elsewhere. It is important, however, that the auditor make his needs known, particularly for audit trail information, at an early stage in systems planning. Otherwise, changes in systems design and programming become difficult and time consuming, and thus expensive, in view of the critical timings and scarcity of quick-access storage usually encountered in a real-time system.

Upon the first review of a real-time installation, the auditor may wish to satisfy himself that the system is adequate for its purpose even during seasonal peaks or, alternatively, that arrangements can be made to handle the expected transaction volume when it exceeds the capacity of the system. Similarly, the auditor should examine the emergency measures which exist for handling the real-time process in case of some calamity such as fire, long-term electrical outage, or catastrophic equipment failure. It is noted that unless such emergency measures have actually been tested under operating conditions, they cannot be relied upon to function when needed. Such a review of the adequacy of the real-time system and the emergency planning is considered necessary, as failure in either of these areas may cause unanticipated losses.

The most important single control available to the auditor for checking on the total system is the processing of test transactions through the system. These test data should be prepared by the auditor to check on the operation of input, processing, and output controls and therefore should include incorrect, incongruous and inconsistent data and data deliberately designed to "beat" the controls. The program may recognize test data by a certain code and refrain from adding them to results, statistics or permanent records. If the program has this capability, it is possible to mingle test data with actual transactions.

Apart from test transactions which check the functioning of the equipment as well as programming and operation, it is easiest to tackle the problem of audit and control of a real-time digital system, or any other EDP system, by examining the separate functions of input, processing and output.

INPUT

There are two basic types of input in a real-time system:

1. *Transaction input.* These are the transactions, status reports, measurements, or other evidences of change which pass from the live process to the real-time system. They are the stimuli to which the real-time system reacts.
2. *Master record and constant input.* These are the types of data which remain permanently either in quick access storage or in bulk storage of the real-time system. These may be subject to continuing change as a result of the real-time transaction input, as in the case of the master file, or may be unaffected by the real-time process and separately updated when needed, as in the case of constants, rate tables, and programs.

TRANSACTION INPUT

In a real-time system, the transaction input poses two main problems of control: (1) It may not be evidenced by independent input data in machine-sensible form which can be separately controlled and audited, and (2) it may be almost impossible to substantiate in which order the transactions from the various input sources are presented to the real-time system and processed by it. Both difficulties are cased or almost eliminated by keeping a transaction log in the real-time system.

This log consists of all transactions accepted by the real-time system, usually in the order of acceptance, including any errors made at the introduction of this data into the system, and contains all detail necessary for complete reprocessing of the transactions in case of loss of data or equipment failure. The transaction log, together with a recent set of master records, also makes possible re-creation or verification of the up-to-date master records. Individual transactions contained in the transaction log can be sorted, by master record, into a daily transaction journal so that, say, last night's master record balance plus today's transactions will verify tonight's balance of the master record. Similarly, the transaction log can be summarized by the type of transaction to confirm the summary information in the control accounts. The daily transaction journal can also be merged into a cumulative transaction journal to show all transactions affecting the individual master record for the month, the quarter, the year, as may be necessary. For these various control purposes, the transaction log is written from time to time into some storage medium outside the real-time system.

In order to have the fullest and most effective use of the log as a back-up device for accounting controls and for subsequent audit, it is usually desirable that the log be posted as the transaction enters the real-time system, and that during processing the master record as well as summary or control records be posted with each individual transaction. As a safeguard against equipment failure, the master records and the pertaining transaction log should be stored, when feasible, in functionally separate storage devices, so that the probability of losing both sets of data simultaneously becomes nil for all practical purposes.

If there is adequate checking from the input device through the central processor in which the log is created, it can be assumed that the log will contain the same information which was introduced into the system. Thus, the log is usually no worse but certainly no better then the original input. It is, therefore, essential that audit procedures be instituted to assure that all data entered represent correctly the actual transaction, and that no transaction has been completely overlooked.

Two methods are open to control the accuracy of transaction data entered. One is the use of data which may be available outside the system, in other departments of the company or from other outside sources. The other method is to use the processing power of the system for as complete a check as the limited time will allow—for consistency, reasonableness and statistical creditability of the data introduced.

Even cursory analysis will show that the problem of overlooking a complete transaction is not as formidable as one might first suppose. Any system where the transaction is introduced into the system as it occurs, by automatic means and without human intervention, or where the transaction input is only a small sample selected from a larger number of data can be ruled out. In the first type of system, proper machine maintenance will assure that no transaction is omitted; in the second type, the individual transaction, usually a measurement, is not significant, only the trend which the measurements establish. Both these presumptions must, of course, be confirmed by audit. The type of system which is most vulnerable in this respect is one in which a separate, deliberate action by an operator is a prerequisite for introduction of a transaction into the system. But even in those systems, complete skipping of a transaction is not likely, for often some inquiry for information contained in bulk storage precedes the transaction.

Depending upon the system, many ingenious methods can be designed to minimize the chances of the omission of a complete transaction and to ascertain afterwards whether any transactions have in fact been missed. Based on the principle that very little happens without leaving an ascertainable trace, evidence will be available if transactions have not been entered, particularly if such omissions tend to occur frequently. For example, missed receipts or issues from an inventory result in differences between the real-time inventory and warehouse contents. Thus, even in the absence of auditable independent records outside the system, the ingenuity of the auditor will enable him to substantiate how reliable the transaction log really is.

If in some system independent auditable input records are provided for all transactions, the well-known techniques of input control such as control totals, batch controls, serial numbers, hash totals, checks on the reasonableness and validity of data input, etc., can, of course, be used. Some of these controls will even be applicable in cases where independent input documents are not always provided. For instance, in an intra-company real-time message communications system, it is usually desirable to sequentially number the messages originated at each terminal.

When input originates, as it normally does, at various individual input terminals, it is possible to tag every transaction record with the identification of the input terminal used. Thus, the transaction input can be analyzed and audited according to the originating terminal. As a consequence the auditor could observe one individual input terminal and subsequently audit the systems operation as far as the input from that individual terminal is concerned.

The most important new element in a real-time system is, of course, time itself. If the system includes an electronic clock, it is possible to time-tag every transaction with the time at which it was accepted by the system. An alternative which is less time and storage space consuming, but only possible in strictly sequential logging, would be to time-tag every fifth, tenth, fiftieth, or other nth transaction, or to write a time record periodically, say every minute, into the master log. It would then be known that all transactions logged between two subsequent time tags or records were received within the same period. If time is thus used as an element of control and audit, it becomes possible to survey the efficiency of operations of the real-time system after the fact, to make meaningful audits of the total operation of the system, notwithstanding the great amount of detail involved by isolating a sufficiently short time span. Such investigations, of course, can become even more meaningful if the output is similarly time-tagged.

In a batch-processing system, transactions covering a relatively long period of time are processed together. It quite frequently occurs, therefore, that we encounter cancellations before the orders, issues of material from inventory before its receipt, and similar incongruities. In a real-time system, such occurrences should be investigated, as they may be indications of improper operations of the system or of irregularities.

One of the main objections raised against reliance on the transaction log is that it is completely and consistently under the control of computer room personnel. This fact, of course, accentuates the importance of such independent input records as may exist in other departments, and of the audit and control procedures carried on to verify the dependability, accuracy and completeness of the master log. It is necessary, therefore, that any such independent input records and/or audit verification of the master log should not be under the control of any person directly connected with central real-time systems operations. Similarly, computer personnel should have no access to terminals which have the capability of originating transaction input. Thus, it is desirable that the control console or other terminal under control of computer room personnel not be used to originate or modify input. The computer can be used to verify the fact that input originates only at terminal stations intended for that purpose.

MASTER RECORD AND CONSTANT INPUT

To guard against loss of data, equipment failure, and for purposes of control and audit, it is absolutely necessary that master records be extracted from the system periodically and stored outside at a location resistant to fire, flood, and other hazards. Contents of the master file can be "dumped" in one operation onto magnetic tape, cards, or other machine-sensible media. In addition, for customer inquiry and other purposes, it is usually necessary to print out the master file from time to time. Another method is to write out the master file on a cyclical basis, each day some part, so that in a complete cycle, say a week, the complete master file has been extracted and the cycle can start all over again. One refinement is to classify the records of the master file according to frequency of usage or criticality of the item. (Criticality here may mean value of an item of inventory or its attractiveness to pilferers, or the importance of a customer.) In this case, extracting and controlling the more often used and more sensitive master records on a more frequent schedule than the remainder of the master file would result in a more economical use of systems time and media.

It is also necessary periodically to dump the control and summary accounts from the system. Thus, there is stored outside the system a recent copy of the master file, a recent set of summary and control accounts, and the transaction log accumulated to a recent date. In addition, these same types of data are available within the system in up-to-the-minute form. This information makes possible most normal accounting checks and allows reconstitution of at least the most essential data if any of these files are lost.

It is also necessary to write out from the system price lists, rate tables and other constants on a periodical and surprise basis. These constants should then be checked against approved data maintained outside the system. For instance, in the case of the rate table of a utility, incorrect rates would cause a tremendous number of incorrect invoices and, hence, complaints. Therefore, all changes in the constants and tables maintained inside the real-time system should be made only in accordance with a regularized procedure, including written approvals and a printed and a machine-sensible change register. Such methods will facilitate subsequent audit verification both by scanning and automatic methods. It is, of course, important to store outside the system sufficient historical constants so that, upon a later audit or outside inquiry, results obtained during the earlier period can be substantiated on the basis of process, rates, or other constants then used. The same regularized change procedures, written approvals and periodic verification should also be applied to the computer program as will be described in more detail below.

One last observation on input: No results can be any better or more accurate than the input from which they were generated, or in the language of computer personnel "garbage in, garbage out" (Gigo).

PROCESSING

Based on satisfactory input, if the *equipment* is in good operating condition; if the *programs* are well designed for the intended purpose, properly controlled, and tested out; and if there is *no unauthorized intervention* in the operation of the system, satisfactory results should be obtained.

EQUIPMENT

Normally, and unless there is information to the contrary, the auditor will assume that the equipment is properly designed, carefully produced, and capable of satisfactory performance. He should, however, make it his business to know enough about the individual pieces of equipment to understand the capabilities and weaknesses of the system. Otherwise, his control and audit procedures may not correspond to actual requirements: For instance, if in a real-time system all equipment and data links contain adequate and reliable checks, built in by the manufacturer, except the lines to the output terminals, then obviously the most elaborate systems controls should be applied to the output data transfer, together with incisive audit procedures to verify that these control procedures are actually being utilized and are adequate for the purpose.

Electrical, electronic or mechanical equipment does not perform satisfactorily forever; it must be properly maintained. In order to rely on equipment performance, the auditor should satisfy himself that dependable maintenance arrangements exist. In the case of equipment leased from a reputable manufacturer, maintenance service is provided as part of the leasing contract for the equipment which continues to be owned by the manufacturer. Similarly, adequate maintenance of common carrier communications equipment and lines is furnished by the common carriers on their tariffed services. It may also be assumed, unless there is information to the contrary, that maintenance is likely to be satisfactory if a regular maintenance agreement exists with an equipment manufacturer or a reputable service organization, or if the equipment is maintained by clients' employees who have been properly trained for this purpose and are regularly assigned to it. Equipment performance, however, is suspect if maintenance arrangements are haphazard and are only made in an extemporaneous and erratic manner when repairs can be put off no longer.

An appropriate source of information on equipment performance, in addition to observation and inquiry, is the operating log which usually is, and should be, kept with the equipment. This log should contain various items of operating and maintenance information such as hours of equipment usage, preventive maintenance, equipment failures, unscheduled maintenance, and names of personnel servicing the equipment. a well-kept log will enable the auditor to assess the condition of the equipment and to what extent he can rely upon proper performance. Clearly, during periods in which there is evidence of equipment malfunction, normal assumptions as to equipment performance cannot be made.

In order to be assured of proper functioning of the equipment while operations are actually carried on and to know when and where maintenance is needed, it is necessary to make arrangements for some or all of these or similar monitoring and testing techniques:

1. *Operating performance statistics.* Errors should be accumulated, by type of failure, for each terminal, communications line and other major systems component. Alarms, display or printout should result if the error rate becomes excessive, and statistics should be printed out periodically.
2. *Test patterns.* It should be possible to originate test patterns at any input/output device to test the input/output device itself and its linkage to the central computer.
3. *Transaction Test.* A test can be programmed which allows origination of dummy transactions at any time at any transaction input point. These transactions should exercise all the parts of the total

system and produce correct results without, however, affecting the processing results of operations. Thus, operating and maintenance personnel can check out at any time whether the system is producing useful results.

PROGRAMS

Programs for a real-time system are often particularly exacting, lengthy and complex. Thus, even if he has knowledge of programming, the auditor will find it a very time consuming and uneconomical employment of his efforts to delve into the details of the program of a real-time system. He should, however, satisfy himself that the programs have been prepared by qualified personnel, that they were properly planned and carefully prepared. To this end, he may review some of the documentation compiled during the planning and programming phase: the training activities and schedules, programming standards and conventions, time schedules, various levels of flow charts, decisions on programming languages to be used, and others.

This review should extend to the systems checking techniques incorporated in the programs. These systems checks are well known and standard and include, among others, such techniques as proof figures, reverse arithmetic, limit checks, accounting checks and check-point routines. The question should be asked whether all conditions which can possibly arise have been provided for. All input errors, combinations of errors, and out-of-the-way conditions, which, however unlikely, are objectively possible, will sooner or later befall. Thus, in such an eventuality, data causing the condition have to be either processed by some special subroutine or have to be ejected by the system for manual handling. If the auditor has had prior experience with the live process which has been converted to the real-time system, he is particularly suited to review whether in fact the program caters to all possible contingencies.

Probably the most important aspect for the auditor to check in detail is the program testing the real-time program has undergone. As indicated earlier, the final testing out of real-time programs is a major undertaking which, in the case of a major system, may take weeks or even months, requires detailed preparation, and even construction of specialized programs that serve only as tools for the final program check-out. The auditor would wish here to review in detail the planning for the program check-out, the data used, and the results obtained. If experienced in the data and results of the process to be automated, he should have competent judgement as to the transaction data to be selected to test out the system. Even where the system is so extensive that test data must be generated by automatic means, he may be able to offer realistic advice as to the relative proportion of various types of test data to be used.

The auditor should be particularly interested in the result of parallel operations, which is the parallel processing of the live process by the real-time system and by the prior manual or semiautomatic system. A comparison of the results of parallel operations by a special computer program will usually furnish an exhaustive study as to the significance of the change in system from an accounting point of view. Manual methods of comparison, although more pedestrian, will be adequate in some cases, except where the wealth of data to be compared precludes a dependable judgment. The auditor will investigate what action was taken by programming personnel in all cases in which the analysis of parallel operations disclosed a major discrepancy, as such differences may significantly affect the consistency of successive financial statements.

However well designed a program may be, in the long-term use, it is no better than the documentation which supports it. Thus, an examination of the real-time system would certainly include a review of available programming documentation, such as flow charts, coding sheets with explanatory notes, program listings in programming and machine language, and adequate and clear operating instructions for the operators. It is desirable that at least one set of up-to-date programming documentation, including the program itself, be kept at a location where it is inaccessible to computer room personnel, so that it can be compared from time to time with program documentation and the program actually used by the operators. The reason for this control is that computer room personnel tend to make quick fixes to the program when some unusual program difficulty occurs. Although such an extemporaneous change during the running of the program may be necessary to maintain the system in operation, there is a danger that such hasty program changes may introduce new errors or invalidate controls programmed into the system.

For dependable operation, it is necessary that every computer installation have a standard method for effecting program modifications. Such changes should be supported by a document explaining the reasons for the program modification sought, the exact nature of the change, any incidental effects, and should be approved in writing by responsible personnel. If a change was originally made under the pressure of a real-time system in operation, it should be subsequently approved in the same formal manner. Programs which have been used at any time productively, i.e., to obtain results used in the business, should not be completely discarded. One copy of every program used and of any appertaining program change documentation should be stored in case substantiation of the operating results obtained becomes necessary.

In order to maintain a real-time system in operation even during equipment failure, stand-by equipment or fall-back procedures may be provided which will result in many cases in an anomalous mode of operation. It is, of course, necessary to design programs and procedures for such a mode of operation and, in particular, to prepare adequate controls for such a contingency. These controls must include a quick but thorough checkout of the newly constituted system when the fall-back mode is entered, and should generally be at least as extensive as the regular controls, for operating personnel as well as other users are unaccustomed to working with the changed system.

UNAUTHORIZED INTERVENTION

Due to the very complexity of a real-time system, its control program, its operating programs, and the interaction between them, the likelihood that an operator or other company personnel would change the program or other operation of the system to achieve some improper purpose is small. It is also unlikely that an operator, in order to lighten his work load, could effectively circumvent the controls programmed into the system if there is adequate supervision of computer operations. To guard against such intervention, it is possible to have the console typewriter print out any manual intervention into the system other than routine introduction of input through the input/output devices programmed to receive them. The information so printed could be kept visible but under lock and key so as to be inaccessible except to control personnel. Alternatively, a "receive only" typewriter could be remotely located, say, in the office of a responsible executive, and be programmed to issue periodically important operating information such as volume of transactions and total amount of money on deposit in a savings system, and to record automatically any intervention in the operation of the system.

OUTPUT

The many different types of real-time systems will also produce many different types of output. Techniques of control and audit of output will vary considerable with the quantity of output produced in a system. Thus, if the only output of a system is answers to inquiries as to status of individual master records or summary accounts, the main output controls needed will be those to assure the correct transfer of data and the security of confidential information. Thus, the program would assure that only output terminals cleared for confidential data could receive them.

If the system produces quantity output, some of the output controls applicable to a batch-processing system will be utilized; thus, output documents may be under numerical or batch control or be subject to some other standard internal control procedure. Exception reports of unusual transactions or abnormal results may be prepared by the system for review by appropriate personnel. Special computer programs can be prepared to sample input, compute the output, and verify that such output, in fact, was created. Conversely, other special programs may sample the output, deduce from the output sample the types of input which could have created it, and verify that, in fact, such input data were introduced into the system. In general, it is always possible to make a statistical review of transactions and results by using the processor to compare them to the equivalent data of the preceding period.

If possible, it is desirable to compare operating results with independent outside data such as physical inventories and positive confirmations of accounts receivable or payable. Differences can then be analyzed by computer and should be investigated in detail, as the early availability of the results through the use of a real-time system makes it possible to find the cause of the differences and to prevent further irregularity, if any.

It may be desirable to permanently record all types of output created. For instance, if the output is merely a display of certain digital information, it is useful to write the information displayed on a permanent medium so that it will be available subsequently to substantiate what data were displayed and for audit.

In some systems, particularly where the amount of output created is large, and where input and output do not match up or are not received by the system in the same order in which they are dispatched from it, an output log may be an effective tool of control. The output log will contain identification of the output record and its salient data and results, sufficient to allow subsequent verification that output data were correct and to recreate transaction input or master file information in case of loss of data or machine failure. Various types of controls can be tied in with the existence of an output log. For instance, in a message communications system the messages received at the switching center (input) less the messages dispatched (output) should equal the number of messages in storage at the time of the control procedure.

Another effective way of using the capability of the real-time system for control is by means of the feedback principle. This principle signifies generally that every change in a process is followed by a response which may act to modify the process; examples are a thermostat or the automatic choke of a car. In a real-time system it implies that, after a transaction occurs, the system returns a positive response to the transaction source, which may influence subsequent transactions. For instance, upon entry of an order a message could be returned that the order has been accepted or, alternatively, that orders for those goods can only be entered for sixty days' delivery. Such a response would furnish a clear-cut commitment and would create an auditable record of systems output.

There is, of course, one factor of prime importance: personnel who have worked on transaction input or on the operation of the real-time system should not be allowed to handle or control output during the same period.

CONCLUSION

The real-time digital system is at the border of engineering and business. It is a highly complex system engineered from various data processing, communications and sometimes other components to accomplish a job in business, industry, science or defense. It has to be understood to be effectively controlled and audited. The CPA must assert his position in this border area or it will be slowly eroded as electronic systems take over more areas in the conduct of business. To maintain and extend his position, he should conceive his purpose in the scheme of things as a professional, independent examiner of business, and should tackle any job existing in the framework of all of these new developments.

8

Auditing Computerized Activities

Extensive use of computer-based accounting systems to produce the financial statements of a firm does not change the basic goal of auditing, which is to verify the reliability of those statements and the degree to which they represent the true financial status of the firm. Extensive use of computers, however, does mean that the auditor must be adequately trained and sufficiently familiar with EDP techniques to adapt new approaches to his needs.

Computers have changed the form of many records and the techniques by which they are processed. In many cases transactions can now be recorded without ever producing a written copy. Audit trails have changed; they will no longer provide convenient "signposts" unless they have been carefully designed for that purpose. The auditor's evidential matter now frequently includes newer forms of documentation such as flowcharts, decision tables, program listings, record layouts, and operator log books. In some instances, the auditor can use the computer itself to perform some auditing tasks such as selection and analysis of items for closer examination.

There have been frequent discussions on the relative merits of "auditing around the computer" versus "auditing through the computer." Most audits involve elements of both. Certainly some procedures such as physical inventories, accounts receivable verification, and verification of cash balances can be done independently of the computer. In other cases, indirect verification can be achieved through examination of the programs and procedures producing the data, rather than through examination of the data itself.

Rapid technological development requires much adjustment and frequently introduces a period of uncertainty while the impact of those changes are being assessed. The material of this chapter is concerned with the changes and uncertainties that computers have caused in audit techniques and procedures.

AN AUDITOR'S VIEW OF DATA PROCESSING

by John P. Harrison

With the emergence of the total integrated information system the data processing function has taken on increased importance and the manager of the system has become the auditor's chief source of information. However, some data processing managers have underestimated the importance of their elevated function. The auditor, too, is not without fault. Some auditor's choose to audit as though the computer is not there. They have not kept abreast of or revised their audit programs to meet this new environment. Let's take a long look at this new information meeting ground where the data processing manager and the auditor must now perform their respective functions.

INFORMATION

Someone has said that information is data that has been processed. I think we should add that this processing must be useful. Management needs information to guide the operation of the business. Management, in turn, accounts for its stewardship through income statements and balance sheets. These financial statements are models of the firm covering the results of operations for various time periods. To be sure, they are not capable of the manipulations of data associated with the mathematical model of the economist. In fact the word manipulation has a sort of sinister meaning to the accountant. Nevertheless, these financial statements are expressed in a common information language so as to be understood both inside and outside the firm. This common language, if you will, is the debits and credits, the assets and liabilities, the deferrals and the accruals of the accounting system. Accounting has been the management information system.

Through the years, data processing has changed from bookkeeping posting machines to wired panel punched card machines to stored program computers. And just as equipment was changing so was the data processing staff. The bookkeeper became the machine accountant. Data

---

Reprinted by permission of the publisher from *Data Management,* September 1968, pp. 32-36.

processing pioneers will recall that the DPMA was previously known as the Machine Accountant's Association. The machine accountant was replaced by the programmer and currently the systems analyst is taking the major responsibilities away from the programmer. For purposes later on, I think it is important that I stress, that for auditing purposes, this change in organization is every bit as important as the equipment which performs the processing. I say this because, whereas the bookkeeper and the machine accountant actually produced the reports upon which the financial statements were based, the programmer and the systems analyst, while not turning out the reports themselves have provided the means of producing these reports through the systems that have been created and the computer programs that are run. These facts, together with the great accuracy of current equipment, have meant that inaccuracies and inadequacies are more likely to result from deficiencies in the systems and programming rather than from the operation of the equipment. Current processing under control of executive routines and operating systems had further reduced the operating man's responsibility.

Before returning to data processing let us now delve into the auditing function in a little more detail.

THE AUDITING FUNCTION

The *Auditing Standards and Procedures* published by the American Institute of Certified Public Accountants states that "the objective of the ordinary examination of financial statements by the independent auditor is the expression of an opinion on the fairness with which they present financial position and results of operations." The auditor conducts his examination in accordance with generally accepted auditing standards. These standards require that a report be submitted either expressing or disclaiming an opinion on whether or not the financial statements are presented in conformity with accepted accounting principles and applied consistently from period to period.

Why is an auditor's opinion necessary? Actually the position of auditor is a result of the development of business organization since the industrial revolution. Business growth had meant hired management and absentee owners and these owners looked to auditors to detect fraud. This concept of fraud detection has been replaced through the years with what is known as the "attest" function. Actually no company would be willing to pay the cost of the systems and auditing required to detect all frauds. In the attest function, the auditor examines the financial statements prepared by company management and the data which supports these statements, and attests to their fairness.

Today's modern business has obtained capital from millions of investors. The stock market conditions of the 1920's gave rise to the creation of the Security Exchange Commission to administer the Securities Act of 1933. This Act, in turn, required an examination by an independent public accountant. If you work for a company listed on a national stock exchange your annual statement must be filed with the SEC which requires strict independence, and public accounting firms pride themselves on this trust.

In summary, the auditor's opinion is desired because it roots from competence, integrity, and independence. These attributes, you recognize, are the typically professional characteristics. Now let us get a little into the audit. We shall begin with the auditor.

THE AUDITOR

The auditor is probably in some phase of becoming a CPA if he is not already one. His goal is to be a partner in his firm—for a partner is CPA top management, since a CPA firm cannot be incorporated. This is to insure responsibility because partners are personally liable whereas corporate officers are not. CPA's can be sued for their opinions.

At the start of an audit, an audit program is prepared. This is a detailed plan of the work to be performed. The size and complexity of modern business requires the auditor to rely on a combination of internal control and sampling techniques as the foundation for his opinion. In the preparation of the audit program, the auditor is guided by the following accepted standard of field work.

"There is to be a proper study and evaluation of the existing internal control as a basis for reliance thereon and for the determination of the resultant extent of the tests to which auditing procedures are to be restricted."

This is where the audit of data processing starts. Much has been mentioned about the audit trail. I think that this is a somewhat overworked phrase in describing what the auditor is looking for. The audit trail can be described as the capability to trace a transaction from the point of origin to its final recording in the accounts or to trace back from the end results to the start. Internal Revenue puts it this way: "the records must provide the opportunity to trace any transaction back to the original source or forward to a final total." The Internal Revenue Service guideline has some other things to say as well.

"If printouts are not made of transactions at the time they are processed, then the system must have the ability to reconstruct these transactions."

"The inherent nature of ADP is such that it may not be possible to trace transactions from source documents to end results or to reconstruct a given account unless the system is designed to provide audit trails."

"The ability to produce in legible form the data necessary to determine at a later date whether or not the correct tax liability has been reported must be carefully considered in designing and programming a machine system," and finally,

"This factor may add to the complexity of the system and require additional cost, but this cost may be negligible in comparison to the expense that may be incurred at a later date if the system cannot practically and readily provide the information needed to support and substantiate the accuracy of the previously reported tax liability."

What this adds up to is that the audit trail is not something required for the auditor. The audit trail is something that is required by good management practice. In fact, some auditors refer to it as the "management trail," because it has come to be a characteristic of good management.

The auditor is not primarily looking for a good audit trail, he is looking for good internal control. Internal control, according to the American Institute of Certified Public Accountants, ". . comprises the plan of organization and all of the co-ordinate methods and measures adopted within a business to safeguard assets, check the accuracy and reliability of its accounting data, promote operational efficiency, and encourage adherence to prescribed managerial policies."

When the auditor encounters your data processing operation it will be to evaluate how adequately the well-being of your organization is being served. How well you are safeguarding your company's assets?

In auditing EDP there are no long standing practices. This is a new field and everyone is still learning. There is, however, a growing body of preferred practices and if these are present, the auditor can logically infer that there is good internal control. These practices can be divided into organization control, input control, hardware control, software control, program control, output control and system control. Now that's quite a composite, so let's go over them one at a time. We will start with organization control.

ORGANIZATION CONTROL

We recognize division of responsibilities as being applicable to EDP. We would prefer, however, to see the programming function and the operating function separated. This would mean that in a payroll application, the man who programmed the job should not be the one to run it. Now you might say that the size of the organization could make this separation uneconomical and I would agree. I merely state the division is the preferable arrangement which reduces the risk.

The auditor would also have more confidence in a system if he knew the operator did not know how to program. I think you recognize that under these circumstances the operator could override program instructions through console changes or program patches. The operations personnel should not have access to program listings. We do not mean the operator-run books. These are extremely necessary. We mean the autocoder-type listings which show the core positions of data stored and the location of instructions. Knowing these facts facilitates operator intervention. It may appear that so many cooks spoil the broth, but I prefer to believe that cooks, waiters, and dishwashers each performing their respective duties, make a better restaurant.

Outside of the personnel area are such factors as:

Is there a schedule of work for the operations group?
Is there a computer usage log?
Is this log the basis of a summarizing report?
Is there evidence of orderly housekeeping?
Are important files and records fire protected?
Are there external tape labels?
Are the rings removed before storage?
Are card files identified?
Is there a record retention program?
Is there adequate backup for important files?
Does there appear to be a sufficient number of people? Or too many?
What training and experience does the staff have?
Are essential positions backed up with competent people?
What has been the turnover rate?

The auditor will have a questionnaire to complete, so he will be recording your answers.

INPUT CONTROLS

Establishing control of input to the data processing operation is usually either very thoroughly followed or completely ignored. Most tape-oriented systems seem to have provided a means to check input control totals. Perhaps this is because the printer is not doing anything else in the preliminary card-to-tape runs. Now control total checking should not be a characteristic associated with a particular configuration of equipment. The console typewriter is also an excellent resource available for printing controls. All reports should have a final total which can be checked against a control figure. Incidentally, control can also be established by counting records to be processed in those instances where totalling a particular field is not practical.

Another control associated with input is key verification, preferably by someone other than the original key punch operator. I know of a data processing installation that doesn't have a key punch. All data is reduced to punched paper tape captured as a by-product from other business equipment. The director of this installation is particularly proud of this arrangement because the user was responsible for the accuracy of the data. So the data was in a machine intelligible format and also verified before arriving at the computer center. Other characteristics of good input control would include the following:

Use of check digits to quickly validate control fields.

Use of a control card to record the batch control total, so that the computer can make the comparison and indicate any difference.

Have the printer show that this comparison was made so that this confirmation will show in the future.

Making a list of all rejected transactions that have not been processed by the system.

Making sure that all rejected transactions are corrected and subsequently reentered.

HARDWARE CONTROLS

The auditor at one time looked upon the computer as a sort of "super-clerk" whose posted columns had to be checked and rechecked. Through experience, the auditor has since grown to respect machine accuracy. Certainly more so than some careless operators or egotistical programmers who usually blame errors on the computer.

I think the manufacturers have provided a very accurate piece of equipment. The auditor in his evaluation may ask you what error checking features are available on your equipment, in which case you should tell him about the validity and parity checks, tape error checking, disk write checks, and whatever else you have.

The auditor is also interested in the downtime log for the equipment. You as the manager should know what kind of trouble you have been experiencing, how often it has occurred, how long you have had to wait for service, and your evaluation of the effectiveness of the manufacturer's preventative maintenance activity.

Any discussion of error detection features leads to a discussion of recovery procedures. Are these steps completely described in the operator's manual or is there a small note saying "see Joe Jones" and incidentally Joe Jones programmed the job 12 months ago and has since left the company.

As I already mentioned, the auditor respects the hardware controls supplied by the manufacturer, so he should spend little time here. However, there are some lemons and there is some deterioration with age. The auditor expects you to know the condition of the equipment and to be able to document any unsatisfactory conditions.

SOFTWARE CONTROLS

In the area of software controls are the facilities supplied by the manufacturer. With third generation equipment the dividing line between hardware and software has become obscured. But let us include in the area of software controls label checking on disk and tape files. This file identification is contained on header labels. A good practice is to check and file before using it.

There are also trailer labels at the end of the file to record hash totals and the like to detect instances where records may not have been processed. Using these features certainly provides the auditor with greater assurance of your ability to process data correctly.

Remember we are discussing these manufacturer's programs under the framework of internal control. Manufacturer's utility programs such as those that sort files or print tape or disk contents means that there is a greater division of duties. So for applications where the use of this software is appropriate, this independence is viewed favorably by the auditor. Current operating systems supplied by the computer manufacturer provide an additional opportunity for system control. The auditor would recommend this as a favorable condition.

PROGRAM CONTROL

Under the heading of program control would be the checks you have in your own written programs. These would be the checks you use to insure the accuracy and the quality of the data. The major difficulty that auditors find in this function is the tendency of some installations to depend too much on the garbage-in, garbage-out explanation. *In these installations the programmer has been made an extension of the hardware rather than an extension of the user,* for the machine will multiply any two figures together and produce an answer. For the programmer to do the same thing is not as excusable. The programmer can add his own intelligence. If the use of 200 hours produced a weekly payroll check of $800 something is probably wrong. If an incentive pay calculation produces work performances of 400%, this too is suspect. If programmers act like the machines rather than like systems analysts, both the installation and the auditor are likely to have trouble.

The judicious use of limit tests, reasonableness test, and cross footings as portions of the processing program gives the auditor greater confidence in the quality of the information prepared.

OUTPUT CONTROLS

The features of output control are those which pertain to the quality and distribution of the reports produced by the system. The auditor may ask for a list of reports. Such a list should be available together with the indication of who gets the report and how often it is due. As data processing gets further into information systems the department will be undoubtedly handling more and more top management information. Some of this will be confidential. The number of copies, who is on the distribution list, and the security of the files, will become of more importance. Someone might question why the operator is running a 2-part confidential report on 4-part paper. Maybe he wants to save putting in the correct part paper, but he is not following company procedures and following procedures is something the auditor is very interested in.

SYSTEM CONTROLS

System controls is likely to get the most attention from the auditor. Included here is the whole function of system documentation. It is in the area of system documentation that the control and efficiency of a data processing installation is most accurately portrayed.

The system objective should be shown in narrative form. This should explain what is being done, why it is being done, and what processes will be used. There should be a systems flowchart showing the design and how the pieces fit together and all the inputs and outputs with the processing runs identified. There should be a listing of valid transaction codes and an explanation of their meaning. There should be operator instructions. In many installations this is the only documentation available outside the program listing itself. There should also be record and card layouts. These are usually available but not always up-to-date.

Some auditors like to ask for program flowcharts. I would too, but only for new applications, preferably before they go on. As time goes on, they become too inaccurate to be reliable.

Of course, the program listing, should be available. It usually is.

The big problem here, particularly with second generation equipment, is the likelihood that the object program contains patches. These patches may not be adequately identified or explained.

Last, we come to a real rarity. The auditor would like to know when and why a program gets changed. He would like to see some kind of request and approval of change forms in use. The auditor might have to vary his audit program to recognize that a program was changed during the year to accommodate a new procedure.

USING THE COMPUTER

The auditor may use the computer at some point during the audit. He may want to test the system to verify its compliance with the stated procedures. The auditor might ask the data processing manager to prepare a special program. Many times this will result in a program that is also useful to management. This could be in the nature of a program aging accounts receivable or a series of programs involving the periodic physical inventory.

Some auditors will have programs of their own to test computer processing. These programs could involve checking extensions of fields, making printouts, or making a statistical sample selection of a file. By their origin one can see that these programs are intended to be generalized.

What is needed in all cases is cooperation between the auditor and the data processing installation. This cooperative effort requires both people time and computer time. It requires a mutual appreciation of the responsibilities of all concerned.

In closing we are reminded that some time ago someone wrote in the *CDP Newsletter* that there should be more accounting questions on the CDP exam because the CPA firms were trying to take over data processing. Well he had the right solution but the wrong reason. I have been submitting accounting questions for this exam now for a number of years. Certainly the accounting profession would like your profession to keep accounting in mind when you design systems. However, you need not be concerned that the CPA wants anything to do with the management of your operation. The CPA has long prided himself on being independent. Without this independence his value is nil. He has managed to keep this professional independence when management reports were produced by the accounting system. He will strive to keep this independence regardless of what kind of information system provides these management reports.

The CPA firm will offer your firm almost any service you want as long as it doesn't interfere with its "attest" function. Because we are professionals, CPA firms respect each other. Because you are professionals, we likewise respect you.

AUDITING IN THE NEW SYSTEMS ENVIRONMENT

by Jerome Lobel

To hit a moving target, you have to aim ahead of it. And if the target is accelerating, you must aim much farther ahead.

In essence, this portrays the dilemma the professional auditor faces today, as a result of the increasing use of electronic computers. Three major questions surround this moving-target problem:

First, what particular aspects of the new data processing systems environment should concern an auditor?

Second, how successfully has the profession demonstrated its ability to audit the present computer systems?

Third, what types of plans and actions are necessary to assure that the profession can carry forward its responsibilities in the new systems environment of the 1970's?

NEW SYSTEMS ENVIRONMENT

The new systems environment has grown out of four generations of computer technology:

1. The first generation of computer systems spanned the years 1946 to 1957 and was characterized by use of the vacuum tube, which represented the first application of electronic components of this type for a computational device.

First-generation computers introduced the concept of the "stored program." They placed emphasis on computing ability rather than upon input-output capabilities.

Input first consisted of punched cards and punched paper tape. Magnetic tape was introduced as an important medium of external storage in 1953.

Reprinted by permission of the publisher from *The Journal of Accountancy*, September 1971, pp. 63-67, copyright 1971 by the American Institute of Certified Public Accountants, Inc.

Storage units employed "electrostatic tubes," "mercury acoustic delay lines," "magnetic drums" and "magnetic core storage."

2. The second generation of computer systems was introduced approximately in 1958, when transistors first were used in commercial computers.

Transistorized—or solid-state—circuitry resulted in improved speed, reliability and lower cost.

Internal storage was characterized by magnetic core elements in most computer systems, magnetic drum storage in some small-scale systems and the introduction of thin-film memory in 1960.

An increased range of input and output capabilities also became available, including magnetic and optical character readers, high-speed magnetic tape units and data transmission devices and communications equipment.

3. The third, or present, generation of computer systems is characterized by integrated circuitry, which makes use of extremely small silicon chips. These chips serve basically the same function as vacuum tubes and transistors in previous generations. Integrated circuitry has increased substantially internal processing speeds and reduced power requirements.

Third-generation computers are also characterized by a considerable change in computer design and system philosophy. These systems combine the capabilities of a scientific computer and a business computer within a single machine. They are modular in design; they provide a broad variety of input-output capabilities—including such features as audio-response units and graphic display and plotters—and they place increased emphasis on communications and the need for data transmission over communication lines.

Systems capabilities include *multiprograming,* which is the processing of several different jobs at the same time within a single machine; *real-time* operation, or the ability to respond immediately to incoming data; *continuous processing* of a job stream; *interrupt capabilities;* and the ability to serve numerous remote terminals which may be transmitting data simultaneously.

We are now supposed to be on the verge of entering the fourth generation, or what might be called the new systems environment.

In concentrating on this new systems environment, the impression may be given that little can be done to improve appreciably the present, or third-generation, systems audits.

Much can be done to improve current computer systems' auditing practices. The problem, however, is that we are presently aiming so far behind the moving target that to change our overall approach it is necessary to advance our sights by a considerable margin.

This means that auditors must now line up their sights on the training that will be needed, and the techniques that will have to be developed, if the same auditing dilemmas of the 1960's and early 1970's are not to be repeated.

FOURTH GENERATION

There is presently a general disagreement in the computer industry about exactly what this new fourth-generation environment is going to look like. There is general unanimity, however, that the new systems will be delivered and implemented long before the present decade is over.

That this is a reasonable prediction may be demonstrated by the fact that IBM, the industry leader, already has announced its IBM 370 product line.

Experts think the fourth-generation hardware/software environment, technically, will look this way:

1. *Graceful degradation.* This means computers will never shut down from a problem such as power failure to the extent of losing the data being processed at a given time.

2. *Advanced memory systems.* The new memories will be able to store much more information in a smaller space at a significantly lower cost.

3. *Information utilities.* Data processing and communication systems are being integrated to improve total information systems, and to provide what is being referred to as "three-dimensional" information systems. These systems permit computing in three modes concurrently: Local and remote batch processing; time-sharing; and remote access to a central data storage facility.

Just as we presently license telephone and electric companies, we may have to license computer communications utilities.

4. *Common or shared data banks and networks.* These will be implemented to permit extensive sharing of information by users who have common information needs. The data banks will be an outgrowth of technical advances in computer memories, communications equipment and related software.

What all of this progress means is this:

1. More information than ever before is going to be stored in smaller and smaller "black boxes."
2. Information will be more quickly and concurrently accessible to users—at their desks, offices and homes—or wherever they may happen to be.
3. Information will be shared to a greater degree than ever thought possible before, by the middle of the 1970's. This means that the shared data bank is essentially on top of us.

Successful technical accomplishment in the areas listed above has been astounding. For instance, a recent laboratory experiment demonstrated a device that is able to store several hundred thousands of computer words on an area as small as the cross-section of a human hair. This device could store on a memory device the size of a human hand a trillion words and figures. This is somewhere near the present storage capacity of all of the world's present computers.

In another case, the ILLIAC IV, presently being built by Dr. Daniel L. Slotnick in Paoli, Pennsylvania, is estimated to have the processing capacity of all of the other computers in the world combined. According to the November 1970 *National Geographic Magazine,* it is estimated that this computer would contain 256 processing elements and should be able to perform a billion calculations every second.

THE AUDITOR

And what effect will these many technical advances have on the auditor?

First, the tremendous additional quantity of information that is going to be held in the new memories and mass storage devices will make the systems more valuable for accounting business data processing purposes. On the other hand, they also will become more susceptible to manipulation and accidental or intentional destruction. Internal control problems become much more critical. Problems involving human error in present systems can become transformed into even more serious problems, if they are allowed to, in the fourth-generation systems environment.

Second, the accessibility of information with the new communication terminals can be considered both a blessing and a catastrophe. For example, we will encounter the potentially serious problem of the disappearing audit trail. Unless planning for this is intentional, it is easy to see how tempting it will be to avoid completely the creation of a source document—or even some form of transaction log—when almost all of the original data comes in through a machine-readable keyboard or other type of input device.

Third, the shared data bank can become a system nightmare in the event of unauthorized or accidental data access.

The whole subject of computer data bank and communications security, all of a sudden, appears as something that should be thoroughly understood by every responsible systems auditor.

PRESENT EDP AUDIT SUCCESS

The second major question surrounding the moving-target problem was, how successful are the audits of our present computer systems?

Auditors have long held themselves responsible for reviewing and appraising the soundness of operating controls; for ascertaining the extent of compliance with established policies, plans and procedures; and for ascertaining the extent to which company assets are accounted for and safe-guarded from losses of all kinds.

With the advent of EDP, many auditors have been somewhat shocked to find so many new business information systems being implemented with what often appears to be serious disregard for basic internal control principles. This dismay is usually justified. Audits normally reveal weak internal controls and raise serious questions about the competence of key data processing personnel.

Although not consistently so, the auditor discovers that the data processing organization simply cannot be relied on to provide adequate controls within the computer systems that they themselves design and implement.

Some of the underlying reasons that tend to support this situation are:

1. EDP personnel often do not have enough detailed familiarity with all of the control requirements directly and indirectly related to the applications that they are responsible for automating.
2. The orientation of most EDP personnel is related more to technical design and accomplishment than operating effectiveness. They think that they are primarily responsible for getting the system designed, debugged and "on the air." In addition, they tend to believe that this is the basis on which they will be evaluated or measured, come salary review time.
3. Important policy and procedural decisions are being made by relatively low levels of staff in the company's EDP operation. Many of these decisions involve controls, but too often the people mak-

ing the decisions do not have sufficient background or authority to make them. They do make these decisions, however, in the absence of other management direction.
4. Controls once included in the initial design or even implemented are occasionally ignored or deleted from the system without the approval or knowledge of responsible individuals.
5. EDP staffs attempt to design systems that will operate at lowest cost and greatest speed. The inclusion of internal control devices works against this objective.

For these reasons, auditors are finally getting involved. They are assigned broader responsibilities and are being directed to participate in EDP systems design, at least to the degree that they outline the controls that need to be incorporated in the new system.

Considerable improvement in data processing systems design and integrity is expected to result from these actions. For example, auditors:

1. Are beginning to have an opportunity to contribute their own strong backgrounds to the design of necessary controls included in the EDP system.
2. Are in a much better position to review the testing, operation and continuance of EDP controls.
3. Can assist in the discovery of EDP control violations.
4. Can assist the EDP operation by adding materially to the overall quality assurance of the computer system. The auditor can design and use his own EDP internal control questionnaire or checklist to assist him when conducting his EDP audits.

In addition, many auditors have become familiar with and are capable of using all of the current or state-of-the-art system auditing techniques, including auditing around the computer, auditing with the computer and auditing through the computer.

Unfortunately, the press of meeting daily schedules has prevented many auditors from taking enough time out from their daily work to acquire the right training and to develop enough confidence in the more advanced techniques. Yet this is exactly the reason for much of the auditing profession's dilemma in dealing with third-generation systems.

With the fourth generation poking its challenging head just around the corner, it would seem that there is a call for some drastic action.

ANTICIPATING FOURTH-GENERATION AUDIT REQUIREMENTS

The solution to the fourth-generation or new systems environment audit problems requires prompt attack in four major areas.

First, there is a language barrier. Like many other professions, including auditing, the data processing industry is full of buzzwords, like multiprogramming, time-sharing, real-time, on-line, multiprocessing and many others. However, none of the basic concepts of business data processing are beyond the capacity of the average auditor. Equally important, there are many data processing professionals who might have more than just a slight problem understanding auditing.

This communications gap between auditing and data processing can easily be cleared up with a concerted training or retraining effort on the part of both professions. And this is not a one-time proposition; it must go on continuously if anyone is going to be able to hit the moving target discussed earlier.

From a training viewpoint, what should an auditor know?

1. He should know and understand what he sees when he enters the computer systems environment. That is, he must recognize how and why the data are manipulated by the system, how the system is organized and how effective are its internal controls.
2. He should be able to identify visually all of the major system components and be able to discuss the functions of these components in a fairly lucid manner with the people who design, program or operate the system.
3. He should be able to recognize the important weaknesses and strengths that affect the internal control of the particular systems he is responsible for auditing.
4. He should be able to recommend changes in the design or operation of the system that may be needed to resolve potential control problems.

Obviously, training cannot make a computer expert in a matter of days and weeks. The value of the training can only enhance the already proven expertise of an auditor.

Second, there is a need to concentrate more on principles. For the most part, there is very little difference between the principles of auditing in an EDP environment and the principles of auditing in a manual systems environment.

For example, EDP does not lessen in any way the need for evaluating and testing the internal control system. The differences that do exist are:

1. The fact that computer hardware is involved.
2. The fact that the auditor may have to acquire new techniques

or tools in order to continue to do his job effectively.

3. The fact that the auditor has a greater opportunity than ever before to contribute his special knowledge to the design of the systems that will eventually be so important to his job.

The basic internal control principles do not change merely because the data are being processed or stored in a computer.

Third, there is a need for auditors to accept more responsibility. Auditors should:

1. Be consulted about the development of new applications.
2. Recommend control features for proposed applications.
3. Introduce any needed control changes to existing applications.
4. Review documentation practices and changes to programs.
5. Review deviations from the planned operations schedule.

Of course, evaluation of the system of internal control, and evaluation of the records produced by the system must be maintained as basic objectives. Also, the classic areas of concern with regard to internal control, including organization, input, processing and output, must remain the same.

The answer to successful computer auditing is learning how to recognize these basic functions wherever they exist in the computer-oriented system.

Incidentally, it would be very helpful if more auditors were familiar enough with the computer to use its own power to make the audit easier, since EDP systems often are much more complex than manual systems.

Fourth, there is the opportunity to implement what is called "on-line auditing." The future will show that after-the-fact auditing will become increasingly more difficult, and that drastic innovation is going to be required if audits in the new system environment are going to have as much meaning as, or even more meaning than, they do today.

On-line auditing involves the implementation of special programmed controls recommended by the auditor. The controls are those which, if always operable, will assure the auditor that the system is continuously guarding against the processing of illegal transactions or of incomplete or inaccurate data.

Periodic audits of a computer-oriented system will be made much easier by use of the on-line auditing concept. This is also a concept which should be considered in all systems which, themselves, are basically on-line or communications-oriented.

Communications-oriented data processing systems often process transactions at very high speeds and in such ways that it is impossible for periodic audits to test adequately the integrity of the system or even the validity of all the records being processed.

Where master records, for instance, are being constantly updated by on-line or real-time processing, there is almost no other way but through on-line auditing to assure that the system is under control at all times. Even where each transaction is recorded or saved for later evaluation, the large number of subsequent transactions may make auditing and recovery extremely difficult.

On-line systems permit the logical extension of traditional audit concepts to a point at which, for the first time, an auditor is able to devote himself *totally* to the concept of "audit by insight."

What makes this possible are the following system features described by Downs, Harlow and Hudson in their article "On-Line Bank Auditing."[1]

1. All the actual record compilation is done remotely [i.e. on magnetic media].
2. The basic elements of audit control (repetitive tasks such as condition verification, totalling, validating and balancing) are separated from the auditor's primary task of investigation.

The result, according to the authors, should be operational program confidence. It is upon the acceptance of this concept that all normal on-line auditing depends.

The authors also contend that the best way to achieve "audit by insight" is for the auditor to demand "program confidence." That is, programs must demonstrate that they:

1. Are designed to maintain the controls desired.
2. Are operating correctly 100 per cent of the time.
3. Are not being tampered with.

The result of this confidence will be the ability to eliminate all the daily or periodic controls necessary in a manual system. The reason for this is that once a computer has been introduced to do something and it is established that the computer is doing it, the computer will continue to do it until instructed to do something else.

---

[1]Melvin T. Downs, Walter A. Harlow, and Charles W. Hudson, "On-Line Bank Auditing," *NAA Bulletin,* January 1965, p. 57.

Further, the authors contend that the information is completely up to date, that criteria are applied instantly during processing and that criteria are applied to every account, not just a sample.

To date, there has not been an adequate amount of research performed or literature published on on-line auditing. This is rather unfortunate, since it is the understanding and rapid implementation of these techniques that will produce the most encouraging results in audits in the new systems environment.

There is still time to take deliberate aim at this advancing new systems environment. But like any accelerating target, it can move by extremely fast if the planning and the aiming are not far enough ahead of it.

EDP AUDITING—THE COMING OF AGE

by Geoffrey B. Horwitz

Lately many auditors have been getting understandably nervous at predictions that clients with computer systems are shortly going to have "unauditable" systems—unauditable, at least, in the traditional sense. They have difficulty reconciling the disparity between what they hear and what they see among their clients, but the apprehension remains.

For some years, auditors have been increasingly confronted by such EDP jargon as "test deck," "on-line systems" and "data bank," yet most of them have problems relating the terms to their own practices.

Auditors, beleaguered by such conflicts, do not yet appear to have found a group identity and, as a result, tend to believe either that nothing of significance is going on in the field of EDP or that the audit of computer systems is an esoteric field best left in the hands of EDP specialists.

Unquestionably, there *is* movement taking place in the field of EDP auditing; it may be a little slow, but the past year has seen some significant new developments. The objective of this article is to bring into focus the subject of EDP auditing and to predict what the immediate future direction will be in this area.

THE CHANGING ENVIRONMENT

The surge of interest in EDP auditing which has taken place in the

---

Reprinted by permission of the publisher from *The Journal of Accountancy,* August 1970, pp. 48-56, copyright 1970 by the American Institute of Certified Public Accountants, Inc.

last three or four years has been the predictable by-product of the increasing use of the computer. Much valuable work has been done to refine techniques for the audit of computer-based accounting systems. Even if the number of computers installed were to remain static—which it will not—there is already enough momentum to sustain a steady flow of new developments in the area of auditing such systems. But the computer field is anything but static, and the expected growth over the next five years will far outdistance anything that has happened in the EDP area to date.

Viewed numerically, the number of computers installed within the United States has doubled, and is expected to continue to double every three years:

1960— 5,000 installations
1963— 11,000 installations
1966— 22,000 installations
1969— 50,000 installations (plus 16,000 on order)
1972—100,000 installations (projection)
1975—200,000 installations (projection)

Recent surveys have shown that, of the above installations, most are being used extensively for the maintenance of accounting records and related financial information. This is likely to remain true for the foreseeable future.

In addition to numerical growth, we are on the brink of significant developments in the areas of systems and hardware. Implementation of the much-heralded Management Information Systems, Integrated Systems and Real-Time Systems is progressing more slowly than anticipated. Nevertheless, progress is being made and, within the near future, new and complex dimensions will be added to the computer system and to the related audit.

Although punched cards have traditionally accounted for about 95 per cent of all computer input, this, too, will be changing. A multitude of new input devices (such as magnetic tape encoders, industrial data collectors, cathode display screens and optical character readers) which have been introduced on the market are rapidly gaining acceptance; these innovations will no doubt lead to novel and increasingly complex systems.

These changes will result in greater involvement on the part of the auditor. Until now a substantial percentage of auditors have avoided meaningful contact with the computer; this will no longer be possible. By weight of numbers alone the computer will force itself onto the auditor's attention, so that a knowledge of EDP is bound to become a requirement of almost every CPA. Beyond this, as new minds focus on the problems, and as the problems themselves become more complex, possibilities will be evolved encompassing:

- New control requirements for the new systems (e.g., memory protection and postfact batch balancing).
- New techniques for gaining audit assurance that the controls are operating effectively (e.g., test decks).
- New methods of using the computer to help automate the audit function (e.g., audit software, test data generators).
- Increasing involvement with preinstallation systems development (e.g., integrated testing facilities).

COMPUTER SPECIALIST OR AUDITOR?

There are many EDP terms which are regarded as commonplace and are easily recognized by most CPAs. Examples are "master file," "software," "memory dump"—even the term "EDP" itself. Yet only five years ago, most of these terms would not have been recognized or understood.

This familiarity with computer terminology is indicative, partly, of a significant transformation in the auditors' *willingness* to become involved in computer operations. One rarely encounters the type of resistance today that was so commonplace in 1965. At that time it was not unusual for the auditor to insist that the computer could be circumnavigated. "I don't have to learn to operate an accounting machine in order to perform an audit, so why do I have to learn about computers?" was a standard comment. There was a feeling that if the adding machine could be built to add correctly, it was only a matter of time before computer output would be equally accurate. In other cases, where grudging recognition was given to the importance of reviewing the programmed controls, it was felt that this was the domain of the computer specialist and not of the auditor.

The former attitude is changing: today the auditor readily recognizes the need for reviewing the computer system and controls. He recognizes the difference between the hardware which is exceedingly reliable and the program which may contain numerous loopholes or other deficiencies.

Nevertheless, there is still a minority of the profession who have had in-depth exposure to computer systems and there is still a considerable reluctance on the part of most auditors to get involved. In too many cases the auditor has not equipped himself with a solid core of technical knowledge, and prefers to turn over to a computer specialist all aspects of the audit that pertain to computer operations. In this context, "computer specialist" does not necessarily mean "EDP audit specialist." The term includes members of the management services staff with diverse backgrounds in the EDP area but with no particular training or experience in auditing. This is regrettable; there is no other aspect of the audit from which the auditor wishes to abdicate.

As a sidelight, it is noteworthy that at the 1969 AICPA Computer Users' Conference a well-respected member of the profession, in a major address, devoted most of his not inconsiderable rhetorical skill to decrying the fact that EDP professionals obscure their meaning by adopting esoteric jargon. The message was as clear as it was well-received: that if only EDP people would speak English, the entire problem of EDP would go away! While part of his attack was made in jest, it does reflect a recurrent attitude on the part of auditors who feel that they ought to be able to absorb whatever is relevant through osmosis. This is not an attitude they normally adopt toward taxes or statistical sampling. Would a standard deviation by any other name be easier to comprehend? But as regards computers, the prevailing mood is still to stop far short of adequate involvement.

This, of course, is a peculiar form of short-sightedness. EDP is *not* a modern hieroglyphic constructed to exclude the uninitiated. It is a precise vocabulary which attempts to describe without ambiguity some very important concepts and techniques, and it behooves the auditor to make an effort to learn it. It does not require a large investment of time, and it is an investment well made. One thing is certain: with the passage of time, the language of the EDP professional will not get any easier!

The AICPA, through its professional development courses and publications, has given some recognition to the problem, and individual members of the profession are lowering their resistance. They will *have* to, to adequately service the fourfold increase in computers between 1969 and 1975. In doing so, they will be propelled by the younger people now entering the profession to whom EDP is a word which conjures up visions of modernity and efficiency, rather than complexity and mystery. It seems highly probable that the wise step of the AICPA in including questions on EDP in the Uniform CPA Examination will give a powerful additional impetus to the younger generation to "do their homework" in the area of computer concepts and terminology.

To fill the gap, a new breed of auditor has emerged: the EDP audit specialist, with a good mix of both skills. At present such people are rare. Ironically, the special insights and techniques which these people have developed is not a source of undiluted satisfaction; many of them would gladly trade their mystique for a more nuts-and-bolts type of mutual understanding with their colleagues. Be that as it may, we should recognize that, in auditing as in any other sphere of human activity, today's brain-tickler becomes tomorrow's platitude. The auditing complexities of today will become the standard tools of tomorrow's generation, and the avant-garde specialists will move on to newer and more challenging fields. There will, of course, always be specialists, but, as the communications gap is closed, their role will change.

However, this narrowing of the communications gap will not take place without the full intellectual commitment of those auditors who feel compelled to move with the tide; the fate of those who do not make this commitment will be to find the communications gap broadening, rather than getting narrower.

THE IMPACT OF EDP ON THE AUDIT APPROACH

The existence of a computer can influence the conduct of the audit in many ways. Stated succinctly, the basic steps in performing an audit (whether or not the system is automated) include:

- Gaining an understanding of the system.
- Reviewing the adequacy of the controls to ensure completeness and accuracy of the recording and processing of accounting data.
- Confirming that the system and related controls are functioning as described.
- Performing additional testing of the closing balances. In determining the scope of such additional work, the auditor would normally take into consideration his evaluation of the effectiveness of the system and its controls.

In each of these broad steps, the computer is likely to have an impact on the audit approach. It is difficult to conceive of an auditor with no familiarity with EDP being able to truly understand the system, let alone come to any meaningful opinion regarding the adequacy of the controls. For example, in a perpetual inventory system, how can an auditor be assured that the correct record on tape (or disk) has been updated unless he has some awareness of file organization, magnetic header labels and file update procedures? How can he satisfy himself that all records have been processed unless he understands the nature of batch controls and trailer records?

In many instances, especially where the system is simple, the auditor may be able to skirt the computer and obtain his audit assurances by means of extensive examination of detailed printouts, where these exist. But what a price to pay for the questionable privilege of conducting an audit without an awareness of the system's weak and strong links.

To the author, then, it is a platitude that an understanding of systems and controls is fundamental to a good audit. It is not a voluntary option which is open to the auditor.

Once the basic review skills have been mastered, there are a number of additional options which are entirely voluntary. These are all in the area of what is called, somewhat misleadingly, "auditing through" the computer. Although relatively new and unexplored, there are many rewards to be gained from an involvement in this area. This subject will be treated later in this article.

WHITHER THE CONTROLS REVIEW?

In reviewing the EDP controls it has become quite standard to use a formal controls questionnaire.[2]

Most of the questionnaires in use today are designed to deal with sequential, batch process operations. Rarely do they include any searching questions pertaining to random process applications, whether in a batch or real-time environment, which are still felt to be the domain of the computer specialist. Inevitably, with the ever-widening spread of random access processing, the emphasis of questionnaires must change.

In the past, these control questionnaires have often not been treated as an integrated part of the audit. The questionnaire has been viewed as an end in itself, designed to serve as a source for comments or suggestions to management. It has not always been viewed as a step in the total audit process. The auditor has not always considered the extent to which the control findings, read in the context of the *total* system with the presence or lack of compensating controls, permit or necessitate changes in the audit program. Further, in performing cradle-to-grave procedural testing, inexperienced auditors tend to treat the computer system as a separate entity. In this way, it is easy to overlook systems weaknesses at the point of transfer of information (and often also of control) between EDP and user groups. Many auditors who have examined the point of interface between departments have identified a control weakness which existed because of misunderstandings between EDP and non-EDP personnel.

As part of the continuous learning process, there are likely to be additional subtle but meaningful changes in emphasis. For example, the pattern of computer frauds (or rather, those few which have received publicity) has focused attention on the need for adequate segregation of duties between computer personnel, especially between the functions of programming, operating and control-checking.

---

[2]An excellent questionnaire is in *Auditing and EDP* by Gordon Davis (AICPA, 1968).

Also, many auditors who assiduously review controls of input into the computer are ambivalent in their attitudes toward checking the run-to-run controls over the numerous programs and processing cycles, especially as one application area may comprise 50 or more individual programs. Little attention has been given to establishing guidelines for the identification and selection of *significant* control points. Clearly, it is neither practical nor necessary to review in detail every program comprising an application area; normally it is possible to balance the final computer output against the appropriate inputs without an in-depth review of all of the intermediate controls.

As a by-product of growing self-confidence, auditors may soon be willing to encounter the more sophisticated type of third-generation system which is beginning to emerge, and the new control patterns that will follow. For instance, the advent of direct entry devices (the movement toward so-called source data automation) is likely, within the next two or three years, to radically alter some of our notions regarding batch controls. Briefly stated, with today's systems it is common to accumulate source documents describing transactions into homogeneous batches, and then move them between departments under batch control (normally an adding-machine tape with an accumulated total). At points in the processing cycle and especially on input into the computer, the individual records are balanced back to the batch control. In the case of direct entry devices, however, there is no delay while a batch is being accumulated. As each transaction occurs, the data is transmitted to the computer. Frequently, by the time the next transaction occurs, the first one has already been completely processed and may have served to update one or more historical records. New, experimental techniques are being devised to assure the accuracy and comprehensiveness of data being so processed; often, this includes postfact batch-proving, with complex procedures for isolating and correcting errors which slipped through.

USING THE COMPUTER IN THE AUDIT

For many years, the auditor has recognized the possibility of using the computer to help perform audit steps. Specifically, he has often spoken about

- Computer programs designed or written by the auditor to help test the client's data.
- Test decks,i.e., hypothetical data designed by the auditor to test the client's programs.

Phrased differently, the former is useful primarily as a tool in the validation of closing balances, whereas the latter is useful as a tool in the procedural testing phase of the audit.

The orientation of our thinking has changed significantly in recent years. For most of the latter part of the sixties, it was believed that these techniques were rapidly becoming obligatory rather than optional.

The argument ran briefly as follows:

The audit trail is eroding. The computer can compute at electronic speeds, but it can print only at mechanical speeds, which are much slower. Further, what is printed can only be read at human speeds. Therefore, effective utilization of the computer demands that we use the computer to perform detailed screening of data and have it print out only that information which is absolutely vital. Also, the advent of direct entry devices is pushing us further into an era in which there will be no hard-copy audit trail.

It seemed ironic that in the middle of a so-called "information explosion" in which the computer was being used to print out more information, and more meaningful information than had ever before been possible, the auditor should be the one person disadvantaged in the sense that he no longer had access to the data he needed. Time has not brought us perceptibly closer to this predicted destiny, and today some auditors are beginning to question seriously whether it ever will. It has been realized that in fact there is no such thing as an audit trail; what there is is a management trail. Management needs information, *detailed* information, not just summarized outputs, for many of its day-to-day operating problems. It uses this data for dealing with customers, vendors, employees—and the auditor merely walks in management's footsteps. There are real doubts regarding the extent to which this management trail will be able to erode.

The realistic expectation is probably the one which lies squarely in the middle of the road. The trail probably *will* erode—but only slightly. Availability of detailed computer printouts may well be restricted; but it seems probable that every well-designed system will have means for obtaining detailed listings on demand. The evolutionary trend may ultimately result in this detailed information being available by means other than on the printed page, such as via video display terminals. If there is to be any significant challenge to the auditor in this regard, it will probably be to those internal auditors or computer audit specialists who are directly involved in the preinstallation systems design aspects of management trail preservation.

For the independent auditor then, there is no immediate evidence of a disappearing audit trail which would *force* him to use test decks or computer programs as the only manner in which the audit could be accomplished. Any decision to use these approaches is likely for the foreseeable future to remain a free choice based on the economics of the situation and the availability of the appropriate EDP skills.

Possibly test decks, and, undoubtedly, computer audit programs will become increasingly commonplace. But this will be because of the interplay between rising costs of manual auditing, larger volumes of computer outputs to audit, and increasing facility in EDP auditing techniques.

THE FUTURE OF TEST DECKS

As mentioned previously, when the auditor has reviewed the system and the related controls as described to him by the client, the next step in the audit is to confirm that the system is functioning as described. This task, normally accomplished manually, is one which can be performed using the computer itself to process test data. The latter method is not much in vogue. There are perceptible developments which, in theory at least, could encourage the test deck approach, so that increasing use of this technique is to be anticipated, though it is unlikely that it will ever become a standard, commonplace tool of the auditor.

To put things into perspective, testing for compliance is normally a relatively simple task, using normal manual "cradle to grave" transaction testing techniques. In performing this phase of the audit, the auditor would make extensive use of computer printouts such as edit lists, transaction listings, control messages, etc. When the auditor has had an opportunity to work with computer printouts, he may find that the highly formalized computer system renders this transaction testing easier to perform than does a manual system. In fact, it is the opinion of the author that there is presently a tendency to give undue emphasis to this topic.

The test deck approach allows the auditor to simulate the types of transactions in which he is interested by means of hypothetical data which he (or the programmer) constructs. Where a test deck is used, it is normally necessary also to construct a hypothetical master file with which the data will interact. The ostensible advantages of a test deck are:

- Where the printed audit trail is difficult to follow, the impact of the test deck on the final report is easier to review.
- It gives the auditor greater freedom of choice over the types and combinations of transactions he wishes to review.

The former argument is valid *where* the audit trail is in fact obscure. As discussed earlier, however, there is no evidence that this is presently a significant problem. Further, the use of test decks poses some very major problems which, in the majority of cases, must outweigh any advantages:

- They are costly in terms of the time and skill required to construct the test data for the transactions and master file.
- They are costly to process, measured in terms of machine and operator time, especially where the system being audited involves a substantial number of programs.
- Alternatively, where test transactions are processed concurrently with "live" transactions, there is a substantial risk involved in the possibility that the accounting records might become accidentally contaminated or distorted. There are cases on record where this has happened, with a considerable resultant cost in tracing errors and correcting them.

In addition, too many unjustifiable claims have been made regarding the test deck's usefulness for testing, in many combinations, the various decision points and branches in the program. As any professional programmer knows only too well, the design of comprehensive test decks of this nature is an extremely challenging and time-consuming exercise; furthermore, the most ingenious and rigorous of test decks virtually never tests all of the functions of a program.

Thus for the foreseeable future, test decks will most likely be useful only in those occasional cases where the audit trail *has* eroded significantly. In virtually all other cases, any transaction types or combinations which have audit significance are likely to be more easily traced from historical hard copy. In exceptional cases where the hard copy does not answer all of the auditor's questions regarding system performance, audit assurance will be sought via a small, limited purpose test deck designed to trace the functioning of the program under a few specified conditions.

As mentioned earlier, there are some new developments which, over the longer term, might facilitate the use of test decks. There are test data generators and integrated test facilities.

TEST DATA GENERATORS

The "test data generator" is a generalized utility program, provided by many computer manufacturers, which generates (on cards, tape or disks) test data conforming to formats specified by the operator (or auditor). These generators are designed for the systems analyst/programmer to use in normal program development and check-out. They do not cater specifically to the auditor. Further, the experience of the author has been that, to date, these programs do not presently provide a satisfactory means for generating a compact set of test data containing a test of each logically feasible condition, though some limited use of them by auditors is to be anticipated.

Human ingenuity being what it is, some creative auditor will one day design a simple, automated way of generating a test deck with a definite audit orientation. Speculatively, it will provide the auditor with a means of describing the format and data content of the master and transaction files, and additional means for defining particular classes or ranges of data and specific relationships which are to be tested. However, any such development is still probably a few years away.

INTEGRATED TEST FACILITIES

The other development of significance concerns the experimentation being performed by a few giant computer users in the area of the so-called "mini-company" or "integrated test facility." In essence, this involves the designing of a new system which integrates permanent test data into the regular master file in a way that permits the auditor, on a demand basis, to process test transactions during normal live processing. This way he can continuously monitor the performance of the system. Safeguards are built into the system to prevent accidental contamination of live data. While systems of this nature provide an exciting intellectual challenge, they are proving to be very costly to construct, and may involve a continuing cost in the form of degraded overall system performance. Nevertheless, for the largest and most complex Management Information Systems, they are likely to prove not only viable but ultimately also valuable as a well-structured technique for guarding against unauthorized programming changes and for measuring the total effect of authorized changes.

THE BREAKTHROUGH: GENERALIZED COMPUTER PROGRAMS

The most important development in recent years—the one that more than any other demonstrates EDP auditing's imminent coming of age—is the generalized audit program. Of these, Auditape is best-known by virtue of its being the first to be made publicly available. Later arrivals, mostly bearing similar names such as Auditpak, Audassist, Audit-thru, Auditronic-16 and Audex have been similar in scope and objectives, though very diverse as regards the methodology.

A generalized computer audit program is a prewritten program designed to automate part of the audit by providing a selection of optional routines which can be readily adapted by the auditor to the requirements of a given audit situation.

The audit programs currently in use are all used to examine the clients' data, where these are stored on computer media such as magnetic tapes or disks or on punched cards. The type of functions they perform include:

- Checking extensions, as in an invoicing or payroll system.
- Checking the footing of a file (to tie back to a general ledger total or a control).
- Selecting items for further audit vouching by such criteria as random sample and stratified sample.
- Testing for certain types of conditions, such as credit balances.
- Comparing and matching data contained in separate computer files (e.g., to compare cost standards over a period of time).

A belief commonly held by auditors who have not used these programs is that they are designed to examine the client's *programs*. This is of course a misconception; the audit program is used to examine the end product of the program, namely the client's data after processing. It merely performs on a rigorous, highly automated basis the same type of audit scrutiny which the auditor has been doing clerically in the past. Of course, insofar as it may result in the auditor's validating the accuracy of the end product, it would give support or "comfort" to the view that the client's programs were operating as described, but this is not the primary objective.

EXAMPLES OF AVAILABLE PROGRAMS

Experience has been that these programs are likely to save substantial amounts of audit time, but only if used on a recurrent basis on the same audit application. The first time around, the set-up time and the time taken for co-ordinating with the client tend to result in minimal savings. Even where first-time savings have not been achieved, the automated approach may nevertheless result in significant benefits in the form of a more rigorous audit, better documentation and an enhanced understanding of the client's computer system.

As mentioned earlier, the methodology used by the numerous available programs is vastly different, and they differ also in terms of the range of equipment on which they can be used. It is beyond the scope of this article to discuss the differences or their implications in any detail, but a few examples will serve to illustrate the point:

- Auditape (Haskins & Sells), originally available only for the IBM 1401 (or 360 with emulator) is now also available for the IBM 360, Honeywell 200 and Spectra 70. Originally available only for tape systems, it can now be used on disk-oriented systems. Audassist (Alexander

Grant) was designed to process clients' tapes on an IBM 360. Auditpak (Lybrand, Ross Bros. & Montgomery) was written in a basic version of COBOL which makes it usable on any tape or disk machine with a COBOL compiler, regardless of the manufacturer.

• Auditape and Auditpak are self-contained programs where the auditor's task involves the filling out of printed specification sheets. Two other systems which are (at the time of writing) in field-testing status will adopt a different approach: they are intended to provide a simple, specialized programming language with which the auditor can develop his own audit programs.

• There are considerable differences in the amount of audit testing which can be performed in one pass of the data. In one benchmark test of which the author has knowledge, a given series of audit tests required in excess of 30 processing passes of the data files using one of the available audit programs, only 12 passes on a different program, and as few as 8 passes on a third.

The above illustrations are but a few of the numerous differences between the available programs. Clearly, there is no one "right" approach; all of them have their advantages and disadvantages, their weaknesses and strengths. Just as clearly, none of them are going to remain as permanent fixtures in their present form; Auditape is already in its second edition and it seems probable that it, and the other programs, will continue evolving and expanding over the years.

Will there ever be a single, universal audit software package in common use by all auditors? Ultimately, yes; in fact the question of joint participation in the design of such a language has already been debated by leading members of the profession, but to date no action has been taken. Probably what will occur (and in the author's opinion what *should* occur) will be that the large national firms will continue experimenting with a multitude of different approaches until a larger core of solid experience has been developed. Given the highly volatile and experimental state that now exists, a co-ordinated focus on only one approach at this time is likely to be premature.

Whatever the future direction, though, generalized computer programs are here to stay. Their potential for long-range time-saving is enormous; they result in a rigorous and well-documented audit; and they involve the auditor in a meaningful fashion with the computer, thus enhancing his knowledge of computers in general and of the client's system in particular. Most auditors who have had the opportunity to use these programs find it quite frankly a more enjoyable way of performing the audit.

SPECIAL-PURPOSE COMPUTER PROGRAMS

Paradoxically, exposure to the computer through generalized programs is bound to kindle a growing interest in specialized programs, i.e., programs especially written by (or for) the auditor for a specific audit objective. Generalized programs, however good they may be, do have and will continue to have limitations. The auditor will always encounter new audit situations for which the generalized program is not well suited. There will be more and more instances of auditors, their interest having been stimulated by experience with generalized programs, who will take the plunge and design (and maybe even code) a special program to cater to the particular audit situation at hand.

Among the most successful innovations of recent years has been the time-shared service bureau, whereby, through the use of terminal devices (normally teletypewriters) subscribers can access, on demand, a remote computer plus a library of programs and subroutines.

Although no statistics are available, there is evidence to suggest that many accounting firms are making extensive use of time-sharing, especially in the area of taxation and for the various functions associated with financial analysis and consulting. Sophisticated accounting firms are using it for model building; others may be using it for routine accounting functions such as accounts receivable or general ledger. In the area of pure and simple auditing, however, it does not seem to have found much relevance.

The major audit-oriented application is connected with statistical sampling: selection of sample sizes, generation of random numbers for sampling, and postsampling analysis of the results. A few firms have dabbled in other audit applications, such as ratio analysis, but with only limited success. A novel approach being used by one of these national accounting firms is in connection with their generalized audit software. Here, the auditor enters his file descriptions and other necessary information via a terminal, and uses the time-shared computer initially to screen this information for logical consistency, and then subsequently (as an optional feature) to compile the actual program deck.

There is room for debate and experimentation, but it seems unlikely that the next few years will lead to any greatly extended use by auditors of time-shared service bureaus for purely audit purposes, except, of course, in the statistical area. The main problem is the present slowness of the input and output functions, which makes remote time-sharing a technique primarily adaptable to complex processing of very limited quantities of data; normally this is the antithesis of what the auditor requires. It has been suggested that auditors might find it useful to load the client's data files into the service bureau computer by means of tape or disk (presumably hand-delivered to the bureau), and then to use the terminal for interrogative purposes only. This approach, which has been used experimentally, is costly and inconvenient, and is probably not going to appeal to many auditors.

On the other side of the coin, there may be increasing use by the auditor of a terminal located on the client's premises and tied on a time-shared basis to the client's computer. This type of usage is of the very essence of Management Information Systems. As mentioned elsewhere in this article, the implementation of MIS is much behind schedule, but progress *is* being made. When these systems arrive, it is entirely feasible that the auditor may use the terminal to refer to data records in the computer's random access files, and possibly even to screen them, or duplicate them and manipulate the copies in various ways for audit purposes (e.g., sort, stratify or subtotal them). Here is where some of the greatest challenges may lie for the creative auditor, especially one who is willing and has the opportunity to participate in the early systems design of new systems. Unfortunately, though, because of the limited number of such MIS systems, such an opportunity will be available to a small handful of only the most sophisticated EDP audit specialists.

SUMMARY: WHERE IT'S AT

Skeptics who have never been convinced that EDP auditing merits their serious study, and non-skeptics who by chance or skilled dodging have avoided a direct working relationship with the computer, are going to find that the "little black box" with all its peripheral trappings will have more and more impact on their professional lives. Professional auditors of some years' standing who have not yet made the commitment to come to grips with the terminology and technology (usually in the hope that it will either go away or get simpler) are likely to find themselves slipping further into the technical void. The outcome is likely to be a new form of generation gap between themselves and the younger, computer-minded graduates who are starting to emerge from college into the auditing field. In their own jargon, these kids know that computers are where it's at!

There is room for speculation and debate regarding the type of new computer systems the burgeoning EDP technology will be producing between now and 1975. To the author, it seems unlikely that these will include any significant number of "unauditable" systems. What there will be, undoubtedly, is a vastly increased number of EDP systems whose control features will require an intelligent and informed review. Beyond this, it seems unlikely that many auditors will find themselves *compelled* to audit "through" the computer, in the sense that they make direct use of the computer as the only effective means for performing the audit. However, many auditors will be electing to make use of the computer as a creative and rigorous way of performing the audit.

Where a computer is used, it will normally be the client's own computer, though there will be some use of remote time-sharing facilities, service bureaus and computer facilities on the auditor's premises. The programs to be used will be drawn from a rapidly expanding pool of sampling, stratification, comparison and analysis routines, some in the public domain and some developed privately. Though there will be increased activity in the area of special-purpose programs, most of the interest will be in the development of new forms of generalized software, possibly including also audit-oriented test data generators. And finally, there is likely to be limited movement into the area of continuous monitoring of EDP systems.

EDP auditing as a legitimate and significant component of the overall audit attest function can no longer be ignored. Five years ago it was viewed as a mysterious and esoteric science of questionable viability, to be nurtured, if at all, by a few intellectually capricious members of the profession. Anyone who still holds to this view had better take a good hard look; yesterday's frail baby is about to come of age!

GENERAL AUDIT TECHNIQUES IN DATA PROCESSING

by Corydon D. Hurtado

Astounding as it may seem, a broad technological gap exists between traditional auditing methods and the requirements imposed by data processing.

Tracing the development of this situation will shed some light on the potential problems of the future, and the requirements necessary to close the existing technological gap. These five questions will be answered:

- When did we first realize the need for auditing data processing as we think of it today?
- Who bears the final responsibility for successful performance of the audit?

Reprinted from *Data Management*, © by the Data Processing Management Association (October 1970).

- What are the current techniques used to audit data processing?
- Why should we be concerned about the auditing techniques?
- How will we face the problems imposed by advanced computer technology?

The auditor, being unfamiliar with the computer or the techniques utilized in data processing, developed his audit procedures to encompass the review of input documents and output reports.

The technological gap between the auditor and the data processor created new requirements for the auditor to complete his audit process. These new requirements were beyond the scope of his knowledge; and it was difficult for him to recognize the inadequacies within the data processing function.

These initial years encompassed what we could think of as "auditing around the computer," rather than "through it." What is the computer in the strictest sense of the word? A tool. A tool used in many different ways. A tool which the auditor failed to exploit to its fullest extent.

Problems began to develop within the computer function, causing erroneous processing and reporting. The auditor was now faced with some unique situations and was not certain about the solutions.

The computer didn't always present problems for the auditor. He soon discovered that it also offered some assistance. For example, it could be used to generate confirmation of account balances which was previously a manual task.

When the computer was utilized as merely an accounting tool, the problems encompassing the flow of input and output information were relatively simple. The necessary computer processing logic was also relatively uncomplicated.

As the computing capabilities increased and the internal processing logic became more complex, review of the input and output functions became substantially more difficult for the auditor.

He soon realized, that unless he was capable of understanding the requirements for controlling the computer process, he was risking the possibility of defalcation or simple operating errors that would otherwise go undetected.

The auditor began to seek solutions to these possible problem areas as they increased in importance and decided to use the computer. He began by extracting information that could be utilized by him for evaluating individual application areas.

For example, he might request a program that would select certain accounts from the accounts receivable master file. These selections would then be utilized to print the accounts receivable confirmations.

CURRENT TECHNIQUES UTILIZED

Current techniques can be categorized into three major areas:

1. The use of exception reporting and analysis — which is often accomplished through the use of input and output controls.
2. The use of sample selection techniques — an example of this technique would be the positive or negative confirmation.
3. The use of detailed testing and computation verification — the test deck and the trial balance are representative of this technique.

These techniques are being utilized primarily for the evaluation of specific applications or individual reporting areas.

The auditor will employ any, or all, of these tools to evaluate the accuracy of a specific computer program within a system. He may also request special file analysis runs to evaluate information that would otherwise be inaccessible.

However, in spite of these tests, the auditor has no assurance that other programs or other controls within a total data processing environment are adequate — nor will they provide him with a reliability factor for the over-all data processing function.

INADEQUACIES OF THE CURRENT TECHNIQUES

If we do not improve our audit techniques, we will not resolve the problems imposed by the present method. Among them:

1. The auditor's practice of evaluating around the computer.
2. Not utilizing the computer as a tool for performing audit functions which consists of more than printing confirmations or trial balances.
3. The auditor does not have complete control over the auditing functions when he utilizes client personnel for writing up his audit programs.
4. Only one part of the whole data processing system is evaluated.
5. The auditor loses the element of surprise associated with other auditing functions, such as a surprise cash count. He usually has to notify the data processing department well in advance of the audit.

MORE ADVANCED AUDIT EDP TECHNIQUES

The most interesting advance in the role played by the auditor involves his escape from the traditional financial audit.

He is now being charged with a broader responsibility for what we could call the "integrated audit program." This program encompasses not only the traditional financial audit, but also includes responsibility for reviews of management and operational functions.

It may well be that this new role will place the auditor in a position which will force him to utilize more computing technology, and so, close the technological gap.

However, individual companies are attempting to bridge this technological gap in their individual approach to auditing their data processing operations. They are evaluating their entire data processing function not just an individual application area. This new interest in a detailed evaluation of the over-all system of controls has been partially inspired by the accountant and partially by management.

Top management has at last begun to awaken to the need for sound control of all company functions and the need for constant review of its internal controls.

The review of these internal controls in data processing can be segregated into three major categories: organizational controls, administrative controls, and procedural controls.

ORGANIZATIONAL CONTROLS

Organizational controls affect the functional operation of each major operating unit in the data processing department. These operating units include: systems and programming, computer operations, the process control group, and the program and file storage library.

The auditor will review the plan of organization and functional responsibilities to determine whether there is a segregation of authorization, record-keeping, and custody of the assets.

Functional segregation is achieved by separating the systems analysis and programming function, the machine-operation function, the process control function, and the file storage library function.

Some questions to be asked about these organizational controls might be:

- Is the data processing department independent of all operating units that it services?
- Are functional units physically as well as organizationally separate?
- Are current organization charts available?
- How removed from top management is the data processing manager?

ADMINISTRATIVE CONTROLS

The auditor's evaluation of administrative controls consists primarily of a review in two major areas:

Systems design and programming—the auditor will be concerned with documentation standards and controls established within a departmental function. He also reviews the general systems procedures and existing programming standards to determine the adequacy of these controls.

Computer operation—the auditor will review and evaluate the production control and production recording methods that are utilized in the day-to-day operation of the computer installation.

During his review, the auditor might ask some of the following questions to evaluate administrative controls:

- Are there written systems standards and procedures?
- Is there a programming standards manual?
- Are program and console run-books adequately documented for each computer program?
- Are file retention procedures adhered to?
- Are master files stored under reasonable protective custody?

PROCEDURAL CONTROLS

A major consideration in the auditor's evaluation of internal control is determining the effectiveness of the data processing system in recording, processing, and reporting data.

These procedural controls could be classified into three major types: input, processing, and output.

Input controls include the procedures utilized in balancing input data to original control figures, and controlling the flow of this data through the data processing system.

Processing controls are associated with the internal computer processing techniques utilized in the programs that process the input data. They would also include the internal balancing techniques that control the flow of information between programs.

It is these highly technical procedural controls that create the most problems for the accountant who is not data-processing oriented. It is this point that has created the need for an intense program of education for the auditor in the techniques of computer processing. In addition, we see the skilled data processing professional being called upon to assist the auditor in his data processing review and analysis.

These procedural reviews are necessary to determine that financial and accounting procedures have been established and to assure that answers are available to the following questions:

- Does the process control group use a control log, or other positive method of recording input control totals?

- Are batch controls established prior to the preparation of input data, and is this data balanced to the controls prior to final processing?

- Do computer programs utilize validity check routines to detect loss or nonprocessing of data?

Output controls are utilized to determine the accuracy of the processing system. Here the auditor may ask:

- Do processing programs report errors or exceptions?

- Are output totals balanced to the original input control totals?

The two flow charts given here describe different auditing approaches to the preparation of accounts receivable confirmations on the computer.

The first flow chart describes a technique that would be utilized in most "traditional" auditing situations. This method is time consuming, expensive and leaves much to be desired.

The second flow chart outlines a considerably more sophisticated technique for accomplishing the same task. Here the computer is utilized to perform all aspects of verification of information in the accounts receivable master file in addition to the simultaneous selection and preparation of the confirmations.

Professional data processing personnel have made significant contributions in developing more sophisticated auditing programs. In the future, we will see the evolution of a new professional—the data processing accountant. He will be skilled in accounting methods and procedures, as well as having a first-hand working knowledge of data processing.

FUTURE PROBLEMS

The audit techniques used today still do not meet management's needs or offer solutions for the auditor. In short—the technological gap still exists. If we are behind in our approach to auditing data processing in the traditional job-shop environment, how will we handle the various control problems imposed by on-line and multiprocessing?

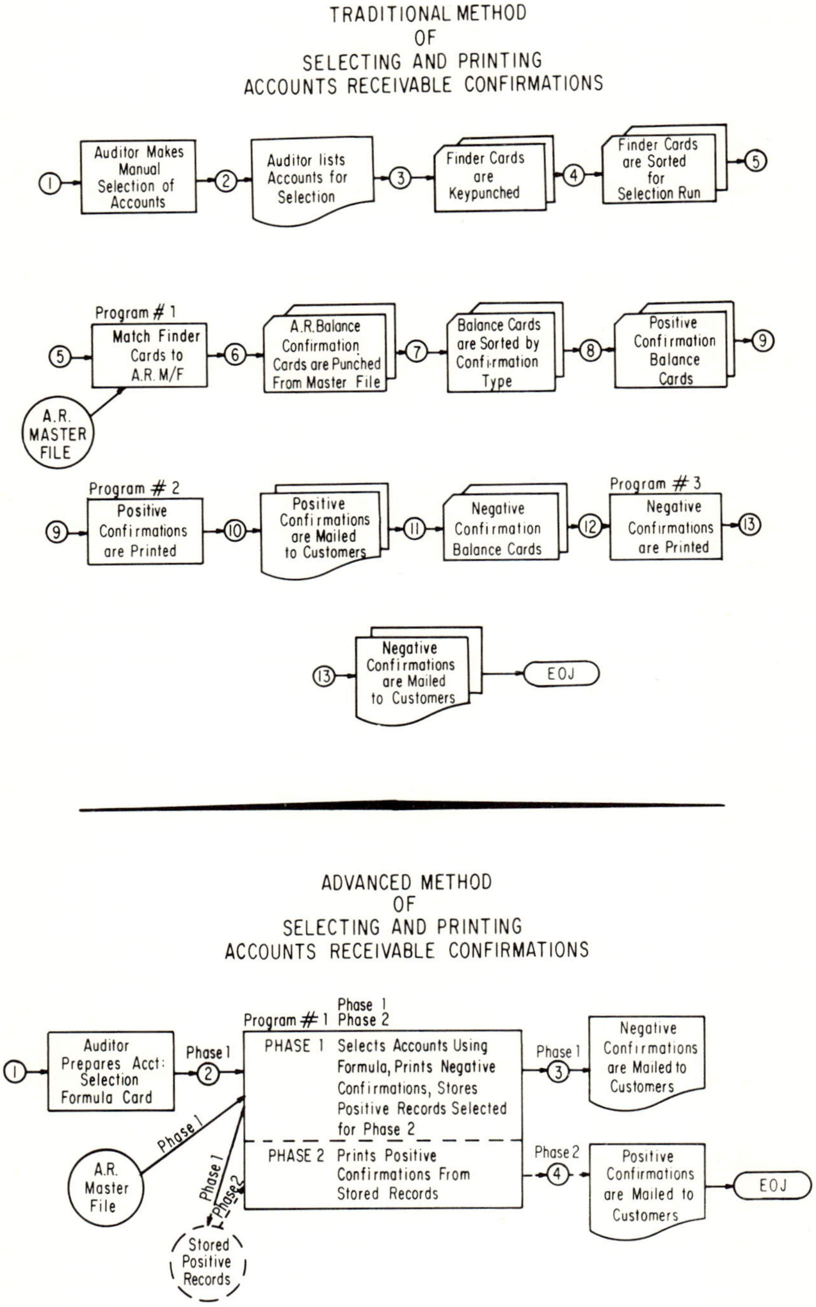
TRADITIONAL METHOD OF SELECTING AND PRINTING ACCOUNTS RECEIVABLE CONFIRMATIONS
1
Auditor Makes Manual Selection of Accounts
2
Auditor lists Accounts for Selection
3
Finder Cards are Keypunched
4
Finder Cards are Sorted for Selection Run
5
Program # 1
Match Finder Cards to A.R. M/F
A.R. MASTER FILE
6
A.R. Balance Confirmation Cards are Punched From Master File
7
Balance Cards are Sorted by Confirmation Type
8
Positive Confirmation Balance Cards
9
Program # 2
Positive Confirmations are Printed
10
Positive Confirmations are Mailed to Customers
11
Negative Confirmation Balance Cards
12
Program # 3
Negative Confirmations are Printed
13
Negative Confirmations are Mailed to Customers
EOJ
ADVANCED METHOD OF SELECTING AND PRINTING ACCOUNTS RECEIVABLE CONFIRMATIONS
Auditor Prepares Acct: Selection Formula Card
Phase 1
Program # 1
Phase 1
Phase 2
PHASE 1 Selects Accounts Using Formula, Prints Negative Confirmations, Stores Positive Records Selected for Phase 2
PHASE 2 Prints Positive Confirmations From Stored Records
A.R. Master File
Phase 1
Phase 2
Stored Positive Records
Negative Confirmations are Mailed to Customers
Positive Confirmations are Mailed to Customers
EOJ

Figure 8-1.

AUDITING: THROUGH THE COMPUTER OR AROUND?

by Edward M. Milko

Conventionally, the auditor tests the accounting system by selecting actual transactions that have been previously processed. He traces representative transactions from the recording of the source documents through whatever intermediate records might exist to the output reports or records produced. This approach is based on the assumptions that if the source data or system input can be proven correct and if the results of the system accurately reflect these source data, then the output must be correct and the manner in which the system processed the data is of little consequence.

THE AROUND-THE-COMPUTER APPROACH

In an EDP-dominated situation, this method is known as the "around-the-computer" approach to testing the system. Auditors have used this approach because it is a familiar method, it does not require technical knowledge of the EDP equipment, and the relatively unchanged audit trail conditions in the EDP installations encountered have not required a different approach. The reason for this is clear. If, as was often the case in the past, that portion of a total procedure which was entrusted to a machine was small and straightforward, the auditor would be taking a risk of insignificant or small proportions by auditing around the machine. As the scope of mechanized work grows, however, it not only takes over more and more of the purely arithmetic functions but also an increasing amount of the work involved in initiating transactions and in checking and controlling individual transactions. There are EDP systems in use, for example, in which the machine detects low inventory balances, itself prepares purchase requisitions and/or purchase orders, matches quantities per receiving reports with quantities per invoices and purchase orders, matches invoice and purchase order prices, prepares remittance advices and checks and signs checks—all with very limited human intervention except when differences occur.

To audit around the machine system has, under these circumstances, considerably different implications and risks for the auditor than when a machine's function is limited solely to maintaining inventory records of balances and transactions. To assume the intervening procedures are

---

Reprint by permission of the publisher from *Management Accounting*, August 1970, pp. 45-48.

satisfactory solely because a limited number of tests from final end product to source document indicates this to be so seems to be a form of leap-frogging at variance with some of our fundamental tenets of what is good auditing.

THE THROUGH-THE-MACHINE APPROACH

The objective should then be to improve the methods of testing by a "through-the-machines" approach. It, too, requires verification of source data, but from that point on it emphasizes review and testing of processing procedures rather than verification of output. In addition to the detailed review of procedures and related internal controls, this approach consists of tests to determine that the procedures and controls are in fact in operation. The basic premise here is that the results can be accepted if input and processing are found to be proper.

NEW OUTLOOK

The through-the-machine approach involves a new outlook. In most large corporations, it is extremely time-consuming to test enough transactions to justify an opinion as to the reliability of the records. Often the transactions selected do not include the unusual ones requiring exception handling. In addition, the auditor can never be certain that the individuals carrying out the system tests actually do what they say they do or are supposed to do. Therefore, according to the through-the-machines approach, auditors should de-emphasize the testing of records and concentrate their tests on the system that produces the records. If the system is found to be reliable, the records can be accepted as being reliable, since the computer, when properly programmed, provides the most reliable accounting system yet devised.

TEST DECKS

Those who favor the through-the-machines approach advocate the use of test decks to audit the computer system. The test deck is developed by preparing machine readable data (i.e., punched cards, magnetic tape) designed to simulate every feasible type of transaction and to test specific program controls. The test deck usually represents imaginary transactions, although it is not uncommon to include actual transactions selected from the Company's files. The correct answers for the "simulated problems" are determined by the auditor and recorded in his working papers. The test deck may include transactions that are deliberately erroneous in one way or another—to test the effectiveness of the programmed controls. Thus, by using a test deck all sorts of good and bad transactions can be fed into the machine and be processed under the auditor's control—to test not only the machine processing but the clerical operations as well.

The purpose of the test deck technique is to determine exactly how a specific processing system will react to particular types of transactions. In effect, the auditor allows the automatic data processing system to audit itself by merely presenting the system with a set of test problems or situations which the system cannot distinguish from normal processing activity, and then ascertaining how these cases are handled.

AUDIT OF COMPUTER RECORDS.

Test decks are normally used as a means of determining whether the program pictured in the flow chart is really in existence on a reel of tape. They also may be used for another purpose—to serve as a means of auditing the records produced by the computer. To do this the auditor first reviews the flow charts and finds out how the transactions are processed and how the processing is controlled. Next, he observes the actual processing. At a given point in the processing the auditor "takes over." He runs his test decks through the machine to check out the program. Then, using this program, he causes the actual transactions to be reprocessed, accounting for any intervention by the console operator. Finally, he compares the results developed under his control with those developed earlier under normal processing conditions. The theory here is that by using a program that has been tested and accepted, the auditor can verify the processing of a great number of live transactions in a matter of minutes.

THE LIMITATION IN THE USE OF TEST DECKS

A word of caution is in order at this point. Test decks, though effective as an audit technique, are not an automatic solution to the audit problems of EDP. Preparation of test decks is neither quick nor simple. It requires close familiarity with the accounting program and record layout, and an understanding of the features of the particular machine involved. In most cases, therefore, the test-deck approach is a matter for specialists in EDP.

PROGRAM CHECKS AND CONTROLS.

In order to prepare an effective test deck, there are two things the auditor needs to know or understand. First, he should obtain complete knowledge, by means of a list, previous training, or by other means of the program checks which can be written into a computer program. Second, the auditor needs to understand the program checks and built-in controls that exist within the machines. These controls are there to protect the malfunctioning of the equipment. They go all the way from ascertaining whether or not it is likely that some magnetic spots have been dropped from the tape, reflecting incorrect information, to checking whether or not tubes have been burnt out or computations are being incorrectly performed. Knowledge of the specific controls available in the equipment is useful in order to appreciate whether or not certain controls need to be made through program checks.

TEST DECK APPLICATION—AN EXAMPLE

Following is an example of how a test deck could be used as part of an inventory audit.

BACKGROUND INFORMATION.

An industrial company is being audited with an ending inventory of 14 million dollars. The inventory contains 6,500 different items which are summarized into 26 categories. Turnover is about three times a year.

The perpetual inventory is posted manually and is maintained only for quantities. The physical inventory counts are first compared to the perpetual record for a quantity check and then priced by the computer. The pricing operation is completed by converting the inventory tickets to magnetic tape and entering the data, together with the pricing table, into the computer. By reference to the pricing table the computer extends each inventory ticket and summarizes the results into twenty-six categories for the final inventory report. An inventory report containing dollars and quantities for each of the 26 categories is prepared by the computer. (Note that it is not possible to obtain a detailed breakdown for each category.)

AUDITING PROCEDURES

The suggested auditing procedures for this case study are:

1. Follow normal auditing procedures in observing the physical inventory and checking quantities to the perpetual records.
2. Have the company prepare a test deck of the various types of inventory transactions including some invalid items. Include some actual

inventory tickets in the test deck to check the clerical accuracy of the input into the computer.

3. Manually price the test items.
4. Observe the computer pricing run as follows:
   a. Obtain a card count before tickets are entered and again after the computer run has been completed. Compare these counts to the physical inventory control count.
   b. Control the inventory tickets until the computer test has been completed.
   c. Obtain explanations for all machine stops.
   d. At the completion of the run utilize the pricing program to run the test items through the computer.
   e. Have the computed test items printed out in the same format as the regular inventory report (26 categories).
   f. Compare the results of the computer run to the manually computed results and follow up differences.

If the company maintains its perpetual inventory records on magnetic tape, it would be possible to utilize the computer to compare the physical count to the book record, i.e., magnetic tape, and print out the differences for followup. By running a test deck through the computer inventory programs, it is also possible to determine if the system posts transactions to the correct categories and assigns the correct prices.

DESIGN OF COMPUTER PROGRAMS TO TEST RECORDS

Whereas test decks are normally used to evaluate the quality of the data processing system in use, computer audit programs are used to determine the quality of information generated by the system. For example, a computer program can be written that will select every "nth" account from the accounts receivable master tape file, print out a confirmation form for mailing to the customer and also, obtain a total dollar amount for all accounts for balancing to the general ledger. This technique actually audits or enables the auditor to audit records contained on magnetic tape by use of a computer program.

COMPUTER AUDIT PROGRAM—AN EXAMPLE

Following is an example of how to use a computer audit program for an audit of payroll.[3]

---

[3]Joseph W. Oberfell, "Case Study of a Computer Program in Action," *The Price Waterhouse Review*, vol. 6 (Summer 1961), pp. 2-5.

The auditor must first determine what audit steps on payroll could be applied to computer operations.

1. Obtain the payroll register (for a particular period) and select names of employees for detail testing of records.
2. Examine approved timecards and signed supporting W-4 forms and other documents authorizing payroll deductions.
3. For employees selected calculate gross pay, overtime, income tax and other withholdings and crossfoot payroll to ascertain correctness of net pay.
4. Check rate of pay to authorized wage listing and to union contract (or other source) to assure that the rate is within the minimum/maximum for the job title.
5. Compare the payroll register with the one which was subject to audit in the prior year and note employee changes for detail testing of documents supporting new hires, transfers and terminations.
6. Foot the payroll register and trace totals through appropriate journal vouchers to the general and/or subsidiary ledger.

All the above steps except number 2 could be applied in some way to a computer audit program. For instance, a sampling of employee names (step 1) is selected by taking every "nth" one. The selection interval is incorporated in the computer audit program so that when the program is processed against the payroll master file the pertinent information relating to the employee names selected is recorded on an output tape. The output tape is later printed in connection with other audit steps. Care must be taken to assure that there is no inadvertent bias in the selection because of grouping of employees. Of course, the selection could also be made by the use of random numbers.

Instructions for calculating federal income tax and FICA withholdings on a year-to-date basis (step 3) are included in the computer audit program. Such mathematical computations are made for all employees on the payroll rather than just tests. The total time required by the computer for these computations is considerably less than that required if such calculations were made on a calculator for fewer employees.

Print-out tapes of employee names or numbers are obtained for those whose (a) cumulative federal income tax does not agree with the computed federal income tax, year-to-date, (b) cumulative FICA tax does not agree with computed 4.8 percent of taxable earnings or exceeded the $374.40 maximum, or (c) title code is not on file. The program can be expanded to include calculations for gross pay, overtime, and other deductions.

Minimum and maximum rates of pay for each job classification (step 4) are also incorporated into the computer audit program. Pay rates which failed the minimum/maximum tests are printed out for investigation.

The computer further compares the payroll with one from the prior year (step 5) which is quite a time-saving procedure. One might reflect here a moment as to the problem of reviewing a payroll journal of several thousand employees and manually comparing it to a prior payroll. To do a thorough job is extremely time consuming. Yet the computer can do this in a matter of minutes and can give output tapes identifying employees: (a) on current payroll only (hires or transfers), (b) on prior payroll only (terminations or transfers), and (c) rate increases (over prior year) exceeding the general wage increase plus maximum progression increases. The tapes containing records of hires, terminations, and transfers are put through a matching operation to separate the transfers before printing.

Totals of the current payroll register and of the charges and credits to various accounts (step 6) are checked through use of the computer audit program and are later traced to the journal entries and general or subsidiary ledgers.

IS A SEPARATE AUDIT PROGRAM WORTH THE EFFORT?

There are some who feel that there is a certain amount of duplication of effort in preparing a computer audit program which is separate and distinct from the company's operating program. While this may be true, auditing has always involved some duplication because it involves reviewing something that has already been completed. It is also true that certain audit tests could be incorporated into the company's operating program by means of subroutines which could be activated as required by depressing a switch on the console.

AUDITING BY EXCEPTION

Computer audit programs are of aid to the auditor by automatically checking routine items and selecting the unusual or incorrect items for the auditor to pursue further with conventional procedures. This type of testing is called auditing by exception. In view of the large number of items normally processed centrally by an EDP system, the value of being able to quickly dispose of the routine and correct items is apparent.

DEVELOPMENT OF STANDARDS

In auditing by exception, the auditor must first develop for the machine standards of criteria as to what is normal for his auditing purposes in the specific situation and state these criteria in some sort of quantitative form. These standards can be based on the dollar amount of a specific item; on volume of transactions; on the percent of variation of expenditures from budget, standard, last year or the average of past several years; on the type of transaction; on the account affected; on the vendor involved; on the department originating the expenditure; on many other types of indicative criteria. They can, in short, be based on the very things which good analytical auditors use to provide themselves with a clue as to the items or areas requiring their special attention. The auditor, like management, can then use the EDP equipment to highlight the problem situations so that he too will not have to spend a lot of his time and energy finding out what the problem areas are and so will be able to spend his time working on significant rather than insignificant matters.

THE LIMITATION TO EXCEPTION REPORTING

One limitation in this approach and a possible danger to the auditor is that the exception listings include only items departing from the standard established within the program. If management changes these standards during the period under review, the exceptions listed will take on a different significance in that they will be exceptions from the new standard. As the details of the processing producing such exceptions will be hidden from the auditor on magnetic tape, he may not readily determine that management has changed the standards. For example, management may decide that it is no longer necessary to list accounts receivable with balances in excess of 30 days old, and instead it may require only those balances over 90 days old. Unless the auditor is aware of this change, his review of what is described as past-due accounts will take on a greatly different significance. Accordingly, it is necessary for the auditor to make tests to detect any changes in important standards and procedures in the EDP system before he can rely on the output of the system to facilitate his review.

THROUGH THE COMPUTER OR AROUND ?

To summarize this chapter, let's set up a comparison of the around-the-machine approach and the through-the-machine approach and draw some conclusion as to the appropriateness of each.

THE AROUND-THE-MACHINE APPROACH

The around-the-machine approach is based on the premise that the method of processing is unimportant as long as the results can be traced back to the input and the input can be proved to be valid. It will no doubt persist for years to come because in many cases it offers a satisfactory way of making the audit without technical training in EDP. However, it does not result in a satisfactory audit in all cases. It is inappropriate, for example, where the major portion of a system of internal control is embodied in the computer programs, or where accounting information is wedded to operating information in a computer program that is too complex to permit identification of inputs and outputs in a straightforward manner.

THE THROUGH-THE-MACHINES APPROACH

It appears likely that the through-the-machine approach will be used more frequently. The basic premise here is that the results can be accepted if the input and processing are found to be proper. It, too, requires verification of source transactions, but from that point on it emphasizes review and testing of procedures rather than verification of output.

CONCLUSION

Typically an audit consists of three phases: (1) the review of internal control, (2) tests of transactions (to substantiate the indicated system of internal control and to test the accounting records), and (3) verification of account balances—the so-called "analysis work." In a given audit it may be necessary to apply the through-the-machines approach in one or two of these phases, but it should seldom be necessary to apply it across the board to the complete exclusion of the around-the-machines approach.

REVIEW OF INTERNAL CONTROL

In the review of internal control for example, the key question is whether or not the work should be extended to include examination of block diagrams and other evidence of the computer programs. It involves a careful review of controls exercised over the EDP department by the outside departments, as well as careful review of the outside controls. In these two situations a review of machine procedures would appear to serve no useful purpose. However, an over-all conclusion regarding the adequacy of internal control cannot be reached without reviewing the computer programs.

TESTING TRANSACTIONS

In the second phase—the testing transactions—the key question is whether to use test decks to verify the accounting records and the purported system of internal control. Where the review of internal control includes examination of the computer programs the purported system can usually be substantiated by simply examining console log sheets, control registers, and other visible components of the system of internal control. Occasionally, however, a system may require the use of test decks. This would be the case, for example, where the audit trail is partially obscured. In any event, a greater use of test decks can be expected as computer applications become more complex and as accountants become more familiar with the potentialities of the computer.

VERIFICATION OF ACCOUNT BALANCES

The final audit phase relates to the verification of account balances, such as inventories, accounts receivable, and accounts payable. At the present stage of EDP technology, audit trails are still in existence in familiar form. Therefore, there is no real need to adopt the through-the-machines approach in this area. Accounting records can still be verified without the assistance of the computer. However, it is clearly evident that the quality of auditing can be improved by harnessing the power of the computer.

AUDITING ON-LINE COMPUTER SYSTEMS

by William F. Lewis

The computer has always posed special problems for the auditor. Its introduction in the mid-1950's produced major changes in the accounting systems that he was examining, in the types of evidence available to him and in the manner in which his clients did business. It also changed the way in which the auditor performed his tasks: He developed techniques for auditing around the computer, for auditing the computer itself and for using the computer to assist him in the audit process.

Early computers were oriented toward the batch processing of transactions. Toward the middle of the 1960's, however, a "third generation"

Reprinted by permission of the publisher from *The Journal of Accountancy,* October 1971, pp. 47-52, copyright 1971 by the American Institute of Certified Public Accountants, Inc.

of computers was introduced. With it came the ability to interact directly with the computer and, accordingly, the possibility of accounting and information systems which would provide for the direct entry of data into the computer system via remote input devices, and for the storage, retrieval and processing of the data within the computer system with a minimum of human intervention.

Systems of this type, with the input, output and storage media connected directly to the computer, or "on line," will present the auditor with an entirely new set of audit problems. The purpose of this article is to examine some of those problems with the objective of isolating those aspects of the on-line audit that cannot be dealt with satisfactorily by present techniques or by variations of those techniques.

INTERNAL CONTROL

The importance of internal control to the audit process has long been known. Before discussing the audit of an on-line system, it would be useful to review briefly the relationship of the internal control evaluation to the audit process.

The primary function of the evaluation of internal control is to provide the auditor with evidence relating to assertions in the financial statements for which compelling evidence is not directly available. Where compelling evidence is available, the auditor can go directly to that evidence to assure himself of the accuracy of the assertions. Where such evidence is not available, he must turn to indirect means. Internal control provides evidence relating directly to assertions involving past occurrences and indirectly to other assertions for which he cannot obtain direct evidence.

In making judgments about the occurrence of past events, the evaluation of internal control is the only evidential tool available to the auditor. Unless he is to examine every transaction for the period—a procedure totally unfeasible in the vast majority of audits—he must rely on a generalized test of the reliability of the records. The degree of importance of the internal control evaluation is directly related to the part that history plays in the financial statements. The income statement accounts are entirely historical in nature, and, while the balance sheet accounts are current, they are an accumulation of past transactions. The auditor must satisfy himself as to the reliability of the accumulation process in judging their accuracy.

Internal control also provides indirect evidence where direct evidence is not available. The auditor will use other evidence to form judgments about the assertions, but his conclusions will be tempered by his evaluation of internal control. The more effective the system, the greater will be the accuracy of the records, and the less opportunity there will be for material irregularities. Thus, a strong judgment regarding internal control will persuade him of the reliability of the records and other evidence that he examines, and the greater will be his confidence in the accuracy of the assertions he is attesting to.

With this in mind, let us consider the special characteristics of on-line computer systems.

ELEMENTS OF AN ON-LINE SYSTEM

In the following paragraphs we will review the present and anticipated computer technology, with the objective of identifying the distinguishing characteristics of an on-line system, and we will define the major difference between on-line and traditional systems.

Generally, an on-line system can be defined as one in which there is direct interaction with the central processing unit of the computer. Data are introduced into the system via devices which are directly connected to the computer. This is different in concept from the batch system which is used in most of the computer installations presently in operation.

In a batch system, similar transactions (e.g., cash receipts, sales, cash disbursements, etc.) are batched together, converted into machine-readable form and translated into a high-speed input medium such as tape. These transactions are then processed against master files using programs specially loaded into the computer for that processing run. The output is usually new master files and one or more activity printouts. With such systems, different types of transactions must be processed in separate runs (or batches), and each run has a different operating program associated with it.

Control procedures are concerned with the integrity of the data and data files and with program integrity. Integrity of data and data files relates to control over the input and output functions to ensure that data are correctly introduced into the system, and to control over tapes and files to ensure that they are not destroyed or tampered with. Program integrity includes the separation of the duties of preparing and running programs from the physical control over the program tapes and backup records so that programs are not altered, either accidentally or purposely.

An on-line system usually provides for the processing of nonaccounting and environmental data as well as accounting data. The operating programs are stored within the system, and data are introduced directly through remote point-of-origin devices (POD), either in batches or as single elements. Data are immediately processed by the system as they are introduced.

An on-line system has special programs that supervise it. The files and operating programs are stored in devices connected directly to the computer's processing units, and they are immediately accessible by the supervisor. As accounting or non-accounting data enter the system, the supervisor determines what type of processing is required and calls upon the appropriate operating programs and files. As each data unit is acted upon, the system updates the records and makes the appropriate accounting entries. Output requirements are provided for within the system. Usually they include periodic summary reports and, as required, accounting documents such as checks and invoices.

In the large-scale information systems presently being built, the accounting system is embodied within the larger information system. Financial statements are prepared by drawing on selected data from the system, and management is provided with periodic summary reports for decision-making. The accounting records are a part of a broader common data bank embracing all the types of information required by the system.

The commonly used input devices are the standard typewriter keyboard, the optical scanner, punched cards and paper tape. A single source document entered via one of these methods will typically provide many data elements for the system. As each data unit is accepted by the system, all of the records related to it are updated. Typically, one source document or data element may initiate several accounting transactions and require the updating of several files. Once the information has entered the system, the source document may or may not be retained. If it is retained, it will usually be filed by date of transaction rather than by the more traditional methods (i.e., by customer, document number, etc.).

The data and files will be stored in one of several ways. Critical data and constantly used files will be stored in on-line devices such as disks or drums. Information required only periodically will be stored in off-line devices such as magnetic tape reels. Rarely used data will be stored in libraries. As data enter the system, the system itself will determine the currency requirements and where the data should be stored. Within this framework one can readily see that almost all the accounting data required by the auditor will be stored in on-line devices.

In a system of this complexity, the authority function will take on new perspective. Authority to enter data or initiate transactions may be in the form of credit cards, special keys or codes. Also, decision rules within the system will be the authority to prepare many documents or make accounting transactions. For example, periodic depreciation entries could be initiated by complex decision rules integrated within the supervisory program.

Future systems can be expected to be even more complex. Present planning is for large-scale information systems to have highly sophisticated information-gathering and -processing phases. Such phases will include edit routines within the system for reviewing, sorting and coding data for storage in the system and subsequent retrieval. The coding pattern will not be predetermined but will be decided by the system. Data sources will be both internal and external to the firm.

Future hardware will increasingly be built under the concept of firmware. This will result in operating programs or micro-programs becoming a built-in part of the computer. Finally, future accounting systems will be more closely integrated with larger information systems, obscuring the distinction between accounting information and other types of information gathered to assist in the decision-making process.

From this analysis, we can conclude that the main differences between an on-line system and a traditional ledger or batch-processing system derive from the fact that information is stored within the on-line computer system. More specifically, accounting data will be integrated with nonaccounting data, and the books, ledgers and computer printouts familiar to the auditor will no longer exist. Records will be maintained within the system, and the auditor will be forced to go to the system for his evidence.

Traditional support documents will also not be as accessible to the auditor. In some cases they may not exist at all. Where they do exist, they may not be stored in a manner permitting easy retrieval. Procedures will be specified and implemented by the system, and authority may be partially or entirely contained within the system. Finally, to the extent that authority and procedures are system-contained, the system will authorize and prepare the output documents normally associated with an accounting system and used by the auditor.

INTERNAL CONTROL IN AN ON-LINE SYSTEM

Earlier we discussed briefly the importance of internal control to the audit process. Basically, little changes in an on-line system. The relationship of internal control to evidence remains the same, and, as in a traditional system, the objectives of the internal control system are the proper safeguarding of assets and assurance that the records are accurate and reliable. However, internal control in an on-line system will reflect the greater degree of reliance placed on the computer. Controls will be designed to prevent the manipulation of the system itself and to ensure the integrity of the input data and the data files. They will also reflect the fact that, although fewer people will be able to tamper with the system, those few who can will be able to do far greater damage.

The plan of organization will remain basically the same, except that it must now provide for the organizational independence of the data processing department as well as the more traditional financial functions. Also, the separation of duties will have to provide for separating the system analysis and design; programing, machine operation and EDP control functions within the department.

Since many of the processes related to a transaction will be automatic after that transaction has been initiated into the system, the importance of segregating the authority and preparation functions will be reduced. However, there will be an increase in the importance of controls over the initiation function. Procedures will also become a part of the system, so internal control will be more concerned with proper methods for updating the system and its operating programs. Internal system controls will be oriented toward hardware and program controls within the system and controls over the input and output of data. Finally, since the system will determine what accounting entries are to be made, there will be more general concern with how data are manipulated rather than with the specific entries themselves.

In evaluating the internal control system, the auditor's objectives will remain essentially the same. As we will see in the following paragraphs, his methods of evaluation and testing may change, but his judgments about the system are still his primary evidential tool in evaluating noncompelling financial statement assertions.

AUDITING AN ON-LINE SYSTEM

We have described the characteristics of an on-line system as being markedly different from those of traditional systems. Nevertheless the auditor will find that many of the traditional audit techniques will still be effective in the audit of an on-line system. It is our purpose here to identify those areas in which the traditional techniques will no longer be effective and in which new ones will have to be developed.

The primary difference between an on-line system and other systems is the manner in which records are kept. For that reason, those audit techniques which do not directly relate to the records will be unchanged. Thus, the auditor can still confirm receivables, payables, bank balances, etc., and make other third-party checks on the system. He can also observe the physical count of inventory, securities and other physical items. In addition, major documents such as mortgages, securities, titles, etc., will still be available and can be examined for terminology, liability, restrictions and other critical covenants.

Those audit techniques relating to the records will be changed, but new techniques will very likely resemble present techniques. As Gordon B. Davis pointed out in a recent AICPA publication,[4] an audit trail will continue to exist because management will require one for its own purposes. For example, questions regarding customer or vendor accounts will require some method of tracing from accounts receivable or accounts payable records to the source documents or to basic transaction data. The form of the trail may not be familiar, but, where a trail exists, the auditor can use it for his own purposes.

Finally, new techniques will become available to the auditor. Where all data are stored within the system in a common data bank, the auditor can develop programs using the system edit routines and storage and retrieval characteristics for selecting evidence. Several such programs have already been developed for certain types of situations, and new ones will certainly be developed as more is understood about the systems.

Thus, it would seem that the auditing of balance sheet and income statement accounts will not provide the auditor with any significantly new problems. Those techniques that have been used for batch-processing systems and for ledger systems can be adapted for on-line systems. In some ways, the auditor's task may become easier, because the more complex computer systems can be utilized to perform more complex audit routines. The initial development of such routines will be difficult, but once they have been developed it should be relatively easy to maintain them.

The major problem area of an on-line system would appear to be internal control. Before an auditor can utilize the techniques discussed above for auditing account balances, he must assure himself that the system is sufficiently strong to provide reliable accounting data. As discussed earlier, the internal control evaluation is the only means available to the auditor for judging assertions of past events, and without assurance of a strong system he cannot be strongly persuaded of the validity of the data drawn from the system. Indeed, the internal control evaluation takes on even greater importance in an on-line system because the extensive reference to source documents and support records used in a traditional audit will not be feasible in an on-line system. The auditor must rely much more heavily on the accounting records themselves; therefore, he must have greater assurance of their accuracy.

---

[4]Gordon B. Davis, *Auditing and EDP,* New York: American Institute of Certified Public Accountants, 1968.

EVALUATION

Of the two basic activities involved in the review of internal control—evaluation and testing—evaluation appears to present fewer new problems to the auditor. As in present audits, his evaluation must allow for judgments regarding the effectiveness of the system procedures and for judgments regarding the effectiveness of system controls. The latter area would include controls wholly outside the EDP system, controls at the input and output points and controls internal to the EDP system. The main considerations are whether the system procedures are adequate to accomplish the objectives of the system and whether the controls are sufficient to provide reliable data and prevent system manipulation.

Obviously, the theoretical and practical skills required to evaluate an on-line system will be different from those required for traditional systems because of the greater use made of computer equipment and systems. In terms of difficulty, there does not appear to be a great difference between evaluating a large-scale information system and a complex batch-processing system of the type now in existence, but there will be a considerable difference in emphasis. The addition of remote input locations and complex supervisory programs to handle communications will complicate the problems of system security and require the auditor to review these functions more carefully.

Initially this will be more difficult, because the profession has had little experience in auditing on-line systems. However, this is no different from other innovations with which auditors have had to cope and, with proper training and some experience, auditors should be able to evaluate such systems with the same degree of skill with which they evaluate existing systems. The degree of judgment and care required in evaluating an on-line internal control system will be greater because of the greater importance of internal control, but this does not change the basic nature of the evaluative process.

TESTING

The major area of change in internal control would appear to be the testing phase. Present testing techniques will not be feasible in an on-line system, and it may be necessary for the auditor to alter his concept of testing. As in traditional systems, the auditor's main objectives will be to determine whether the system is working properly and whether system controls are functioning to preserve system integrity, but he will not be able to trace individual transactions through the system or to utilize statistical testing as it is presently understood.

For those portions of the system that lie entirely outside the computer system, it should be possible for the auditor to test the system using traditional methods; however, testing at the input and output points and testing within the computer cannot be done directly. In a batch system, testing is done by devising test transactions, processing them through the computer system, and comparing the output with predetermined results. In order to test an on-line system, it will be necessary to devise transactions that will not alter the data base or the records. This is important because, if the tests do alter the data base, then the auditor is introducing error into the system. It might be possible to devise tests that reverse the errors introduced, but it is doubtful that the client would allow such tampering with the records. The rate at which data are introduced into the system and the complexity of the processing programs would make it almost impossible to guarantee data integrity.

It is equally difficult to test the system controls. Tests will have to be developed to insure that illegal transactions are rejected; however, if they are not rejected, the test objective is again achieved at the expense of tampering with the data base. More important, whenever erroneous data are introduced into the system, there is no way to guarantee that the data base will not be affected or that the error can be corrected.

Finally, where tests are designed to insure that records are being properly updated, it will be necessary to establish some form of control over the records being tested. In a system in which hundreds of transactions are being processed each hour, it will not be possible to establish such control without halting the system, and that is not feasible.

Monitoring is a possible alternative to testing, but monitoring is not a sufficient test in and of itself—the primary reason being that monitoring will provide the auditor with evidence only for those controls and procedures that happen to be used during the monitoring period. It will yield no evidence regarding controls that were not called upon.

The problem of testing is a difficult one, but it should be remembered that, in a system of the complexity described, the client will be required to set up an extensive test system to assure himself of data integrity. On-line systems will have complex programs, decision rules and authorization procedures, and they will utilize a considerable amount of computer equipment—all of it subject to breakdown. At the same time, the quantity of data flowing into the system, even in a very short period of time, will be enormous. For these reasons, the client will be required to set up extensive monitoring systems so that system malfunctions can be detected before serious error is introduced into the data base. Merely monitoring output will be insufficient because of the time lags involved in the system.

The client's emphasis in such a system will be on the processing of data and on data control rather than on the possibility of outside manipulation; however, the auditor can still utilize the system for his own testing purposes. He can set up his own monitoring programs for reviewing the system, and he can also evaluate the client's internal audit staff to determine their effectiveness. These kinds of tests should provide him with sufficient evidence for basic conclusions as to the system's effectiveness.

At present, there does not seem to be any feasible way of testing those parts of the system not reviewed during the monitoring period. This is the major part of the audit in which traditional audit techniques cannot be adapted to the on-line system. The auditor will either have to find realistic test procedures or devise some other way of assuring himself that the system is operating properly. Answers will require greater experience with these types of systems and more basic research into the nature of system testing. It may become necessary to build testing routines into the systems as they are designed.

CONCLUSION

On-line systems will undoubtedly change the nature of the audit process. It seems highly likely that the internal control evaluation will become a year-round effort. The magnitude of the errors possible in the system will require that the auditor assure himself of the effectiveness of the internal audit staff continuously rather than once each year. He will also have to keep abreast of system changes and assure himself that changes are made in accordance with prescribed procedures. Testing at any one point in time will be no guarantee that the system is operating in that same manner either before or after the test. Indeed, similar considerations have already dictated year-round auditing for some very large batch-type systems.

At the beginning of this article we indicated that our objective would be to identify those problem areas that the auditor could expect to encounter in auditing an on-line system. We conclude that the major problem area is the testing of the system. In other parts of the audit process, it appears either that the audit will not change appreciably or that present techniques can be altered to meet the requirements of the new system. Testing will require the development of new techniques and, perhaps, new conceptual approaches to the problem.

THE AUDIT OF REAL-TIME SYSTEMS

by Jack F. Thorne

Although certain aspects of the audit of real-time accounting are the same as those of batch processing systems, other factors are unique to the audit of real-time applications. These factors require new audit approaches and techniques.

THE NATURE OF REAL-TIME SYSTEMS

Various connotations have been attached to the concept of real-time operation and real-time computer systems. In this discussion a real-time system is considered to be one or more digital computers and other devices which control or monitor an environment by receiving data, processing them, and returning the results in sufficient time to affect the function of the environment at that time. In order to control or monitor an environment, a short response time from the computer is necessary. The speed of the response differs from one type of system to another as needed.

Real-time systems range from very small single computers with relatively simple programs to the largest and most expensive multi-computer systems in the world. Regardless of the complexity of a real-time system, the following major components are the same:

The computer which accepts data, applies prescribed processes to the data, and supplies the results of these processes

The files which have random access to a large store of information in order to provide the data necessary for processing

The terminals which are attached to the communications network

The communications network which links the remote terminals with the computer

The software which is the collection of programs and program segments or sub-routines which enables the system to respond to its constantly changing environment

THE AUDIT ENVIRONMENT

The operating environment of a real-time system is more complex than that of a batch processing system. In most real-time systems com-

---

plicated supervisory programs are required which can inject errors into the data or the application programs. Under the time constraint of a real-time system, the transactions may not be thoroughly validated. In some batch processing systems, where the time constraint is not critical, as many as 4,000 executed steps are used to validate one transaction.

With remote terminals, identification procedures are required to identify both the terminal and the operator and to check requests against lists of authorized users. Personnel turnover necessitates frequent changes of these identification codes and operating procedures.

When hardware failures occur, the fall-back and recovery procedures are more complex with a real-time system than with a batch processing system. If a computer in a batch processing system breaks down and two hours are required to repair it, the operating staff may have to work overtime to complete the day's processing. However, if a real-time system is not operating for two hours, the organization or the control of a situation which depends upon the information provided by the system is disrupted.

In order to decrease this disruption, three basic methods are possible. First, equipment is duplicated so that when a component of the system fails, another takes over its work. Second, fall-back procedures are devised which allow the system to modify its mode of operation to circumvent the failure thus providing a degraded form of service while still furnishing the most urgent information. Third, bypass procedures are designed which enable the functions usually performed by the system to continue without real-time assistance. However, in all three of these methods, a greater chance exists for transactions to be missed, duplicated, or erroneously processed than exists during normal operation.

Because of its complexity, the conversion of a real-time system is a difficult task. An audit during this period is especially troublesome. First of all, complete documentation on certain phases of the system is not available and some of the existing documentation is difficult to review. This problem is complicated by two additional factors. Communication with operating personnel or programmers is difficult due to the auditor's lack of knowledge and experience in electronic data processing in general and particularly real-time systems. Secondly, the pressures under which the computer personnel operate leaves little time for lengthy explanations and time consuming conferences with auditors. Another contributing factor to the difficulties in the audit process is due to the frequent changes which are made in programs; changes which affect the auditor's understanding of the system and require many amendments to the write-up of the system. In addition, the master files are often incomplete thus increasing the difficulties of an audit during the conversion period.

INPUT CONTROLS

Because of the nature of real-time systems in general and of the terminals and the communications networks specifically, many of the input controls usually found in batch processing systems, such as batch totals, hash totals, and record counts, are not applicable in real-time systems. Nevertheless, controls must be devised to ensure that all transactions are properly entered at the terminals and transmitted to the computer.

Multiprogramming is a technique for handling several programs simultaneously by overlapping or interleaving their execution. Since a multiprogrammed system has a number of application programs in the core storage at any given time, it's often difficult to determine the particular program that is used to process a transaction. Dynamic core allocation is another factor that greatly increases the difficulty of this determination. Storage is frequently allocated in such a way that specified data may occupy one part of storage at one time, and a different location at another.

Because of the large number of terminals that are usually part of the real-time system, more people are involved with the system and are aware that the system is malfunctioning. Since internal controls are often less effective during these periods, greater opportunities exist for defalcation. Because installation and operation of a real-time system require more highly skilled people than a batch processing system, the auditor should be aware that troubles may occur if such personnel are not available. With many remote terminals, the likelihood exists that incompetent, untrained, or unauthorized people may use the terminals. For example, confidential company performance data might be obtained by competitors, union officials, or proxy fight participants, by way of the terminals.

In a real-time system the chances for accidental or deliberate modification to the data are greater than those in a batch processing system. A number of factors which are related to the input of data into the system account partially for this fact. First, remote terminal operators may have no confirmation of the receipt by the computer of the transactions. Second, controls totals may not be used for verifying the number of transactions and the quantity figures. Third, because of the communications network, unauthorized access to the system may exist. Finally, if the system must accept transactions, some transactions might unknowingly be lost or damaged during peak loads or equipment malfunctions. Other factors also contribute to the possibility of damage to the data in a real-time system. The files' exposure to damage to the data in a real-time system. The files' exposure to damage is increased since they are on line to the computer at all times. Even the use of test transactions by the auditors may damage actual records.

Because of the above factors, the audit environment of a real-time system is more complex than that of a batch processing system. All of the factors do not apply to every real-time system, particularly to the simpler and less sophisticated systems. However, as real-time systems grow in complexity, more of these factors will prove to be pertinent.

THE AUDIT TRAIL

Traditionally, the audit trail includes the source documents supporting entries in the journals, the chronological journals used in the posting process, and the ledger accounts showing both current status and historical data. The audit trail is used in tracing accounting transactions through to the final statements, or tracing accounting transactions from the final statements to the source documents. Auditors are accustomed to a visible audit trail and usually insist on procedures for maintaining that trail.

The availability of the audit trail in a real-time system depends to a great extent on the participation of the auditor in the system design. The auditor must make his needs known in the early stages of implementation since once the system is installed changes in the system design and in programming become difficult, time consuming, and expensive.

Since the real-time system permits direct input without the use of a specific source document, the use of a transaction log which describes all inputs is mandatory. These logs are not prepared for the sole convenience of the auditor but also for the system protection. Since these logs are available, the auditor uses them as the focal point of the audit trail.

IMPORTANCE OF INDEPENDENT LOG RECORDS

The objection raised against reliance on the transaction log, that it is completely under the control of the computer room personnel, accentuates the importance of independent input records that may exist in other departments and of the audit and control procedures carried on to verify the accuracy and completeness of the log. Among the procedures is the requirement that independent input records and audit verification of the log must not be under the control of any person directly connected with the central real-time system operations. Increased reliance may be placed on the transaction log if the computer operating personnel do not have access to terminals from which transactions can be originated. Verification that transactions originate only at terminals intended for that purpose can be accomplished by the computer.

Usually the information recorded at the terminals is the result of a business transaction which creates a printed document, such as a sales slip or an invoice. However, in some real-time systems, no printed evidence of the transaction is produced. In such cases, one method of verifying the transaction's originality is by providing for terminals which prepare records of all transactions entering through them that are inaccessible to the operators. A transaction log at the computer along with periodic recordings of the files are necessary for reconstruction of the files in the event of loss or extensive file damage from erroneous processing. If these recordings are retained for a sufficient period of time, they normally provide ample source records for the auditor.

Although the capability exists in a real-time system to eliminate the audit trail, the system designer is constrained by the requirements of customers, governmental agencies, auditors, and management. Because of these requirements the visible audit trail will probably be provided for some time to come, by means of printing transactions, files, and worksheets. For example, the real-time system of the Lockheed-Georgia Company prints a daily listing, by department and by employee number, of all attendance and labor transactions. In order to maintain an audit trail, the real-time wired book closing program of the Westinghouse Electric Corporation produces complete consolidated worksheets.

Even if the visible audit trail is retained, its nature is changed with real-time systems. Source documents may not exist when transactions are directly recorded via the terminals. If source documents do exist, they may be retained at the sites of the terminals and may not be as convenient for the auditor as when they are processed through central keypunch operation. Printed listings of transactions or printouts of the files may not be available. In some cases, printed evidence of system-initiated transactions, such as purchase orders initiated by the computer and transmitted by the communications network, is not provided. Important historical data may be stored only on an erasable medium such as magnetic tape.

TESTING THE SYSTEM

Many of the audit approaches and methods used with batch processing systems may also be applied to real-time systems. However, the application of these techniques will normally require that the auditor examining the real-time systems have greater knowledge of computers and systems than is typically necessary with batch processing. The problems and techniques which are peculiar to the testing of real-time systems are defined here.

The design of the real-time system should provide the ability to expand or contract the system. The system should have the ability to handle a substantially increased workload for extended periods of time without the loss of data. During the system design, the auditor should investigate certain aspects of the system to decrease the possibility of the loss of data. Included in these aspects are the ability of the system to handle peak loads, the accommodation of long duration equipment breakdowns, the possible loss of data from the operation of the priority system, the existence of data movement controls throughout the whole system, and the adequate design of fall-back and recovery procedures.

Since the testing phase of the implementation of the real-time system is of major importance, the auditor should review in detail the testing planned, the data used, and the results obtained. The result of parallel operations, which is the parallel processing of the live process by the real-time system and by the prior manual or batch processing system, is of particular interest. In all cases where the analysis of parallel operations disclosed a major discrepancy the auditor should investigate what action was taken.

GUARDING AGAINST THE LOSS OF DATA

During each audit a number of factors should be checked to guard against the loss of data. These factors include the procedures for file and data protection, the actual operating experience during periods of equipment malfunction, the operator intervention procedures, and the possibility of "concurrent updating" in programs. Where the same record is being updated by two transactions concurrently, the effect may be the loss of one transaction.

The problems created by the changed nature of the audit trail in a real-time system can be solved by concentrating on logical units, such as all of the invoices and payments of a particular customer and all of the receipts and issues of a particular inventory item for the period. This procedure requires that all such transactions be available by name and type, which is extremely unlikely. However, the auditor can have a computer program to scan the transaction log pulling out all similar records, thus providing a list of specific transactions which the auditor can trace to source documents.

When verifying a master file, two generations of the file — one as of the beginning of the period and one as of the end of the period — are desirable since comparison of the two provides all differences of interest. Further analysis determines whether all of the differences are supported by legitimate transactions and usually detects the insertions of fictitious master files into the system.

The audit trail in a real-time system can change from day to day. Some of these changes are caused by alterations in the system design and programming, while others are due to the variability of human behavior. Whatever the cause, the adequacy of the audit trail must be determined during every audit. This determination can be made by answering the following questions: Can all transactions be traced through the system to final reports? Can a trace be made from any final report back to the originating transaction? Are two generations of file available that can be compared to detect all differences?

As indicated above, the proper handling of transactions in a real-time system is of the utmost importance to the auditor. During the system design stage he should insist that the transaction coding system used provide for proper classifications of transactions and for the addition of new codes and that adequate plans are laid for testing the system both during and after conversion.

During each audit certain investigations should be made to ascertain that all transactions are handled properly. Procedures should be checked to ensure that all transactions are recorded correctly, that all recorded transactions are authorized and legitimate, that remote terminals are used properly, and that all recorded transactions are transmitted to the computer. The proper functioning of privacy safeguards should be tested because if the safeguards can be bypassed, fraud can occur. The procedures for the handling of garbled and erroneous transactions should be checked to make sure they do not get into the main processing stream and that proper corrective action is taken.

HAZARDS IN USING CORE, DRUMS AND DISKS

In a batch processing system transactions covering a relatively long period of time are processed together. Quite frequently, cancellations are encountered before the orders, issues of material from inventory are encountered before receipt of the material, and similar incongruities. With real-time processing such occurrences should be investigated since they may be indications of improper operations of the system or of irregularities.

The possibility of writing over and destroying a previous record is one of the greatest hazards in using storage devices such as core, drums, and disks. The auditor should satisfy himself that all instructions to write information on such devices are preceded by an order to compare identifying data such as account number. The auditor also should see that the programmer has included instructions for subsequent comparison of the record written on drum, disk, or tape with the same data as it exists in core storage.

The most important single technique available for auditing the real-time system is the processing of test transactions. These test data should be prepared by the auditor to check on the operation of input, processing, and output controls. Therefore, they should include incorrect, incongruous, and inconsistent data, and data deliberately designed to circumvent the controls.

PROBLEM OF TEST TRANSACTIONS AND MASTER RECORDS

In the use of test transactions, a problem exists as to the master records to which they should be posted. With a batch processing system the problem usually is not complex. However, with real-time systems, where the master records are stored in random-access storage and where records are updated and replaced, the problem is complex since damage can occur if actual master records are updated by the test transactions. One procedure is to use actual but obsolete records if they can be obtained, or to set up fictitious master records. With this procedure, the test transactions do not damage actual file data.

Since thousands of test transactions may be involved in auditing a computer system, obtaining the time for processing these transactions may be a problem. With a batch processing system, the usual answer is that the auditor is allotted some scheduled computer time, perhaps after regular working hours. With a real-time system that operates only during regular working hours the same solution may be used. When the real-time system operates around the clock the answer seems to be that the auditor must inject the test transactions during normal working hours.

However, if test transactions are injected during normal working hours, other complications arise. If the auditor is trying to add a new employee to the employee file, some clerk ought to spot the fact and report the matter. If this event does not occur, the auditor has found a weak spot in the internal control system. Since the clerks should be tested under normal working conditions, they should not be forewarned of what is going to happen. Certain key managers should be forewarned, so that when the tampering is detected, they will have knowledge of the situation.

If a real-time system is used for customer order entry, the auditor may want to check the internal control by entering a number of fictitious customer orders. However, some means must be set up for intercepting the orders after they have been entered since he does not want those orders shipped and billed. The auditor also is interested in seeing how new orders, order changes, order cancellations, returns for credit, returns not for credit, and other transactions are handled and how they appear in the financial summaries. He does not want test transactions to affect the regular reports or to appear in the official business backlog. Since the auditor may be entering test transactions into the real-time system during normal working hours new auditing problems are encountered.

With a real-time system the auditor cannot be content just to create test transactions and feed them into the system from magnetic tape or punched cards since to check the over-all performance of the system, many of the transactions must enter via a remote terminal. If access to the terminal is controlled, the auditor should try to gain access to it in some reasonable but unauthorized manner. If the terminal is not controlled, but instead is used by an employee to report a transaction, the auditor will want to check to see if improper use is detected by the computer.

SURPRISE AUDIT CHECKS ARE DESIRABLE

Several types of surprise audit checks are desirable with real-time systems. One such check, which is used by the internal auditors of the Lockheed-Georgia Company, is for the proper recording of transactions. An auditor walks up unannounced to an employee and asks him to identify the job on which he is currently working. Information relative to the employee and the job is recorded via a terminal in the system. At the end of the day, the computer compares the recording by the auditor against the last recording made by the employee. If they are not the same, an exception report is produced which is used for follow-up and subsequent necessary corrective action.

Another surprise check is aimed at determining which application programs actually are being used for processing data. In real-time systems this type of surprise check proves to be more complicated than with batch processing systems. With multiprogramming the computer works on a number of jobs concurrently and uses programs or segments of programs as required. Since the input is heterogeneous the computer must have access to all of these programs. Usually, the majority of the programs will be kept in some secondary storage such as drum or disk. Since a program or program segment may be used for more than one application, the auditor will not find a well-defined program residing in storage for any particular application.

The use of test transactions, which can be used as part of a surprise check, has already been discussed. The auditor might try to enter test transactions by way of remote terminals that he is not authorized to operate. This attempt might be made both with and without a knowledge of the supervisory programs used in the system.

A surprise test may be used to check the fall-back and recovery procedures of the system. The auditor might identify a piece of equipment as being down and have the operating staff go through fall-back and recovery procedures. If sufficient actual cases have arisen to convince the auditor that the procedures are satisfactory, this surprise test would not be necessary.

A comparison of operating results with independent outside data such as physical inventories and positive confirmations of accounts receivable is desirable. Differences can be analyzed by the computer and the early availability of the results through the use of the real-time system makes it possible to find the cause of the differences and to prevent further irregularities.

AUDITOR NEEDS SYSTEMS KNOWLEDGE

Since the number of real-time systems in the accounting area are relatively small, the audit experience with these systems is limited. However, from this experience two conclusions are made.

First, in order for the auditor to have the necessary competence to audit real-time systems, he must have a knowledge of the nature of and the components of these systems as well as the advantages and disadvantages of real-time processing. If the auditor evaluates the adequacy of the provisions made for the audit trail and internal control during the installation of these systems, he needs a general knowledge of the complete implementation process and more specific knowledge of the system design phase. Even if the auditor does not participate in the implementation of these systems, a knowledge of the system design considerations which relate to internal control is desirable.

Second, some of the problems which are unique to the audit of real-time systems seem to lack satisfactory solutions. First, since many of the input controls usually found in batch processing systems are not applicable in real-time systems, new controls must be devised to ensure that all transactions are properly entered at the terminals and transmitted to the computer. Second, a need exists for a technique of determining which program is used to process a transaction in a multiprogrammed system. Third, because random-access files are always on line, control methods are needed to ensure the security of their data. Finally, even though most current real-time systems provide a visible audit trail, audit procedures should be developed which are applicable to systems with little or no visible audit trail since the trend in these systems is to have fewer printed documents.

9

Using the Computer as an Audit Tool

The same advantages of speed, reliability, and storage capacity which make computers desirable and useful tools for information handling also make them convenient tools for the auditor. Efficient use of computer techniques can reduce the time and cost of an audit engagement and at the same time increase the coverage given in the audit by providing access to actual machine records and by making more complete examinations practical.

Basically, the computer can be used in two areas: to test the information processing system and to test the actual data. In the first case, the effort is concentrated on testing and validating the processing system, on the assumption that if the system which produces information is complete, accurate, and well controlled, the results that that system produces will be correct. Thus, for example, the computer can be used to process test data against existing programs to determine if the programs and their related procedures produce predictable results.

The second approach concentrates on verifying the data itself. In this case the auditor can use the computer to test extensions and footings, to select and print confirmations, to select and print audit samples, to compare duplicate data for consistency, to compare audit data with company records, and to make and print analyses of audit samples.

Use of the computer to perform certain testing functions has become so widespread that many firms have developed generalized programs for such use. As with any good tool, these generalized audit packages have been adapted for use not only by the auditors but also by installations themselves for abstracting management data and formulating it into special reports.

AUDITING EDP—BY COMPUTER

"The adoption of the computer as an audit tool is one of the visible hallmarks of a progressive internal audit staff," says William F. Smith, international controller for Mattel Inc.

Most experts agree. There are several ways, they say, to use the speed and accuracy of the computer to full auditing advantage. One technique, called "through the machine," utilizes a spot-check system. Every Nth record from a file is pulled out for inspection. This allows an auditor to evaluate a situation through a representative sampling—but using the high-speed facilities of the computer to extract the sample.

Another technique is the "test check," a series of fictitious transactions specifically designed to test a system's logic. An offshoot of the programmer's normal testing procedures, the test deck can check all operations built into the system. A disadvantage is that it soaks up valuable computer time and is difficult to maintain if frequent computer program changes are made.

An expansion of the test deck method is the "mini-company," a total model subsystem run concurrently on the computer with the regular live system. By comparing known data from the live system with test data from the fictitious mini-company, auditors can discover irregularities in processing within the machine.

According to Joseph J. Wasserman, president of Computer Audit Systems, East Orange, New Jersey, the mini-company can be defined as "a means of passing fictitious test transactions through a computer simultaneously with live data, without adversely affecting the live files or outputs. A separate set of outputs, including statistics and reports, are produced for the mini-company. This ensures that the test material does not interfere with any outputs concerning the real company."

Wasserman, whose firm specializes in computer audit retrieval systems, feels the EDP auditor should be actively engaged in the design of a computer system, not as a designer but as a "devil's advocate, to evaluate the procedures and facilities being designed. It is the auditor's responsibility to ensure that computer systems are auditable when they become operational. He should be continually on the alert for possible effects that a proposed system will have on internal controls, and should develop all consequent audit requirements accordingly."

Some auditing techniques which can be used in addition to the ones described above are:

Reprinted by permission of the publisher from *Administrative Management,* December 1970, pp. 61-62.

Comparison — compares two duplicate files contained on magnetic tape, cards, or discs; ascertains if they are the same, and singles out any unmatched records. The advantages of the comparison program are its ability to perform 100 percent confirmation and identify for the auditor any exceptions for more detailed review.

Sampling — samples records in a file on a random basis.

Extraction — extracts specific records from the file.

Compilation — verifies mathematical calculations done by the computer. This type of program is especially helpful in determining the proper application of formulas in computer runs. For instance, if employee group insurance deductions are set up in a payroll system by multiplying yearly salary by a fixed rate, the compilation program can figure these calculations independent of the regular programs. Next, the comparison program described above can determine if the results of the compilation program and the normal payroll runs are the same.

The methods described are programs that can be written into a computer either at the time the system is first established or afterwards when the system is in operation. According to Jerald Greenberg of Worldwide Computer Services Inc., a software package manufacturer in Hartsdale, New York, "The right time to write in an audit program depends on the company's sophistication. If a firm is experienced in handling computers, then having an audit program built in with a new system is fine. But if there is some doubt as to the problems that might be confronted with conversion to a new system, even if a firm *is* experienced, it is best to wait."

AUDASSIST

by Richard Webb

Approximately five years ago, it was apparent to a number of us at Alexander Grant that many businesses—both large and small—would soon be using data processing equipment for their business records either in their own installations or at a service center. There was a clear implication that we as practitioners would have to learn to cope with a computerized audit environment or face the possibility of losing clients to firms which possessed such capabilities.

Reprinted by permission of the publisher from *The Journal of Accountancy,* November 1970, pp. 53-58, copyright 1970 by the American Institute of Certified Public Accountants, Inc.

Our intensive investigation of this subject indicated that the major problem areas in obtaining specially prepared audit programs to deal with the variety of computer audit environments are as follows:

1. Communication. The auditor was spending an inordinate amount of time making his needs known to data processing personnel.
2. Training. A substantial investment in initial and subsequent special training was required to maintain, review, evaluate and/or write special computer programs.
3. Client involvement. In our opinion, depending heavily on the client for assistance might impair independence. It was also concluded that the day would come when it would be inefficient and probably ineffective to audit "around" the computer. Testing and evaluating the client's data processing procedures were as vital as testing the client's printed reports. We also desired the capability to use the computer as an audit tool.
4. Computer audit-time scheduling. Problems were encountered since the client's own programming or processing requirements took priority.

In April 1968, it was determined that a *generalized* computer audit system was the best solution to our problems in this area. Shortly thereafter, the development of a generalized audit program was begun. It was decided to develop an appropriate computer audit language and to perform the processing at a central location.

We believe the combination of an audit language and a central processing capability provides two distinct economics:

1. The auditor is placed in direct communication with an audit-oriented computer facility. The need to communicate with data processing personnel apart from obtaining basic information relating to the organization of their computer records is largely bypassed. The auditor now can communicate his requirements to an audit-oriented data processing group—reducing substantially the possibility of misunderstanding.
2. In addition, audit-oriented central processing provides the auditor with an available resource of data processing/audit expertise which he can use to solve his technical or processing problems. The auditor need not be concerned with the difference between the various computers since compatibility problems are resolved by the AUDASSIST staff.

Development of an audit language thus became the basis of the design of the AUDASSIST system. More importantly, it added significantly to the attainment of the goals of the project: minimizing problems, optimizing services, improving efficiency and effectiveness of the staff in computer audit engagements.

In order to give the auditor the necessary background for using the language, as well as to set aside any fears he might have of computers, a series of brief audit-oriented commands was developed. With these, the auditor could communicate his audit requirements to the computer directly and would need to use client personnel only to obtain the required information regarding internal control and the format of the client's computer files.

It should be noted that AUDASSIST is merely a tool to help the auditor with a phase of the audit. It is neither a substitute for the auditor's judgment, nor for his review of internal control and the other traditional aspects of the audit. In fact, it is impossible for the auditor to use AUDASSIST without properly exercising his audit judgment.

Described below are the essential elements of AUDASSIST along with an indication of when and how it is used.

WHAT IS AUDASSIST?

As indicated above, AUDASSIST is a *generalized* audit program using accounting-oriented terminology to extract in usable form, through an audit-oriented central processing facility, client data useful to auditors. Functions such as aging, confirming, sampling, stratification and calculation can be performed.

DETERMINATION OF AUDIT OBJECTIVES AND SELECTION CRITERIA

The selection of the data to be extracted from the client's files and the formats of the reports to be prepared remain within the auditor's control, as do his audit objectives. AUDASSIST addresses the work to be performed in the third standard of field work. "Sufficient competent evidential matter is to be obtained through inspection, observation, inquiries and confirmations to afford a reasonable basis for an opinion regarding the financial statements under examination."[1] In the auditing of computer-based accounting systems, AUDASSIST allows the auditor to extract for validation, review, inspection, etc., data which are maintained in electronic format (i.e., tapes, disks, drums, etc.).

---

[1]AICPA, "Auditing Standards and Procedures," 1963, p. 16.

As clients have computerized their systems, the auditor has had to have increasing liaison with data processing personnel. In the examination of the computer systems that process financial information in order to satisfy the second standard of field work,[2] we have gained an increasing awareness and respect for the tremendous capabilities of computers. A computer can be motivated by precise sets of instructions, called programs, to operate on data stored in electronic form. The auditor's ability to establish, reorganize and test his client's records has thus been geometrically increased.

The auditor using this powerful tool can also increase his confidence through much more complete review of his client's records, increasing both the stratification and summarization of criteria for judgment and the collection of evidential matter. Using the capabilities of a computer will certainly cut down on the drudgery of accumulating this form of data.

With this background, let us examine how AUDASSIST can fulfill these goals, and what is required on the part of the auditor to use AUDASSIST.

First, it is definitely not a system to be used to program clients' applications nor does it perform audits by itself. It has nothing to do with the actual checking of clients' programs. It *is,* however, a tool to be used on computer records to extract, rearrange, calculate or otherwise perform operations which have a direct relation and use in the performance of an audit. AUDASSIST allows the auditor, after he understands the rules for its use, to use the computer as an electronic extension of his thought pattern. If the auditor's thought pattern can be structured into a format recognizable by a computer, its capabilities can serve his needs. How does the auditor instruct the computer to achieve his audit objective?

INPUT PHASE

To communicate with a computer, it must be informed about the type of media on which the data are stored. Computers are capable of receiving many forms of data. (The most recognizable form to the auditor is the punched card. Other data-storage media include paper and magnetic tapes, disks, and drums.) As the computer can recognize all of these forms of information, the auditor must specify which media are

---

[2] "There is to be a proper study and evaluation of the existing internal controls as a basis for reliance thereon and for the determination of the resultant extent of tests on which auditing procedures are to be restricted." AICPA, "Auditing Standards and Procedures," 1963, p. 16.

being used—punched card, paper tape, disk, drum or magnetic tape—and how the data are recorded on these media. In this area, the auditor has the same concern as the data processing department itself.

Because the data processing department must be able to tell the computer what form of data is being introduced into the system, each data processing department must have an explanation of not only what type of data is being recorded, but also the coding formats of the data and their location on the media used. Therefore, the client can assist the auditor in developing a record layout (the location of the various data fields). Once a record layout has been established, the auditor is in a position to instruct the computer to anticipate a certain type of data and to recognize it when it is presented. If the record layout is *incorrectly* prepared, *incorrect* results will be obtained—such is the accuracy of computers. However, this is not a situation unique to the computer environment. On an audit in a manual environment, if we were to instruct someone to foot the accounts payable ledger and expect to receive the accounts receivable balance, we would not receive accurate results. AUDASSIST asks these questions (regarding record layout) through the use of preprinted forms.

The completed forms indicate what type of media is involved, and where, within that medium, the information of interest to the auditor is located. This is done by addressing fields of data. For illustrative purposes only, fields can be compared to columnar information on accounting worksheets. If the accounting worksheet has four columns with the following headings—customer name, customer number, invoice number and amount—and we wished to total the amount column, we would indicate that column four was an amount column with so many digits of information.

After the forms specifying the type of media to be used (punched card, paper tape, disk, drum or magnetic tape) and the location of the areas having data of interest to the auditor have been completed, the way in which he will use this information to obtain his audit objective can be determined.

PROCESSING PHASE

The processing phase utilizes several techniques to provide both an adequate communication trail between the auditor and the central AUDASSIST installation—including, in descriptive form, a statement of the audit objective and a method of determining how this objective will be achieved using AUDASSIST.

To communicate his objective, the auditor describes, in a simple straightforward manner, what he wants to do with the data. Normally, this can be accomplished by a few brief specifications. The auditor represents the way in which data will be used to obtain his audit objective by using program flowchart techniques. These techniques are certainly not unique to AUDASSIST. They are the normal means of graphically illustrating the computer steps required to reach a stated objective (or those required to describe the elements of a manual system).

Gordon Davis, in *Auditing & EDP,* defines a program flowchart as "a diagram showing by means of symbols and interconnecting lines the structure and general sequence of operations of a program."[3] The use of program flowcharting is a key element in the effective use of

The objective of this program is to select all items from a client's inventory file which have had a unit price increase of 6 per cent or more over last year. Also, items with less than 6 per cent increase are to be statistically sampled.

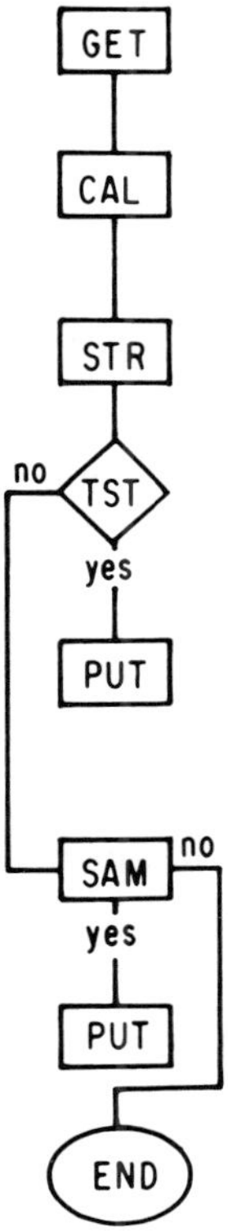

This instruction (GET) retrieves data from the inventory file, accumulates a control total and counts the number of records it has read.

The instruction to calculate (CAL) divides this year's unit cost by last year's unit cost and inserts this ratio into the record. The resulting ratio is available for further audit use.

The instruction to stratify (STR) determines whether the ratio is greater than or equal to 1.06. If it is, a "standard tick mark" is set which can be used later by the auditor.

The instruction to test (TST) is used by the auditor to look at "standard tick marks" created by other instructions. In this case the auditor would look for a mark set by the stratification instruction. Based on the results of this test, the auditor instructs the computer to proceed (branch) to an appropriate audit procedure.

If the condition of the previous test instruction is met, the PUT instruction is used to store the data on an output file. It is also marked for identification purposes, counted and a control total accumulated. This file is used later to create the worksheet listing of items selected.

If the condition of the test above was not met, that is, the ratio was less than 1.06, the computer is instructed to sample (SAM) the remaining portion of the file. The sample instruction indicates which records it has selected. Based on the results of this test, the auditor instructs the computer to proceed to an appropriate audit procedure.

If the sample instruction above indicates the item is to be selected, this instruction is used to store the data on an output file.

This instruction (END) indicates that all processing has been completed for a given amount of data (an inventory record) and to proceed to the GET instruction to obtain another record. This procedure continues until all records on the input file have been processed.

Figure 9-1. Illustration of Audassist Processing.

---

[3] *Auditing & EDP,* Gordon Davis, AICPA, 1968, p. 310.

AUDASSIST as it is in the effective use of computers in any environment. Therefore, this statement will be examined in greater detail to illustrate the essentially logical underpinnings of flowcharting and to further illustrate that an auditor should be quite comfortable in using these techniques.

Flowcharting basically is a schematic representation of the steps required to obtain a desired result. The value of using a flowchart is that it enables one to concentrate his thoughts into a detailed presentation showing each step which must be provided for in order to properly use the data to obtain the stated objective. This is important since, in writing a computer program, each step must be specified because computers will perform exactly the operations they are told to do—no more and no less.

As a simple illustration, if we wish to use confirmations on an engagement but do not indicate this to the computer, even though it is obvious to us, the computer will not prepare confirmations. The flowchart enables the auditor to visualize the output he will receive from the computer and also forces him to concentrate on the detailed steps in order to obtain his objective.

Figure 9-1 illustrates how a flowchart would be used in conjunction with AUDASSIST commands.

In the processing phase, the use of flowcharting, problem description and an illustration of the commands available in the AUDASSIST system have been discussed. The output phase will now be considered.

OUTPUT PHASE

The output phase is that part of AUDASSIST concerned with the structuring of the reports to be printed by the computer to present the results of the processing.

Once again, through the use of preprinted forms, the auditor selects the type of report that he desires—including the manner in which the data should be displayed within the framework of the AUDASSIST system. These are basically general listings, stratification listings and confirmations. Within these three broad categories, many options are available. In order to show more concretely how the auditor would use AUDASSIST, two shortened case studies are printed in Appendixes A and B.

After the input and output have been specified and the AUDASSIST program written, the auditor obtains the appropriate client data tapes and forwards them with the related AUDASSIST program to the central processing center.

The steps in the AUDASSIST process, in the order in which they are performed rather than the order in which they have been described here, may be summarized as follows:

1. Determine audit objectives.
2. Determine required output data.
3. Determine selection criteria.
4. Determine input data required.
5. Write AUDASSIST program.
6. Obtain copy of client's data tape.
7. Send AUDASSIST program and client tapes to processing center.

In conclusion it might be useful to review some of the principal advantages of AUDASSIST:

1. The communications problem is minimized because the AUDASSIST system doesn't require a special program to extract information from a client's computer files.
2. The auditor can express his objectives in the same way he expresses his objectives in auditing a noncomputerized client.
3. Because of centralized processing, the auditor's involvement in computer technology is minimized. He can thus devote all of his time to solving auditing and accounting problems.
4. The auditor doesn't impose upon the client's data processing department except to request a copy of the tape files that he wishes to audit.
5. AUDASSIST requires minimal training. All that is required is a 3 1/2-day AICPA AUDASSIST course.

APPENDIX A

INVENTORY CASE STUDY

This application points out the value of saving a client's prior year's tape for comparison with the current year. A case study application was run in the prior year to select items for inventory observation. The same application was repeated again this year. In addition, a second program was run in which last year's tape was merged with the current year's inventory tape to enable the auditor to use the items selected for price testing and to augment his obsolescence review.

Background. The client is a manufacturer of overhead cranes and trackmobiles. Sales volume is approximately $45 million with an inventory of approximately 10,000 different items.

Objective of Application. The application consisted of merging the client's 1969 inventory file with the 1970 file to compare increases or decreases in unit price per part. The 1969 and 1970 quantities on hand were also included for comparison.

Client File Formats. The inventory file is maintained on an IBM 360 tape-oriented system.

Summary. In this application the auditor was able to use the items selected for price testing in order to determine the validity of the changes and the fair presentation of the inventory as to pricing.

The auditor was also able to test the client's obsolescence program.

The number of items printed was 3,200. Because of the large number of items, the auditor used a judgmental sample to select items to be price tested. It was suggested that a second listing be prepared in future years which would be a random sample of the first listing. This would limit the number of items for price testing and further reduce the manual effort required by the auditor.

At the client's request, a copy of the AUDASSIST run was given to him. The client felt that this listing would be of assistance to him in analyzing further the trend of prices in the inventory items selected.

APPENDIX B

ACCOUNTS RECEIVABLE CASE STUDY

Summary. This application points out the feasibility of processing small client files which are kept in punched-card form. This application also shows that, although AUDASSIST is a tape-oriented system, conversion from another input form (cards) to tape is not difficult and requires little time. This fact also holds true for other forms of input (paper tape, disk, noncompatible tape from other manufacturers). Since more than one audit function was performed with this one application, the economics of using AUDASSIST were easily justified.

Background. The client is a dairy with approximately 1,200 customer balances maintained on punched cards.

Objective of the Application. This application consisted of two separate phases:

1. A selection of all accounts with balances over $300 for confirmation as of 11-30-69 and selection of approximately 4 per cent of the items between $0 and $300 using a statistical selection method. Credit balances were not confirmed.

2. Matching of cash receipts for December against accounts selected for confirmation.

Selection of Receivables Phase. Processing Phase. The file was stratified into: (a) balances over $300, (b) those between $0 and $300 and (c) credit balances. All accounts over $300 were selected. Every 28th item (about 4 per cent) of the items between $0 and $300 were statistically selected.

This stratification and sampling produced the following results:

Records in 1,200
Records out 230
Dollar coverage of total file was about 97%

Output Phase. A confirmation control listing, in order by customer number and reasons for selection, was printed showing customer number, name and balance. Totals were printed for the accounts over $300, for the accounts statistically selected along with a grand total of all items selected. After the list, accounts receivable confirmations were printed in duplicate. *Note:* One month later AUDASSIST was used to apply subsequent cash.

EDP AUDIT IMPLEMENTATION WITH GENERAL PURPOSE SOFTWARE

by George F. Reid and James A. Demcak

The auditor can bring the power of the computer under his direct control and apply it to the fulfillment of certain audit responsibilities through the use of recently developed, general purpose software packages.

This conclusion is based on experience dating back to March 1970 in the audit department of The Marine Corporation, a Wisconsin-based registered bank holding company. Since then, the audit staff has written computer audit procedures and applied computers to the auditing process without either intervention by or technical support from programmers or other data processing personnel. This approach has been applied to the preparation of a number of EDP audit applications. The major advantage of using computers to assist the auditor is that he gains an overview of the total system from initiation of transaction or source data through to the delivery of final financial and management reports. The auditor acquires the capability to extend audit tests beyond financial data verification. This is accomplished by delegating detailed clerical audit procedures to the computer. He gains the ability to address computer files directly, to access data and prepare reports as required by the objectives of a given audit and to provide the documentation necessary to satisfy audit standards.

The degree or level of detail presented to the auditor for his review is based upon his own judgment and the criteria of the individual examination. In some cases, an auditor calls for and receives computer-generated documents, listing the entire content of information files. In other cases, he may choose to have the computer select and report only exceptions or deviations[4] identified through comparison of files and data with audit application specifications.

The ability of an auditor to access and screen the detailed content of computer files on his own represents a new degree of EDP audit capability—broader than any previously available to most of the auditing profession. This statement is based on an extensive survey conducted by The Marine Corporation in the last half of 1969 during which many EDP software systems applicable to audits and other uses were reviewed. The software was studied in terms of its use for a number of audit functions, including the test of internal controls. During the survey, two alternative methods of testing internal control as well as the use of generalized software were considered—test decks and inspection of program listings.

The test deck approach was not feasible for The Marine Corporation. Test decks would be time-consuming to prepare and would have a rapid obsolescence factor as a result of normal program changes. In addition, this approach requires a detailed understanding of all computer programs in a system. Further, test deck information could alter data contained in a file.

Detailed inspection of program listings or block diagrams would involve a degree of complexity which would make this approach time-consuming and subject to error. In addition, program documentation is not always current. More importantly, however, this approach limits the auditor's independence, since he must rely solely on documentation prepared by others without being able to perform tests directly.

In contrast to test decks and detailed inspections, generalized audit software—such as the STRATA system used by The Marine Corporation—allows the auditor directly and independently to test inter-

---

[4]As the term is used here, an exception item is one for which conditions are outside the parameters of acceptability, or normalcy, established for data files. A deviation refers to a difference from stated management policies. Computerized audit procedures can be used to identify either exceptions or deviations. For example, an error in computation would be an exception. Interest calculated under directives other than those stipulated by management would be a deviation. This distinction emphasizes the ability of the new computerized techniques to perform management, as well as financial, audits.

nal control and to perform other audit functions. This approach, which is described later in greater detail, requires that the auditor understand user requirements, procedures and file content.

This discussion will not review the background of EDP auditing further detail because the Principles are not new in themselves. *The Journal of Accountancy* carried articles on this subject in February, July, August and November 1970.[5] However, these previous articles have dealt chiefly with internal control and mentioned only briefly the potential for computerized audit techniques. The authors believe that the significance of the present discussion lies in the fact that the methods described have been applied in actual audit situations and have proved effective. The application described below relies heavily on the exception reporting concept.

DIMENSIONS OF AUDIT TASK

The Marine Corporation is a registered bank holding company with total deposits of approximately $600 million among 14 banks with deposits ranging from $4 million up to $270 million. Data processing for all banks has been centralized. Applications supported by the data processing department include demand deposits, time deposits, proof and transit, commercial loans, mortgage loans, installment loans, personal trust and corporate trust. The data processing installation includes two IBM System/360 Model 40s with 256,000 bytes of main memory and an IBM System/360 Model 30 with a 65,000-byte main memory. From an auditing standpoint, it is important to recognize that this installation services both on-line and batch processing applications.

Prior to the availability of general purpose software, audit practices were limited largely to working around the computer. Auditing was done chiefly by tying user source records to documents generated by computer applications. This made for the traditional difficulties which required auditors to review voluminous computer printouts to substantiate the existence of the necessary processing controls and balances. These former procedures required the auditor to spend more time in clerical than professional evaluation activities.

Under the new audit approach, the computer is applied directly to the auditing function. Auditors work with computer users to determine

---

[5]Richard C. John and Thomas J. Nissen, "Evaluating Internal Control in EDP Audits," *JofA,* February 1970, p. 31; Jerome Farmer, "Auditing and the Computer—A Suggested Program," *JofA,* July 1970, p. 53; Geoffrey B. Horowitz,"EDP Auditing—The Coming of Age," *JofA,* August 1970, p. 48; and Richard Webb, "Audassist," *JofA,* November 1970, p. 53.

the policies and procedures applied to individual jobs, records or files. Then the auditors themselves develop the computer application which will test record content and substantiate the existence of programmed controls and agreement of file detail with general ledger control totals. Further, the computer generates all of the working papers necessary to establish evidence supporting completed audit procedures.

It is worthwhile to note that the computer can scan data fields for reasonableness and thus provide the auditor with some assurance of the reliability of data. A reasonableness test may be one in which the data to be verified are compared to an acceptable value. If the data fail the comparison, perhaps by some predetermined margin, they are treated as exceptions requiring further review by the auditor. Also, the existence of valid data at this point in an audit does not immediately imply acceptable internal control throughout the system. Only when the results of the general purpose software are considered with all the other audit procedures—including manual audit procedures—may conclusions be properly drawn.

AUDIT POLICIES ESTABLISHED

Prior to introducing the new EDP audit techniques, several audit policy decisions were made. Objectives were primarily aimed toward broadening the scope of audit activities, particularly in the area of testing management information. Rather than simply transferring existing clerical audit procedures to the computer, it was decided to use the power of the computer to identify and report exception situations. The auditor, then, will review the exceptions to determine whether deviations from management policy exist. These basic policies provided the justification for adoption of the EDP audit methods. Further, it was decided that testing EDP controls, such as crossfooting and balancing, could be best accomplished by the computer itself—under the control of audit software.

Once the basic decision to install the EDP audit techniques was reached, the audit group studied its role and responsibilities in detail and defined its operating methods in an EDP audit environment. For instance, it was decided that members of the audit staff, rather than programmers from the EDP department, would develop, test and operate audit applications. This approach was considered essential for the maintenance of audit independence. In addition, and of particular importance, several management-type criteria were established to guide all EDP applications. These criteria established that all computer audit programs would test:

1. Compliance with written management policies.
2. Compliance with established plans.
3. Compliance with user system specifications.
4. Compliance with approved procedures and existing documentation.

To achieve the first two of these management-oriented objectives, the corporation's written policies and plans were to be tested with computer-implemented audit systems. Management policies and plans, as communicated directly to audit personnel, were tested by the auditors. That is, management's policies and plans were used as a decision model to simulate the corporation's position on the basis of transactions which occurred during the period under audit. The last two management-oriented objectives were to be achieved through a detailed review of existing user documentation and by interviewing key members of user departments. The resulting information was incorporated into the computer audit programs.

AUDITING AN INVESTMENT PORTFOLIO SYSTEM

The specific example discussed in this article is the actual review of a computer application at The Marine Corporation of an investment portfolio of approximately $150 million in securities. A number of audit procedures were performed on this system. However, in the interest of clarity and brevity, this discussion will deal primarily with the test of accrued interest receivable. This application was designed to meet three audit objectives:

1. To total the record balances in the file. The total obtained for each of the 14 corporation banks must agree with its corresponding general ledger control account total.
2. To test the accuracy of each record balance and related income earned for each security. This required a statement from management of income recognition policies and formulas. These earnings conditions were then simulated using STRATA and the results were compared with the results produced by the user system. Differences between simulated interest totals and records in the computer file were then reported.
3. To provide audit procedures suitable for incorporation within the tests for the directors' examination at each bank. It was further stipulated that the corporation's independent public accountants

must be satisfied, after appropriate review, with these procedures and could therefore rely upon them in reducing the scope of their audit work.

Figure 9-2 illustrates the accrued interest exception report prepared after simulation of the calculation of accrued interest for the entire file. The figures in Figure 9-2, of course, represent test data. However, they illustrate the principle of having the auditor use the computer to identify and list exception situations—in this case, the records for which accrued interest receivable calculated using the audit software work files do not agree with the corresponding figures in the investment portfolio system master computer files.

The value of such reports in focusing audit attention to exception situations is substantial, since the auditor can spend his time reviewing exception conditions rather than performing clerical functions. The auditor can instruct the computer to generate this type and caliber of report for any exception condition he is able to describe and for which record data exist. Several specific exception situations are considered in the accrued interest receivable application:

1. The validity of identification numbers for the 14 separate banks included in the investment portfolio system are tested, and invalid identification numbers are reported as an exception in the bank number exception report.
2. Records for securities that have been sold but not removed from active computer files are reported in the closed record exception report. (System specifications required that records for sold securities be purged from the files.)
3. Types of records that should not be processed by the system are recorded in the reports of invalid record types.
4. Numbers of investment security types which should not be processed within the system are listed in a report as security group exceptions.
5. Invalid date exceptions are listed on a separate report.

In short, the auditor defines possible exception parameters. These are then communicated to the general purpose software in terms readily understandable to the auditor. The computer then performs detailed inspection and processing and reports the results in a specified format. Of course, the auditor must then follow up on the reported exceptions to determine their cause.

In considering the value of these reports, it is worth emphasizing the speed with which they are generated by the computer. As a specific example, the schedule of securities held for one bank is 14 pages long and last year required five hours of manual audit effort to list and bal-

Touche Ross & Co. 02/15/71
STRATA/360 Page 1
Version 4.1A Run 0001 Report 03

Bank No.	Sequence No.	Coupon	Par Value	P	Next Amount	Audit Amount	Difference
100	6010	.05000	100,000.00	S	2,000.00	2,500.00	500.00
101	7020	.04750	15,000.00	S	712.50	356.25	356.25–
102	8130	.06000	5,000.00	A	150.00	300.00	150.00
103	9015	.03210	10,000.00	S	321.00	160.50	160.50–
110	5860	.06500	4,000.00	S	260.00	130.00	130.00–
250	7310	.07250	1,000.00	S	72.50	36.25	36.25–
481	0100	.05125	100,000.00	A	2,562.50	5,125.00	2,562.50
632	0992	.06250	250,000.00	A	7,812.50	15,625.00	7,812.50
632	0981	.04500	9,000.00	S	405.00	202.50	202.50–
632	0977	.02500	8,500.00	S	212.50	106.25	106.25–
810	6710	.10000	25,000.00	S	2,500.00	1,250.00	1,250.00–
999	0782	.08500	10,000.00	S	1,700.00	425.00	1,275.00–
Grand							7,508.25

Figure 9-2. Bond Department System Test of Accrued Interest Exception Report.

ance. Today these schedules are prepared in minutes on a computer, which in addition foots and tests computations.

APPLICATION OF GENERAL PURPOSE SOFTWARE

The software package STRATA (developed by Touche Ross & Co.) is a group of programs for the implementation of general purpose file and information processing. It was designed principally for creating and processing files, and printing reports to assist in computerized auditing.

Implementation of EDP audit techniques started in the spring of 1970, after a three-month test of the software. After initial tests proved acceptable, five members of the audit staff attended an intensive one-week course. Approximately one-third of this course was devoted to the specification and computer processing of sample problems by the participants. This initial group then became the nucleus for helping the entire staff implement computerized audit procedures. At this writing, six additional members of the audit staff are scheduled for the one-week course.

An example of the documentation used to initiate the computerized audit procedure for accrued interest testing is shown in Figure 9-3, a logical flowchart of the EDP audit procedure. This type of flow diagram is prepared through techniques much like those of systems analysts. Prior to preparation of such a flowchart, the auditor must define his audit objectives and report requirements.

The flowcharts prepared in the design of an EDP audit procedure help with both the planning and communication aspects of the audit. In a planning sense, the flowchart is an outline of the logical steps for computer assistance in completing the audit. This document becomes a working guide in the preparation of the EDP audit procedure itself. The communication value of the flowchart lies in the fact that this is a graphic representation of the audit process which can be understood clearly by users, EDP personnel, management and the audit staff.

As a further aid to planning and communication for the EDP audit procedure, a form such as the one shown in Figure 9-4, which describes the accrued interest test application, is prepared by the auditor. This form is a summary of the required audit procedures for the computerized application. Space is provided to describe the purpose of the application, the input records, the output requirements and general comments pertinent to the program.

Specification of computer operations for audit implementation is performed through a series of preprinted forms which describe the computer configuration, the files to be processed, the processing functions to be performed and the format of reports to be printed. It is possible

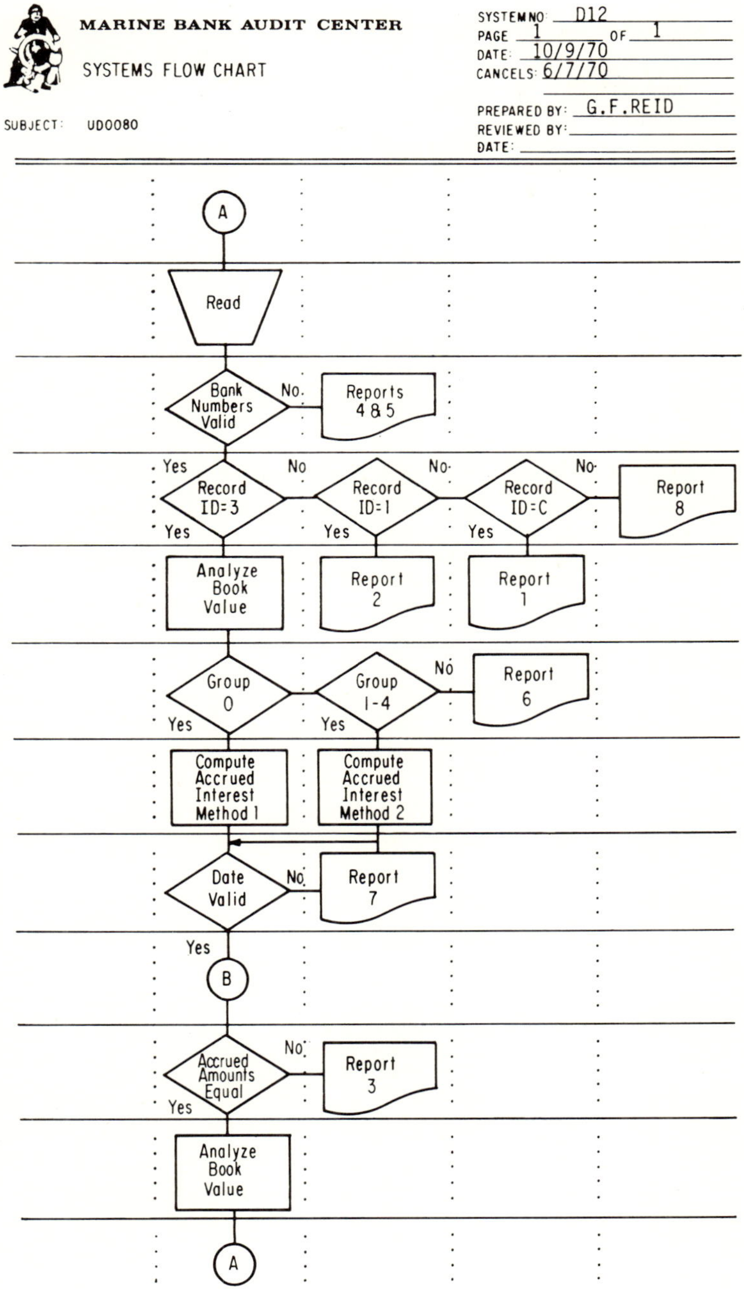

Figure 9-3. Systems Flow Chart.

MARINE BANK AUDIT CENTER

AUDIT PROCEDURE INSTRUCTIONS
COMPUTER AUDIT APPLICATION DESCRIPTION

SUBJECT: Test of Accrued Interest Receivable
UD0080

SYSTEM NO: D12
STEP NO: 001-006
DATE: 10-15-70
CANCELS: Nil
PREPARED BY: G.F. Reid
REVIEWED BY:
DATE:
PAGE 1 OF 1

STEP	
001	APPLICATION NAME AND NUMBER: Test of Accrued Interest Receivable UD0080
002	APPLICATION DATE: 10-14-70
003	APPLICATION PURPOSE: Will ANL Automated Investment file by Marine Banks for: book value and accrued to date. Will list records coded "C" (Report 1) or "1" (Report 2) or other than "3" (Report 8). Will list any bank number not provided in program (Report 4) or bank number not in sequence (Report 5). Will list detail of record having group number other than 0 to 4 inclusive (Report 6). Will list record having date not provided for in program (Report 7). Will compute accrued interest receivable at audit date; compare computed amount with record field "accrued to date"; amounts that are equal will be accepted and ANL. Amounts not agreeing will be listed (Report 3).
004	INPUT Magnetic tape: 890000.
005	OUTPUT Report #1 - Closed Record Report 2 - Bank Header Record Report 3 - Interest Exception Report 4 - Bank Sequence Exception Report 5 - Bank Sequence Exception Report 6 - Group Number Exception Report 7 - Invalid Date Exception Report 8 - Record Number Exception Report
006	ADDITIONAL COMMENTS: Audit date used to compute days held in formula is 11-30-70. Daily accrual and "days left" field in record also compared with computed figures. Those not agreeing will be listed in Report 8. STRATA application.

Figure 9-4. Audit Procedure Instructions: Computer Audit Application Description.

to generate a complete EDP audit application through use of combinations of specification sheets, three of which are shown in the accompanying illustrations.

To illustrate, Figure 9-5 is the General System Specification form, which describes the computer configuration used in connection with the test of accrued interest receivable. The Calculate-Stratify form in Figure 9-6 identifies the fields of data to be processed, the arithmetic or logical operations to be performed and the field specified for computer-derived results. One of the reports to be generated for the auditor is specified on the Select & Print form illustrated in Figure 9-7. This form identifies the fields to be selected and printed by the computer. Output formats are at the discretion of the auditor.

When the specification forms have been completed, the data in the entry boxes on these forms are keypunched and entered into the computer system. Processing of data from the cards is under control of the audit software package stored on a disk pack kept in the audit department and brought to the computer center for processing runs. The software programs are also catalogued on the computer library and may be used in a multiprogramming environment if desired.

EDP AUDIT PROCESSING

Processing of a computerized audit program is handled in two stages. First, software applied diagnostic routines verify the validity of the auditor-specified instructions. Where applicable, error notices are generated by the computer and returned to the auditor for adjustment of input cards. The diagnostic phase, which requires just a few minutes of computer time, also calls for printing of sample report lines. This technique gives the auditor a chance to evaluate the format of the data as it is presented to him and the completeness and applicability of the report requirements he has specified. When the specifications are error free, the program to execute the instructions is automatically prepared. Diagnostic routines also create computer-printed flow diagrams to document the processing to be performed in execution of the audit program. The flowchart is important, since the auditor can then determine whether all computer program phases have been executed as planned. One of the computer-generated flowcharts associated with the investment portfolio program is shown in Figure 9-8.

Successful completion of a diagnostic run for an audit program indicates that the specifications are suitable for processing. However, diagnostic acceptance does not guarantee that the objectives of the audit procedures will be met. It is still possible that a logical flaw exists in the specifications. This remains the auditor's responsibility. For this reason,

TOUCHE ROSS
STRATA
360

GENERAL SYSTEM SPECIFICATION

Sequence Number: G D 0 1 (1–4)

1 (5)

1. DATE — MO. 10 (6–7) DAY 14 (8–9) YR 70 (10–11)
2. COMPANY HEADING — BOND DEPARTMENT SYST (12–31)
3. APPLICATION HEADING — TEST OF ACCRUED INTR (32–51)
4. COMPUTER CORE STORAGE (enter right justified with leading zeros) — 065 (52–54)
5. FILE ASSIGNMENT (1)
   Use code T9 for 9 TRACK TAPE
   T7 for 7 TRACK TAPE
   D1 for 2311 DISK
   D2 for 2314 DISK

   WORK File — T9 (55–56)
   SORT File — D2 (57–58)

6. DEVICES AVAILABLE FOR *STRATA* USE (2)

5	DEVICE NAME (6–16)	MODEL NUMBER (17–20)	DEVICE NUMBER (21–23)
2	PRINTER		00F
2	CARD READER		00C
2	9 TAPE DRIVE		180
2	9 TAPE DRIVE		181
2	9 TAPE DRIVE		182
2	9 TAPE DRIVE		
2	9 TAPE DRIVE		
2	9 TAPE DRIVE		
2	7 TAPE DRIVE (2)		
2	7 TAPE DRIVE (2)		
2	7 TAPE DRIVE (2)		
2	7 TAPE DRIVE (2)		
2	7 TAPE DRIVE (2)		
2	7 TAPE DRIVE (2)		
2	DISK DRIVE	2314	231
2	DISK DRIVE		
2	DISK DRIVE		
2	DISK DRIVE		
2	DISK DRIVE		
2	DISK DRIVE		
2	STRATA PACK	2314	230

7. DISK VOLUME SERIAL NUMBERS FOR *WORK* OR *SORT* FILES

5	6	12	18	24	30	36
3	002314					

(1) Always assign both *WORK* and *SORT* file types. Do not assign the *WORK SORT* file combination of Disk *WORK* and Tape *SORT*.

(2) Use "Initial *STRATA* Program Load-Device Assignment" procedures and *PUB* Table in Reference Manual to add or delete devices not shown here. Add and Delete procedures must be used if 7 Track Tape is assigned.

10-9-1

Figure 9-5. General System Specification.

TOUCHE ROSS
STRATA
360

CALCULATE-STRATIFY

Sequence Number: C S 1 0 (1–4)

LINE NO. (5–7)	FIELD A (8–10)	OPERATION (1) (11–13)	FIELD B (14–16)	CONSTANT VALUE (2) (3) NUMERIC / ALPHA-NUMERIC (17–24)	DEC. PL. (25)	FIELD C RESULT (26–28)	GO TO (1) (29–32)
110	T01	SUB	T01			T01	
115	W03	MUL	W04			T01	
120	W05	E		S			CS12
125	T01	DIV		2		T01	
130	T01	E	W06				CS14
135		ANL	W04				READ
140							
145							
150							
155							
160							
165							
170							
175							
180							
185							
190							
195							

CONDITIONAL OPERATIONS (1)	MATHEMATICAL AND MOVE OPERATIONS	GO TO OPTIONS (1)
L - A less than B LE - A less than or Equal to B E - A equal to B NE - A not equal to B G - A greater than B GE - A greater than or equal to B RS Random Selection of nn %. nn is a numeric constant from 01 to 99. For nn % of the records chosen at random, the condition is met. (2) SC Tests *STRATA* Code field of the *WORK* record. If equal to the two-digit Alpha-Numeric Constant, the condition is met. (3)	ADD A + B → C SUB A − B → C MUL A X B → C DIV A ÷ B → C ANL Analyze Field B MOV B→A, Moves Alpha-Numeric field B or Constant to field A. COD Enters any two digit Alpha-Numeric Constant in the *STRATA* Code field of the *WORK* record. (3) After performing a mathematical operation, *STRATA* performs the next sequential operation <u>unless</u> the "Go To" field is <u>non-blank</u>.	END pass current *WORK* record to next *STRATA* function. (After Calculate/Stratify.) READ reject current *WORK* record from any further *STRATA* function by getting the next record. CSnn branch to page number nn. EX CSnn Perform steps on page nn and return. Put EX in "Operation Field" and CSnn in "Go To" field. blank if any conditional operation fails, a blank "Go To" will cause a branch to the next page.

(1) In Conditional Operations
- if the tested condition is <u>met</u>, the next sequential operation is performed.
- if the tested condition <u>fails</u>, *STRATA* takes "Go To" option.

(2) Enter Numeric Constants and Random Selection percent right justified in Constant Value field.
(3) Enter Alpha-Numeric Constants and two digit *STRATA* Codes left justified in Constant Value field.

5/0-8

DECEMBER, 1969
REV. MAY, 1970

Figure 9-6. Calculate-Stratify.

TOUCHE ROSS
STRATA
360

SELECT & PRINT

Sequence Number: P S 9 2 (1 … 4)

REPORT SELECTION CRITERIA (1)

LINE NO. (5–7)	FIELD A (8–10)	OPERATION (11–13)	FIELD B (11–13)	CONSTANT VALUE NUMERIC / ALPHA-NUMERIC (17–24)	DEC. PL. (25)	FIELD C RESULT (26–28)
110		SC		RI		
115						
120						
125						
130						
135						
140						
145						
150						
155						

ALLOWED OPERATIONS

Conditional

- L Less Than
- LE Less Than or Equal to
- E Equal to
- NE Not Equal to
- G Greater Than
- GE Greater Than or Equal to
- RS Random Select
- SC Test Strata Code Field

Mathematical and Move

- ADD Add
- SUB Subtract
- MUL Multiply
- DIV Divide
- ANL Analyze
- Mov Move
- COD Fill Strata Code Field

PRINT SPECIFICATIONS

2 (5) REPORT NO. 01 (6–7) REPORT NAME CLOSED ACCOUNT REPORT (8–35)

3 (5) REPORT SEQUENCE W02 (6–8) W01 (9–11) W13 (12–14)

4 (5) LINES TO BE PRINTED (enter Y for Yes)

Details (6)	Major Totals (7)	Intermediate Totals (8)	Minor Totals (9)	Page Totals (10)	Grand Totals (11)
					Y

CONTENTS OF COLUMN (2)

Column	Description	NO.	FIELD	LOW-ORDER POSITION	Card columns
COLUMN 1	CONTROL FIELD FOR MAJOR TOTALS	5 01	W02	005	5–13
COLUMN 2	CONTROL FIELD FOR INTERMEDIATE TOTALS	02	W27	022	14–21
COLUMN 3	CONTROL FIELD FOR MINOR TOTALS	03	W06	054	22–29
COLUMN 4		04	W13	071	30–37
COLUMN 5		5 05	W		5–13
COLUMN 6		06	W		14–21
COLUMN 7		07	W		22–29
COLUMN 8		08	W		30–37
COLUMN 9		5 09	W		5–13
COLUMN 10		10	W		14–21
COLUMN 11		11	W		22–29
COLUMN 12		12	W		30–37

(1) See explanation on Calculate-Stratify form of Report Selection Criteria fields and Allowed Operations.

(2) Do not use low-order position of less than 002 when specifying column positioning

5/0-9

DECEMBER, 1969
REV. MAY, 1970

Figure 9-7. Select & Print.

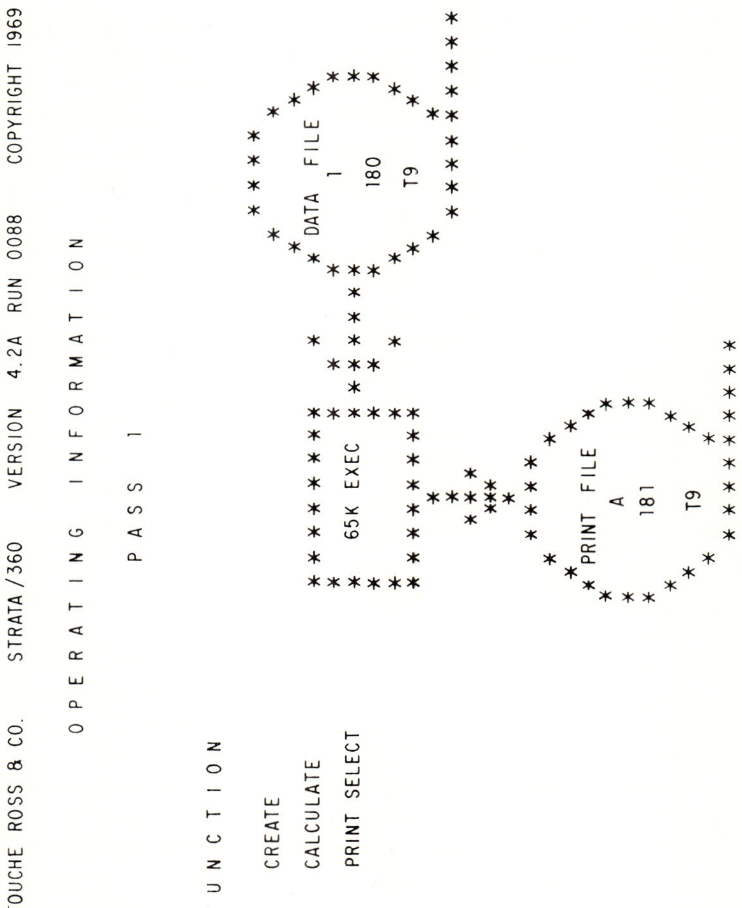
TOUCHE ROSS & CO. STRATA/360 VERSION 4.2A RUN 0088 COPYRIGHT 1969
O P E R A T I N G I N F O R M A T I O N
P A S S 1
F U N C T I O N
CREATE
CALCULATE
PRINT SELECT
65K EXEC
DATA FILE
1
180
T9
PRINT FILE
A
181
T9

Figure 9-8.

the second or execute phase includes an initial test capability. At the auditor's discretion, the execution of the program can be tested using a specified number of items read from the computer files being audited. At this point, the auditor has an opportunity to review and challenge the results prior to commitment for the computer time necessary for performance of the complete file audit.

File examination with EDP programs can be either on a complete content basis or through random sampling. Up to this writing, all computerized audit programs run at The Marine Corporation have selected all records within the files being examined. However, random sampling techniques are available at the discretion of the auditor.

The ability of the computer to process EDP files for audit purposes leaves the auditor himself free to devote the major portion of his time to the examination of exception situations in depth. With the computer reviewing file content, more records can be examined more thoroughly and reliably than was possible under manual procedures. The auditor's time can thus be devoted to professional probing of situations or conditions identified by the computer—and to testing the overall systems under review.

As indicated, EDP audit techniques have been applied to the full spectrum of computerized banking applications. The accrued interest receivable test used for the purpose of illustration is a small part of total EDP audit activities. At this writing, EDP audit application areas include:

1. Tests of premium and discount amortization in the investment securities portfolio audit.
2. Time deposit audits covering both regular savings and other savings accounts of deposit. Reports delivered to support these audits include exceptions in file or record content.
3. Commercial and installment loans accounts.
4. Fixed asset depreciation audits, which recalculate and compare all pertinent general ledger figures and compare the figures in computer application files with the audit-derived amounts. Exceptions in asset identification or depreciation amounts are reported.
5. Trust security audits, which match the list of securities not in the vault with the list of security transactions in process. Thus only those items that are unmatched are reported as exceptions.

In addition, demand deposit EDP audit procedures are under development at this writing. They will include account balance verification, confirmation and exception reporting.

It is also worth noting that STRATA has been used by other departments within the banks. These include:

1. The operations department, which has developed an extensive project reporting system utilizing the general purpose file management software. This system is used to report on the budgeted and actual hours, completion dates, variance and responsibility for all projects under development.
2. The marketing department, which has used this software package to analyze the effectiveness of promotional programs and to stratify demand deposit accounts for management analysis.
3. The commercial banking department, which has used the software to prepare one-time management reports.

CONCLUSION

The ability of the auditor to work directly with the computer has greatly improved rapport between auditors and EDP personnel because the main communication barrier, data processing terminology, has been eliminated. The auditor is no longer dependent on programmers to communicate with the computer. Under the new methods, he works directly with management and system users to develop his own application routines for computerized audits. Interaction with systems analysts and programmers is now carried out on an independent, peer level since auditors are self-sufficient in the development of jobs for computer processing.

This approach also meets the standards for virtually any EDP installation. There is no need to interrupt EDP operations for the development of audit reports, since the new methodology addresses system files without requiring alteration of processing methods. The software does not alter the content of files for established EDP applications. Rather, information required for audit programs is abstracted from existing files and used to create working files specifically to support the computerized audit.

Computerized audit procedures make it possible to expand the scope of audit activities substantially. Capabilities for testing and verifying internal controls are greatly expanded. New potential for control review has been opened by the ability of the auditor to test controls within EDP application programs, machine function and software, EDP audit procedures address and utilize the official records of a corporation as they are stored on machine-processable data files.

This management emphasis for auditing is possible largely because of the ability of the computer to alleviate clerical workloads. Computers take over such routine clerical functions as the calculation and verification of footings, the preparation of confirmations, the testing of extensions and the preparation of reports.

The results of the application described in this article and other applications converted to EDP audit techniques have been fully satisfactory. In particular, a reduction in clerical audit test time has been noted. This, in turn, has permitted increased internal control appraisal. Staff auditors have a greater opportunity to achieve an understanding of the total system and are more effective in evaluating the total system. They are also more familiar with the problems encountered between the user and the data processing department.

Particularly impressive has been the quality of internal control recommendations made at the conclusion of each system audit. These recommendations are more pertinent to the user and salient to management because of the improved understanding brought to system audits. Increasing numbers of postaudit comments include administrative control recommendations. Audit practices are closer to the management auditing level, which presents a real challenge to the auditing profession.

GENERALIZED COMPUTER-AUDIT PROGRAMS

by W. Thomas Porter

Much has been written about auditing electronic systems in the past few years. Most of the techniques recommended for the auditor who uses the computer require some specialized knowledge about computers and programming.[6]

The purpose of this article is to discuss the use of generalized computer-audit programs in evaluating and testing records produced by the client's system. In my discussion, some analysis will be made of the Auditape system, developed by Haskins & Sells, since this system is an important example of generalized computer-audit programs.

USES OF COMPUTER PROGRAMS IN AUDITING

A computer program can be used for any computational or comparison task for which quantitative criteria can be established. Examples of these types of tasks in auditing are:

Reprinted by permission of the publisher from *The Journal of Accountancy*, January 1969, pp. 54-62, copyright 1969 by the American Institute of Certified Public Accountants, Inc.

[6]Many authors have advocated the use of test decks and specialized computer-audit programs by the auditor. Both these techniques require extensive knowledge about the computer and the programming process for the design and implementation to be effective.

1. Testing extensions and footings
2. Summarizing data and performing analyses useful to the auditor
3. Examining records for quality—completeness, consistency, invalid conditions, etc.
4. Selecting and printing confirmations
5. Selecting and printing audit samples
6. Comparing the same data maintained in separate files for correctness and consistency
7. Comparing audit data with company records.

A common characteristic of these applications is the fact that the auditor can define clearly and precisely what is to be computed, compared, summarized, printed, etc.

TESTING EXTENSIONS AND FOOTINGS

The computer can be used to perform the simple summations and other computations in order to test the correctness of extensions and footings. The speed and low cost per computation of the computer means that it takes only a small amount of extra time and expense to perform the test in all records rather than a sample.

SUMMARIZING DATA AND PERFORMING ANALYSES USEFUL TO THE AUDITOR

The auditor frequently needs to have the client's data summarized in different ways for analysis. Examples are aging of accounts receivable, preparation of annual usage, requirements of parts and inventory, listing all credit balances in accounts receivable and all debit balances in accounts payable, etc.

EXAMINING RECORDS FOR QUALITY

The quality in visible records is readily apparent as the auditor makes use of them in his examination. Sloppy record-keeping, lack of completeness, and other conditions affecting the quality of the records are observed by the auditor in the normal course of the audit. If the auditor obtains a complete printout for use in manual evaluation methods, the records can be tested for evidence of unsatisfactory recordkeeping. If the records are in machine-readable form, the auditor has the option of using the computer for testing the records. In using the computer, a program is written to examine the records for completeness. For example, the customer file records might be examined to determine the number of records in which there is no credit limit specified. The records can also be tested for consistency between different items in valid conditions; e.g., account balances exceeding credit limit in unreasonable amounts (more than ten dependents for payroll deduction purposes on a man's payroll record).

SELECTING AND PRINTING CONFIRMATIONS

Based on quantifiable selection criteria, the computer can select and print out the confirmation requests. As an example, one auditing firm has designed a multi-part form which is prepared on a computer. A single printing prepares a first request, a mailing envelope, a return envelope, a control copy and a second request should it be needed. The form is designed so that the first request is stuffed in the mailing envelope which contains the return envelope. The savings in audit time when preparing large numbers of confirmations is substantial. A computer program can be written to select the accounts according to any criteria desired and using any sampling plan.

SELECTING AND PRINTING AUDIT SAMPLES

A computer can be programmed to select audit samples either through the use of random numbers or systematic selection techniques. The sample selection may be programmed to use multiple criteria, such as random samples of items under a certain dollar amount plus all items having certain characteristics such as high dollar values. The samples selected in this way can be used for audit tests such as confirmation, price tests of inventory items, etc.

COMPARING THE SAME DATA MAINTAINED IN SEPARATE FILES FOR CORRECTNESS AND CONSISTENCY

Where there are two or more separate records having data fields which should be the same, the computer can be used for testing for consistency. For example, the pay rates on the payroll master tape may be compared with the pay rates used in computing the payroll as shown on a transaction tape.

COMPARING AUDIT DATA WITH COMPANY RECORDS

Audit data such as inventory test counts can be compared to the inventory records by using computer programs. This requires that the audit data be converted to machine-readable records. Other examples of this use are tracing case receipts to accounts receivable records or comparison of inventory costs with the master file cost data.

OBTAINING AN AUDIT PROGRAM

Three approaches have been used in obtaining suitable computer programs for use in the evaluation and testing of records: (1) programs written by the client, (2) programs written by or under supervision of the auditor and (3) generalized audit programs.

PROGRAMS WRITTEN BY CLIENT

Much analysis desired by the auditor is sometimes useful to the client. Therefore, the client will frequently write computer programs for his own use or will prepare the program for the installation if the auditor requests the analysis and there is also internal use for it. Examples are programs to age accounts receivable, analyze inventory turnover and obsolescence, review open order files, etc. Obviously, to use such programs the auditor will need to test the client's program. The extent of testing would depend, of course, on the reliance the auditor can place on the installation's control over programs and operations. As a general rule, the auditor should, at the minimum, obtain a copy of the run book for the application, review the documentation for the run and be present when the program is run.[7]

WRITING AN AUDIT PROGRAM

Since a computer-audit program is written in the same way as any other computer program and since the programming process is explained

---

[7]For a discussion of programming documentation, see W. Thomas Porter, "A Control Framework for Electronic Systems." *JofA*, October 1965, p. 56.

very well in other literature,[8] I will not discuss, in any detail, the steps involved in preparing a computer program to perform audit activities. Basically, there are four aspects of developing computer-audit programs: (1) determining audit objectives and procedures, (2) developing systems flowcharts, (3) developing program flowcharts and (4) coding, assembling and testing programs. The extent to which the auditor can or should perform each of these tasks depends upon many factors, such as the auditor's knowledge of data processing and competence in developing computer programs, the complexity of the programs being developed, the source language being used and the availability of client programming assistance.[9]

GENERALIZED AUDIT PROGRAMS

It has become apparent to auditors involved in computerized systems that there are many audit functions which change very little from client to client. This is not really a very novel observation. Indeed, public accounting firms have guides to the preparation of audit programs which are issued to all audit personnel. The guides suggest an outline of procedures to be employed in audit examinations and to be included in the individual audit programs prepared for each client.

The idea of generalized computer programs is also not a novel one. Equipment manufacturers and other organizations involved in supplying computer programs to clients have been involved in developing generalized programs or software for a number of years. These programs perform activities related both to the operation of the computer system (systems programs) and to the manipulation and processing of data used in the management of the business (applications programs). Generalized programs, such as assembly routines, utility routines and compilers, and application programs, such as payroll, inventory control and demand deposit accounting, find widespread use in many computer installations today. The availability of such programs is a great aid to personnel trying to use the computer in that these programs preclude the develop-

---

[8]There are several excellent references available if one is interested in understanding the programming process. For example: Gordon B. Davis, *An Introduction to Electronic Computers,* McGraw-Hill Book Company; Gregory and Van Horn, *Automatic Data-Processing Systems,* Wadsworth Publishing Company, Inc.; Frederic G. Withington, *The Use of Computers in Business Organizations,* Addison-Wesley Publishing Company.

[9]For a detailed discussion of the development and use of computer-audit programs, see W. Thomas Porter, *Auditing Electronic Systems,* Wadsworth Publishing Company, Inc., chap. 5.

ment of systems flowcharts, programming flowcharts, source language instruction and the assembling and testing of programs. Generalized programs, if developed, designed and tested properly, are available for use in performing functions designed to be performed by the computer with a minimum of preparation on the part of the user.

Until recently, generalized computer-audit programs have been used to a limited extent. One approach has been the use of an industry program which is applicable to all clients in an industry. The best example is the brokerage audit where generalized audit programs have been used to perform standard audit procedures having to do with confirmation, margin computations, etc. The client's files are transferred to a standard format on magnetic tape. The conversion program is unique for each client having a different computer; the data file in standard form is processed by an audit program used for all clients. The client's computer is used only if it fits the model and configuration specifications for which the audit processing program was written. It should be noted that even though two computer systems are not program compatible, they are probably data compatible if the data are put on magnetic tape.

THE AUDITAPE SYSTEM

The second approach is a generalized set of audit routines which can be useful for a variety of audit and management purposes and used on a restricted set of compatible computers meeting specified configuration requirements. Currently the best and most promising example of this approach is the Haskins & Sells Auditape system, designed to be used:

> By persons having no specialized knowledge of computers or programming languages, and having only a nominal amount of simple instruction.
>
> On a wide variety of records interchangeably, without any need for preparation of special programs for each type of application to be processed.[10]

The primary component of the system is Auditape itself, a series of audit routines written in machine language which are executed by virtue of specification cards developed by the auditor. In addition, the system includes an instruction sheet for computer operators, specification

---

[10]*Haskins & Sells Auditape System Manual,* sec. 1, p. 1.

sheets and an operating manual. The operating manual includes a general discussion of the Auditape system, excerpts of which follow:

> The Auditape is in machine language, ready for immediate use, and includes several programs or what might be better referred to as routines to perform specific operations and a monitor routine to control the selection of these several operating routines.
>
> The instruction sheet for the computer operator includes all explanations necessary for operation of the equipment. The person using the Auditape system need not be concerned with any actions taken by the computer operator unless the application is being made for an audit purpose that requires control against possible manipulation of data by intervention of the operator.[11]
>
> The specification sheets are the means by which the person using the Auditape system adapts it to his purpose and to the input records available for each application. The specification sheets are used as a source document from which specification cards are key punched and read into the computer memory and combined with instructions read from the Auditape to complete the program for the particular routine being processed.

The routines, other than the monitor routine, comprising the Auditape are:

1. Edit routine, including the subtotal subroutine and an include-exclude subroutine.
2. Print/punch routine
3. Summarize routine
4. Mathematical routine
5. Audit sample routine.

EDIT ROUTINE

The principal problem in developing the Auditape system, or any set of generalized programs, arises from the wide variety

---

[11]Haskins & Sells has recommended that the auditor using the system observe all processing with the system since it is possible for the operator to alter the contents of the computer core memory during processing by switches on the console of the central processing unit. The system as designed does not require any such manipulation during the auditor's processing of any routine. Accordingly, physical observation of the processing should be sufficient to maintain control.

in the format of the computer records to be processed. This variety occurs not only in the records used by different companies for similar applications, but also for different applications by any one company. . . . In the absence of a generalized program, a separate program is required for each specific record format to be processed, even though the basic operation to be performed by each of the specific programs might be the same.

This problem is solved in the Auditape system by the use of the Edit Routine, which causes selected data to be read from any specified position in the input record regardless of its format and written in any specified field on an output tape in the Auditape record format. This output tape then becomes the input for any of the other routines in the system.

The Subtotal or Include/Exclude Subroutine can be processed simultaneously with the Edit Routine at the option of the person using the Auditape system. These subroutines can be used for special analyses and other purposes by providing subtotals of input data in certain specified classifications and by including or excluding input data based on certain specified criteria.

PRINT/PUNCH ROUTINE

Aside from control totals and processing messages, the results from each of the other routines are written on an output tape in the Auditape record format. With any of these tapes as input, the Print/Punch Routine can be used to provide printed or punched card output or both. This routine also includes options to permit the fields in the Auditape record to be printed out in any desired order, and to print appropriate descriptive headings over each column of data.

SUMMARIZE ROUTINE

The Summarize Routine can be used to summarize details of records by some identifying characteristic such as customer number or inventory part number.

MATHEMATICAL ROUTINE

The Mathematical Routine performs addition, subtraction, multiplication, or division of amounts in any two quantitative fields in the Auditape record, or of amounts in one of such fields and a specified constant amount.

AUDIT SAMPLE ROUTINE

The Audit Sample Routine computes the approximate optimum sample size required to obtain the statistical precision and reliability specified for a particular sample and selects the items to be included in the sample.[12]

USE OF AUDITAPE SYSTEM

There is evidence that the Auditape system has been used very successfully by Haskins & Sells in performing audit tasks and by their clients in analyzing files for management purposes. My objective in using the system was to confirm my understanding of the system and to compare it with the approach of using programs written by or under the supervision of the auditor. The situation I used was an accounts receivable application for which special computer-audit programs had previously been written to perform certain audit procedures. The audit procedures included in these specialized audit programs were accounts receivable year-end procedures in a medium-sized manufacturing company. The auditor's objectives were (1) to determine the validity of the client's year-end accounts receivable amount and (2) to evaluate the collectibility of the accounts.

The company processed accounting and operational data on an IBM 1401 data processing system. This system included a teletypewriter order entry network, 1011 paper tape reader, 7330 magnetic tape units, a 1402 card-read punch and a 1403 printer. The central processing unit had a storage capacity of 16,000 characters.

Trade accounts receivable, in the aggregate, averaged approximately $2,500,000 and consisted of over 6,000 accounts, approximately 5 per cent of which represented about 80 per cent of the total dollar value. The accounts receivable were on two magnetic tape files, one being the basic record file that contained data records for each customer as shown in Figure 9-9; the other tape file was the item record file that contained the details—i.e., invoices, unidentified cash payments—which supported the basic record account balance (see Figure 9-10, for item record of unpaid invoices).

---

[12] *Ibid.*, sec. 3, pp. 1 and 2.

Data Field	*Number of Characters*
Customer number	7
Current A/R balance	9
Amount on order	
Steel	9
Tungsten	9
Sundry	9
Credit Limit	
Amount	7
Date limit established	6
Credit history	
Date account opened	6
Highest credit extended	9
Date highest credit extended	6

Figure 9-9. Accounts Receivable Basic Record (Sheet 1 of 2).

AUDIT PROCEDURES

In performing the year-end audit procedures for the accounts receivable files, the auditor developed certain computer programs using the client's accounts receivable basic record file and the item record file. These files were then processed with the computer-audit programs as shown in Figure 9-11. The procedures performed by the three programs were:

1. Select for positive confirmation and print, on the circularization report, accounts with:
   a. Balance ≥$5,000 (type Code 1).
   b. Balance ≥$1,000 but ≤$5,000 and with any portion of the account 30 or more days delinquent (type Code 2).
   c. Balance ≥$1,000 and with sales this year 500 per cent ≥last year's sales or ≤20 per cent of last year's sales (type Code 3).
2. Randomly select for negative confirmation and print, on the circularization report, 10 per cent of the remaining accounts (type Code 0).
3. Age all accounts.
4. Select and print on the exception report all accounts:
   a. Over credit limit (type Code 4).
   b. Whose basic record balance is not in agreement with the total amount of all items in its item record (type Code 5).

Data Field	*Number of Characters*
Original credit limit	9
Date original credit limit established	6
Previous credit limit	9
Date previous credit limit established	4
Number of months of previous credit limit	2
Number of items currently delinquent	3
Amount currently delinquent	9
Delinquency history	
Months reporting	2
Months delinquent	2
Consecutive months delinquent	2
Last month delinquent	4
Highest delinquency	
Number of items	3
Amount	9
Date	4
Date last sale	6
Sales history (material amount only) (By-product line—steel, tungsten, sundry)	
3rd prior year	9
2d prior year	9
1st prior year	9
This year to date	9
This month	9
Potential	9
Profit at standard—year to date	9
Payment history	
Payment ratings (company establishes payment ratings 0-9 based on payments for each quarter):	
3rd prior year—by quarter	4
2d prior year—by quarter	4
1st prior year—by quarter	4
This year—by quarter	4
Dollars paid this quarter:	
By discount date	9
By due date	9
Customer name and address	136

Figure 9-9. Accounts Receivable Basic Record (Sheet 2 of 2).

Data Field	*Number of Characters*
Item record code	1
Customer number	7
Date	5
Invoice number	12
Gross amount of invoice	9
Net amount of invoice	9
Cash discount	7

Figure 9-10. A/R Item Record for Unpaid Invoices.

c. With credit balance ≥$500 (type Code 6).

5. Accumulate and print, on the circularization report:
   a. Number of accounts in basic record file.
   b. Aged totals of all accounts in basic record file.
   c. Number of items in item record file.
   d. Total balance of all items in item record file.
   e. Total balance of all accounts with credit balances.
   f. Number of accounts selected for negative confirmation and aged totals for these accounts.
   g. Number of accounts selected for positive confirmation and aged totals for these accounts.

DEVELOPING COMPUTER-AUDIT PROGRAMS

After formulating the audit procedures for the accounts receivable work and the systems flowcharts, the auditor prepared program flowcharts and designed output records to include the required audit information.

Of the three programs shown on the system flowcharts, Program I includes most of the processing logic and decision criteria. Programs II and III merely print machine-readable output resulting from Program I.

The primary output from the computer processing is the accounts receivable circulation report (see Figure 9-12). The report was set up in working paper form ready for the auditor's analysis. The digit under the "T" column in the report corresponds to the type of confirmation request—that is, 1 represents a positive confirmation request. File totals are printed at the end of the report for comparison with file totals shown on the client's aged trial balance.

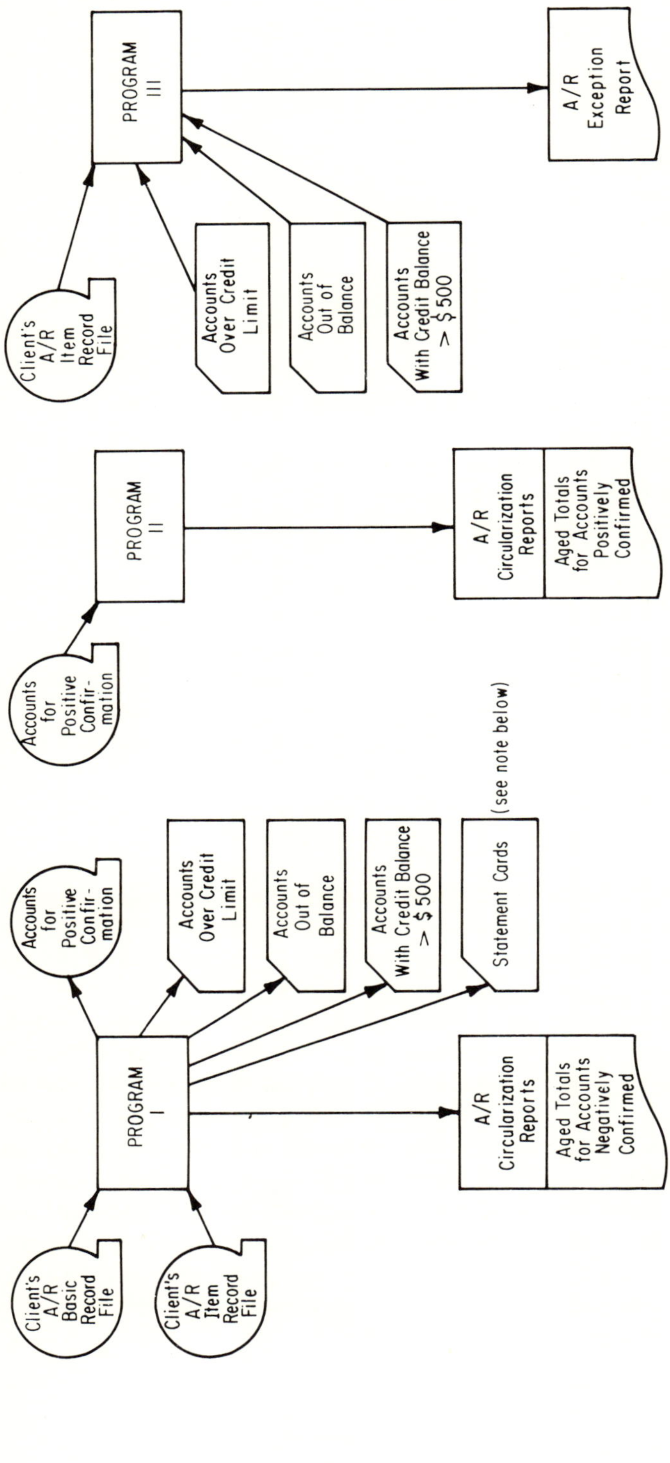

Note: Statement cards are processed with the client's statement preparation program to produce customer statements for mailing with confirmation requests.

Figure 9-11. System Flow Chart—Computer Audit Programs.

Number	*Name and Address*	*T*	*S*	*Balances*	*Difference*	*No Reply*	*Explanation and Disposition*
0333500	ACE INC.	1	0	7,280.31	BALANCE		
	2105 WINSPEAR AVE.			937.41	30 DAYS		
	MADISON, ILL.				60 DAYS		
					90 DAYS		
0350000	ACME COMPANY	1	0	12,408.47	BALANCE		
	7055 BEST RD.			2,463.94	30 DAYS		
	LANSING 4, MICH.				60 DAYS		
					90 DAYS		
0514000	ADDER CO.	1	0	33,347.91	BALANCE		
	YAKIMA, WASH.			23,180.43	30 DAYS		
					60 DAYS		
					90 DAYS		
1161000	BOOM TOOLS	1	0	6,037.19	BALANCE		
	12360 ASPEN LANE			3,022.76	30 DAYS		
	BOULDER, COLO.				60 DAYS		
					90 DAYS		
1466000	CRISP FORGING MFG.	1	0	34,246.84	BALANCE		
	LOWELL, MASS.			23,082.57	30 DAYS		
					60 DAYS		
					90 DAYS		
2511000	DUNHILL SUPPLY	1	0	5,772.28	BALANCE		
	4890 SOUTH CANTON ST.			2,236.99	30 DAYS		
	CANTON, OHIO				60 DAYS		
					90 DAYS		
2620075	EARTH-MOVERS INC.	1	0	11,784.47	BALANCE		
	PUYALLUP, WASH.			7,121.74	30 DAYS		
					60 DAYS		
					90 DAYS		
2646000	ESTHER TOOLS	1	0	7,234.73	BALANCE		
	COLLEGE LANE			255.96	30 DAYS		
	WILLIAMS, PA.				60 DAYS		
					90 DAYS		
3170000	FIRST SUPPLY	1	0	8.098.33	BALANCE		
	6360 DIVISION RD.			75.20	30 DAYS		
	BATTLE CREEK, MICH.				60 DAYS		
					90 DAYS		
3262310	GUNN FORGING	1	0	6,738.26	BALANCE		
	BARNESVILLE, IND.			3,212.17	30 DAYS		
					60 DAYS		
					90 DAYS		

PAGE TOTAL 10 ACCOUNTS BALANCE 132,948.79 30 DAYS 65,589.17 60 DAYS 90 DAYS

Figure 9-12. Accounts Receivable Circularization Sept. 30, 19XX.

THE AUDITAPE SYSTEM APPLIED

In using the Auditape system to perform the audit procedures enumerated above, I completed the relevant specification sheets required to use the system. There were 38 separate computer runs required to perform the necessary audit procedures. Many of these runs were necessary to get the data into the Auditape record format for performing the audit procedures. The scope of this article does not permit any discussion of the technical aspects related to the completion of the specification sheets and details of operating the system.[13]

Based on my analysis, I concluded that the Auditape system can perform all of the significant procedures included in the specialized programs. It does not provide the same flexibility in report format—i.e., aged information on the circularization report, type code—but this seems to be a rather insignificant item.

As to a comparison of time requirements of both approaches my analysis indicates:

	Specialized Programs	*Auditape*	
Analysis of problem (including flowcharting, input-output design)	150.0	30-50	(estimated)
Programming (including coding, key-punching, assembly and testing)	70.0		
Completion and key-punching of specification sheets		12	(estimated 2 hours for keypunching)
Run time	.5	2.5	
	220.5	44.5—64.5	

One footnote to the above time analysis should be added. The actual time for the analysis of the problem originally was 230 hours; this reflected some developmental and learning time. Discounting this time, it is more realistic to think in terms of 150 hours, which I have shown above, for the analysis of the problem. Approximately 100-120 of the 150 hours would be required for flowcharting and input-output design and would be unnecessary when using the Auditape system; hence the 30-50 hours for analysis under Auditape.

[13]For those who wish such details, they may contact the AICPA's professional development division about courses on the H&S Auditape system, Haskins & Sells, or W. Thomas Porter on the specifics of this research.

CONCLUSIONS ABOUT AUDITAPE

Based on my knowledge of and experimentation with the Auditape system, my major conclusions are:

1. The Auditape system, by virtue of the Edit Routine, can be applied to a variety of EDP installations involving a variety of record and file formats "without any need for preparation of special programs for each type of application to be processed."
2. The system, by virtue of the Include/Exclude Subroutine of the Edit Routine, can be a very powerful auditing tool in a variety of auditing situations that require examination of records for qualitative characteristics and conditions. In relation to the auditing uses of computer programs discussed earlier in this article, my analysis indicates that the Auditape system can be used to:
   a. Test extensions and footings through its Edit Routine and Mathematical Routine.
   b. Summarize data and perform analyses according to specified criteria by virtue of the Include/Exclude or Subtotal Subroutines of the Edit Routine and the Summarize Routine.
   c. Examine records for quality through the use of the Include/Exclude Subroutine.
   d. Select and print audit samples through the use of the Audit Sample Routine and Print/Punch Routine.

   At the present time, the Auditape system cannot print confirmation requests, and it cannot very easily compare data maintained in separate files. However, Haskins & Sells plans to develop routines in the near future which will print confirmation requests and which will handle multiple input files and permit comparisons of data in separate files.
3. The system has been developed for use with the following equipment:
   a. Processing units—IBM 1400 series tape systems or system 360 with 1401 emulators, with memory capacity of at least 8,000 characters. Honeywell Series 200 tape systems, with memory capacity of at least 8,000 characters. IBM System 360 tape or disk systems, with memory capacity of at least 32,000. Certain other equipment for which 1401 simulators are provided by the manufacturers.
   b. Card read-punch.
   c. Printer or a console typewriter.
   d. Input/output units—at least three units for applications requiring an output tape or disk; at least two units for other applications.

However, the nonavailability of the above equipment at a particular location may not be a limitation if the input data are available on tapes or disks that can be transcribed into punched card or IBM tape format and the required equipment is available at another location (such as a service bureau). For example, in using the system for internal audit purposes at the University of Washington, we analyzed, on the university's IBM 1401 computer system, files previously generated on the university's Burroughs B5500 computer system.

4. The system significantly reduces the time required by the auditor in using the computer in auditing as compared to the alternative approach of developing specialized computer programs for individual client situations without any significant decrease in effectiveness in performing audit procedures with a computer.
5. The system, although requiring no programming on the part of the auditor, does require some knowledge of the computer and programming to allow *efficient* completion of the specification sheets. For example, terms and activities such as low-order positions, data fields, record formats, control cards and character manipulation all require more than a basic knowledge of the computer and programming on the part of the user of the Auditape system to effectively and efficiently use the system. Haskins & Sells, in recognition of this problem, has designed and conducted an Auditape System Seminar sponsored by the AICPA's professional development division. This program provides instruction for practicing CPAs in the use of the system. This program coupled with a few on-the-job experiences in using the system should be sufficient to allow efficient use of Auditape.
6. The system requires that even auditors experienced in the use of the computer have a nominal amount of instructions about the system in addition to knowledge gained by reading the operating manual. This is extremely evident when trying to use the Include/Exclude Subroutine. This was borne out in a recent classroom experiment with M.B.A. candidates most of whom had previous knowledge of computers and actual programming experience. All of the students had difficulty in applying the Include/Exclude Subroutine to an auditing application. Comments on problems they encountered in using the system included:

> I was not able to determine from the information provided in the operating manual how one indicates the information pertinent to the Include/Exclude operations on the specification sheets.
>
> In relationship to the Include/Exclude Subroutine, it

would appear advisable to include in the operating manual an appendix which demonstrates how a simple representative problem is worked out.

7. The system as currently designed is somewhat cumbersome to use and would be greatly improved if certain functions could be combined so as to minimize the number of runs. The current version of the Auditape system was designed for the IBM 1400 series with a minimum of 8,000 characters of memory. It is obvious to users of EDP equipment that such a small memory capacity places constraints on the design and running of computer programs, particularly generalized computer programs. Haskins & Sells is working on a new version of the system which will combine certain routines so as to minimize the number of runs required for some audit applications.

SUMMARY

This article has examined the development and use of generalized computer-audit programs with particular emphasis on the Haskins & Sells Auditape system. The idea of generalized audit programs is a good one. H&S has taken one approach; other but not mutually exclusive possibilities include:

1. Generalized industry programs to perform audit steps common to an industry.

2. Generalized programs to perform common tasks such as confirmation, aging, testing for obsolete items, examination of file quality, etc.

3. Standard COBOL subroutines which the auditor combines to develop an individualized program for a particular client.

4. An audit language, based perhaps on a special version of the RPG (Report Program Generator) language.

I believe that there will be considerable activity in the area of generalized audit programs by different CPA firms and perhaps by software companies. In view of the high costs involved in developing such programs, the duplication of effort that may result from individual firms' developmental activities and the relevance of such programs for the entire profession, it is comforting to know that the AICPA has appointed a computer users committee which, among other things, is looking into this entire problem area.

AUDITING ACCOUNTS RECEIVABLE BY COMPUTER—A CASE HISTORY

by Joe R. Fritzemeyer and Carmen C. Spinelli

Much has been done in the past three years in the computer field in the development and use of generalized audit programs, specialized audit programs and time-sharing as an aid to the auditor.

Our experience in a recent case clearly indicates that these different techniques can be a powerful tool in performing a more effective audit, developing more complete information, reaching more logical conclusions and bolstering the judgment of the responsible auditor.

What is perhaps even more important is that our experience demonstrates that these techniques can be used to reduce the cost of the audit while doing a more effective job.

The following is based on a true case history, although it has been broadened to some extent to permit the introduction of related techniques. Actually a new client with whom we had no previous audit experience was involved.

CLIENT DATA

The client's principal asset consists of accounts receivable arising from the sale of subscriptions. The two major items on the balance sheet of interest to the auditors are the accounts receivable and deferred subscription income.

The normal accumulation of other balance sheet items also exists. Because of their size and lack of significance, however, they did not lend themselves to the type of approach which we would utilize in applying computer audit techniques.

The initial information developed by the audit group indicated that the accounts receivable represented a gross value of over $2.5 million, involving approximately 30,000 accounts. No information was available on the average distribution of the dollar value or on the aging of these accounts.

The client maintained the accounts receivable records on a unit record system, using a series of IBM 407 accounting machines to accumulate the schedule and other distributions periodically. This is significant, because this was a situation in which the record-keeping techniques were not unique or unusual. And yet the method in which we

---

Reprinted by permission of the publisher from *The Journal of Accountancy,* April 1970, pp. 73-78, copyright 1970 by the American Institute of Certified Public Accountants, Inc.

utilized the computer audit techniques capitalized on the available knowledge of tape and disc systems. This knowledge was used to extend the information available on a unit record system.

PLANNING DECISIONS

In the initial discussions with the audit group, it was decided that statistical sampling techniques would be applied to the total universe of the accounts receivable.

It was also decided that Auditape would be used for the following purposes:

- For examining the content of individual accounts.
- For stratifying the dollar value of the accounts.
- For re-summarizing the account totals.
- For selecting as well as identifying the audit sample.

We further decided that the preparation of the accounts receivable confirmation notices could be performed as a by-product of the computer approach. This initially presented a problem, because the client's file system maintained the name and address files separately from the account balance file, the only common factor being the account identification number. Accordingly, a specialized audit program had to be written to transfer the information from the two files to the confirmation forms.

Finally—and most importantly—the next step was to determine the most efficient and the least expensive way of evaluating the audit responses. This was necessary in order to reach a conclusion as to the amount of the reserve to be established and to evaluate the adequacy of the internal control system. Certain programs available on General Electric's time-sharing system were selected for this purpose.

PROCESSING THE CLIENT'S FILES

Initial discussions with the client's controller led to the conclusion that the most effective approach would be to duplicate the client's unit record file as of their closing date. This would provide sufficient flexibility without impeding the client's subsequent updating of their files.

When the files were reproduced by the client, the records were moved to a service bureau and the cards reproduced on tape. Only then did we proceed with the Auditape approach.

As a result of the first run, it was established that certain data were being introduced into the client's card format which were not susceptible to tape treatment. At this point, special programs to modify and adapt the card image to tape format in the necessary arrangement were required. Reprocessing the tapes also effected an initial examination of the client file, which showed approximately a $900,000 difference between the total amount in the file and the amount represented as being the correct balance. Upon examination, it was determined that the client had inadvertently given us an incorrect control balance.

We also discovered certain problems about the segregation of credit balances from debit balances because of the client's card format. Therefore, modification of the tape files was necessary to permit further processing.

As we continued to process the files and segregated the credit balances from the debit balances, we came to certain startling conclusions. The first was that the client's personnel had been filing the cards representing the cash receipts without removing the offsetting debit balances. We found that the file contained approximately $1 million in unapplied cash balances! This, of course, was not readily discernible in the client's schedules because these amounts would cancel themselves against debit balances in producing the trial balance of the accounts receivable. This was a significant observation on the internal control system which obviously had elements of inadequacy. These internal control problems were quickly brought to the attention of the client's personnel with a recommendation that immediate steps be taken to correct this situation.

While this situation was being corrected, we established that there remained certain large credit balances which were unusual. Since these items required further investigation, the information was conveyed to the audit group.

At this stage, we proceeded with our determination of the stratification of accounts and the selection of the statistical sample. Two or three passes were made before a stratification was established that was considered satisfactory by the audit and computer personnel involved. The results of the final stratification are shown in Figure 9-13. The upper portion reflects the stratification of the universe and the lower portion shows the sample selected by stratum. It can be seen that, of 30,217 accounts in the universe, only 644 accounts, or 2 per cent, were selected, but that the dollar value for those accounts represents approximately 25 per cent of the total dollar value.

Upon selection of the sample size, the particular accounts within each stratum were identified and printed out, and we moved on to the program which prepared the accounts receivable confirmations.

SUMMARIZING VERIFICATIONS

As confirmation responses were received, the data were introduced into the General Electric time-sharing system. In this way we could keep control over the trend and the deviation in the indicated reserve for

POPULATION DATA

	BOTTOM STRATUM	MIDDLE STRATUM	TOP STRATUM	TOTAL
REC. COUNT	26,145	4,059	13	30,217
FIELD 9				
POS.	674,317.20	1,325,382.20	198,913.77	2,198,613.17
NEG.	112,189.44 CR	162,978.32 CR	7,951.37 CR	283,119.13 CR
NET	562,127.76	1,162,403.88	190,962.40	1,915,494.04

SAMPLE DATA

	BOTTOM STRATUM	MIDDLE STRATUM	TOP STRATUM	TOTAL
RFC. COUNT	237	394	13	644
FIELD 9				
POS.	10,528.63	308,351.30	198,913.77	517,793.70
NEG.	1,612.87 CR	20,785.74 CR	7,951.37 CR	30,349.98 CR
NET	8,915.76	287,565.56	190,962.40	487,443.72

Figure 9-13. Audit Sample Routine—Monetary Sample.

doubtful accounts as well as evaluate the internal control system.

Upon completion, the computer was programmed to list in detail the items confirmed or tested as partially shown in Figure 9-14:

```
J.K. LASSER


GE TIME-SHARING SERVICE


ON AT   15:19   G   MON 01/27/69    TTY 12

USER NUMBER--H00000
SYSTEM--BASIC
NEW OR OLD--OLD
OLD FILE NAME--MARSHA


READY.

LIST


MARSHA     15:19   G   MON 01/27/69

5REMARK NUMBER OF STRATA + QUANTITY IN EACH IS NEXT
10DATA 3,12,395,217
15 REMARK TOTAL ITEMS IN STRATUM 1 + VALUE OF STRATUM IS NEXT
20DATA 12,176790
25REMARK BOOK VALUES STRATUM 1 ITEMS, RECOM. ADJS. ARE NEXT
30DATA 7500,1,12543,0,12229,0,34860,191,8781,0
31DATA 9734,0,9200,9200,17323,0,11073,0,-7951,0,17470,0,44028,0
35REMARK TOTAL ITEMS IN STRATUM 2 + VALUE OF STRATUM IS NEXT
40DATA 4060,1162229
45REMARK BOOK VALUES STRATUM 2 ITEMS, RECOM. ADJS. ARE NEXT
50DATA [illegible]
[illegible] 20,20,78,[illegible],84,64,0,0,22,[illegible],54,0,[illegible],96,0,[illegible]
226DATA 96,0,20,20,-96,0,18,18,21,0,72,0,75,0,20,0,66,66,48,0
227DATA 25,0,22,0,35,0,29,0,21,0,-53,0,20,20,-100,0,90,90,20,0
228DATA 20,20,20,0,57,0,96,0,96,0,29,0,21,0,76,0,20,0,20,20,24,0

280DATA -91,-91,96,0,21,0,20,0,-95,0,82,0,-13,0,20,0,53,3,67,0
285DATA 20,20,72,0,75,0,72,0,39,39,72,0,96,0,22,22,99,99,72,72
290DATA 20,0,72,72,20,0,73,0,82,82,-24,0,20,0,61,61,72,72,58,0
295DATA 22,0,-24,0,20,0


BYE

***OFF AT 15:29   ELAPSED TERMINAL TIME =    10 MIN.
```

Figure 9-14. Summary of Accounts Receivable Verifications.

1. At the top is certain information necessary in using the GE time-sharing system. The time and date are always automatically printed out when the system is accessed, and the time at the end of the run is recorded at the bottom. It is of interest that the program run began at 15:19 and ended at 15:29, representing a

total elapsed time of only ten minutes. This interval is the actual time taken to transmit the data, and the cost for terminal time was approximately $2. No computer usage time is charged for this listing.

2. The first two lines of the summary indicate that there are three strata and that the number of accounts in each stratum is: 12; 395; and 237, respectively. The 237 has been manually changed to 217 as an indication to reduce stratum three in order to keep the total accounts within the number which the subsequent program could handle.
3. The third and fourth lines indicate that there are 12 items in stratum one and that their total value is $176,790.
4. Lines five through nine list the value of each stratum one item and the value of the recommended adjustment that resulted from the confirmation. Thus it can be seen that the value of item one was $7,500 and the confirmation showed a $1 difference, the value of item two was $12,543 and the verification showed no difference, and so on.
5. Lines ten and eleven are the beginning of the listing of values for stratum two items and the recommended adjustments that resulted from the verifications.
6. It should be noted that at the end of the listing, the values for 20 items are marked for deletion in order to reduce stratum three items to 217 as discussed above.

APPRAISING SAMPLE RESULTS

The data summarized in Figure 9-14 printout were then run through the computer program for appraising sample results, producing the printout shown in Figures 9-15 and 9-16.

Figure 9-15 shows the instructions to the computer:

1. Note the words, "List-280," which are the instruction to the system to print out saved data commencing with data line 280, so that we could visually verify the removal of data rejected by this program because of data file size restrictions.

2. The program run begins at 10:43. Following the listed data, the words "999 Call Apsam," are the instructions to the system to call in the appraisal of sample results program. The word "Run" is our instruction to proceed.

```
J.K. LASSER


GE TIME-SHARING SERVICE


ON AT  10:42   G  THU 01/30/69   TTY 17

USER NUMBER--H00000
SYSTEM--BASIC
NEW OR OLD--OLD
OLD FILE NAME--MARSHA
WAIT.

READY.

LIST--280
WAIT.



MARSHA    10:43   G  THU 01/30/69

280DATA -91,-91,96,0,21,0,20,0,-95,0,82,0,-13,0,20,0,53,3,67,0
285DATA 20,20
290DATA 20,0
295DATA 22,0
999 RETURN


999 CALL APSAM$***
RUN



MARSHA    10:45   G  THU 01/30/69
```

Figure 9-15. Computer Instructions for Appraisal of Sample Results Program.

In Figure 9-16, which shows the appraisal results, note that the program analyzes data for each stratum by two different methods:

1. Under the Difference Method, the total value of differences reported is divided by the number of items in the stratum to determine the average value of Unit Cost Questioned for each item. Thus, in stratum one the total value of Unit Cost Questioned was \$9,392, divided by the 12 items in the stratum, yielding an average of \$782.67.
2. Under the Ratio Method, the total value of differences reported is divided by the total value of all items to determine the ratio of sample differences to the total value. Thus, in stratum one the \$9,392 Unit Cost Questioned is divided by \$176,790, the value

```
APPRAISAL OF SAMPLE RESULTS
                                                  DIFFERENCE      RATIO
                                                  METHOD          METHOD
STRATUM 1 OF 3
  UNIT COST QUESTIONED-- 9392 / 12                                782.667
  RATIO QUESTIONED-- 9392 / 176790                                .053125
  TOTAL COST QUESTIONED
                 782.667 X 12                     9392.
                 .053125 X 176790                                 9391.97
  STANDARD DEVIATION                              2651.34         2826.13
  STANDARD ERROR OF ESTIMATE                      0               0
  CONFIDENCE INTERVALS--PLUS OR MINUS
   70 PC LEVEL-- 1.088    X STD ERROR             0               0
   80 PC LEVEL-- 1.363    X STD ERROR             0               0
   90 PC LEVEL-- 1.795    X STD ERROR             0               0
   95 PC LEVEL-- 2.199    X STD ERROR             0               0

STRATUM 2 OF 3
  UNIT COST QUESTIONED-- 35507  / 395                             89.8911
  RATIO QUESTIONED-- 35507   / 287389                             .12355
  TOTAL COST QUESTIONED
                 89.8911 X 4060                   364958.
                 .12355  X 1162229                                143593.
  STANDARD DEVIATION                              422.866         408.473
  STANDARD ERROR OF ESTIMATE                      82083.8         79289.9
  CONFIDENCE INTERVALS--PLUS OR MINUS
   70 PC LEVEL-- 1.038    X STD ERROR             85203.          82302.9
   80 PC LEVEL-- 1.284    X STD ERROR             105396.         101808.
   90 PC LEVEL-- 1.649    X STD ERROR             135356.         130749.
   95 PC LEVEL-- 1.966    X STD ERROR             161377.         155884.

STRATUM 3 OF 3
  UNIT COST QUESTIONED-- 1215 / 217                               5.59908
  RATIO QUESTIONED-- 1215 / 8153                                  .149025
  TOTAL COST QUESTIONED
                 5.59908 X 26145                  146388.
                 .149025 X 562128                                 83771.1
  STANDARD DEVIATION                              25.0522         23.2398
  STANDARD ERROR OF ESTIMATE                      44279.5         41076.1
  CONFIDENCE INTERVALS--PLUS OR MINUS
   70 PC LEVEL-- 1.039    X STD ERROR             46006.4         42678.1
   80 PC LEVEL-- 1.285    X STD ERROR             56899.2         52782.8
   90 PC LEVEL-- 1.652    X STD ERROR             73149.7         67857.7
   95 PC LEVEL-- 1.971    X STD ERROR             87274.9         80961.

ALL STRATA SAMPLED
  TOTAL COST QUESTIONED                           520738.         236756.
  CONFIDENCE INTERVALS--PLUS OR MINUS
   70 PC LEVEL                                    96830.4         92710.3
   80 PC LEVEL                                    119774.         114678.
   90 PC LEVEL                                    153858.         147309.
   95 PC LEVEL                                    183465.         175654.

USED          24.83 UNITS.
BYE

***OFF AT 10:50    ELAPSED TERMINAL TIME =     7 MIN.
```

Figure 9-16. Printout of Appraisal of Sample Results Program.

of all items, yielding a ratio of .053125.

3. For each stratum, the Unit Cost Questioned and Ratio Questioned are then converted into Total Cost Questioned for the stratum. Since all of the items in stratum one were selected, the calculation results in the actual value questioned, $9,392. In stratum two, the Total Cost Questioned is $364,958 under the Difference Method ($89.8911 average cost questioned times 4060 items) and $143,593 under the Ratio Method (.12355 sample ratio times $1,162,229 total value for all items in the stratum).
4. The appraisal program next computes Standard Deviation, Standard Error of Estimate and Confidence Intervals for each stratum and finally summarizes results for all strata. The summary shows that the Total Cost Questioned for all three strata was $520,738 under the Difference Method and $236,756 under the ratio method.
5. It can be seen that results under the Ratio Method were preferable for audit judgments in this case, because the Ratio Method is based upon dollar value, as was the selection of our sample.
6. Note at the bottom of the listing that the number of computer time units came to 24.83. In going off the system at 10:50, we used a total elapsed terminal and computer time of 7 minutes. Our total cost for computer and terminal time for this appraisal run came to approximately $3—a remarkably modest expense.

The timing of each of these runs is truly phenomenal when compared to the amount of effort which would have been required to perform the same functions by longhand. The response time of the terminals, as well as the case with which the information was developed, also permitted the continued evaluation of the data as it was received.

The true payoff to all this processing and analysis comes both from the knowledge that a better job has been done professionally and also in the final test of the economies of the situation.

TIME REQUIREMENTS—MANUAL VS COMPUTER

In order to compare our computer approach with a manual approach, we estimated the time that we would have budgeted for this engagement, if we had done it on a straight-manual basis. Figure 9-17 shows the time requirements for each step of the audit on a manual basis and on a computer basis.

It can be seen that for preliminary investigation and discussions, the manual approach would have required only four hours compared to the ten hours required for the computer approach, but that for the steps

	Audit Staff Time Manual Approach (Hours)	Audit and Computer Staff Time Computer Approach (Hours)
Preliminary Investigation and Discussion	4	10
Footing Accounts Receivable File and Audit of File Contents	35	3
Selecting Confirmation Sample and Preparing List	28	1
Preparing Confirmations, Stuffing and Mailing	31	2
Accumulating and Appraising Sample Results	45	21
TOTAL	143 Hours	37 Hours

Figure 9-17. Comparison of Time Requirements Audit of Accounts Receivable.

thereafter, the manual approach would have required vastly more time than we used in our computer approach:

Footing Accounts Receivable File and Audit of File Contents	1000% more time
Selecting Confirmation Sample and Preparing List	2800% more time
Preparing Confirmations, Stuffing and Mailing	1500% more time
Accumulating and Appraising Sample Results	200% more time

The budgeted manual approach comes to 143 hours. The computer approach adds up to only 37 hours—dramatic evidence that the computer is indeed a powerful audit tool.

CONCLUSION

As it is abundantly clear from the broad outline of this case study, the client's record-keeping techniques were in the "dark ages" of computer approaches and yet we were able to apply the computer to auditing the accounts receivable in a much shorter time than would have been required for a manual audit.

By the same token, we believe that the accounting profession may also be in the "dark ages" of relating audit techniques to data processing. In this particular case, we have used the computer for only one of the many items on the balance sheet. The others were dealt with in a normal, routine way, solely because the economies did not dictate the application of other techniques.

It is entirely feasible to foresee the day when all this information will be readily available for some form of computer processing. And that is the ultimate goal to which the profession should dedicate itself, because this direction represents the true professional challenge as well as the true economic payback.

PART FOUR

Improving EDP Effectiveness

10

Controlling Application Selection and Development

Most organizations have already seized the opportunities for quick, tangible returns from data processing applications. Despite the advances in performance and capacity, profitable use of the computer has become more difficult to achieve.

A successful project must be feasible at three levels: technical, operational, and economic. Each of these levels of feasibility is harder to assess and accomplish when advanced applications are undertaken.

Outside resources, in the form of consulting, facilities management, and purchased application software, are growing in importance. They can bring skills, experience, and results which are not always available internally. Special care in contracting is required.

Achieving the economic potential of the computer calls for new dimensions of managerial involvement and broader professional skills in the information systems activity. Control and audit skills can assist management and the data processing activity. There is an important contribution to be made during project selection and in the final postinstallation audit of costs and results. Major projects also offer an additional opportunity for control and audit inputs at key checkpoints in the long and costly development process.

UNLOCKING THE COMPUTER'S PROFIT POTENTIAL

McKinsey & Company, Inc.

ABOUT THE STUDY

In the course of this study, we interviewed staff and line executives, up to and frequently including the chief executive officer, in 36 large U.S. and European companies representing 13 industries. Some but not all of these companies were clients of McKinsey & Company. Their distribution by industry, sales volume, and relative level of computer expenditure is shown in Figure 10-1.

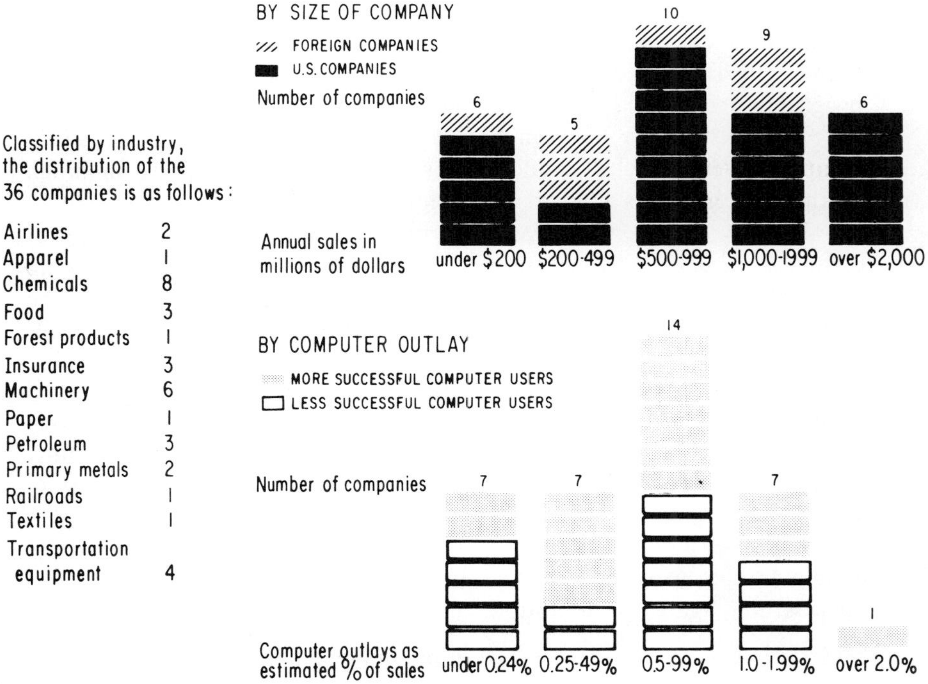

Figure 10-1. Profile of the Study Sample.

Reprinted by permission from "Unlocking the Computer's Profit Potential," copyright 1968 by McKinsey & Company, Inc. New York, N.Y.

The companies represent all levels of achievement and experience with computers. One of them, a major European manufacturer, installed its first computer as recently as 1963. Several others have more than a dozen years' experience, and some of these have computer applications in almost every major department.

The computer practices and achievements of these companies are so diverse that quantitative performance measures are both difficult to formulate and easy to misinterpret. In this report, therefore, we have relied mainly on anecdotal evidence to exemplify the problems that can beset computer development efforts and the means that have proved most effective for solving or avoiding them.

Our findings strongly indicate that "keys to success" in the use of computers can be expressed only in very general terms. Even for a particular industry, it is seldom possible to pinpoint inventory management, or financial planning, or sales performance measurement as the application holding most immediate promise of profit in 1968 and beyond. And, as Figure 10-1 indicates, success with the computer shows no consistent correlation with level of computer expenditures. Some companies are spending heavily for a very dubious payoff; others with less ambitious programs are reaping major rewards.

The distinction between "more successful" and "less successful" computer users, which is explicit in several figures and implicit in much of the text, requires a word of explanation.

In view of the many variables involved, any absolute standard of computer success must necessarily be arbitrary. Instead of attempting to legislate such a standard, therefore, we decided to let "success" be defined by the range of performance observed in the survey sample itself.

For this purpose, we ranked the 36 companies judgmentally on their overall achievement with the computer, taking into account such factors as measurable return on the computer investment over time, range of meaningful functional applications, and chief executive satisfaction with the computer effort to date. The companies identified in Figure 10-1 and elsewhere as "more successful computer users" are simply those falling in the upper half of this order-of-performance ranking. The "less successful," again by definition, are those in the lower half.

As any executive experienced in the management of large-scale computer efforts will recognize, an element of subjectivity inevitably enters into judgments of this kind, and there is almost always room for legitimate difference of opinion on the rankings assigned to individual companies. However, we believe that any experienced analyst having access to the same data would arrive at essentially the same results.

INTRODUCTION

In terms of technical achievement, the computer revolution in U.S. business is outrunning expectations. In terms of economic payoff on new applications, it is rapidly losing momentum. Such is the evidence of a new study by McKinsey & Company of computer systems management in 36 major companies.

From a profit standpoint, our findings indicate, computer efforts in all but a few exceptional companies are in real, if often unacknowledged, trouble. Faster, costlier, more sophisticated hardware; larger and increasingly costly computer staffs; increasingly complex and ingenious applications: these are in evidence everywhere. Less and less in evidence, as these new applications proliferate, are profitable results. This is the familiar phenomenon of diminishing returns. But there is one crucial difference: As yet, the real profit potential of the computer has barely begun to be tapped.

Almost 20 years ago the first computers for business use made their debut. In 1963, when we published our first research report on the computer,[1] business was well on the way to exploiting the awesome clerical and arithmetical talents of its new tool. Today the early goals have for all practical purposes been attained. Most large companies have successfully mechanized the bulk of their routine clerical and accounting procedures, and many have moved out into operating applications.

As a super-clerk, the computer has more than paid its way. For most large organizations, going back to punch cards and keyboard machines would be as unthinkable as giving up the typewriter for the quill pen. Yet in these same companies—including many that pioneered in the mechanization of paperwork operations—mounting computer expenditures are no longer matched by rising economic returns.

What has gone wrong? The answer, our findings suggest, lies in a failure to adapt to new conditions. The rules of the game have been changing, but management's strategies have not.

There was a time, less than a decade ago, when management could afford to leave the direction of the corporate computer effort largely in the hands of technical staff people. That time is past. Yet the identification and selection of new computer applications are still predominantly in the hands of computer specialists, who—despite their professional expertise—are poorly qualified to set the course of the corporate computer effort.

---

[1]McKinsey & Company, Inc., *Getting the Most Out of Your Computer*, 1963.

It is not hard to understand how this situation has come about. Historically, profit-oriented companies have undertaken computer development work for the sake of a single ultimate objective: improved financial results. There are just three ways such results can be reflected in the income statement, and three general categories of computer applications by which this can be accomplished directly:

	Purpose	Application
1.	To reduce general and administrative expenses	Administrative and accounting uses
2.	To reduce cost of goods sold	Operations control systems
3.	To increase revenues	Product innovation and improved customer service

Improved financial results, of course, can also be achieved indirectly, through better management information and control. This gives rise to a final purpose and application category:

4.	To improve staff work and management decisions	Information systems and simulation models

Mainly because of rising clerical costs and the desire to cut clerical staffs, the practical history of computers in U.S. business to date has been dominated by the first of these four purposes. A look at current computer development projects shows that the prime objective in many computer departments is still the refinement of administrative systems and the reduction of G&A expenses. But this, our study indicates, is an area where the cream (and some of the milk) has already been skimmed. It is high time for a change in emphasis, if not a change of course, in the computer development effort. And the next move is up to management.

Many senior executives are already beginning to recognize their dilemma. "How can I keep on justifying major computer expenditures when I can't show a dollar saved to date from our last three applications?" asks the president of a large consumer goods company. "Maybe I'm a fool to let it worry me—after all, who tries to find a dollar justification for telephones and typewriters? But I do worry. After all, we know that what we're doing with telephones and typewriters makes sense. But that's more than I can say for some of the things we're doing with the computer, at many times the cost."

The ill-justified expenditures, however, are insignificant compared to the opportunity costs. Though it has transformed the administrative and accounting operations of U.S. business, the computer has had little impact on most companies' key operating and management problems. Yet, as Figure 10-2 suggests, this is where its greatest potential lies.

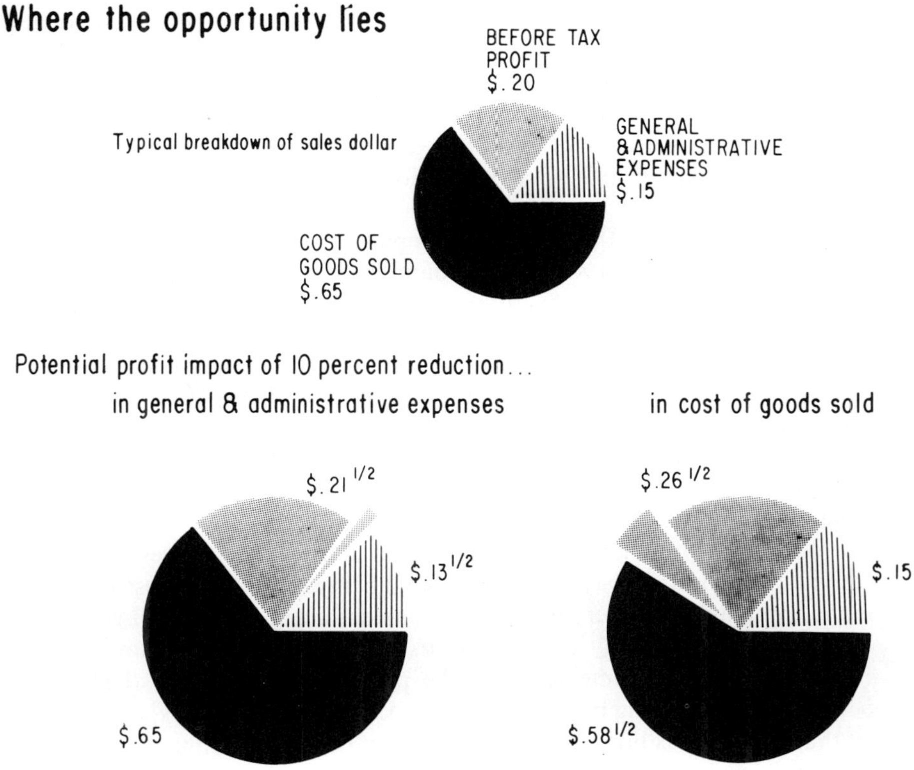

Figure 10-2. Where the Opportunity Lies.

In our 1963 report, we noted that no company had yet come anywhere near exhausting the computer's potential. Today the gap between technical capability and practical achievement is still wider, and the stakes have risen sharply. Until the computer is put to work where the leverage on profits is high, the penalty of lost opportunities and lost profits will continue to mount.

Subsequent sections of this report will set forth the dimensions and implications of the issue. We shall outline the developments that have shaped it, explore the current problems to which it has given rise, and indicate some of the future opportunities open to companies that take timely action to resolve it. Finally, we shall offer a few practical guidelines for the chief executive who recognizes his own vital personal responsibility for the success and profitability of his company's computer effort.

THE STAKES AND THE PROBLEM

In 1963, computer manufacturers shipped hardware worth $1.3 billion to their U.S. customers. By 1967, the value of computer shipments had risen to $3.9 billion, an increase of no less than 200 percent in four years.[2] Of every $1 million that business laid out on new plant and equipment in 1963, $33,000 went for computers and computer-associated hardware. By 1967, the computer's share had risen to $63,000, and each dollar was buying at least half as much again in capacity. Computer spending, both absolutely and as a proportion of all plant and equipment outlays, is still rising.

Another index to the growth of computers as a factor in the national economy from 1963 to 1966 can be found in the published accounts of the largest computer manufacturer, the International Business Machines Corporation. IBM's gross investment in "factory and office equipment, rental machines and parts" grew from just under $2 billion in 1963 (double the 1957 figure) to just over $5 billion in 1966. In its annual report for 1966, IBM chose for the first time to report separately the value of its investment in machines on rental. Valued at cost, that investment had grown from $3.3 billion to $4.4 billion during the previous 12 months, a one-year growth of 33 percent.

Massive as it looks and rapidly as it is growing, the investment in computer hardware is far from an adequate measure of business's stake in the computer. For every dollar spent on equipment, the typical company in our current study spent close to $2.00 on people and supplies in 1967, as Figure 10-3 indicates; and the payroll component of the total outlay is clearly rising more rapidly than the rental bills. Thus, a company that is paying as little as $125,000 a year to rent equipment of very modest capacity is probably spending upwards of a third of a million dollars on its total effort. It is a fair estimate that well over a hundred industrial companies have rental bills running into seven figures, and there are a handful whose total computer outlays approach $100 million a year.

Because so much of the total cost is payroll, and because staffs are dispersed and personnel classifications and accounting conventions differ from company to company, attempts to formulate "yardsticks" for corporate computer outlays (e.g., as a percentage of assets, capital expenditures, administrative expenses, or sales volume) are likely to end in confusion. Even if precision in such figures were possible, what a particular company "ought" to be spending on computers will not be discovered

---

[2] *EDP Industry and Market Report*, January 26, 1968.

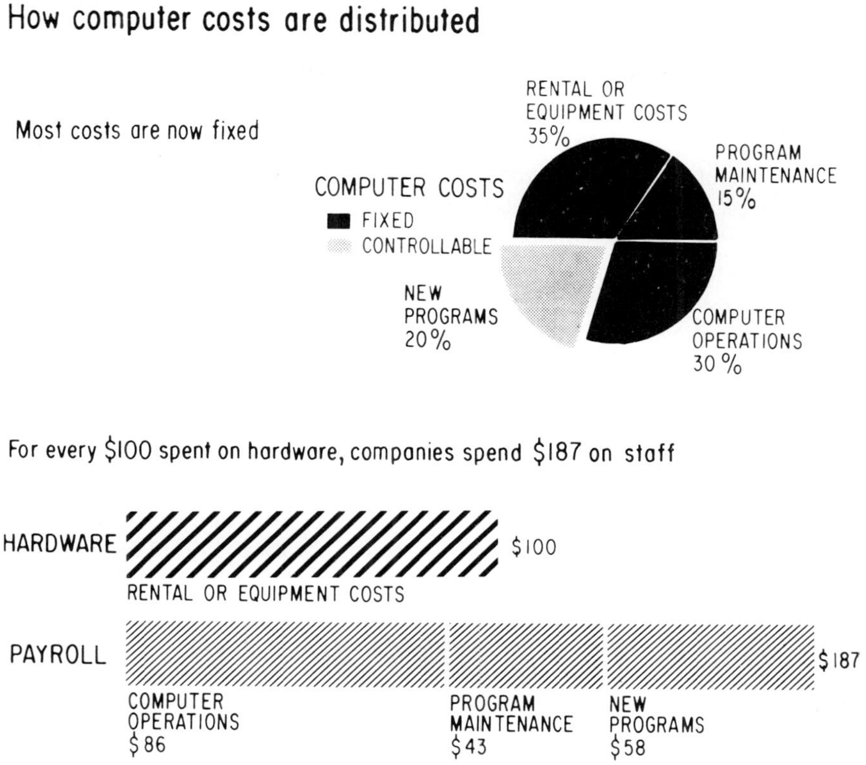

Figure 10-3. How Computer Costs Are Distributed.

by studying industry averages or the outlays of individual competitors. At best, such yardsticks will provide a bench mark from which to start; but the final answer can only be determined in the light of the company's own situation, strategy, and resources (including the depth and sophistication of its computer experience).

The distribution of costs which go to make up total computer expenditures is, however, fairly consistent among the companies participating in our study. Figure 10-3 indicates this distribution. Of every $100,000 of total computer expenditures about $35,000 goes for hardware; $30,000 for computer operations staff payroll; $15,000 for maintenance programming (i.e., keeping current systems updated); and the remaining $20,000 for development programming and other staff time devoted to new applications.

These development dollars, the only computer outlays subject to significant short-term management control, are typically a smaller fraction of the total than the company's annual bill for hardware rentals. Yet their leverage on future costs and benefits is enormous; in fact, they hold the key to the company's long-range success or failure with its computer effort. For unless management segregates these costs and understands the nature of the resources they buy, the direction of future computer developments will be in doubt, and the whole activity will be vulnerable to precipitate, perhaps emotional, review.

The computer management problem as it confronts corporate executives today, then, is a matter of future direction rather than current effectiveness. The key question is not "How are we doing?" but "Where are we heading, and why?"

Five years ago this was a less critical issue at the top-management level. As long as computer developments were largely confined to accounting departments there was less reason for corporate executives to concern themselves with direction setting: If the controller carried out his function and kept his costs in line, no one outside his department worried very much about *how* he did it. The situation is very different today. Now that the conversion of accounting work to computer processing is virtually complete—as it is in 30 of the 36 companies in our study—the question "What next?" comes into urgent focus. Many of the alternatives currently being proposed are complex and costly enough to require executive approval, but their justification is obscure at best. When top management, reviewing a proposal, looks in vain for the promise of profit, it is right to hesitate.

For example, the following three proposals, submitted for approval during 1967 in one company we studied, would have consumed 80 percent of the computer staff time available for development:

1. *Design a computer-based "strategic management information system."* This was candidly described by its sponsor, the manager of the Systems & Procedures Department, as "a basic research project," as indeed it would have been. Management's information needs had not been determined; the cost of making information available was uncertain; and the proposed techniques for putting the manager (assuming he was interested) in a position to manipulate the information (if it could be provided) had never really been tried out.
2. *Design a model of the corporate distribution system, to be used in both long-range planning and daily management of operations.* Cost data on the present distribution system were scanty and out of date. Moreover, responsibility for distribution lay with the marketing vice president, a man who had made no major changes in distribution policy or practice for 15 years, and had a well-

earned reputation for being hostile to innovation. Perhaps understandably, he had not been consulted on the proposal. Yet his support would obviously be indispensable to its success.

3. *Design a revised system of sales call reporting.* As this project was envisioned, the computer would analyze salesmen's routes and product and customer profitability; it would then print out detailed instructions to salesmen each week, specifying customers to be called on, sequence of calls, target sales by product, and weekly sales quotas. This project looked promising, but it had not been evaluated by the very sales people for whom it was intended. And its assumptions were based on present account volume, not future potential.

All these proposals were listed, without specific cost or benefit estimates, in the annual request for budget approval submitted by the Systems & Procedures Department. The president, when they were presented to him for review, reacted with irritation. Were they the best opportunities available for the application of the computer resources? What economic results could realistically be expected? No good answers were available.

Essentially the same questions are raised by any computer development proposal. They are basically questions of *feasibility* — a concept often misunderstood and even more often misapplied where computer projects are concerned. It is this concept, crucial to soundly based computer development efforts, that we will now briefly consider.

THE THREE TESTS OF FEASIBILITY

Recently the president of a German chemical company was asked to examine and approve a proposal for an exciting new management information system. Featuring a desk-side cathode-ray tube inquiry terminal that would display on demand any data in the computer files, the system would enable the president to compare current production figures, by product and/or by plant, against plan; it would break down current sales figures in half a dozen different ways; it would display inventory levels, current labor costs and trends, material costs—in short, just about any kind of operating data he might care to request. A few years earlier such a project would have looked like science fiction; in 1967, its technical feasibility was assured.

Nevertheless, the president turned the proposal down. As he explained his decision to a McKinsey interviewer, "I care more about what will happen five years from now than what happened yesterday. Anyway, I already get all the routine data I can handle. What would I do with more?"

The incident is significant because it typifies a trend. Computer technology has made great strides in just the past few years. Fewer and fewer applications are excluded from consideration because of limits on computer file capacity, internal speed, or input/output ability; more and more technically exciting projects are being proposed for management approval.

Particularly when corporate management is unaccustomed to dealing with the computer department, it takes a certain amount of hard-boiled skepticism to insist on proof of a payoff. Yet the fact is that technical virtuosity is no guarantee of problem-solving potential. The most ingenious new proposal may be merely a fancy new wrapping for an outmoded product. Instant access to data generated by an outmoded cost accounting system, for example, is at best a dubious blessing.

Back in the days when the computer's full potential, and hence its full impact on operating systems, was not foreseen, the overall feasibility of a proposed computer application was generally equated with its technical feasibility. That being the case, it made sense to let the computer professionals decide how to use the computer. Today, judging from the findings of our study, this same policy of delegation is being followed in most companies. But it no longer makes the same kind of sense. Technical feasibility is only one aspect of overall feasibility. For the great majority of business applications, it is no longer an important stumbling block.

The concept of "feasibility" really takes in three separate questions. There is the test of *technical feasibility:* "Is this application possible within the limits of available technology and our own resources?" There is the test of *economic feasibility:* "Will this application return more dollar value in benefits than it will cost to develop?" And there is the test of *operational feasibility:* "If the system is successfully developed, will it be successfully used? Will managers adapt to the system, or will they resist or ignore it?"

Particularly on complex and ambitious computer development projects, these key questions of feasibility can seldom be answered once and for all at the time the project is proposed. Continuous reassessment of the technical and economic risks and payoff probabilities may be vital to keeping such a project on the right track. But a careful initial assessment can go far to avert costly misapplication of scarce computer resources.

It is dangerously easy, however, to avoid confronting the full implications of feasibility until a project is well under way. Technical feasibility, though less often a question mark today, is still the test most commonly considered at the start. The issue of operational feasibility is far too often neglected until the new application is actually tried out in practice and perhaps found wanting—the costliest kind of feasibility test. And economic feasibility—the measure of how much expected dollar returns will exceed expected costs—is frequently given only superficial examination.

Since a company's computer resources are seldom equal to its computer opportunities, economic feasibility should almost always be a key criterion in weighing the merits of technically feasible projects. Yet it is frequently assessed rather casually, on the grounds that the important benefits are intangible, and intangible benefits can't really be evaluated. Actually, of course, the very difficulty of measuring intangible payoffs is the best argument for imposing on managers the discipline of explicit evaluation.

In assessing the cost-benefit balance of a proposed application, computer personnel can, of course, provide the needed input on costs. The assessment of benefits, however, requires a full understanding of the operations affected and the policies that govern them—an understanding that only operating executives can really bring to bear.

To achieve its economic potential, a computer project may also require substantial operational changes—changes in corporate policies, staff reorganizations, the construction of new facilities and the phasing out of the old. It will certainly require the support of operating managers and their staffs, and it may also depend on the cooperation of dealers, suppliers, and even customers. Consider the case of a hardware distributor who requires his customers to submit orders on coded forms designed for the computer. All his customers may want the faster service promised by the system, but some may balk if it entails a messy problem of staff retraining.

Corporate computer staffs cannot really judge the necessity of such changes, much less implement them. At most, they can advise the operating managers who must make the final assessment of operational feasibility.

Against this background, let us look more closely at the problems and opportunities confronting the companies in our study.

PAST SUCCESSES AND PRESENT PROBLEMS

Ironically, the basic problems currently besetting the management of the computer effort in most of the companies we studied have their origin in the successes of the past. In 30 of the 36 companies, conversions of routine administrative and accounting operations to computer systems are already complete, or so close to completion that only minor incremental savings are expected from the mechanization of remaining manual procedures. Typically, most of the people who accomplished these conversions are still operating and maintaining the systems they helped to install. But others who participated in the early installations now enjoy a different organizational status. They constitute the nucleus of a corporate computer staff. Instead of reporting to the controller, in some cases they now report directly to top management.

For obvious reasons, these computer department staffs are under pressure to show results in the form of new computer systems. Technically speaking, they may be superbly equipped to respond to management's expectations. Typically, they are highly skilled in computer systems design, and their status as professionals is unchallengeable. But they are seldom strategically placed (or managerially trained) to assess the economics of operations fully or to judge operational feasibility. These limitations, although they reflect no discredit on the corporate computer staff, are raising ever more serious obstacles to the success of new corporate computer efforts, our findings indicate.

Another obstacle to future success, also stemming from past experience, is management's lack of exposure to the feasibility problem. Back in the days when corporate computer efforts centered on the conversion of accounting and administrative systems, management seldom had to concern itself with the issue of feasibility. With a relatively orderly manual system, the feasibility question centered on the technical problems of programming the computer. Economic benefits could be determined with relative ease in terms of clerical payroll reductions: Once a company had learned how to estimate conversion costs realistically, assessing economic feasibility was relatively simple. And operational feasibility was assured when a single executive, such as the controller, had charge of both the development and operating phases of the new system.

Today the situation is very different. Applications are not only more complex, but also more far-reaching in their impact on different operating departments. Feasibility is no longer an issue that operating managers can ignore, for it is affected by complex economic and operational questions that the staff specialists are unequipped to answer. Yet many managers—far too many—are still leaving the whole question of feasibility to the computer professionals. At the same time, they are neglecting their own responsibility for setting the direction of the company development efforts.

The background sketched above, then, typically affects the computer effort today in two ways.

First, today's management practices and attitudes, inherited from a time when the full scope of the computer's potential was not foreseen in most companies, are falling short of the demands of today's task. Over the past five years, computer staffs have typically doubled. The department that had 40 people in 1962 has 80 or 85 now, and expects to double again by 1975. Yet no overhaul of the management practices of earlier years has taken place. In 14 of the 36 companies we studied, as Figure 10-4 indicates, nothing deserving the name of an overall plan for a full range of computer applications is yet in evidence, and the economic and operational feasibility of individual projects is seldom fully explored. Ten companies, including a number that do have a computer plan, are providing few if any short-term objectives against which the progress of individual computer projects can be measured.

Second, the range of computer projects now open to the company is circumscribed by the limited background of its computer personnel and the limited initiative of its managers. Consider a list of four proposed applications recently submitted to the president of a midwestern electric machinery manufacturer:

1. Put labor records on random-access files, so that production department or machine group efficiency (now the subject of a weekly report) can be measured daily.

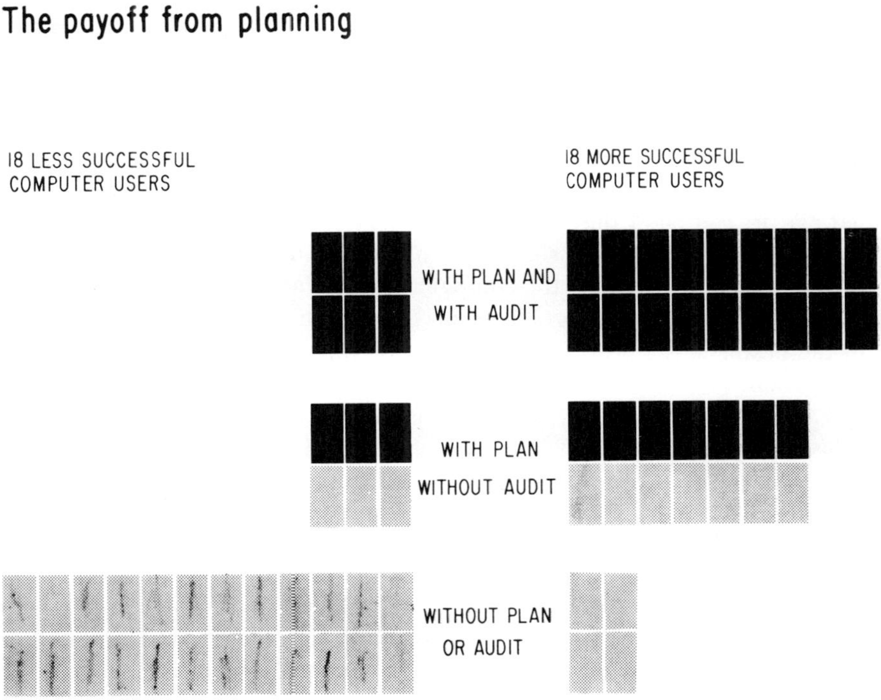

Figure 10-4. The Payoff from Planning.

2. Mechanize the follow-up of delinquent accounts receivable. (At present the computer lists delinquent accounts and shows the age of outstanding debits, but clerks review the list and handle the follow-up.)
3. Install a data-transmission terminal at the warehouse receiving dock so that receipts can be recorded immediately on the computer file when shipments are unloaded. (At present good pieces are counted and the count punched into cards only after a quality control inspection.)
4. Double the core memory of the computer to permit multiprocessing of data processing jobs instead of running them one at a time as at present. (The computer is currently loaded less than two shifts, five days a week.)

None of these proposals had much relevance to the well-being of the corporation. Individual machine shop efficiencies, for example, had long been appallingly low, and the vice president for production was convinced that efficient production runs would be impossible until the design department learned to reduce the catalog of parts used in assemblies. But no attempt had ever been made to put bills of material on computer files, and an overall analysis of the catalog of parts would have to be done manually, an excessively time-consuming job. Accordingly, the president decided to postpone Proposal No. 1, making his reasons quite clear to both the computer department manager and the production head. Later, these two men came up jointly with a project, which was promptly approved, to transfer bill-of-material descriptions from a manual file to computer files. With this application "on stream," production managers are beginning to show real interest in making more extensive use of the computer, and the computer staff is gaining a valuable understanding of the practical problems of production. At least in this area of the business, the prospects for profitable future computer applications look good.

Operational feasibility was the Achilles heel of Proposal No. 2. The sales vice president firmly opposes automatic dunning of delinquent accounts. The clerks who now analyze the delinquent listing are pensioned salesmen who make collections by phone and call personally on seriously delinquent customers. This system of debt collection will not be changed until there is a change at the top—and that is unlikely to happen until 1971 at the earliest.

As for Proposal No. 3, the quality control inspection is essential since high-value components make up 40 percent of all receipts at the dock, and typically between 3 and 5 percent of all items received are returned to the manufacturer or held pending billing adjustments. Thus, although a data-transmission terminal would put data on the computer file two to three days earlier and might avoid some of the interruptions in work flow that now result from reported stock-outs, the data would be faulty and would require detailed subsequent correction and audit.

Such examples, symptomatic of the unbridged gap between computer staff and operating management, could probably be duplicated in most corporations. They are as discouraging to computer professionals as they are to operating management, and they doubtless account for the tendency, observable in many of the companies we studied, for computer staffs to take refuge in refining the internal operating efficiency of the computer department itself (as in Proposal No. 4).

If computer systems design must be so closely linked to operating procedures even in apparently simple applications, it should not be surprising that the more ambitious projects conceived by computer staffs so seldom meet the tests of economic and operational feasibility. To make better use of computers in the future will require expanding the scope and capabilities of computer professionals and bringing managers to a fuller awareness of the computer's vast potential. The history of computer developments to date has limited both.

THE OPPORTUNITIES: NEAR AND FAR-OUT

The computer's credentials as a cutter of clerical payrolls are now beyond dispute. On the evidence of its achievements in a few exceptional corporations, we believe that the computer can make an equal or greater contribution to corporate profits by reducing the cost of goods sold.

The more successful companies in our study have recognized this potential and are already beginning to exploit it. The dominant lesson of their experience so far is that this second stage of the computer revolution, unlike the first, entails real operational changes—new, and at first uncomfortable, ways of doing business that will quite possibly encounter resistance within the company.

For the companies moving into operating system applications, moreover, the issue of feasibility has emerged on a new level of importance. They have found that technical feasibility is often a problem because marketing, production, and distribution systems are subject to outside influence and therefore less orderly than accounting systems. Since the benefits do not derive from reductions in payroll dollars, they have often found it harder to determine economic feasibility. Most significantly, they have found that the operational feasibility of a project is vitally dependent on the attitude of operating managers.

Teamwork, then, is the key. Where top management provides leadership, and operating managers actively and enthusiastically cooperate with professional computer staffs, major economic achievements can result. Even a fairly commonplace computer application such as inventory control requires such cooperation. Design engineers must give adequate notice of design changes; sales planners must furnish detailed product sales forecasts; and management must give guidance on spares requirements and desired customer service levels. But once developed on the early projects, cooperation between managers and professional computer staffs becomes an important stimulus to the development of profitable further applications.

Consider the case of one manufacturer of heavy construction equipment. In this company, whose first computer-based inventory control system went into operation well over a decade ago, computers now play such an integral role in production planning and control that it is difficult to picture the company without them. These are some of the jobs now being done by computer:

1. *Consolidating sales forecasts from 31 countries.* Forecast data are first consolidated by region, product, and model; then they are correlated with figures for seven previous years. Trends are established for each product group, and forecasts that seem not to "fit" are pulled out for further staff review. The president and the vice president for sales use these staff analyses in their annual budgeting discussions with division heads at corporate headquarters.
2. *Establishing a quarterly manufacturing plan for each of 13 plants.* These plans are updated monthly by reconciling revised sales forecasts with records of finished goods inventory and work in process in final assembly. The revised manufacturing program is then exploded into component requirements, and a "net component requirement" analysis is prepared. Extensive manual analysis by production planners is still required to supplement these computer analyses, but lead time between customer order and delivery has been reduced, and the cost of shipping finished goods from depots in surplus to those with shortages has been cut drastically.
3. *Maintaining cost schedules in all plants showing the economics of make-or-buy decisions.* In conjunction with the "net component requirement" report, these cost schedules make possible intelligent work-load leveling and allocation among plants. Where there is an option to contract work out, managers can make their decisions with full knowledge of both the costs and the effect on specific work centers within each plant where bottlenecks are predicted.

4. *Central recording of all engineering changes.* Before an engineering change is put into effect, components in stock are exhausted first wherever possible. With changes occurring at a rate of about 2,000 a month, the costs of writing off obsolete stock used to run as high as $1.5 million annually before the advent of the computer. In the past three years, these costs have been reduced to approximately $500,000 a year.
5. *Maintaining cumulative records on labor efficiency.* In addition to detailed information on direct labor costs and trends, this system provides production planners with data on the work content of each component by work center. These data have been invaluable for scheduling manpower requirements to meet a varying production schedule, and particularly in planning the start-up of two new plants, which required the transfer of hundreds of skilled manufacturing workers.

The complex network of systems which produces such results has been evolving for 12 years now, and its net benefits to date have been outstanding. Overall, management credits computers with reducing lead time between order receipt and delivery by three to five months for U.S. customers, and with cutting direct labor requirements by 2 percent through improved materials availability and better control of work flow. Since direct labor costs are approximately $100 million per year, this fractional saving is significant both in absolute terms ($2 million) and as a percentage of before-tax profits (5 percent).

Another example of evolutionary development is offered by a major consumer goods corporation. This company gives its product managers and marketing staffs access to a comprehensive, detailed sales history file, in which total U.S. sales over three years are cross-referenced to show product sales data by geographic region, type of outlet, timing with relation to promotions, and packaging. This system evolved from an order entry and billing system that recorded sales solely by customer number.

The direction of this company's development effort was set early in 1959 by a product manager who foresaw the potential value of a comprehensive marketing information system. Today, in addition to recording orders centrally, the system he envisioned is used to schedule production at nine plants and to coordinate shipments from 13 warehouses. One gauge of its usefulness is the willingness of marketing men to pay the salaries of the programmers who prepare on demand whatever analyses may be needed by marketing managers.

Evolutionary development is typical of systems requiring audited data bases, since these cannot be built up overnight. But other systems, equally ambitious, can sometimes be developed quite rapidly where management recognizes that the data-base approach is not the only, nor necessarily the best, way to develop advanced computer applications.

A manufacturer of high-style clothing, with national outlets and multiple plants, decided two years ago that computers, hitherto used only for accounting purposes, could furnish major help in forecasting sales and establishing preliminary cutting schedules at the beginning of each season. The resulting computer forecasting model has already proved so successful in matching production to demand that a project is now under way to put computer forecasting methods to work in planning purchasing decisions.

Similarly, a number of oil companies have moved quickly into new fields unrelated to previous computer development work. Several have successfully undertaken crash programs to develop computer-based seismic analysis techniques to assist in the planning of exploratory drilling, and more than one has developed a computer model of the crude oil distribution system in order to improve the scheduling of its tanker fleet, at potentially vast savings.

In a matter of months, one oil company moved to transfer the production and maintenance records of thousands of domestic oil wells to computer files where they can be correlated and analyzed. This system enables production decline curves of wells and fields to be plotted and future production forecast under various alternative secondary recovery programs. It also calls management's attention to wells that are no longer producing enough to cover marginal costs. The principal task in developing this computer system was one of data reduction and file design, and here there was ideal matching of the talents of the computer systems men and petroleum engineers. With the engineers' enthusiastic support, the computer staff is now exploring the feasibility of making the same data accessible to engineers in the field through graphic display units. The obstacles are great, but the potential payoff from improving the effectiveness of operating engineers, who control expenditures in the hundreds of millions of dollars per year, is greater still.

Finally, in industry after industry where such data are critical, the science of communications is being wedded to the science of computing to centralize record keeping, planning, and control in an ever more complex economic environment. Railroads have "control centers" where up-to-the-minute central records are maintained on the movement of freight and rolling stock. Retail chains are using teleprinters and central computer-based dispatch systems to reduce branch-store inventories by cutting the stock-replenishment cycle. A wood-products company is coordinating production at its nine mills to match sales orders transmitted by branch offices throughout the United States directly to a central computer. Banks are handling branch accounting centrally; it is interesting to note that one of the main reasons cited for the recent merger of three large British banks was the opportunity to consolidate the banks' computers and computer knowhow. And virtually all the major airlines now have their own versions of the seat reservation system that first proved computers able to control large communications networks on a commercially feasible basis.

It is often extremely difficult to assess the overall economic effects of these advanced computer applications, for the simple reason that where the corporation would be now *without* its computers is well-nigh impossible to determine. But many of these companies are convinced that they have the computer to thank for the fact that they are beginning to outdistance their competitiors.

The resources—computers, professional computer systems men and programmers, management scientists, and communications experts—are available to all. But the team needs leadership. Advanced computer application concepts, with potential impact on the central activities of a corporation, must have sponsors high in the management pyramid to plead their case. The leadership of enthusiastic managers will gain the commitment of operating men—and teamwork between operating men and computer preofessionals will turn concepts into practical reality.

If the situation prevailing in the companies we studied is typical of U.S. industry as a whole, it is a fair guess that more than half of the proposed computer applications currently awaiting management approval were not originated by operating managers in consultation with computer staffs but proposed independently by systems and programming professionals. Yet as Figure 10-5 indicates, the experience of the more successful computer users leaves little doubt that operating managers, well motivated and equipped with some knowledge of computer capabilities, are likely to be a better source of ideas for profitable changes in operations than are computer professionals. The most profitable applications uncovered in our study had originated with operating executives pondering such ideas as these:

• If only we had a way to test the reliability of the sales forecasts made by these regional managers of ours, we might not find ourselves out of manufacturing capacity in Italy at the same time that we're laying off valuable skilled labor in Brazil.

• If only we had a way of recording and analyzing all our customer orders in one place, we ought to be able to allocate our production better—improve mill efficiencies and raise the yield from our raw materials.

• If only we could easily check out our historical sales performance by product, package, and so on, maybe we could interpret our test marketing results faster and more reliably.

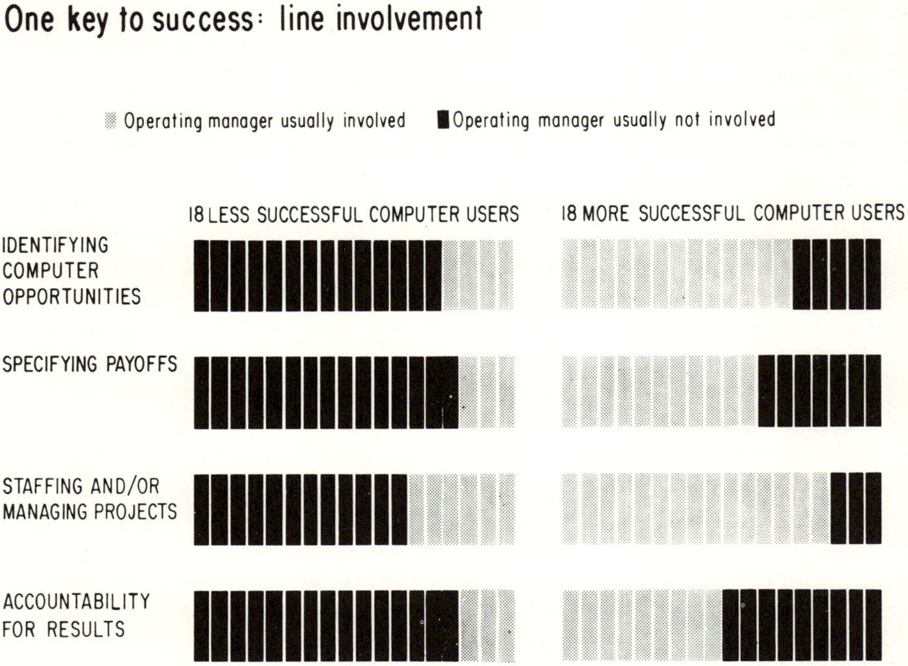

Figure 10-5. One Key to Success: Line Involvement.

- If only we could play with alternatives on our tanker deployment, we might use our capacity better—charter in less and charter out more.
- If only we could project our needs for skilled labor three months out, we could save the expense of these crash recruiting and training programs.

Two lessons emerge from all the varieties of successful computer experience that we have studied. First, there is a unique set of *feasible and profitable* computer applications for each company. Second, most of these applications are closely related to the key strategic opportunities that the top executives are really concerned about: marketing and distribution operations in the package goods company; production operations in the capital equipment concern; facilities planning operations in the chemicals maker; exploration and producing operations in the petroleum company; financial planning in the conglomerate; and so on. Such applications may be designed to reduce costs of goods sold, or to increase revenues by changing operating methods directly. Or, as already noted, they may seek to improve the staff work and analyses available to decision makers.

These lessons, in turn, have important implications for the top manager. Since each corporation has its own unique pattern of problems and opportunities, there is danger in trying to duplicate the successes of others: The computer development strategy that has worked well for one company may not work at all for its competitor. For the same reason, a company would be unwise to pin all its hopes on vendor-produced "applications packages" where major development projects are at stake. Nor can the answers be left to the professionals. No top executive is going to turn over the operation of his key departments to specialists with little or no operational experience.

In almost every industry, at least one company can now be found that is pioneering in profitable new uses of computers. In such companies, our findings suggest, the key to success has been a strong thrust of constructive interest from corporate operating executives who have put their own staffs to work on computer development projects. (See Figure 10-5 for evidence on this point.)

We believe that other companies will follow their lead. Indeed, it may soon be a nearly universal practice to transfer operating staff to computer development projects, either by making them members of a project team or by attaching them for a year or two to the corporate computer staff.

Another much-discussed area of computer use is management information and control. A few companies have already succeeded, by means of computer systems that sort out and speed routine data to the user, in notably improving the quality and quantity of specific information available to operating managers. Others, as noted earlier, have made profitable use of the computer in decision making through simulation models designed to improve decision making by predicting the impact of alternative actions on economic and operating realities. Skills in the construction of such models are widespread and growing, and their results have frequently been noteworthy.

A fertilizer manufacturer has used computer-based simulation to help top management answer such questions as these:

• How much should we plan to manufacture, ship, and store at the plant location in order to minimize total accumulated costs of production, distribution, and storage over a one-year period?

• How much, if at all, could we reduce total costs by renting additional storage in outlying locations? What would be the effect on our present production, shipping, and storage program?

• How large a market area should be served from each of our warehouse locations?

• Where should new plants be located with respect to warehousing locations and market areas?

A well-known food products company has constructed and used a computer-based simulation model enabling it to assess, under various possible 1970 and 1975 environments: (1) the relative profitability of different product markets; (2) the desirability of investing in new-market development; (3) the impact of investment in added plant capacity; and (4) detailed income statements based on these projections.

Again, computer-based risk analysis techniques have demonstrated their value in a wide range of capital investment situations. The industrial chemicals industry is known for the magnitude of both its investment and its risks. Since industry capacity directly affects market price, these risks are aggravated by the uncertainty of industry intelligence regarding competitors' plans for adding new capacity. Risk analysis, made practical by computers, has proven invaluable for evaluating alternative strategic plans with the help of simulation models, sometimes even including simulation of alternative competitive responses by the application of game theory. To exploit the potential of these and related techniques, an increasing number of corporations are finding it necessary to supplement the professional skills of computer men by recruiting specialists in the management sciences.

What is true of simulation models, however, is hardly true of the so-called total management information systems that have beguiled some computer theorists in recent years. Much effort and ingenuity have been devoted to the design and promotion of such systems, and many businessmen are understandably intrigued by their possibilities. Yet in terms of economic payoff and operational feasibility they are as yet ill-defined, and certainly they are a long way from practical realization in business.

Doubtless the computer's information processing capabilities will one day eliminate the need for large staffs occupied with collecting and interpreting information from various sources for the use of decision makers. But whether the computer will ever be able to evaluate strategic opportunities or indicate the proper timing for corporate actions is by no means assured. Nor are man-machine dialogs via desk-side consoles likely to become a feature of life in the executive suite any time in the foreseeable future; top management's "interface" with the computer is unlikely to be anything more exotic than a telephone, with a human information specialist at the other end of the line. What counts, of course, is not the sophistication of the interface but the responsiveness of computer-based systems to management's information needs, and the quality and timeliness of the information they can provide. Here, without doubt, the potential of the computer is only beginning to be realized. But "integrated total management information systems" drawing on a single data base, which have so often been touted as the wave of the future, are another matter. They have not yet come to pass—and it is far from clear that they ever will.

In short, the potential of comprehensive computer-based information systems and the role of the computer in decision making are still surrounded by question marks. Research in these areas may be a sound investment for some companies, even though the costs of experimentation are high. But no company should embark on a program to develop a major management information system except to meet a specific, well-defined need. Even then it should carefully weigh its options—including the option of applying its scarce computer resources to areas where operating success and economic payoff can be predicted with greater confidence.

KEYS TO THE FUTURE

In embarking on the present study, McKinsey & Company analysts were not seeking fresh evidence of a gap between potential and performance with respect to the management of the computer effort. The existence of such a gap has been obvious for some time to most informed observers. We were concerned, rather, with determining the present dimensions of the gap, analyzing its background and causes, and synthesizing from the practices of the top performers a few succinct management guidelines for maximizing the computer's effectiveness and unlocking its profit potential.

Evidence on the first two points—the performance gap and its underlying causes—has been reviewed in the earlier pages, and the general nature of the remedies has been indicated. Against this background, certain lessons emerge for the senior executive who is dissatisfied with the performance gap he sees in his own company and is determined to do what he can to close it.

In the computer field, as in other areas of management, the usefulness of generalizations from successful experience is rather sharply limited. It is possible to state *some* of the principles a company must follow to have a reasonable chance of success with the computer. But there will always be other factors—constraints, needs, or opportunities—which are peculiar to each company and can only be determined in the light of the individual situation. Hence it is useful to state general precepts only if their neglect is rather widespread and the consequences of that neglect are costly. This is the case in the management of the computer effort today.

The common denominators of successful computer practice, as seen in the companies we have examined, may be expressed in terms of three principles: the rule of high expectations, the rule of diversified staffing, and the rule of top-management involvement.

THE RULE OF HIGH EXPECTATIONS

In all of the companies that are realizing outstanding *economic* results from computer applications, top management is simply unwilling to settle for anything less. In the less successful companies, many managers exhibit a tendency to keep the computer at arm's length for fear of exposing their technical inadequacies. This tendency is conspicuously absent among the top computer users. Departmental and divisional managers in these companies know that top management will insist on economic results—and that they will be held personally responsible for achieving those results.

The new president of a capital equipment manufacturer, who has succeeded in getting a badly stalled computer program in his company moving again, typifies the prevailing tone of management expectations in the better-performing companies. Said he: "I ask my department heads to give me regular formal reports on their current successes and failures with computers and their future objectives. Right now they're a bunch of sheep with computers. I aim to convert them into enthusiasts, so that later I can be jockey, not herdsman."

THE RULE OF DIVERSIFIED STAFFING

A computer staff whose experience is limited to successful conversion of accounting and administrative operations is seldom really qualified to design and install new systems in major operating functions such as manufacturing and marketing. Computer professionals alone seldom constitute an adequate corporate support staff.

To make the most of their opportunities for profitable corporation-wide use of the computer, therefore, the top-performing companies take one of two organizational approaches. Some assign to the corporate computer staff—along with the usual operations research specialists and other professionals—at least one talented individual with experience in each of the major functions of the business. Others, relying on the project approach to computer development, use project teams staffed by temporary transfers from operating departments. This arrangement, too, encourages good support from all levels of management.

To head up the computer staff and assume responsibility for the implementation of development plans, the outstanding companies have in all cases been careful to pick a manager who commands, or can quickly learn to command, respect and confidence throughout the organization. The appointment of the right man to this position is seen as a key contribution that top management can make to the success of the computer effort. It is also recognized that this individual's effectiveness depends more on his personal stature and professional skills than on the precise location of his unit in the corporate hierarchy. We found no evidence, statistical or otherwise, to suggest that high organizational status assures effective performance on the part of the corporate computer staff.

THE RULE OF TOP-MANAGEMENT INVOLVEMENT

If any one man can be said to hold the key to the computer's profit potential, it is probably the chief executive. He has a very definite responsibility for the success of the computer development effort, and it is not a responsibility that he can safely delegate.

At a minimum, the chief executive who wants maximum results from his company's computer effort must do five things. *First,* he must approve objectives, criteria, and priorities for the corporate computer effort, with special attention to the development program. *Second,* he must decide on the organizational arrangements to carry out these policies and achieve these objectives. *Third,* he must assign responsibility for results to the line and functional executives served by the computer systems—and see to it that they exercise this responsibility. *Fourth,* he must insist that detailed and thorough computer systems plans are made an integral part of operating plans and budgets. *Fifth,* he must follow through to see that planned results are achieved.

There is nothing novel in any of these recommendations; they are standard operating practice for most chief executives in most of their traditional areas of responsibility. Many otherwise effective top managements, however, are in trouble with their computer efforts because they have abdicated control to staff specialists—good technicians who have neither the operational experience to know the jobs that need doing nor the authority to get them done right.

Only managers can manage the computer in the best interests of the business. The companies that take this lesson to heart today will be the computer profit leaders of tomorrow.

COMPUTER PROJECT SELECTION IN THE BUSINESS ENTERPRISE

by M. H. Schwartz

With continued speeding up of both the tempo of American enterprise and the introduction of new technology, controllers and other financial managers in business and government are becoming increasingly conscious of competing investment demands. Computer projects are rapidly becoming significant competitors both with one another and with all other investment demands. For some time, it has been the rare, larger organization that has not generated more computer project ideas than available resources could deliver, that has not been confronted by more project demands than it could fulfill.

This problem is now filtering down to smaller organizations. Recently a bank controller told me that he could either convert his present "second generation" automated demand deposit accounting system to a lower-cost third generation system or he could automate his manual loan accounting system. He could not do both this next year. He asked my views on which to do. I advised him to do the loan accounting project for two reasons—to innovate for large new opportunities rather than improve marginally on opportunities from which the cream has already been skimmed and to focus on information potentials rather than on paper pushing.

No matter what the size of the organization, deciding what to do and what comes first is a perplexing task. In the face of increasing competitive drives and increasing competitive opportunities and threats, the financial manager must come to grips with computer project selection on a measured, analytic basis.

The effective screening, selection and evaluation of computer projects require: (1) criteria for making judgments, recommendations, and decisions about authorizing and maintaining projects, and for assigning and shifting resources and (2) a system, a method, a set of procedures. These requirements are compelling. In many ways, the requirements are identical with those associated with any major investment. Considerable thinking has been focused for years on clarifying the issues and attempting to solve the problems that have been identified. The literature

---

Reprinted by permission of the publisher from *The Journal of Accountancy*, vol. 127, no. 4 (April 1969), pp. 35-43. The views expressed in this article are the author's and should not be considered as an official statement representing the views of the U. S. Atomic Energy Commission.

on the subject, which is now quite large, emerged when business managers recognized the need for careful rationalization of decisions on plant and equipment expenditures. Improved accounting systems were of great value in improving these decisions. The literature has recently been considerably expanded in association with growth in the number and variety of competing opportunities for research and development.

We can now expect that serious attention will increasingly be given to the selection of computer projects, and we can no longer afford to plunge into the beckoning opportunity without a serious reckoning of costs and returns. We must focus on producing the most valuable output of our available human and machine resources. The role of the accountant is important, for he must shape the information that is needed for proper analysis in the selection of de novo computer projects and in the determination of which ongoing projects should be continued and which put on the shelf.

CRITERIA

Authorization for computer projects in a business enterprise should be based upon: (1) quantifiable impact on profit and loss, whether in the form of new earnings or savings, (2) qualitative factors and (3) institutional criteria. (Special cost-effectiveness analysis is required in government enterprise in lieu of P&L impacts.) "Quantifiable impact" means that we have been able to estimate, with reasonable confidence, the *explicit* cost/earnings relationship for a project. Qualitative factors really represent *implicit* future dollar values—presently invisible, unspecifiable dollars that we feel reasonably confident the business will earn from improved financial analysis, improved marketing and improved operations. Qualitative factors must be analyzed not only for projects whose benefits cannot be specified in dollar terms, but also for projects measurable in dollar terms—management may frequently override dollar comparisons in favor of compelling qualitative comparisons. We should beware of monolithic dependence on the "strictly business' appeal of estimated dollar figures (whose crudeness and inadequacy are often neglected). The essence of qualitative factors is their nonquantifiable but ultimately very significant impact upon P&L in the business organization and upon the quality of performance at a given level of expenditure in the government organization.

Institutional criteria also relate, ultimately, to improved earnings and performance. These criteria are mainly concerned with keeping balance in the organization by deliberately distributing projects over the longer run in accordance with corporate objectives, corporate organization and other institutional factors.

Another factor of institutional importance is the availability of particular human resources for particular projects and the significance of projects to the human beings in the computer complex.

DOLLAR IMPACT ON P&L

Upon satisfactory completion of preliminary analysis, broad design and technical feasibility of a particular application or system, and following establishment of development plans, economic and financial feasibility may be examined. This involves a careful accounting estimation of annual and cumulated cash flows of costs and returns. Such figures bear on both the overall feasibility of particular applications and also on the priority analysis upon which choices among feasible alternatives must depend. Needless to say, the cost figures (people, equipment, etc.) should be painfully comprehensive. Too frequently many real dollar costs of implementing and running a new computer system are not adequately allowed for in systems planning. Efforts to ferret out all the potential returns are often far greater than efforts to identify and estimate all the potential costs. The potential contribution of the accountant is clearly significant.

The left-hand columns of Table 10-1 show a possible cash-flow summary for a particular project in a way that is often presented to management. Such figures, taken at face value, may be seriously misleading, however. Is a return of $1,300,000 over five years adequate for an investment of $900,000? Is the project really worth undertaking? Is the $400,000 cash advantage fully meaningful?

There are two techniques for answering these questions. One is to compute the implied rate of return on the outlay. If the rate at least equals the institution's rate of return objective, the project begins to show financial appeal. Holding other things equal, the greater rate of return, the higher the priority of the project and the greater the resources which should be applied to it.

Rate of return calculations sometimes have tricky effects and many people, including the author, prefer to compute the "present value" of the future net earnings stream, using the institution's rate of return objective for the discount calculations. Costs for projects whose development lives exceed one year should also be discounted. The purpose of the discount is, of course, to bring consideration of the time value of money into the financial presentation. It is remarkable how neglected this imperative accounting analysis can be! The author has seen huge proposals made, even in financial organizations, that present only the unadjusted streams of earnings or savings, thus exaggerating the dimension of earnings or savings.

Table 10-1. Cost-Earnings Analysis—Quantifiable Dollar Impact Basis. (In Thousands of Dollars)

Year	Project Costs	Earnings #	Cash Flow	Cash Flow Discounted* to "Present Value"
1969	500.0	0.0	−500.0	−416.5
1970	400.0	100.0	−300.0	−208.2
1971		350.0	+350.0	+202.7
1972		400.0	+400.0	+192.8
1973		450.0	+450.0	+180.9
Five Year Total	900.0	1,300.0	+400.0	− 48.3

#Net of all operating costs other than taxes
*Cash flow discounted at 20 per cent return, before taxes

The right-hand column of the table shows the effect of discounting the cash flow for the illustrated project. In contrast to net earnings of $400,000 over the anticipated life of the system, discounting shows that the present value of the system is negative in sign. Compared to alternative typical uses of funds in the organization, the project will lose $48,000. On the basis of a proper accounting analysis, other things being equal, this project should not be undertaken. A more fully rounded analysis of the potentials of the project, say for the qualitative improvement of management information, may demonstrate that despite the apparent negative dollar picture, the project should be undertaken. But that is a different matter. Alternatively, more complete analysis may reveal that particularly in view of the "true" dollar implications, the project is very definitely not worthwhile. The point is that the data processing manager, the financial manager and the top manager should not be misled into selecting a project on the basis of inadequate accounting only for simple undiscounted cash flow.

ALTERNATIVE PROJECTS

So far we have dealt only with the dollar significance of a single project. Most of the time, top management must make choices from a number of alternative projects. Better decisions will be made when management is presented at planning and budget sessions with alternatives in two senses—alternative projects that would serve alternative purposes and alternative approaches to individual projects. Only then can management deal adequately with decision-making for computer activities.

When two or more possibilities are being considered, a bit more refinement of the discounted cash-flow figures is useful. A million dollar project and a half-million dollar project may show similar discounted returns, say a quarter of a million dollars. It is obvious that the half-million dollar project is preferable, other things being equal. When a large number of projects and approaches are being reviewed, the relationships are not so obvious. A relative measure of discounted returns is needed for lining up priorities. A very convenient and significant priority measure is the computed present value dollars of net savings (or of net earnings) per present value dollar of project costs. In strictly dollar terms, the ratio tells management what dollar output is yielded per dollar of input. Other things equal, projects should be ranked according to this measure.

A comprehensive annual budget review should also embrace ongoing projects, partly to bring new information and the lessons of experience with the projects into play and partly to determine if any existing project is of lower priority than one or more possible new projects. Should one or more ongoing projects be shelved? The ratio is highly useful in making this determination. The numerator should contain the latest revised figures of savings or earnings, discounted from the present time, and the denominator should show only remaining costs. Sometimes the financial officer must remind top management that spent costs are sunk costs—they are gone—and, while they may teach valuable lessons, they have nothing to do with determining current priorities. Thus, a project with costs behind it is worth continuing if additional costs in relation to returns are low. High past costs should not be considered as supporting a project in the effort to "make the costs good"—they are gone; nor should they work against a project whose remaining costs are now favorable in relation to payoff.

Visible, estimable dollars are not alone sufficient, however, for adequate priority determination. There are many highly desirable computer projects that management senses the need for without being able to specify explicit dollar returns. A banker, for example, may decide to put teller operations "on-line" to a computer in order to speed up window transactions, thereby reducing customer waiting time and increasing teller productivity. The costs of such a project can certainly be identified but the returns are virtually impossible either to predict in advance or to measure afterward. Compelling competitive threats or opportunities often justifiably stimulate action on *qualitative* grounds that importantly bear upon earnings in ways presently unspecifiable in strict quantitative terms.

The judgmental weighing of qualitative factors is the best presently available substitute for dollar measures where dollar measures cannot be made with confidence but where dollar earnings high in relation to costs may nevertheless be anticipated with confidence.

QUALITATIVE FACTORS

A number of qualitative factors may be revealed by study of the potential contributions of the computer to the activities and problems of a business enterprise. Increasingly, we are focusing on what can be done to strengthen management, in contrast to the focus of the past on improving paperwork processing. This article is limited to noting four broad categories of qualitative contributions of computers, the first of which is, appropriately, management information for decision-making. But before moving on to particular qualitative considerations, it should be stressed that qualitative analysis must always also present the fullest possible cost statement, because economic feasibility and economic implications are the ultimate basis for resource expenditures.

DECISION-MAKING

Decision-making stands upon four foundations—human attributes, skills, information and analysis. Decision-making in business occurs within many broad areas—personnel, finance, production, marketing. Improved summary statistical information and sharpened analysis will surely add to business earnings by improving decisions and hence performance. Projects that show significant promise of contributing substantially to the information flows and analytic procedures available to management should be given a high priority status. For example, an automated accounts receivable system not only provides for reduced costs of processing and speeded up billing; perhaps more importantly it can be a first step toward automating information flows that will help improve corporate cash management, that will significantly contribute to more effective use of the corporation's cash resources.

It is hard to quantify in advance the payoff of successive automation projects that increasingly enhance the financial manager's capabilities of minimizing deposit balances by the synchronization as much as possible of the streams of payables and receivables and of maximizing short-run investment earnings from freed-up cash. But a cash management information system can be a most important profit-yielding reward of computer-based financial transactions processing.

OPERATIONS

Earnings from production and marketing are heavily dependent upon the speed, quality and accuracy of transactions data processing. Projects that show significant promise of contributing substantially to the speed, quality and accuracy of data processing should be given a high priority status. Of course, judgment must be brought to bear on the expense side—gilding the lily must be avoided. Achieving speed where speed is not profitable is a waste of resources.

COMPETITION

Judgments about the competition are difficult, but they are necessary in the priority setting process. Suppose a firm has to choose which of two automation opportunities to exploit this year, say systems S1 and S2; suppose further that S1 is an innovation in the industry while S2 is already in use by a major competitor; suppose the dollar cost/earnings analysis is similar for the two systems; and suppose overall budgetary considerations dictate that only one of the two be implemented this year. Management would need to analyze and judge between S1, which opens up the opportunity for leadership and an early start, and S2, which is demanded in response to a competitive threat. Even if the two systems were of greatly different dollar benefits, management would want to weigh the competitive angles in setting final priorities for it may find that it prefers the project with the lower quantifiable dollar benefit in favor of competitive intangibles.

THE FIRM'S IMAGE

This is a self-explanatory qualitative factor. Nowadays all companies are eager to show leadership—in using computers as well as in other ways. This is a meritorious factor that calls for balance. No organization can be first, or even among the first, in all activities.

INSTITUTIONAL CRITERIA

Analysis of the dollar impact upon P&L and of the qualitative factors of a project deals with the more visible benefits of the project. Effective management and effective priority setting also depend upon maintaining institutional balance in the allocation of computer resources beyond the more visible benefits.

Certainly some kind of balance must be maintained among the various organizational units of a firm. Nobody, nor mathematics, can say what a "fair" share is; the solution to this problem requires great judgment and "give and take." This means, operationally, that a project of less visible benefit may occasionally be given priority over a project with presumably more visible benefit if the latter comes from an area already well endowed with projects and the former comes from an area for which little computer work has been done. The historic record is clear in too many firms: Operating potentials have starved information and analytic potentials, seemingly because the visibility of the operating payoff swamped all the rest.

There are a number of institutional criteria that make for an institutionally balanced set of projects over time. Among the criteria are:

1. *Corporate objectives and corporate plans.* Certainly no project should be undertaken that is at variance with corporate objectives or corporate plans. In a sense, overall objectives and plans are constraints. But they are more than constraints. It is the other side of the coin that is less obvious—namely, that the full spectrum of objectives and plans is often forgotten. Sometimes a costly computer project would justifiably support a fundamental business objective that bears only very generally and in no way measurably on the fortunes of the business. A commercial bank, or any business firm for that matter, may deliberately seek to develop a system in support of a community need in the interests of fulfilling an objective to participate constructively in community affairs even though the system is "unprofitable." This is a broad institutional objective. Such objectives belong among the considerations in determining project priorities.
2. *Management aspirations.* Management by hunch is playing a decreasing role in American business enterprise. But it is not, nor should it be, always inappropriate. The instincts of the manager are among his most valued attributes. While every effort should be made within a business enterprise to lay out the analytical basis for computer projects, if only to keep application tweakers at bay, there are occasions when an idea of a far-seeing manager should be pursued despite skimpy evidence. While this argument runs contrary to the basic theme of this article, room must be left for human beings to work out their affairs in the human context. All too often, and this is regrettable, technicians are capable of working against good ideas that come from line managers.

In the same vein, top management must occasionally give in to technical drives. At least a limited number of "way-out" projects must be pursued. Overemphasis on "sure things" and on conservative criteria is likely to lead to long-run weakness. "Crazy" ideas should not be allowed to drain off resources, but ideas should be openly explored before they are classed as "crazy."

3. *Divisions and departments.* Some kind of balance must be maintained in project allocation among various major units of a business; there is some kind of "fair" share for each major activity. In the end, of course, division of resources must be on the basis of efficiency in their use. But how can it be ascertained that all the alternatives are being considered? One way is consciously to study potentials in relation to the structure of the organization. A bank controller might ask: Are we doing enough for loan accounting and loan management? Are we neglecting our correspondent responsibilities? What alternatives might we explore for presently unattended areas? This kind of review leads to the opening up of new potentials and to the widening of long-range systems planning.

There is no need to labor the notion of institutional criteria any further than to note that others include customers, markets, services and products, improvements vs. innovations. A final institutional criterion that merits special attention, however, has to do with the human resources that make up the electronic data processing effort.

HUMAN RESOURCES

Current work has to be geared to the resources available—mainly the skills and abilities of the staff. To be sure, consultant organizations are a useful extension of the existing staff, but effective use of consultants does depend in part on the ability of the user organization to negotiate with, monitor the progress of, and implement consultants' work. Consequently, some (managerial) local resources are also required for effective use of external resources. The human resources upon which computer projects depend involve:

1. Project management
   a. For internal projects
   b. For consultant projects
2. Project technical staff (could be furnished by consultant)
3. Project administrative staff
4. User area staff
5. Affected area staff

On balance, a project is best not undertaken, no matter its seeming priority, if there are not adequate supervision and staff to prevent wholesale waste of resources. The emergence of desirable projects that the present staff cannot handle should be recognized and staff resources should be augmented or reshaped accordingly.

A CONCLUDING NOTE ON CRITERIA

The discounted cash-flow analysis, and priority analysis in general, may be extended several degrees of sophistication in the effort to portray and to cope with the uncertainty of future events: (1) ranges of costs and earnings may be specified in lieu of single figures; (2) probabilities may be assigned to the single figures or to ranges; and (3) the costs and earnings figures, along with weighted criteria, may be analyzed with the help of operations research models. Each of the three advanced methods has its advantages, notably to provide for sensitivity analysis of possible errors of estimate as well as to make clear to all parties that the estimates are in fact literally estimates and therefore subject to inevitable errors.

The notion of modeling the possible consequences and impacts of each of a set of projects and approaches is appealing, and we can look forward to improvements in project selection in the large organization along these lines. Great strides have been made in government and in a number of large corporations with the use of mathematical systems analysis for cost/benefit studies and for probing the alternative implications of possible decisions across the whole spectrum of planning and budgeting. We can expect recently developed methodologies, now actually about 10 to 15 years old, to filter down to major decisions in business generally, including decisions concerning computer systems design and implementation.

We want to fortify the judgment of top management with as sharp an analysis as possible; and management will be looking for an increasingly systematic study of alternatives and consequences. In the meantime, great improvements can be made simply by laying out the variables, their best estimated values and their likely significance to the organization.

IMPROVING PROJECT SELECTION SYSTEMS

All organizations have some kind of project selection system, whether they recognize it or not. Too many systems, however, are highly informal, nonquantitative, discontinuous, and highly personal. Many firms that study product and services development and marketing in great cost and earnings detail fail to give similar attention to computer project development. This we may take to be transitional, reflecting the newness of the computer in business. Sooner or later most business firms will put individual computer systems development projects through the same sort of wringer that other capital and major expenditure projects go through. In fact, a few organizations have already swung too far toward the other pole: they have selection systems that are rigorously structured to the point of inflexibility and they demand quantitative explicitness that is unreasonable.

The purely informal kind of system—which is not "systematic" and can only be called a "system" in the broadest sense of the term—is to be deplored, for its major output is frustration and misdirected efforts. The alternative extreme is much less undesirable; but when it focuses on form rather than content—a not uncommon sump for intelligence among the affairs of men—it, too, generates more frustration than enlightenment. Between the poles there is a reasonably broad band within which effective project selection is feasible.

The major ingredients of a meaningful project selection system are:

1. Selection criteria, which are the bedrock of a system
2. Project generation and formation, which stem mainly from research into potentials and problems and from planning for uses and solutions
3. Documentation, which conveys systems plans, purposes, implications, and justifications to top management
4. Organized review and analysis, which is conducted by top management against the background of explicit criteria in the contexts of the annual budget cycle and long-range plans
5. Project decisions, which are made by top management

The crucial underlying element of each of the five ingredients is management involvement. Top management must lay down the criteria, must guide and support research and planning, must communicate its desires on documentation, and must become enmeshed in the review as well as in the decision-making in which priority analysis terminates. Line management must participate directly, substantively and deeply in research and planning and, of course, should contribute wherever feasible elsewhere in the range of activities that lead to priority determination. Above all, line management must share greatly in the shaping of individual computer projects: each manager is no less responsible for his information system than he is for any other aspect of his sphere of activities.

We have already reviewed selection criteria in considerable detail. Research and planning have been treated in other articles so they will not be dealt with extensively in this one.

There is one aspect of research and planning, however, that should be considered here for it is intimately tied to the project selection process. In all but the smallest organizations, the results of research and the broad planning for project proposals should be shared by some sort of users' committee drawn from line management throughout the organization. Such a committee might be named the systems planning committee or the systems steering committee. It should be chaired by either the senior data processing officer or by a superior who is either a member of top management or is especially close to top management. All proposals for computer projects should be approved by such a committee, if indeed the project proposals are not generated by this group. Final recommendations should be prepared by the committee, acting on behalf of the entire organization, for top management review and decision. The role of the committee is a vital one, for only through such a committee can an organization that has reached mature use of computers be reasonably sure that computer resources are institutionally directed in a balanced way.

This brings us to the matter of documentation of project proposals for management study and decision.

PROJECT DOCUMENTATION

For management to be adequately informed on the significance and desirability of alternative computer projects, or even of a single project if only one is proposed within a particular budget cycle, they need broad information (for each project) about (1) objectives, (2) costs and returns over the life of the application or system to be spun out of the project, (3) qualitative and institutional factors and (4) plans for development and operations. Project proposal documentation can be visualized as a four-part package, each part devoted to a major aspect of the proposal. Similar documentation should be presented for both ongoing projects and proposed projects, except that history and status information should be embedded in the documentation of ongoing projects. Finally, in addition to individual project packages, there should be the summary recommendations of the systems planning committee. While prepared last, the summary should be the initial package presented to top management.

PART I, OBJECTIVES

The statement of project objectives is best handled in *narrative* form. It should specify no less than the problem and the feasibility analysis that presumably have triggered the project proposal, the various purposes to be served and the contributions of the project, the nature of the new system, the bases for financial and technical feasibility, and place of the project in the long-range automation plans of the organization. The narrative should also point up problems that are likely to emerge, particularly the potential impacts on people, and on organizational structure. Anticipating all the problems is, of course, virtually impossible, but every reasonable effort should be made to perceive negative fall-outs both as a result of the sheer conduct of the project and as a result of implementation and operations.

PART II, FINANCIAL OVERVIEW

Like the narrative statement on objectives, the financial overview should be presented in rather broad terms. A good overall electronic data processing framework will contain institutional standards for estimating costs and returns and presumably estimates for each project will be consistent with those standards. Proposal documentation should show annual total costs of the development project, broken down by salaries (including fringe benefits), consultant fees, machine costs, space costs, data conversion costs, training costs and all the rest. The financial plan should also present estimated financial magnitudes associated with utilizing the system to be developed.

Any proposals for replacement systems should show the annual net financial impact of the new system based upon a presented comparison of projected total costs of both the old and new systems over the anticipated life of the new system, also in terms of salaries, equipment and other major costs. Improved earnings, say from improved marketing capability, should also be specified where feasible. The mass of details that necessarily underlie summary figures should not be loaded onto management, but they should be organized and presentable in the event that the need arises for an examination of the basis for the summary estimates. The grand summary financial table for each project should be similar to Table 10-1, which contains annual figures for costs, earnings or savings, raw cash flows and discounted cash flows.

It should be noted that *annual* cash flows are particularly important, in contrast to lump sums. The timing, as well as the magnitude, of expenditures and/or earnings may bear importantly on the selection decision. There is a danger here, however, because constant skimming of the cream in favor of short-run payoffs may leave a residue of sour milk.

PART III, QUALITATIVE AND INSTITUTIONAL CONSIDERATIONS

Table 10-2 shows one useful way that qualitative and institutional considerations may be brought into summary focus. For each criterion, qualitative and institutional, either "high" value or "low" value may be checked off, the choice depending of course upon subjective and intuitive measures. The purposes of the form shown in the table are, specifically, to force out the analytical basis for subjective values and generally to cast qualitative and institutional considerations into as specific and analytic a framework as possible.

Table 10-2. Computer Project Proposal.

(Part III—Qualitative and Institutional Considerations)

Criteria	Value: High	Value: Low	Comments
Qualitative:			
Decision making, information	____	____	________
Decision-making, analysis	____	____	________
Operations data processing, speed	____	____	________
Operations data processing, quality	____	____	________
Operations data processing, accuracy	____	____	________
Competitive factors, take lead	____	____	________
Competitive factors, catch up	____	____	________
Image of firm	____	____	________
Institutional:			
Corporate objectives	____	____	________
Corporate plans	____	____	________
Balance among firm's units	____	____	________
Customer relationships	____	____	________
Markets	____	____	________
Balance among services and products	____	____	________
Improvements to existing system	____	____	________
Innovative system	____	____	________
Human resources	____	____	________

The form may be used in at least two ways. Projects with a large number of "high" checks are in general more valuable to the organization than projects with a small number of "high" checks. Alternatively, in the interest of bringing some sort of balance into a long-range sequence of projects, certain projects may be selected because they are the *only* ones that give high checks to otherwise neglected particular criteria.

Many organizations that have formal procedures for selecting industrial research and development projects go so far as to assign relative weights to each criterion, computer a total weighted score for each project, and rank projects accordingly. There are certain advantages to scoring systems, but they certainly do not avoid subjective valuations—the assignment of weights and the checking of criteria are still subjective.

No doubt the handling of qualitative and institutional criteria must be shaped in accordance with the character and modes of the particular business enterprise. The choice of criteria—the table shows only *one possible set*—and the weighing of criteria are really evolutionary within each enterprise. The main issues are not which criteria and how to weigh them, for these issues can be worked out with experience. The central issue is criteria or not; the central issue deals with bringing as much analysis to bear as is possible in the effort to minimize *ad hoc* influences in the development of corporate computer and information systems.

PART IV, PLANS

Three project subplans belong in presentations to top management. These are (1) the systems development plan, (2) the systems conversion plan and (3) the systems operating plan. They may be presented in broad tabular form, largely in terms of phases, stages and milestones. Overall Gantt charts or overall PERT charts are very useful supplements to tabular formats. Review of the plans helps give management insight into the whole systems development activity and provides them some firm bases for performance measurement and evaluation as well as enriching their information basis for current project selection. Plans also stimulate questions on alternative approaches, thereby contributing to the formulation of the eventual project and implementation of the new system. As in the case of the financial overview, management should not be swamped with details of the technical planning apparatus. Rather, details should be collated and held in stand-by should particular discussions call for greater detail.

SUMMARY DOCUMENTATION

While last in preparation, first in presentation to top management should be a recommended total package. The recommendation should be structured parallel to the individual project packages so as to facilitate analysis of the parts in the context of the total. The narrative, the financial statement, the analyses of criteria and the project plans for recommended projects should be presented in aggregated form so that the entire systems effort may be appreciated as a whole both for the coming budget year and for the years ahead covered by the proposals. The recommendation should deal with ongoing projects that should be shelved and with potentially new projects that should be deferred. The individual project documents now appear as supporting evidence and justification for the recommendation.

While burdensome to prepare, the documentation is invaluable. Top management will be in a position effectively to review and to accept or modify the proposed plans and budgets either in the aggregate or in terms of particular projects. This is the final station of the project selection system—rational, measured, analytic decisions for action.

This article has been kept as practical and pragmatic as possible. It should be remembered, however, that there is a powerful theoretical foundation for solving the broad problem we have been considering. Implementation of the theoretical principle may go beyond our present accounting information-generating capabilities, but that difficulty, although perhaps presently insurmountable, should not stand in the way of conscious attention to the principle.

THE BROAD PRINCIPLE FOR RESOURCE ALLOCATION

In principle, a business should adjust expenses of each project activity—whether computer, marketing, branching, acquisitions or new products—so that estimated marginal discounted net incomes are equal throughout the firm. Budget allocations should be shifted so that a dollar spent for any project will not yield a lower net income than if it were spent anyplace else. This will yield the greatest net institutional income for any given total budget.

Thus, expenses for computer projects should be increased as long as the estimated marginal discounted net income from those expenses exceeds that for the rest of the firm and should be decreased as long as the estimated marginal discounted net income is less than that for the rest of the firm. The principle for resource allocation among computer projects is, of course, identical: expenses for each computer project should be increased so long as the estimated marginal discounted net income from those expenses exceeds that for other computer projects and should be decreased so long as the estimated marginal discounted net income is less than that for other computer projects.

While accounting systems may not yet specify the marginal values, especially for qualitative and broad institutional improvements, the essential logic belongs in the forefront of our thinking when we attempt to determine what is the most efficient way to reach institutional profit objectives.

GET THE COMPUTER SYSTEM YOU WANT

by Roy N. Freed

In April 1969, a data-processing service company was ordered to pay three automotive and electrical parts-distributing customers $480,811 in damages for losses suffered from misrepresentations concerning the capabilities of an inventory system which had been used to serve the company's customers; the misrepresentations were considered tantamount to fraud.[3] That incident is fast becoming merely another example of the large lawsuits brought by unhappy customers against suppliers of computers and computer service. It shows how unwise it can be for top management to leave the purchasing and leasing of computers or data-processing services in the wrong hands. Too often these decisions are turned over to subordinate financial, procurement, and engineering personnel, who then proceed on their own without guidance.

Senior managers must exercise control over the acquisition of computer services for their companies. Bitter experience now is proving what ordinary business judgment should have indicated long ago: guidance and oversight from the very top is essential in most cases if mistakes in contracting are to be avoided and if full advantage is to be taken of new approaches to securing the use of the computer.

The accelerating pace at which lawsuits are being brought by users against practically all types of suppliers of computers and computer services is fair warning that customary contracting practices have been grossly deficient and need prompt change; usually, recourse to litigation indicates inadequate contracting. The proper procurement method is relatively easy to adopt. Essentially all that is required is a genuine policy determination by top management to procure computer services in the same businesslike way used to buy less complicated (and less critical) goods and services. Strange as it seems, failure to do just that is largely the root of current difficulties.

Originally published in the *Harvard Business Review,* November-December 1969, pp. 99-108.

[3] *Clements Auto Co. et al. v. Service Bureau Corp.,* 298 F. Supp. 115 (D. Minn. 1969). Decision reported in *The Wall Street Journal,* April 19, 1969.

HIGH PRICE OF FAILURE

It is not necessary to recount all of the computer contracts that have gone sour and ended up in court in order to demonstrate the advisability of using proper procurement practices. Let me note only a few cases which, in addition to the introductory example, point up elements in the acquisition process that need particular attention from management:

- A food wholesaler recovered damages of $53,200 (and a remission of rent) in 1968 from a computer manufacturer because of a breach of warranty involving faulty software supplied in connection with a leased computer system.[4]
- In 1964, a hardgoods distributor overturned a sales agreement in court because of a breach of warranty by a data-processing equipment manufacturer. The distributor received a refund of the purchase price for equipment delivered in 1957.[5]
- In 1967, a computer manufacturer was sued by a textile manufacturer for $4 million in damages for breach of contract and fraudulent representations in connection with the lease of a large computer system in 1964. An injunction was granted against the removal of the equipment until alternative arrangements could be made by the lessee.[6]
- A computer manufacturer was held liable to a cement manufacturer in 1968 for failure to deliver a computer system under a contract entered into in 1961.[7] Damage claims of about $138,700 were settled.

Corporate buyers may get some solace from the realization that their difficulties are shared by others. Even the federal government (probably the world's largest customer for computers) and computer system manufacturers themselves have not been immune from contractual blunders such as those described. For instance:

---

[4] *Food Center Wholesale Grocers, Inc. v. International Business Machines Corp.*, U.S. District Court for District of Massachusetts (Docket No. C.A. 64-45-C). Jury verdict reported in *The Wall Street Journal*, March 27, 1968.

[5] *Sperry Rand Corp. v. Industrial Supply Corp.*, 337 F. 2d 363 (5th Cir. 1964).

[6] *Spring Mills, Inc. v. General Electric Co.*, U.S. District Court for District of South Carolina (Docket No. C.A. 67-544). Suit reported in *Electronic News*, September 11 and 25, 1967, and October 3, 1967.

[7] *Lone Star Cement Corp. v. Royal McBee Corp.*, Supreme Court of New York, New York County, Index No. 7250, 1967.

• In 1965, a computer manufacturer that failed to deliver a computer in 1957 was required to pay the federal government $235,806 (consisting of $46,300 for liquidated damages, $179,450 for excess reprocurement expense, and $10,056 for unnecessary preparation costs), plus interest.[8]

• A manufacturer of peripheral equipment was sued by a producer of computer systems in 1967 for breach of warranty between 1965 and that year. The $145,000 damage claim was settled out of court.[9]

Undoubtedly, countless situations of the same nature either have been resolved short of litigation or could not be taken to court for some reason. Certainly my own experience has been that court cases reflect only a part of the controversies created by poor contracting.

STEPS TO BETTER CONTRACTING

Improvements in contracting are required at this time not merely to "tighten up" procurement and avoid costly errors, but also, more importantly, to enable computer users to benefit from the variety of new offerings in the marketplace today. Before most of us have learned how to lease or buy a computer system properly from a single source, we are tempted by the apparent advantages of securing central processing units, peripheral equipment, and software from different sources and making up the systems ourselves. We are also invited to leap into time-sharing systems. Instant sophistication seems to be required of computer users.

The effort to assess the economic advantages of acquiring software separately is dramatizing for some executives the serious deficiencies in their contracting practices. As they examine the hardware and software offered by their suppliers, many of them are amazed to discover that their contracts for entire systems have not stated the type or quality of the software to be furnished. For example, the lease of one major manufacturer simply assures "the use of the below listed machines" and its sale agreement refers only to the "machines . . . listed below."

Sound procurement of computer services, regardless of the nature of the transaction, involves three primary steps:

---

[8] *U.S. v. Wegematic Corp.*, 360 F. 2d 674 (2nd Cir. 1966).

[9] *Astrodata, Inc. v. Bolt, Beranek & Newman;* U.S. District Court for District of California (Docket No. 67-1486 CC). Suit reported in *Electronic News*, December 25, 1967.

1. Establishing basic company objectives for computer utilization.
2. Conducting negotiations so that the objectives will be achieved.
3. Writing a usable contract that really describes the transaction negotiated.

Senior management probably can make its greatest contribution simply by steering procurement back on the right route. Management should help to choose the objectives and evaluate the procurement team's performance during and after each acquisition. To perform such evaluations effectively, executives must be thoroughly acquainted with the proper subjective matter and techniques of negotiations and with the related contract drafting. The discussion that follows is intended to remind senior management of those items, not to qualify them to do the negotiating.

OBJECTIVES AND IMPLEMENTATION

Early establishment of objectives for computer utilization is indispensable if management is to make the best possible arrangements. Computer users have a wider choice of approaches than many people realize. Bear in mind that, regardless of the form of the transaction, all that is being acquired in essence in the *use* of a computer system. The system comprises both hardware and software, rather than simply the machines making up the central processing unit and related peripheral equipment. So long as this basic fact is recognized, computer users are free to survey the entire market for the best approach to satisfy their particular needs. They should regard the different types of transactions as merely means to that end.

The present market basket includes, in addition to the traditional lease or purchase of entire computer systems, the lease or purchase of separate system components (such as central processing units; peripheral equipment; compilers, sort routines, and similar programs; application software; and maintenance) and the purchase of time sharing, batch data processing, or merely time on someone else's computer. Entire systems may be bought from special system houses as well as from the manufacturers, and some systems may be leased from third-party lessors. Moreover, with the growth of the used system market, it is possible to buy used equipment (as well as to sell it).

Each of the possible arrangements mentioned has qualities that might either promote or frustrate efforts to obtain specific company objectives such as (to mention only a few):

- Smallest possible capital investment.
- Minimization of effects of technological obsolescence.
- Lowest possible net cost of computer system use.
- Greatest possible privacy of company records.
- Maximum ability to enlarge or improve the system.
- Maximum assurance of continued operation of the system.
- Protection against losses from data-processing errors.

CHOOSING THE RIGHT APPROACH

In view of the multiplicity of factors that are pertinent in selecting the right approach, it is impractical to try to designate which procurement arrangements will best achieve particular objectives. However, some examples can be provided:

- A company's initial capital investment can be kept down by using almost any approach other than outright purchase.
- It is easier to assure privacy of company records if they remain under the company's control rather than being sent outside (as in, say, a time-sharing system).
- The impact of technological obsolescence can be lessened either by using a short-term lease or by buying with a readiness to resell in the used system market.
- Losses resulting from errors and omissions of employees can be avoided by buying data-processing services under a contract that imposes liability on the supplier. (Data-processing service companies can buy errors and omissions insurance that is not available to companies using computer systems for their own work.)

In view of the increasing rate of change in the marketplace, continuing thought must be given to the question of ways and means. A particular acquisition method should not be routinely repeated by a user from one transaction to the next; rather, the selection process should be performed afresh each time in the light of prevailing market offerings as well as current company objectives. For example:

- Short-term leasing was the logical hedge against early obsolescence—until a market for used computers developed. In years past, leasing could be prohibitively expensive for some users. But then third-party leasing evolved. Also, manufacturers started to offer long-term leases. Likewise, third-party leasing is satisfactory only if the bundle of "support services," consisting of system design, programming, and maintenance, can be secured on economical and satisfactory terms and conditions from some source.

Despite the insistence of a supplier on its "standard" lease or sale contract form, each customer must make a strenuous effort to secure contractual provisions that protect its interests. More than ever before, it is possible to shop around if the suppliers first approached turn out to be inflexible or unreasonable.

EFFECTIVE NEGOTIATIONS

Computer contract negotiations (and inevitably the resulting agreements themselves) have tended to be seriously deficient in many critical respects. To illustrate:

- Although customers almost invariably procure computer systems, not just individual machines, few if any agreements with nongovernment users have specified the software to be provided. In fact, many customers actually accept computer systems that are "blanketed in" under leases of tabulating equipment which involve no internally stored programs. (The failure to describe the software involved probably results from habits developed in using punched-card system lease forms for computers.)
- Contracts with nongovernment users usually do not contain specifications describing either the design or the performance of the items to be delivered or the precise nature of the services to be furnished. Software and engineering service contracts should at least specify the items they cover.
- Very few agreements state objective acceptance test for determining whether delivered items are exactly what the customer was to receive.
- Agreements practically never include meaningful milestones for the production of systems or software, or for the commencement of subcontracted services, so that the customer cannot spot delivery failures early enough to arrange for their correction or, as a last resort, to go to another supplier.

But, some may ask, do not all corporate users receive basically the same treatment from supplier companies? Actually, despite apparent insistence on standard supplier forms which tend to leave little room for negotiation, suppliers do *not* treat all customers alike. Up to now, at least, many customers have secured special treatment in practice. Such treatment usually is camouflaged in a number of ways, such as by supplying greater amounts of system designing and programming without extra charge and without specifying any of it in the contract, or by giving lower prices under the guise of buying back the right of the supplier to use the system for demonstrations or information-processing work.

Of course, achieving uniform treatment for all customers in itself would be no major improvement as long as the forms used and the resulting contracts are deficient. It merely would perpetuate the basic difficulties resulting from the lack of understanding concerning what is to be delivered and what may be done in case of nonperformance.

As past cases of substantial damage awards to disgruntled customers show, deficient contracts can be harmful to suppliers as well as to computer users. Frequently, suppliers suffer in court largely because, in the absence of positive, well-considered contractual statements of what goods or services are to be delivered,customers are able to introduce into evidence the substantially less precise and occasionally somewhat exaggerated statements of salesmen attempting to make a sale. When unhappy customers seek redress from contracts that limit the supplier's warranty liability, they are charging fraudulent misrepresentation and are permitted to use salesmen's statements as proof. Clearly, *both* parties to a contract should prefer to live with specific, comprehensive provisions based upon careful negotiations and written formulation.

MAKEUP OF THE TEAM

Negotiations can be effective only if conducted by a properly qualified and supported team. The team should include the different types of specialists necessary to handle the complex aspects of the transaction, and all team members should be sophisticated in computer-communications technology.

More specifically, a team should include, as a minimum, a financial man, a purchasing agent, a computer system specialist, and a contracting or legal expert (just as in any major procurement). And each specialist should be qualified to deal with the unique subject of computers. For example, the legal specialist should appreciate, at the very least, the significance of these facts:

1. Systems, not merely machines, are involved.
2. Thorough program debugging is extremely difficult.
3. Acceptance tests should include objective criteria that readily and adequately reveal acceptability.
4. Computer use usually makes management substantially more dependent on the continued operation of the system than does practically any other form of mechanization.

Lack of sophistication about computers is far more significant than many people have been willing to acknowledge. It is, in my opinion, the major cause of inadequate computer contracts. It shows up in other ways, too, as the following case illustrates:

• In a suit involving the failure of a computer system to provide proper inventory control and correctly calculated invoices, it was alleged that the computer was not as ordered. Actually, the testimony indicated that the machine itself was entirely satisfactory. It was the *programming* that was deficient. Hence, the complaint properly should have charged that the delivered system, rather than the machine, failed to satisfy contractual requirements.

Obviously, it is the negotiating team that must think of all the technical and business requirements of the user and see that they are provided for.

KEY POINTS TO COVER

What matters should be taken up in the negotiations? The talks should deal completely with the usual variety of provisions appropriate for leasing, purchasing, or other types of transactions—and agreements on these points should, of course, be recorded in the contract. As indicated earlier, computer-use contracts are plagued by omission or inadequate treatment of a number of provisions that normally are found in well-drawn documents for the acquisition of complex machinery. I shall discuss these provisions briefly, not in the expectation that senior management will do the negotiating but rather to help it make certain that the negotiating team does its work properly.

When all of the appropriate kinds of provisions are included, it is essential that the scope and content of each be developed in as much detail as the state of the art requires. In short, individual attention is extremely important. A number of characteristics of computer system use justify such attention. The technology is still very novel and has numerous qualities that differ substantially from the more traditional items of machinery acquired by companies. For example:

• It can be extremely difficult to achieve complete accuracy in many software packages. Despite the frequent assurances of salesmen to the contrary, people simply do not have the ability to anticipate the wide range of possible circumstances that must be provided for in designing and programming many varieties of systems.

• Computer systems frequently constitute a more integral part of a company's operations than do other types of machines, and the user quickly becomes completely dependent on their scheduled availability, continued functioning, and easy expandability.

The creation and adoption of computer systems can require very substantial periods of time and major financial investments. Yet, at the same time, computer technology is extremely dynamic, and its most significant qualities can change from time to time.

Accordingly, experience proves the advisability of paying close attention to the following items even though they may appear elementary:

Descriptions of *all* goods and services to be furnished
Specifications of those goods and services
Acceptance tests
Time of delivery
Penalties for unexcused delays and other defaults
Place of delivery
Price, including discounts
Terms of payment
Warranties
Protection against patent and copyright infringement
Limitation of the supplier's liability
Action to be performed by the customer
Options
Duration of agreement

Full lists of all potential provisions for each of the above would, of course, be too extensive to include here. I shall limit myself to making general suggestions concerning the listed provisions and to providing some general observations on the acquisition of computer use.

ADEQUATE SPECIFICATIONS

All goods and services to be furnished to the customer should be stated, so that complete strangers to the transaction (including court judges) can find in the agreement exactly what is included. The deliverable items should be described well enough so that receiving clerks can prepare adequate receiving reports for all items, and accounts payable clerks can authorize proper payment for them solely on the basis of routine paperwork. This means that contract negotiators should, in addition to identifying and listing all such items, establish acceptance procedures. In the case of software, for example, it is frequently advisable to specify not only the names of the items but also such components as flow diagrams, print-outs, punched-card decks or reels of punched-paper tape, and sample inputs and outputs.

In a great many cases there should be adequate descriptions of goods and services to be furnished so that delivery of them can be determined by proper inspection procedures at a specific time and place. Such descriptions are familiar ones in procurement. They might show either how the deliverable items are composed, in which case they are called design specifications, or how the items will function, in which case they are called performance specifications. Often, either type of description is feasible, and the parties simply choose which one they want. On occasion, however, performance specifications really are preferable from the customer's standpoint, as he does not care how the item is made up so long as it produces the required results. A case in point is certain types of time-sharing services. (Suppliers, in contrast, usually prefer to work to design specifications.)

Incidentally, it should be noted that the sale of software to a customer usually constitutes the delivery of goods rather than the performance of services. Software packages are tangible items that are delivered physically. Consequently, they satisfy the definition of "goods" in the Sales Article of the Uniform Commercial Code, and contracts for their production and delivery are subject to that law. This is important because it automatically incorporates warranties into transactions and requires that certain warranty exclusions be stated prominently. Moreover, characterization as "goods" may affect the application of sales taxes and have other legal consequences, such as expanding the scope of legal liability of the software producer.

CONFORMANCE WITH STANDARDS

In addition to describing the things to be delivered, negotiators should establish the means for determining whether each delivered item meets its standards before payment is due. Invariably, an inspection procedure of some sort is utilized in major business purchases of equipment. The criteria for computer system or component acceptance should be selected not only so that they will assure that the specifications are met but also so that their fulfillment can be determined objectively and unequivocally, even by an outsider. Except in very unusual cases, the exercise of judgment or discretion should not be necessary to determine acceptability.

In its Federal Supply Schedule contracts covering computers, the federal government insists on actual performance of installed systems in accordance with the manufacturer's technical specifications at effectiveness levels of at least 90% for 30 consecutive days and involving at least 100 hours of productive time. The model lease of the Council of State Governments has a similar requirement and provides for the listing in the lease of the supplier's documents containing specifications.

Preparation of specifications and acceptance test routines for special computer systems or software can be laborious, expensive, and time-consuming (even for the most highly skilled specialists). Nevertheless, these matters are critical elements and well worth considerable effort. In many proposals, their preparation is postponed until after the contract is entered into. This is done in order to avoid incurring expenses for designing a test until a contract for the system is assured. However, the eventual contracts should require that preparation of specifications be completed early enough so that the customer can escape from his obligation if acceptable test criteria cannot be agreed on promptly. When a supplier has had sufficient experience with similar systems to permit economical formulation of a test at the proposal stage, the test should be included in the offer.

DELIVERY AND DAMAGES

Delivery is another important contract factor to be negotiated. It triggers the customer's obligation to pay; frequently it is also the time when the customer starts running the risk of loss and should insure the property involved.

As for the place of delivery, in some cases sellers prefer this to be at their own plants. However, buyers sometimes find that unacceptable, especially when performance standards are to be met by the new system. As for the time of delivery, agreement should be reached on precisely what the supplier must do with respect to the system or other items on or before the delivery date. Bear in mind that, since use of the system is the important thing to the buyer, delivery of such individual components as line printers or other terminals is, by itself, of no value to him; nor is he interested in delivery of a full complement of components that do not perform as specified.

When a computer system becomes a key part of the customer's operations and he must make lengthy and elaborate preparations for its introduction (particularly programming and coding of records), normal legal remedies for delivery default are not likely to provide adequate protection. Once contract performance has been under way for a significant period of time, the customer usually cannot attempt reprocurement elsewhere because of the long production lead times he would have to face anew. This is especially true when default is not discovered until the delivery date has arrived. The receipt of money damages rarely compensates for the expense and inconvenience suffered, many aspects of which are not measurable in dollars.

Consequently, a wise customer will try to establish meaningful concrete performance milestones throughout the period of production of the computer system. This enables him to spot many delivery failures (or potential failures) early, before his bargaining power is weakened;

also, he can take advantage of actual or anticipatory contract breaches, depending on how the contract is written. Designing those milestones is a very important item for negotiations. They might include the receipt of confirmations of delivery dates for major items procured outside, the successful passing of in-process tests of critical elements, or the completion of design steps.

The establishment of such milestones can be essential even when buying time-sharing service under a short-term contract. I know of one situation in which the customer had to accept grossly deficient service because it could not abandon the supplier and get prompt help from another company. Moreover, it could not prove monetary damages for the clear breach of contract because of the difficulty of valuing in money its great inconvenience and the burdens of providing makeshift complementary arrangements.

Since, as suggested, the normal judicial type of damages measured by provable loss frequently is not adequate, consideration should be given to using liquidated damages in amounts large enough to serve as "prods" for on-time delivery. The federal government customarily uses the remedy, especially in its contracts under thich computer systems are placed on federal supply schedules for easy ordering by agencies. Currently, the penalty is set at the greater of $100 per machine or 1/30th of the basic monthly rental, with a deiling of 180 days. Admittedly, the government enjoys substantial bargaining power by virtue of its large volume of acquisitions. Commercial customers might encounter supplier resistance to that approach.

PAYMENTS AND WARRANTIES

When very large systems are bought, it is important to consider how payment will have to be made. The supplier might be entitled to some payments as his work progresses and before final performance. However, any such payments should be made as advances (the so-called progress payments under government contracts) conditional upon acceptance of the entire system. Individual components of a system bought as such should not be paid for finally unless the customer is willing to keep them in any event, whether or not the whole system is accepted.

Meaningful operational warranties are probably even more important for computer systems than for many other items of equipment. Failure of electronic components of computers during the initial "burn in" period probably is more common than for parts of mechanical items. More significantly, many software packages require considerable tinkering because of the great difficulty of designing and debugging complicated programs. Hence, it is essential to secure a proper scope for warranties on a system as well as to specify that they remain in effect for a suitable length of time. In current contracts that do not identify the software furnished, the express warranty provisions probably do not cover the programs. However, implied warranties might apply.

When system elements are obtained from different sources, it may not be easy to take advantage of operational warranties; many times it is difficult to identify the source of a system failure. In such cases the negotiation of warranties obviously calls for special care.

Traditionally, computer system suppliers have given adequate protection to users against patent infringement claims affecting the hardware furnished. But until recently the software supplied was neither specified nor protected by patents or copyrights. The situation has now changed radically, largely because many software houses are undertaking to get patent or copyright coverage on their proprietary products. Hence, system users should seek such indemnification commitments covering software and, in the process, should identify the software so protected.

LIMITING LIABILITY

A very important point to cover is the limitation of the supplier's liability. Although in years past suppliers secured merely waivers of claims for consequential and special damages, they now seek to exclude also the broader liabilities introduced in the fraud suits of customers. For example:

- A major manufacturer states that its warranty obligation to keep leased machines in good working order is "in lieu of . . . all obligations or liabilities . . . for damages, including but not limited to consequential damages, arising out of or in connection with the use or performance of the machines." Interestingly, the failure to mention liability in connection with software might have the effect of not achieving any limitation for the manufacturer in that area.
- The same manufacturer imposes the following obligation (or one like it) on purchasers of equipment:

"The purchaser will be responsible for assuring the proper use, management, and supervision of the machines and programs, audit controls, operating methods, and office procedures, and for establishing all proper check points necessary for the intended use of the machines."

This relatively unobtrusive approach probably is taken in an effort to escape from claims for losses that could be avoided by programming techniques and other measures for verifying the accuracy of system operations at relatively frequent intervals. It thus is another attempt at limiting liability.

PUTTING AGREEMENTS IN PRINT

Skillful negotiations can be futile if not summarized well in written agreements. These agreements not only must cover all of the points agreed on, but also must do so in simple language that can (a) guide the people on both sides who carry out the transactions and (b) communicate adequately to nontechnologically oriented tribunals that might be called in to resolve any disputes.

Obvious as the need for completeness in contracts may be, it is difficult to achieve in practice. Points hammered out orally in negotiations often are not reduced to writing for these reasons:

1. It usually is much more difficult to formulate understandings in writing than to arrive at them orally, because absence of precision becomes more apparent in writing. Prompt feedback and superficial analysis in oral discussions tend to create an illusion of full coverage.
2. Statements on highly technical subjects such as specifications and acceptance tests are difficult to write; relatively few people have the patience and the skill to work them out.
3. Some aspects of oral agreement may seem so clear to the participants who have "lived with" the negotiations that their restatement in writing is considered to be unnecessary. Even lawyers can be lulled into such a false sense of security.

The written agreement must tell the entire story to an outsider, preferably one who is nontechnically oriented. It is remarkable how quickly negotiators' memories of details fade and how rapidly they cease to be available for interpretations of agreements. The ultimate test of the adequacy of documentation, of course, is how well the interests of a party to the contract would fare before a judge.

Incidentally, applicable written sources of information, such as specification sheets, test routines, and the like, should be identified precisely if they are not included in the agreement physically. For example, the model computer lease of the Council of State Governments requires, in the case of equipment specifications, the "manufacturer's document name, number, and date which defines the physical performance characteristics of the machine." Titles of documents alone are not enough; dates of revising the material also are essential.

Exhibit 10-1. Examples of Information to Keep in a Central File.

Items generated by the customer:
- Requests to supplier for proposals
- Letters to supplier
- Document drafts submitted to supplier
- Memoranda of conversations with personnel of supplier
- Memoranda of other actions of supplier

Items received from the supplier:
- Advertisements
- Brochures
- Letters
- Proposals
- Document drafts
- Manuals
- Specifications

Formal agreements signed by the parties.

Simplicity of statement in agreements has many virtues. If written in the language of laymen, agreements will not repel or defy understanding by the persons who are intended to use them. They then can serve the purposes for which they are created, namely, day-to-day guidance on action to be taken. This requires that the words should be nonlegalistic and that the statements should be more complete than "tight" legal writing, even at the risk of redundancy. Laymen are not as adept as lawyers with implied conditions or exclusions; they function better when points are made expressly. Technical jargon and buzz-words must be avoided as much as legalistic words. Most of the former have no clear definitions and merely create a dangerous illusion of expertness or precision. If the use of technical terms is unavoidable, they should be defined clearly and precisely.

SUPPLEMENTARY FILES

In many situations it is not possible to achieve the ideal of completeness in a formal written agreement. If so, all is not lost. Many legal as well as business purposes can be served by contracts made up of numerous components, some formal and others informal, oral as well as written.

To provide for this possibility, the parties to a contract should start building a central contract file just as soon as possible. That file should contain relevant items such as those listed in Exhibit 10-1. This data will be useful while the transaction is being carried out—and invaluable if litigation is necessary. Responsibility for its maintenance should be assigned carefully.

EVALUATING PROGRESS

How can top management best evaluate the work of the acquisition team while the negotiations and contract drafting are in process and after completion? Mere general attention to the activities of the team is not enough. Attention must be focused on specific goals and steps toward those goals.

As a minimum step, management should have an acquisition timetable and budget drawn up. This timetable will provide a means for determining whether adequate progress is being made. Moreover, since one of the chronic and serious problems of buying the use of computers has been unexpected delays in delivery, the timetable should be tied in to any milestones established for contract performance. It should include such steps as those listed in Exhibit 10-2.

Exhibit 10-2. Topics for a Timetable.

- Preparation of specifications of the system to be used
- Selection of type of procurement transaction to be used
- Receipt of proposals from potential suppliers
- Choice of supplier for negotiation
- Commencement of negotiations
- Completion of negotiations
- Drafting of agreement
- Approval of draft
- Signing of agreement
- Adoption of acceptance test procedures
- Activities in connection with delivery:
  - Availability of hardware for advance programming
  - Training in programming, operation, and maintenance
  - Delivery of hardware and software
  - Start of acceptance tests
  - End of acceptance tests
- Start of operation of computer system
- End of parallel operation of system being replaced
- Evaluation of cost of the procurement effort

Since the financial aspects of the acquisition process also should be reviewed periodically, a budget should be established at the outset (and revised periodically as new data become available) to reflect both the cost of the acquisition activity and the cost of utilizing the system. By this device, effectiveness of the effort can be measured and efficiency in its performance can be promoted by discouraging recourse to costly spur-of-the-moment decisions when delays or other difficulties crop up.

CONCLUSION

As the record indicates, there has been a serious, inexcusable failure to use normal contracting practices in acquiring the use of computer systems. This failure has been harmful to computer suppliers (the possibly unwitting perpetrators of the errors) as well as to customers, at least where litigation has occurred.

Fortunately, the remedy is relatively easy to adopt. Top management must take the reins and require the use of recommended procurement practices, much as it does in the case of other major purchases of equipment. The apparent complexity of computer technology is not a valid objection to such a policy. In fact, that complexity makes care in contracting even *more* important than in other areas of procurement.

Management's involvement in buying computer services will be rewarding in itself by making executives more familiar with the devices that are already reshaping the structure of many businesses. It will pay substantial dividends by reducing the unnecessary expenses that have resulted from poorly chosen systems, delivery delays, and disputes. And it will help computer users to take full advantage of the rapidly enlarging variety of procurement approaches becoming available in the marketplace.

MANAGEMENT OF SYSTEMS ANALYSIS

by Richard G. Canning

In managing the systems effort, management would like to know in advance, and with reasonable accuracy, *what* will be accomplished and *when* it will be accomplished. In short, management would like to be

---

This material has been adapted from the July 1968 issue of *EDP Analyzer;*

able to realistically plan the system analysis and design phases of a project and then be able to control progress according to the plan.

In the past, the planning and control of the systems effort has run into difficulties. That is, the job of system analysis often required so much more time than expected that the original plan was useless. One cause of the difficulty has been the mass of detail that potentially can be studied, when studying the present system. Few guidelines exist for system analysts on what to study and what not to study; if the analyst has a cautious and conservative nature, he wants "more" data about the present system—and sometimes, it seems that he can continue to uncover new data until the end of time.

Another reason that actual progress deviates from plan has been that system design turns out to be more difficult than anticipated. That is, the initial designs fall far short of meeting the performance or economic criteria for acceptance, so new designs have to be created and evaluated.

And still another reason for difficulty has been that operating managers many times warm up slowly to the project. Their first reviews of project plans tend to be superficial and they give a "tentative" OK to the plans. (A "wise" manager, if he realizes that he doesn't fully comprehend the new system, always conditions his approval of the system. It gives him something to fall back on later, when he uncovers problems.) Then, as these managers gradually begin to come to grips with the new system and try to visualize how they will operate their departments using it, they begin to see things they would like changed. These requested changes can play havoc with project schedules and costs. Data processing analysts, of course, can't disregard operating management's requests—but we will have more to say about the handling of changes later in this report.

Thus it appears that the systems effort still is not as subject to discipline as is the programming effort. Even so, steps can be taken to reduce the difficulties. To this end, we will discuss the following:

Three main steps in analysis and design
Controlling progress and costs
Project organization
Freezing design and handling changes
Documentation

THREE STEPS IN ANALYSIS AND DESIGN

The three main steps in the analysis and design phase are: studying the present system, analysis of requirements, and design of the new system. We will discuss each briefly, from the standpoint of effective management.

STUDYING THE PRESENT SYSTEM

The dominant characteristic of a study of an existing information system is the tremendous amount of detail that *can* be explored. From the standpoint of management, the question is: how much of this detail *should* be explored?

One of the first steps in studying an existing information system is to gather copies of each of the forms and reports currently in use. In saying this, one normally thinks of the "formal" or "official" reports and forms, recognizing that there probably are some "informal" or "unofficial" forms and reports in use. The actual situation may be staggering. We saw figures recently pertaining to the official and unofficial forms and reports in use at three medium size companies. These figures were:

Company	*Official forms*	*Unofficial forms*
Electronics co.	566	1145
Insurance co.	3120	2672
Aircraft co.	2249	2683

In another instance, a division of a major aerospace firm found that data processing was preparing some 1500 different "reports" for the accounting function alone.

While it is likely that the number of unofficial forms and reports could be reduced by careful analysis, consolidation, and elimination, the point to keep in mind is that each one of these was created to meet some particular need. Just searching out and obtaining copies of all the official and unofficial reports and forms is a big job in itself; gaining an understanding of the need for and use of each of these is an even bigger job—and charting the flow of each one of these would be a tremendous job.

How should the systems effort be managed, with respect to the study of the existing information system? The answer to this question is influenced by the degree of participation by the operating managers.

Heavy participation by operating managers. If operating managers participate heavily during the analysis and design stages—through what we have called "design sessions"—much of the formal data gathering tends to be bypassed. The managers tend to enter immediately into the definition of requirements and then the design of the new system. In the course of this work, if data is needed about the present system, they know who to call and what to ask.

In the design sessions with which we are familiar, the managers normally concentrated on the desired outputs. They frequently came to the sessions armed with copies of all reports and operating documents currently in use, and could answer many questions about those documents. When questions arose which they could not answer, they knew how to get the answers quickly. Frequently other people, knowledgeable in specific areas, would be invited to attend the sessions when their areas were being discussed. The end result was that the system analysts were spared the necessity of gathering much data about the present system.

Study performed primarily by system analysts. In those instances where operating managers do not participate heavily in the analysis and design stages, then the system analysts must study the present system so as to determine the requirements for the new system. Here, too, the approach can follow two main courses, depending on whether or not the analysts have a broad familiarity with the company's operations.

If the analysts are quite familiar with the company, the normal approach is for them to immediately become engaged in studying the area under consideration. As we pointed out earlier in this report, the mass of detail that they *could* gather is staggering, so data processing management should see to it that a careful selection is made of what data to gather. We favor a structured approach such as is found in IBM's Study Organization Plan (SOP) for gathering this data. SOP provides procedures for studying the existing forms and reports (messages), files, and operations, without the need to chart the flow of all forms and reports. Experience with SOP has demonstrated that an effective study of the existing system can be made without getting trapped by too much detail.

If the analysts are not familiar with the operation being studied—as is the case with consultants, system engineers from the computer manufacturer, newly hired analysts, etc.—then SOP recommends a brief, broad study of the enterprise. This broad study has a further benefit: if substantial improvements are to be made by means of improved system design, they must be made in relation to the basic goals of the enterprise.

So where big improvements are desired, or where the analysts are unfamiliar with the enterprise, SOP advocates that such information as the following be gathered at the outset: history and background of the enterprise; industry background; business objectives and goals; major policies and practices; pertinent government regulations; business structure (its inputs, outputs, and resources); and projections of markets, products, budgets, and facilities.

Following the broad study, SOP calls for gathering the information already described—forms and reports, files, and operations.

ANALYSIS OF REQUIREMENTS

The main reason for studying the existing system is to determine the information requirements that the new system must satisfy. One goal here is to determine what is logically necessary, as opposed to information that is requested "because we have always had it." A related goal is to perform a simplification and streamlining of the information system by attempting to remove unimportant variations or complexities.

The new data management systems will help solve the problem of report contents and sort sequences. Reports can be prepared on a demand basis—and if an operating department wants a report in a particular sequence, they should get it in that sequence. The price paid will be in extra computer time but often that is becoming a secondary item of cost. If the new information system will operate under data management software, the analysis step will be primarily concerned more with the contents of the data files than with the exact format of the output reports.

The National Cash Register Company has recently developed a new technique that appears to be a powerful tool for the analysis step. Called Accurately Defined Systems (ADS), this technique is concerned with identifying the required outputs, inputs, historical data, and processes for the new system. It is basically simple in concept and easy to use; it is equipment independent and can be easily understood by operating managers and personnel. Thus they can review the specifications for the new system and can make necessary changes and corrections. At the same time, the technique gives the system analysts and programmers a clear definition of the system for the purposes of design and programming.

Another aspect of the analysis step is the identification of performance criteria and tradeoffs between performance factors in the new system. It is hard to pin managers down as to what they will deem poor-versus-good performance and the tradeoff between performance factors, but this information will be invaluable to the system designers. As an illustration, the performance criteria for an order entry system might include the following: anything over a four hour order entry cycle is unacceptable; a one hour order entry cycle is reasonable; we would not be willing to pay extra money for an order entry cycle faster than 15 minutes. In connection with tradeoffs, the relative amounts of money that management is willing to pay for the different levels of performance would be stated.

Finally, the analysis step is the time that improved decision-type methods should be selected, if desired. For instance, if improved short range forecasting is desired in an inventory control application, this would be the time to investigate different approaches and select the preferred one. Thus a management science study might be conducted in parallel with the information system study, and timed so that the methods selections are made during the analysis step of the information system study.

SYSTEM DESIGN

The prime goal of the system design stage is to consider alternative designs and select the one that best meets management's needs—best, that is, in relation to the alternatives considered.

The most common approach to this stage has been for the system analysts to conceive and manually evaluate alternative designs. When they find a design that seems to meet the needs, they tend to lock on to that design and attempt to sell it as *the* solution. Because manual evaluation—timing and costing many computer runs, for instance—is so slow and costly, few alternative solutions are investigated. We feel that this approach always has been a poor one—and in these days of more complex systems, it is becoming less and less tenable.

A better approach is to make use of a mechanized evaluation method, so that many alternative designs can be considered. One such method is SCERT.

An even better approach, in our opinion, is to obtain heavy participation by operating managers in the analysis and design stages—as discussed above—and then use a mechanized evaluation method for evaluating alternative designs. We should emphasize, of course, that skilled data processing system designers should participate; the operating managers cannot do the job by themselves.

GENERAL PATTERN

Usually these three steps—studying the present system, analysis of requirements, and design of the new system—are performed twice, in most cases with which we are familiar. They are performed once during the feasibility study, in a fairly limited fashion. Then, if the project is approved for implementation, they are performed again in greater depth during the system design phase.

Ideally, of course, it would be desirable to perform these steps in sufficient depth during the feasibility study so that very little repetition would be needed during the subsequent phases. The question, though, is the probability of obtaining approval for project implementation. If there is a good chance of not proceeding with the project, then feasibility study costs should be limited. On the other hand, if the feasibility study is limited, the chance exists that something has been overlooked that will significantly influence performance or costs.

As far as we know, there is no "right" answer to the length of a feasibility study. All that can be said is it is usually not long enough, so time must be spent as effectively as possible. In our opinion, the charting of existing procedures is largely a waste of manpower and should be avoided.

TESTING AND CONVERSION

It is essential that the detailed plans for testing and conversion be developed during the design phase. For testing, this includes a listing of all test cases that will be used, the conditions that each test case will test for, and the dates by which each test should be completed. Conversion plans should include the decision on how conversion will be accomplished (immediate cut-over versus gradual cut-over, for instance), the conversion schedule, and the user training that will be necessary.

CONTROLLING PROGRESS AND COSTS

As discussed above, most of the effort during the design phase can go into studying the present system, so that plans and controls should be carefully laid out for this step. The best approach with which we are familiar is to break down this study into relatively small segments of work and then estimate the man-hours of time required for each segment. A Gantt chart can be constructed to show the sequence and personnel assignments.

How big is a segment of work? In studies with which we are familiar, a segment has been some logical group of operations. For instance, an accounts receivable application system might be broken down into segments having such names as: opening new accounts, checking credit, posting daily sales, posting cash receipts, billing, making bill adjustments, etc. The man-days required to study segments of this size can usually be estimated with reasonable accuracy. The chance still exists, of course, that a segment will turn out to be far more complex than originally estimated. But during the planning of the studies, conversations with operating managers should pinpoint areas of unusual complexity.

We have seen small PERT charts used effectively in the planning of such studies. Once the segments have been identified and the personnel assignments made, a PERT chart can be laid out. In many instances, a chart of 30 to 50 activities will be adequate and can thus be developed and maintained manually.

A point of critical importance in meeting project schedules and costs: a system design freeze point must be set and enforced. This freeze point should occur at the end of detailed system design. The main effect on the systems effort, of course, is the need to get requirements and specifications crystallized as much as possible during system design, to cut down on the number of mandatory changes after the design freeze point.

Another point to consider is that of expected operating costs of the new system. It is not unusual for changes in system design to be made during the detailed design phase that will increase the eventual operating costs over what was estimated in the feasibility study. In well-managed system efforts that we have observed, the manager does not just accept such increases, but challenges the system designers to find other design changes which will offset the increased costs. A mechanized method for timing runs or jobs would be most desirable, for frequently reassessing the impact of design changes on operating costs.

PROJECT ORGANIZATION

We have just mentioned the importance of effectively freezing the design of the new system at the end of the detailed design phase, if programming schedules and costs are to be controlled. But to made a "design freeze" philosophy work, it is essential that most of the causes of later changes be eliminated or greatly reduced. One of the major causes of requested changes is that of operating managers who do not begin to grasp the full implications of the new system until they see conversion approaching. So it is most important to achieve meaningful communications between the design staff and the operating managers during the design phase.

How can meaningful communications be achieved between these two groups? A variety of ways have been tried:

An operating manager is made the project manager.

Co-managers are assigned, on a partnership basis, one an operating manager, one from data processing.

Full-time liaison persons are assigned from key operating departments.

System analysts are selected from operating departments.

Operating managers participate in system design via design sessions.

Frequent reviews are held with operating managers during design phase, pointing out implications of the new system.

There is no magic formula for solving this problem of communications. All of the above solutions have worked effectively when used with sincerity and intelligence. None of them will work automatically.

A final point: in order to have operating managers participate more effectively during the design phase, it would be well to give them background training in data processing.

FREEZING DESIGN AND HANDLING CHANGES

As we have pointed out, it is important to institute a system design freeze point at the end of the detailed analysis and design phase if schedules and costs are to be met for the remainder of the project. A program design freeze point is also necessary at the conclusion of the program design phase.

Freezing design means that henceforth any proposed changes must go through a formal submission, evaluation, and implementation procedure. It does *not* mean that no further changes can be made. However, during evaluation the proposed changes are separated into two major categories—mandatory or desirable. If mandatory, the timing is investigated; some might be delayed until the new system is working. If urgent, then the change will have to be made. What design freeze *does* mean is that someone—say, an operating manager—does not informally request a change and a system designer informally agrees to make it.

We have discussed one major cause of changes—inadequate communications between the system designers and the operating managers during the detailed design phase. If operating managers really begin to comprehend the new system only after programming has commenced, delays and extra costs are sure to occur.

But there are other causes of changes. Programming is a slow process and it stretches out the implementation cycle. A long implementation cycle means that business conditions can change and the information system may have to be modified to accommodate the changed conditions. The system analysts and programmer may see ways in which the design can be changed to achieve operating economies. And sometimes the need for a change is caused by a clear oversight during the detailed design phase.

We see the new data management systems as playing an important role in handling changes. Data management systems promise to drastically cut the implementation cycle for new applications. This means, for one thing, that there is less chance for business conditions to change during the shorter implementation cycle. It also means that when a change is necessary or is desired, it often will be made much more easily—because if a data management system helps create the new application system more rapidly, it can help change the new system more rapidly also.

DOCUMENTATION

The conversion to third generation equipment has spotlighted the fact that program documentation too frequently is inadequate. The same can be said of system documentation. Only the minimum documentation may be developed in the eagerness to get on with the more interesting parts of the project.

What does good documentation consist of, for system analysis and design?

1. Charter or work statement for the project, setting out what is to be accomplished, the goals and objectives, what resources will be used, and so on.
2. The project plan and budget, both in original form and in updated form.
3. Data gathering documentation, for each segment of work—including scope and boundary definition of the segment, the file, message, and operation sheets, volume data, etc.
4. The analysis documentation, including ADS documents (if used), any operations research studies leading to new decision rules, and documentation supporting system requirements.
5. Design documentation, including overall system design diagrams, data designs (inputs, outputs, records, file organization), overall program logic, performance criteria, supporting clerical procedures, equipment requirements, and operating time estimates. If

alternative designs are being submitted for selection, schedules and budgets for each design should be documented.

6. Testing documentation including identification of all conditions that must be tested, the test cases designed to test those conditions, and the dates when the various tests are expected to be completed.
7. Conversion documentation including the overall plan of conversion, the schedule, user training schedule, and broad plans of action in case serious troubles are encountered.

11

Controlling Computer Performance and Costs

Profitable use of the computer requires many steps: systems study, design, programming, and operations. Each of these steps can do no more than pass on, undiminished, whatever quality was embodied in the previous steps.

The previous chapter examined ways to improve the quality and predictability of systems development. This chapter reviews the importance of the operational phase and explores possibilities for raising operational performance and reducing cost.

Data processing cost has often been the fastest-growing segment of corporate expense. The magnitude of these costs and the frequent discoveries of poor utilization of equipment and personnel have prompted new efforts in planning and control.

Some operational decisions such as equipment selection call for new and complex tools such as performance monitoring and simulation. Many areas, however, are amenable to improvement through managerial and control techniques used successfully in engineering and manufacturing.

For years computer activity contributed to change and improvement elsewhere in the organization. Now there is an opportunity for outside experience and skills to have a healthy and valuable impact on the data processing component.

A GUIDE TO COMPUTER CENTER EFFICIENCY

by Gordon C. MacKenzie

In today's rapidly-expanding business world, it is no longer enough to

Reprinted by permission from the publisher from *Modern Data,* vol. 4, no. 5 (May 1971), pp. 62-64.

purchase and install a computer, train its operators, and write programs that will provide useful information. Because of the large increase in the number of computers being installed, one must consider yet another aspect of computer installation and usage if an efficient computing organization is to be achieved. That aspect is systems support.

By systems support we mean an organization that will undertake the day-to-day clerical jobs that enable a computing center to function effectively. Such an organization is normally staffed by several nontechnical clerks, supervised by an administrator or clerical manager. The purpose of this organization is to relieve machine operators, programmers, or managers of the clerical tasks necessary for smooth operation.

The organization should consist of groups or individuals assigned to the following tasks: tape library supervision, job control, time accounting, equipment (hardware) inventory, material supply, and clerical administration. The organization's duties would be to gather time charges for billing; to maintain control of tapes (and disk packs and data cells); to forecast workload and equipment requirements, and types of runs to be made on the system; and to generate reports that will enable management to manage their computing center more effectively. The interrelationship of these groups is shown in Figure 11-1.

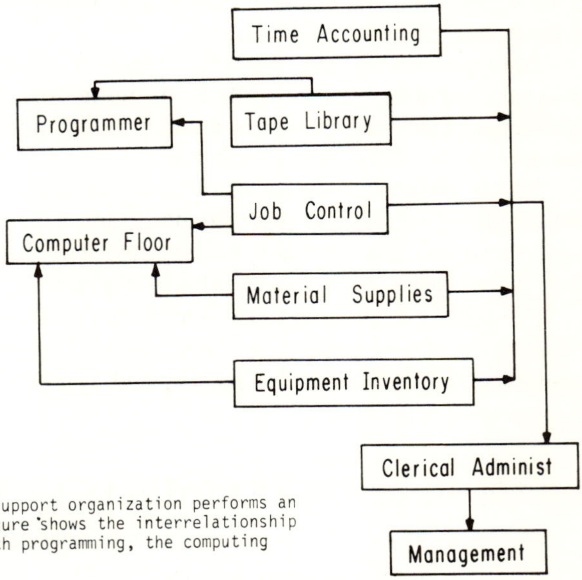

Each group in a systems support organization performs an essential task. This figure shows the interrelationship of the various groups with programming, the computing floor, and management.

Figure 11-1.

TAPE LIBRARY

The storage of tapes should be given great consideration. While the means by which the library is laid out and arranged is important, it is not as critical as the system used in storing and identifying tapes. We have found that a sequentially numbered library is the most practical and manageable since it allows for programmed record-keeping. Numbering the library tapes sequentially also makes the day-to-day jobs—such as scratching, assigning, auditing, and inventory—simpler and less time-consuming.

The labeling of tapes lends itself to several different approaches. We have found that the following system works well for us:

New tape labels are created on the system by the operator at the time that the tape is created. A duplicate of the newly-created tape label is forwarded to the tape library twice daily (or when sufficient labels have been created to make such pickups a necessity). The tape library will record the tape number, the individual to whom it is assigned, the date assigned, the system it was assigned on, the scratch date, and a brief description of the information on the tape—unless the programmer has requested special labeling information via his job request card. After the tape label has been created, it is affixed to the tape and will remain as part of the tape's records until the tape is scratched.The pre-numbered tape will be restored in its pre-numbered storage location.

Audits of the tapes held by each programmer are sent out to the tape library users on a bimonthly schedule. The returned audits, indicating those tapes that the programmers want scratched, account for 90% of the tape library's available scratch tapes. Disk packs and data cells can be handled in much the same manner.

JOB CONTROL

To simplify the duty of "in-house" job control, a system based upon the use of credit cards can be employed. Its operation is straightforward and is described as follows:

Each programmer who uses the facilities of the computing center is issued a credit card. This card is ordered by his manager and is the responsibility of his manager. It contains the programmer's project or problem number, his department, his name, his telephone extension, his room and building address and the name of his project.

The reason for using a credit card is to insure correct delivery of completed jobs and the charging of computer time to the correct project and individual; and to provide the machine operator with the telephone extension where the programmer can be reached. A Job Request Card can be used in conjunction with the credit card. The job request card, filled out by the programmer, gives the machine operator all the necessary information he needs to run the job and label the tapes, disk packs, and/or data cells that might be created. The job card is arranged to provide an area that the programmer can stamp with his credit card, and no jobs are accepted for processing by job control personnel unless the job request card is stamped. In special cases, the time accounting office may issue a temporary credit card to be used on a restricted basis.

Job control personnel receive and log jobs into the computing center. The job control office will issue a sequential job number to the job, request the appropriate tapes, disks, disk packs, and data cells from the tape library, and transport the job to its specific system (correct core size, correct I/O devices, etc.). When the job is completed, it is transported back to the job control office and logged out. The log will provide management with a turn-around time report and control over job flow. It also enables a trace to be placed on jobs that are in-shop, making it possible to run down "lost" jobs.

TIME ACCOUNTING

This group is responsible for the accurate accumulation of charges arising out of computer usage. When a user's job is run on a system, the operator or system must record the times that the job started and finished as well as the system's idle time, engineering change time, and malfunction time. By maintaining time records on type of job, type of system, and the dollar worth of the machine time used, the time accounting group provides local and higher management with information that is not only important from the standpoint of decision-making, but also from the legal standpoint since some of this time might be taxable under state and/or federal laws.

The time accounting group also computes the "rate" at which time should be charged in order to pay the expenses of operating the computing center, and produces and oversees the credit card system. Their control of the credit card system is appropriate because they are the group that is responsible for charges made against individuals and/or departments.

EQUIPMENT INVENTORY

The equipment inventory clerk will maintain an inventory of the computers and equipment in the computing center. He prepares and maintains a full set of records and issues management reports on machine type, machine features, purchase or rental price, installation date, and termination date (if known or anticipated). He records any moves that take place on his computing floor—what machines have been moved and their new location—and maintains records pertaining to equipment transferred to other locations.

MATERIAL SUPPLY

The stock clerk requests the paper, tape, etc. required by the computing center to carry on its normal business. He maintains a running inventory of stock in order to allow the clerical administration group to place orders with sufficient lead time to insure delivery before his regular "on hand" stock is depleted. He prepares a monthly management report on items in stock, items on order, items received, and monthly expenses.

CLERICAL ADMINISTRATION

The duties of the clerical administration group vary depending upon the overall computing center organization. In general, this group performs the actual ordering, exercises cost control, and suggests alternatives.

One of the clerical administration group's most important duties is to prepare and distribute a forecast of the machine time to be used. They do this by polling the various users of the computing center for their projected needs during the ensuing year. This forecast is broken down by group, department, project, and type of system required. From this forecast, clerical administration prepares reports for management for scheduling. With the assistance of time accounting, this group also prepares a monthly report comparing the amount of time forecast with the amount of time actually used.

SUMMARY

The foregoing is but one possible approach to achieving computer center efficiency. The proper functioning of the groups or individuals that comprise a well-rounded systems support organization provide for effective delegation of the many responsibilities involved in setting up and running a computing organization. The solution offered is by no means a cure-all, but is one tested approach to the problem.

THE EDP MANAGER—AND THE COMPUTER PROFIT DRAIN

by Walter J. Schroeder

PART 1

THE PRESENT AND FUTURE STATUS OF THE EDP MANAGER IN THE CORPORATE ORGANIZATION

The status or condition of the EDP manager can be viewed from various perspectives:

1. We could look at his status vis a vis other top corporate management positions in the organization.
2. We could review the status of the EDP Manager from the view of the public. Much has been said on that subject in the press recently.
3. We can inspect his status from the perspective of the computer professional's expectations for the position.

It is the third perspective that I have chosen for my theme. Compared with the expectations of the field, how has the EDP Manager fared in the corporate organization and what is the prognosis?

A LOOK AT THE PAST

In order to do this it is necessary first to take a brief look at the past. Predictions concerning the future of the computer are not difficult to find. Everyone it seems has at one time or another felt compelled to make a prognostication about where electronics would lead us in managing business enterprises. It is an intriguing fact that about the only major forecast to be achieved was the number of computers installed. There we have exceeded expectations.

But in other, more fundamental aspects, the predictions have largely failed to materialize. Consider some of the following which were widely held beliefs during the 1960's:

Reprinted with permission from *Computers and Automation,* January 1971, copyright 1971 by and published by Berkeley Enterprises Incorporated, 815 Washington St., Newtonville, Mass. 02160.

1. That there would be a reduction in the numbers of middle-management personnel required by corporations as the computer began to take over routine decision-making functions. There is certainly no evidence to support any conclusion this has been achieved. If anything, there are more middle-management positions today than there were five years ago.
2. That profitability and return on investment will improve when EDP functions fulfill their primary purpose of providing faster and better information. High-speed information should result in better management decisions and improved performance. Although there are some instances where improved information has led to improved performance, I can name many more where it did not come to pass.

What many top management people and most EDP personnel have overlooked is the fact that decisions are made by people. If people are going to become more effective, they not only need good information but:

(a) they need to be motivated to change, and

(b) they need to be taught how to change.

Few EDP functions adequately address this problem, let alone even recognize it as the really fundamental objective of their activity. In case after case, from hundreds of interviews and consulting assignments in this field, I have found the EDP manager turning more and more into a technician and less and less into a business manager.

Many people have believed that the EDP manager, by virtue of his analytical training and understanding of the business through the information systems, will become the general manager of the enterprise. A few EDP managers have crossed the barrier into the ranks of functional or operations management positions. Most of these are in staff jobs and only a very few in line positions. Those who achieved top management did it mostly by starting their own businesses in the EDP service industry. A large number of these have proven to be less than sufficiently capable—as testified by the large number of business failures in this industry.

LACK OF TRAINING FOR BUSINESS MANAGEMENT

My own observation is that, in general, there is little about the systems and data processing field which trains a man to join future top management of the company. He learns little about the true nature of competition, choosing product or pricing strategies, and the use of risk capital. Many in the EDP field have become so engulfed with the hardware and software they do not even relate well with their fellow men — an important ingredient in leadership needed at top corporate levels.

Some EDP managers, particularly those under 35 years of age, have had work experience only in the EDP function where they started their careers as computer programmers. Unfortunately they often know very little about the business.

I conclude that the major expectations of the past have largely not come to pass. What then is the current status of the EDP manager?

THE CURRENT SITUATION

To assess the current situation, I would like first to draw upon several personal observations.

1. *The EDP Organization.* Recent surveys indicate a trend toward moving the EDP organization out of the corporate accounting or financial area and placing it higher in the overall corporate structure. Many EDP departments located in the financial areas of the business have concentrated on financial information systems and have done very little to help in other problem areas. About 50% of the EDP Managers now report to non-financial executives. The larger the corporation, the more likely the EDP manager will report to the President or other high ranking officer.

2. *Systems Planning.* The effectiveness of the service to solve problems and develop application systems provided by EDP functions is heavily dependent upon the way in which the EDP manager views his own role in the business.

Some consider their proper role one which is closely related to the technical computer environment. They concentrate on the development of highly capable computer complexes and rely upon the users to ensure the realization of economic benefits. The EDP manager with this view is likely to describe his function as one of supplying better information faster.

The other perspective is to view the job as one of solving user problems — problems which can be stated in terms of:

- Too much inventory,
- Excessively high cost of operation, or
- Inadequate customer service.

Personally, I endorse this latter view as the proper role of the EDP manager. However, to fulfill that role effectively requires the EDP function to be fully absorbed into the operations of the business. EDP cannot stand alone or be isolated from the line and other staff activities. We have found the degree of EDP absorption into the business is revealed by the extent of its planning for the future and how well those plans are integrated with the plans of the operating functions of the business.

LONG-RANGE PLANS

Only a minority of EDP departments have a really effective long-range plan. At A.T. Kearney, we define a long-range systems plan as containing:

1. An overview of the systems as they are intended to function by the end of the planning period.
2. A list and description of the projects which will be undertaken.
3. Estimates of personnel requirements by skill categories.
4. Plans for hardware and software changes within known state of the art.
5. Estimates of benefits and costs.

Even this degree of detail of planning will not be effective where there is no corporate planning activity. If top management lacks the vision, desire, or understanding to establish objectives of performance and to integrate planning across functions, the EDP plan will be better than nothing, but not truly viable.

We often are called upon to help clients prepare EDP plans. Presidents of client companies have commented later they did not realize the far-reaching consequences of such a project. While systems planning of this type is on the increase, there are a pitifully small number of companies which do it.

PART 2

THE COMPUTER PROFIT DRAIN

The other main topic I would like to discuss is the effectiveness with which EDP managers manage computer operations.

Whether EDP managers in general do a good job with the tools they have was revealed by a research study which we conducted recently at A.T. Kearney and Co., Inc. The study was entitled, "The Computer Profit Drain". Because of the significance of the findings, the rest of this article will summarize that study.

COMPUTING COSTS IN THE U.S.

On the basis of the 1969 World Computer Census published by *Computers and Automation,* a conservative estimate of annual equipment rental in the United States is $3 billion.

Generally accepted rules of thumb indicate a company may expect to spend one-third of its systems and computer expenditures for rental, another one-third in operating costs in the computing center (personnel, supplies, power and space) and the balance on system development and programming. It appears therefore that at least $9 billion are spent annually in the United States for computers and related costs.

THE BURDEN OF EXCESS COMPUTING CAPACITY

It has long been suspected that our national economy bears a heavy burden of excess computing capacity. There also are indications that a substantial number of users are not effectively managing computer operations, and, as a result, may be paying a heavy penalty. The Kearney study provides substantial evidence that two-thirds of annual expenditures for computer rental and operating costs (about $6 billion in the U.S.) are poorly managed. It further reveals that the average computer installation in the United States uses its equipment productively less than half the time it is available. Idle time and rerunning of poor quality work alone is costing the average company in this study over $100,000 each year.

ABOUT THE STUDY

The A.T. Kearney study covered 155 computers used by 89 organizations. A stratified, random sample of companies in several major industries (see Exhibit 1) was chosen from the mailing list of a well-known financial service. Each company was asked to provide explicit information about their computer operations. First, a small sample of companies was contacted and results summarized. Later, a larger sample was analyzed and the results compared with the earlier sample to test the validity of the study. The two groups were highly correlated, indicating the results are statistically valid.

SIGNIFICANT FINDINGS

Interestingly, though the study sample was broken down by industry, the data revealed no significant differences among industry groups. Briefly, the six most revealing findings are:

1. Only 48% of available time is used productively.
2. Computers are operated only 64% of available time.
3. 25% of manned hours are wasted.
4. Large centers have the poorest performance in all categories of lost time.
5. 42% of the companies reporting do not maintain accurate records on computer performance.
6. Firms using multi-programming achieve higher production.

However, of much more significance are differences in performance between small, medium and large computer installations.

PRODUCTIVE USE OF AVAILABLE COMPUTER TIME

Of the total available machine hours (three shifts, thirty days per month = 720 hours) the average computer in the study performs productive work only 48% of the time.

Productive work is defined as the time equipment is used to process Production Runs and Testing, without regard for how effectively the computing power of the machine is being used at any one time or the value of the information produced. Based on our experience, there is a high probability that the computers are not working to capacity when doing productive work. Therefore, productivity is even less than indicated by the study results.

OPERATION DURING AVAILABLE TIME

Computing centers are manned and operated only 64% of available time, a major factor contributing to low computer utilization. Significant differences exist in hours manned as between large and small installations. The larger installations tend to operate much longer hours. Several companies reported that their computer centers hardly ever close.

The percentages of manned hours to total hours convert into shifts per week as follows:

Size of Installation	*Number of Shifts Per Week*
Small	10
Medium	14
Large	16
Average	13
Available	21

WASTE OF MANNED HOURS

A comparison of productive time with total hours that a computing center is manned and operated is most revealing. This comparison indicates that 25% of all costs are wasted due to Idleness, Reruns, Machine Maintenance, and Down Time.

LARGEST CENTERS LOSE THE MOST TIME

Significantly, larger installations suffer about 40% greater losses for these reasons than smaller ones. This suggests that huge computing centers are less efficient, experience greater scheduling problems, are more difficult to manage and are more likely to have highly structured, inflexible organizations resulting in lack of coordination and a negative impact on efficiency.

The substantially higher rerun percentage suggests that large installations need better controls and need to provide improved training for personnel.

From other studies of individual computing centers we have seen that the technology of massive hardware and complex configurations of devices create an environment which may not be fully understood and controlled by its staff. Trial and error play major roles in managing these installations.

It is readily apparent that EDP management should evaluate the productivity ratios of its computer installation before authorizing multiple shifts and new equipment. During the time the computers are manned but idle, the company is paying for both rental and payroll. Sixteen percent idle time translates into a cost to U.S. businesses of about $960 million annually. The four percent average reruns costs American industry $240 million per year.

On the average the companies in the study are incurring the following annual losses due to idleness and reruns:

Size of Computer Installation	*Annual Costs due to:*	
	(1) Idle Time	*(2) Reruns*
Small	$30,000	$2,000
Medium	84,000	18,000
Large	280,000	94,000

These costs represent inadequate management in the truest sense. In our experience, they result from such factors as:

1. Inadequate instructions for computer operators.

2. Absence of internal controls.
3. Improper or non-existent computer scheduling.

All of these require management attention.

MAINTAINING ACCURATE RECORDS

The 155 computers in the survey represent a total capital investment of approximately $110 million at purchase price. The low utilization indicates that management is not giving its attention to the performance of this expensive equipment. This is substantiated by the fact that 42% of the respondents report the data submitted are *estimated* because accurate records of computer utilization are not maintained.

Clearly management has written the computing center off as being outside of its management technique, and have left the center for the technician to manage.

MULTI-PROGRAMMING BRINGS HIGHER PRODUCTION

Approximately 28% of the computers in the study are operated in a multi-programming or multi-processing mode (processing more than one application program at any one time). Those with multi-programming achieve a ratio of productive time (production and testing) to total available hours of 62% compared with only 42% for non-multi-programming operations. This indicates that, as companies require processing in multiple shifts, they also seek more ways to increase throughput per hour of processing.

To validate this conclusion, we compared meter hours with total operating time. Meter hours are widely held to be the only convenient measure of how near capacity a computer is operating. Multi-programming computers have a 94% relationship between meter hours and operating hours. Non-multi-programming computers have only a 75% ratio.

It is easier (but more costly) for managers to increase throughput by going to multiple shifts, than it is to install multi-programming.

Although many installations have the technical competence and hardware/software capability to increase throughput of their computers with multi-programming, they do not avail themselves of this added capacity due to:

1. Desire by technicians for more powerful and costly equipment.
2. A large residue of computer programs written in second generation or non-compatible programming languages.
3. Management's inability to understand the true capacity of equipment on hand.

PERFORMANCE OBJECTIVES

Only 22 companies, out of the 89 in the study, reported productive time compared with available hours exceeding 60%. The results of the 22 companies with the highest ratio of productive time (production and testing) to available hours, were segregated from the total sample to establish performance criteria that might suggest goals or objectives for less efficient operations. As a group, they operate their computers longer hours and achieve 68% productive time compared with only 40% for the other respondents.

As a percentage of manned hours these high performance companies turned in the following results:

Performance Indicator	*Percent of Manned Hours*
Productive Time	81%
Idle Time	10%
Reruns	6%
Machine Maintenance and Down Time	3%

All industry groups and all size classifications were represented among these high performers. Only in rerun performance did this group have a poorer result than the rest of the respondents. It appears that even the best computing installation can find opportunities to cut waste.

THE CHALLENGE FOR MANAGEMENT

It has become more and more apparent, to both EDP specialists and general management, that selection and management of computer systems projects has suffered from lack of management attention and direction during the decade of the sixties. It has often seemed that frustrations generated by delays and escalating costs of systems projects causes executives to breathe deep sighs of relief once the systems are installed. They quickly and gladly turn attention elsewhere, and the result is waste and inefficiency in the computer room.

This study demonstrates clearly the opportunity available to the executive who has the interest, determination and know-how to measure and improve the performance of his computer operations. Simple tools can be utilized to monitor the computing center. Once such tools are in use, goals can be established and performance gradually improved. This is the approach taken by several of our clients.

> *Case.* The computer was manned initially 100% of the time. Outside rental of computer time had risen sharply and was being used to justify a proposal to increase computing power. Initial analysis of throughput revealed very low utilization of the installed computer. By instituting monthly management review of several performance indicators management began to establish specific goals.
>
> EDP personnel, working diligently to achieve these goals, discovered numerous ingenious ways to increase throughput and eliminate outside rental time. They successfully delayed acquisition of a new, larger computer for two years, created much better rapport and communication with management, and developed a more professional EDP group.

Regardless of industry, managing a computing center has virtually all the characteristics of managing a manufacturing plant. Many of the same disciplines and techniques apply.

It is time to apply some of the concepts of Management Information Systems to the management of computers. Although millions upon millions of words have been written about information systems that schedule and control manufacturing processes, and millions upon millions of dollars have been invested in such systems, there is seeming reluctance to apply similar techniques to the data center.

A machine tool costing $50,000 may be scheduled, loaded and measured in terms of minutes and mills. A complex of accounting, routing, standards and methods are used in the process. But even a modest size computer, costing ten times that amount, is often operated with inadequate or non-existent management tools.

FACILITIES MANAGEMENT?

Management has the option of applying generally known planning and control techniques to the computer center, or employing one of the more recently developed services—facilities management—where an outside vendor takes over operation of the customer's computer center, sometimes including systems and programming activities, and physically removes operations to the vendor's data center. Such an approach is not without trial and tribulation.

> One of the largest financial institutions in the world has for years operated its business without an internal computer or systems and programming staff. It has been using a local service bureau installation for all systems design, programming and computer operations.

Unfortunately, the proprietor of the service bureau recently decided to retire. He, therefore, opened negotiations to sell the service bureau, including the applications programs, to a third company that intended to market them to competitors of the financial institution. There has been considerable concern about how to regain independence from this operator so the company can become master of its own destiny.

When the computer is used effectively and becomes an integral part of the business, it usually is due to an intense involvement by top management. The systems and information with which the business is operated are as vital to its success as the products or services it sells. Thus management does not have the choice of:

1. Managing these systems and computer activities, or
2. Turning them over to someone else.

They must be well managed irrespective of where they are performed, and those responsible for the success of the enterprise are responsible for the successful conduct of all its vital functions.

AN EFFECTIVE APPROACH

The findings of this study suggest that the EDP manager of the seventies must become a much more effective manager of his resources. At the same time he must continue to struggle with user relationship problems. A great deal of credibility is lost by the EDP manager who does not look to the effectiveness of his own managing techniques, while trying to advise others on how to solve their problems.

Those who have seen the opportunity have been rewarded by substantial improvement. They have usually accomplished that by following a five-step process:

1. Find out where you are. The first step is to determine what the current situation is. How good or bad is it? Which aspects are satisfactory? Which are not? This can usually be established by a brief survey and elementary measurement of current performance. Five broad areas to be reviewed are:

— Objectives, Goals, Long-Range Plans, Organization
— Relationships with Major Users
— Quality of Design Concepts Employed
— Efficiency of Machine and Manpower Utilization
— Administration of the Function

2. *Define Objectives*. Executives need to determine the role and mission of the EDP effort within the organization. Without defining these and specific objectives for accomplishment, effectiveness will be seriously hampered. It is important that these be:

— Put into writing for analysis, study and modification as necessary.
— Understood and accepted by senior management, user members of the organization and systems and data processing personnel.

Overemphasis on the service-to-users aspect of data processing objectives may contribute to inadequate understanding of the cost trade-offs which service involves. It is important that all affected persons view these conflicts in proper perspective. Development of objectives can materially assist.

3. *Establish Measures of Performance*. On the basis of objectives, systems and data processing activities should be analyzed to establish those specific performance factors that will be measures of effectiveness. Care must be taken to identify items that can be measured with some precision and accuracy. Major categories of measured activities are:

— Costs
— Quality
— Schedule Adherence
— Utilization of Personnel
— Utilization of Machinery

4. *Develop Goals and Plans*. For each measured activity, standards of acceptable performance should be agreed upon between senior management and EDP management. Where the standard represents significant improvement over current performance, interim goals and plans for their accomplishment should be developed. The goals represent gradually improving performance each month until the standard is reached. EDP management should then set forth in detail the actions to be taken to achieve each increment of change.

5. *Measure and Motivate*. Senior management should demonstrate its sincere desire in seeing that standards are achieved. This requires the personal time of the interested executive to:

— Hold regular meetings and review progress.
— Ensure that the reporting system is accurate and objective.
— Review proposed plans.

— Aid in diagnosing successes and failures.
— Provide motivation (reward and punishment) for EDP personnel to achieve the standards.
— Reexamine and modify standards, measurements and reporting systems as conditions change.

Our study, "The Computer Profit Drain", indicates that the total burden of excess computing capacity in the United States is nearly $3.5 billion. Elimination of idle time and reruns would increase throughput about 20% and reduce costs by about $1.2 billion per year. Elimination of unmanned hours would provide a 75% increase in computer throughput. This is the equivalent of about $2.25 billion in computer rental per year.

These projections do not even consider the improvements which can result through use of available technology in the equipment now installed.

Thus while the A.T. Kearney study presents only a portion of the EDP manager's responsibility and performance level, it seems quite clear that the wave of criticism—of both computers and those who work with them—is in at least some ways justified. Perhaps, then, the status of the EDP manager can best be characterized by one word: opportunity.

PERFORMANCE EVALUATION AND MONITORING

by Henry C. Lucas, Jr.

Three major purposes for evaluating the hardware and software performance of computer systems—selection evaluation, performance projection, and performance monitoring—are described. Eight techniques that have been used or suggested for evaluating performance are discussed. Each of these techniques is rated on its suitability for the three purposes of evaluation. Recommendations are made on the most appropriate technique for each evaluation purpose. These suggestions include the development of a comprehensive set of synthetic programs on an industry-wide basis for selection evaluation purposes. Simulation is recommended as the most suitable technique for performance projection. Finally, a number of hardware and software monitors are available for performance monitoring.

INTRODUCTION

The evaluation of computer performance is of vital importance in the selection of computer systems, the design of applications and equipment, and the analysis of existing systems. Evaluation is usually undertaken for a specific purpose, and the techniques employed must be considered in light of the objectives of the evaluator. The goals of the evaluation may be to maximize the throughput of the system, process a given workload for a minimum cost, or any number of other objective functions. These goals furnish the overall environment for evaluation and determine what level of effort can be devoted to the measurement of performance.

Historically, only computer hardware performance was evaluated. Though there is probably little agreement on all of the parameters, any evaluation procedure should consider a wide range of hardware characteristics. Attention must be paid to the organization of the machine, for example the word size, data path, number of addresses per instruction, and character versus digit orientation. Secondary storage, I/O channel, and peripheral unit performance should also be evaluated. Special features, such as lookahead, memory interleaving, scatter gather I/O, scratchpad memories, and special registers, may make a difference in operations.

Because the programming system is an integral part of modern computers, the evaluation process must now consider software as well as hardware in assessing performance. The capabilities of the operating system are central to the performance of the computer; particularly crucial are any multiprogramming and multiprocessing features. The speed of assembly and compilation plus the execution of the resultant output code are also of great importance. Application programs, special telecommunications packages, and utilities are also a part of the computer system, and their performance is a component of total systems performance.

THE PURPOSE OF EVALUATION

There are three general purposes of performance evaluation: selection evaluation, performance projection, and performance monitoring. Selection evaluation in which the evaluator plans to include performance as a major criterion in the decision to obtain a particular system from a vendor is the most frequent case.[1] The procedure includes both hardware and software evaluation. For this analysis at least one prototype of the proposed system must exist.

Performance projection is oriented toward designing a new system, either a hardware component or a software package. The goal here is to estimate the performance of a system that does not yet exist. For example, the central processing unit for a new computer or the executive system for a dedicated, time-sharing system may be evaluated prior to final development in order to estimate the feasibility and performance of the design. A secondary application is the projection of the performance of a given system on a new workload.

Monitoring provides data on the actual performance of an existing system. These data can be used to forecast the impact of changes in the system, such as a reconfiguration of the hardware or an improvement in the frequently executed software modules. Such evaluation may also be concerned with obtaining a profile of the use of a system in order to make strategic decisions, for example, on the characteristics of a job priority system.

EVALUATION TECHNIQUES

Table 11-1 lists the major evaluation techniques, which are discussed more fully below, and rates their suitability for the three main purposes of evaluation. The purposes appear as column headings, and the specific techniques of performance evaluation appear as row entries. The number in each cell is an attempt to indicate the suitability of each technique for the given purpose. Certain techniques have not been applied to some of the evaluations or are inapplicable; a dash indicates that nothing is contributed by the technique to the evaluation purpose. A "1" means that the evaluation method has been used, but is inadequate in providing a valid picture of performance. A "2" means that the technique provides some assistance in evaluation, but is insufficient by itself. Lastly, a "3" indicates that the technique is satisfactory for the purpose indicated.

---

[1] Other factors besides performance also enter into the vendor selection process. For example, it is usually necessary to consider the training provided, the maintenance, applications programs, expandability of the proposed configuration, etc. These are separate issues of one particular use for performance evaluation and will not be considered further.

Table 11-1. Suitability of Techniques to Purposes of Performance Evaluation.

Evaluation technique	*Purposes of evaluation*					
	Selection evaluation (system exists elsewhere)		*Performance projection (system does not yet exist)*		*Performance monitoring (system in operation)*	
	New hardware	*New software*	*Design new hardware*	*Design new software*	*Reconfigure hardware*	*Change software*
Timings	1	—	1	—	—	—
Mixes	1	—	1	—	—	—
Kernels	2	1	2	1	—	1
Models	2	1	2	1	2	—
Benchmarks	3	3	—	2	2	2
Synthetic programs	3	3	2	2	2	2
Simulation	3	3	3	3	3	3
Monitor (hardware & software)	2	2	2	2	3	3

—: Technique not applicable
1: Has been used but is inadequate
2: Provides some assistance but is insufficient; should be used in conjunction with other techniques
3: Satisfactory

CYCLE AND ADD TIMES

Early evaluations were often based on a comparison of CPU cycle time and add times. The shorter the memory access time, CPU cycle time, and add time, the higher the rating of the computer. These figures were supposed to provide an estimate of raw computing power and were used during a period in which most programming was done in machine language. This method is insufficient for a number of reasons. First, the organization of the machine is completely ignored; a character-oriented machine may perform differently from one with a digit organization [3, 13]. Similarly, word sizes and special features, such as hardware instruction lookahead, are ignored [3]. The data path of a particular machine may be different from that of the comparison system, making cycle times for the machines non-comparable. For a modern machine, no one instruction, such as add, can be considered an adequate representation of the hardware system [13]. The add criterion also ignores any differences in machines that are related to the number of addresses included in an instruction [3]. Finally, the technique totally ignores any consideration of software.

Although this technique has been used in the past, as shown in Table 11-1, it is clearly inadequate for evaluating current computers. It is too incomplete for either selection evaluation or projecting the performance of a new system. It is also not applicable to determining existing performance since it can only compare, not monitor.

INSTRUCTION MIXES

The instruction mix is an attempt to provide a broader range for evaluation than cycle or add times. A frequency of execution is specified for certain types of instructions, and timings are weighted accordingly to produce a figure of merit. For example, a business mix may give heavy weight to instructions concerned with editing, table look-up, and data moves. A scientific mix would emphasize raw computation, such as add, multiply, and divide times. A simple scientific mix may weight floating-point add and subtract at 20%, multiply at 30%, and divide at 25%, with other instructions making up the remaining 25%. The time provided by the manufacturer's specifications for each of the operations is multiplied by the weight, and the totals are summed to provide the figure of merit.

The technique of mixes represents some improvement over cycle and add times. First, it considers more of the instructions of the machine, which means that more factors are taken into account in arriving at an estimate of the speed of operations. However, mixes are subject to many of the same criticisms that apply to cycle and add times: items such as word size, data path, addressing logic, special features, and software are not considered [35]. Also, the various mixes usually do not include any I/O considerations, which are very important in business and many scientific applications [35].

Another major difficulty with mixes is that there is no accepted criterion for determining the weight for each instruction in the mix [13]. The timings are subjective unless existing programs are monitored to provide data on the frequency of execution for instructions in the present or proposed system [42]. Current medium-scale machines are used for both business and scientific work; thus the distinction between a business and a scientific mix is not meaningful for many installations. Instruction sets differ, but all of them must be weighted in the same way, according to the mix [18]. It is also difficult to show the effects of different instructions that may be used by two central units to perform the same task [13]. Mixes are designed for simple comparisons and cannot help to monitor existing operations. Therefore, although they represent some improvement over simple cycle and add times, they are still inadequate for hardware comparisons and completely inapplicable for software evaluation.

KERNEL PROGRAMS

A kernel program is a typical program that has been partially or completely coded and timed. The timings are based on the manufacturer's stated execution times for the instructions that comprise the kernel program for a given machine. Both simple algorithms and quite elaborate data processing applications have been coded and timed as kernel programs. These routines range from complete payroll systems to matrix inversions. Perhaps the most extensive set of kernels appears in the Auerbach *EDP standards,* described in [53]. (Auerbach calls these kernels "benchmark" programs, but in this paper that term is reserved for programs that are actually coded and executed.) The kernel can include more parameters than the previous techniques because it utilizes the computer's instruction set more fully, whereas cycle and add times and mixes are restricted to a standard set of machine instructions. A kernel program may use the entire instruction set of a machine permitting consideration of characteristics that may be unique to the particular machine, such as differences in addressing logic, special index registers, number of addresses, etc., which are overlooked by the previous techniques [3].

However, kernel programs usually do not include adequate I/O considerations [3]. Including I/O operations in kernels is tedious, and timing estimates are much less certain because of the asynchronous nature of data channels. Besides, kernels are restricted to user program operations, and administrative functions are ignored. Overlap among units, CPU interference from a data channel, and multiprogramming and multiprocessing are very difficult to estimate [35]. Also, a kernel can be designed to make a given CPU look either attractive or unattractive [13]. There is no one typical kernel, and there are no accepted or standardized weights for combining kernels. Much effort is required to code and time a large number of kernels, and it is difficult to determine if equal programming skill was used for each [18].

A kernel can be helpful as a component in assessing hardware performance, as shown in Table 11-1. Kernels can also provide some data on software; for example, the quality of the compiler output code can be judged by programming and compiling the kernel and examining the object code. Kernels cannot, however, provide data on the effects of the operating system. They can contribute to monitoring by using a revision in an algorithm to illustrate timing changes, but they cannot help in evaluating the quality of vendor supplied software and are inadequate for the evaluation of either present or projected software performance. The technique is an improvement over the previous methods for hardware evaluation for selection purposes or performance projection.

ANALYTIC MODELS

An analytic model is a mathematical representation of a computing system [49, 54]. A number of such models have been developed; those based on queueing theory are particularly numerous. Models vary according to the type of mathematical analysis used. They are frequently employed to provide performance data on one particular component of a system, such as a disk unit.

It is difficult to evaluate these models as a class because of their diversity; a new model is usually created for each system.

On the plus side, an analytic model is useful as an additional point of reference in hardware analysis for all of the major evaluation purposes, as shown in Table 11-1. Some models can be altered easily to reflect new parameters, making this the first evaluation technique so far discussed that can be of value in monitoring existing systems.

For the disadvantages, analytic models do not generally include a comprehensive set of operating system functions, nor do they consider the quality of software performance. While some of the techniques include software algorithms, these are generally at the machine language level [18]. It is hard to include the random effects of multiprogramming and multiprocessing in an analytic model. For many of the models, it is difficult to change the parameters for testing different aspects of the system. The development and, particularly, the revision of models are tedious and time consuming [22]. In many cases, the entire system may be too complex for modeling, given the interaction among hardware, software, applications programs, and a sophisticated interrupt structure. The simplifying assumptions necessary to develop models in these instances tend to reduce their validity.

BENCHMARKS

A benchmark is an existing program that is coded in a specific language and executed on the machine being evaluated. A comprehensive series of benchmark runs can demonstrate differences in machine organization and evaluate the performance of I/O equipment and secondary storage as long as a variety of instructions are used by the test programs. The benchmark is also the first evaluation technique that includes a satisfactory consideration of software. This method allows for evaluation of the speed of compilation and execution. The same program can be coded and executed in assembly language in a higher-level language to evaluate the speed of the compiler output code. A series of benchmark runs can be made sequentially, under control of an operating system and then under multiprogramming, the ratio of these times indicating the increased throughput provided by a multiprogramming capability [18].

A benchmark series can be extremely helpful in analyzing hardware before choosing a new machine. Benchmarks can also help in designing a new system by coding modules and executing them on several machines, but experience may be too limited at that point to forecast which routines will be representative of the behavior of the new system.

Benchmarks, however, have to be used with caution. For example, the design point of the software must be taken into consideration. Is the compiler intended for fast compilation and slow execution, or is it one in which time is taken to optimize the object code [40]? Software often improves over the expected life of a system as new revisions or sources become available. Such improvement is hard for benchmarks to predict. The benchmarks selected must be representative of the current job mix of the installation. The proportion of compilation to execution must be considered, and this should be related to each class of program (for example, the class of I/O-bound programs and the class of compute-bound programs). The equipment required must also be included; routines to handle disk and tape operations in proportion to their representation in the job mix are necessary. Finally, the priority of various runs (order of presentation) must be in proportion to the real job mix in arriving at a final evaluation of the benchmarks [26].

A major problem with a benchmark is that it may not be typical of the user's real job mix [3]. A large number of benchmarks is needed to be representative; two or three are not sufficient [40]. It is difficult to weight the series of tests that may be required to guarantee the proper proportion of compilation versus execution, types or classes of jobs, equipment requirements, and priority considerations [28]. It is also difficult to adequately appraise the complete effect of the programming system on benchmark performance [3].

The technique is not helpful in developing new hardware except insofar as it provides data on which to base design, that is, what the existing mix of applications is like. Benchmarks are of limited use in monitoring performance unless the proposed changes in the hardware configuration are available elsewhere for a test. The only way to test a proposed software change with benchmarks is to program it, which defeats the purpose of projection. Benchmarks can be used as before-and-after tests to monitor performance following system changes.

SYNTHETIC PROGRAMS

Like a benchmark, a synthetic program is one that is coded and executed, but it differs in that it does not necessarily exist beforehand [8]. Like a kernel program, the synthetic program does not represent a real program, but, unlike a kernel program, it is coded and does include I/O considerations, files, and the environment provided by the operating system. Thus, in a sense, it combines the attributes of a kernel program and a benchmark.

The activities represented in a synthetic program must cover a wide range; some segments of the program will have to depend heavily on computational facilities, while others will have to make high I/O demands. It is suggested that these programs be highly cyclic so that comparisons can be based on ratios: for example, I/O to compute time [8]. The programs can be written in both assembly and higher-level languages to demonstrate the speed of the compiler output code. As with benchmarks, throughput can be evaluated by running a series of synthetic jobs sequentially and then using full multiprogramming capabilities, the comparison between the two times indicating the increased throughput for multiprogramming [8].

The major advantage of a synthetic program is the flexibility it provides, since jobs can be designed to include almost any desired measurement parameters. However, some of the problems of benchmarks also apply to synthetic programs. These difficulties include the representation of the current or projected job mix, run priority, run selection, the weighting of different synthetic programs, and the adequate attention to the effects of the programming system. It is also difficult to develop synthetic programs for terminal-based systems that respond on-line. This technique requires a mobilization of manpower to code and debug the appropriate synthetic programs. Without any overall coordinating authority, there is the danger of a lack of standardization. If the use of synthetic programs were to become widespread, inadequate standards would reduce their value for making comparisons among systems.

As shown in Table 11-1, synthetic programs make their greatest contribution to selection evaluation. If a group of synthetic routines is readily available, a user can select a representative subset for his evaluation problems. Software design can be advanced by the availability of synthetic programs that can be run on the proposed hardware for comparison. For designing new hardware and projecting performance, synthetic programs can be used to determine which hardware features have the greatest potential for improving performance. If alternative modules are available, synthetic programs can be used to help reconfigure software during performance monitoring. As with benchmarks, synthetic programs can be used as before-and-after tests when performance monitoring indicates the need for changes in hardware, or if proposed changes exist as synthetic modules they can be tried on the appropriate hardware.

SIMULATION

The most potentially powerful and flexible of the evaluation techniques is simulation, which provides a testing ground for and insight into the functioning of the system [13]. There are two basic types of simulation that have been used to evaluate computer performance. An event-oriented simulation models the actual operations of a computer system. A calendar of events is maintained, and probability distributions are generally used to describe the performance of the components of the system being evaluated. The second type of simulation uses empirically derived data which are manipulated to correspond with the specific configuration and job load to be evaluated.

The ideal parameterized program capable of simulating any proposed computer configuration is probably not feasible under existing technology [22]. Computers differ so much in their organization and operations that each simulation would probably have to be custom tailored to the individual machine. There are systems that purport to measure both the hardware and software performance of a number of different machines. In one of these programs, SCERT, the processing consists of a series of table lookups, and empirical equations are used to estimate the behavior of the simulated job mix [22]. Although it is not primarily a clock-oriented event simulator, the system does attempt to assess the degree of concurrency and to include real-time factors using a clock-oriented event simulator [25, 21, 20]. These empirical simulators are highly dependent upon the prior existence of the hardware and software to be studied.

Event-oriented simulations have been more often directed toward the design of a single system [59, 44, 36, 34, 30, 29, 19], but at least one of those developed can be generalized, by parameter changes and some rewriting [38], to apply to computer systems other than the one it was designed to evaluate. Some of the simulators have been designed to model a range of compatible equipment, such as the IBM 360 series [47]. Finally, one of the systems developed by Lockheed (LOMUSS) is a more general-purpose language that views the computer facility as a job shop or PERT network [23,24].

Probably the greatest drawback of simulation is its relatively high cost. Many of the simulations used for evaluation have been designed specifically around existing or proposed systems, and major changes to include other systems would entail a complete rewriting. Deciding how many items to include in the simulation is a difficult design question. If the level of detail in the simulation is too fine, the simulator may be too expensive to use; too much machine time or capacity may be required. If the level of detail is too gross, the results may be misleading because important details might be aggregated to such an extent that their impact is lost [13]. With empirical simulators, like SCERT, it is difficult to adequately consider the effects of software, multiprogramming, time-sharing, and terminal-oriented operations [2]. It is also possible that adequate time may not be available for development; in one case the simulation lagged behind the actual development work of the system and was of little use [14]. The validation of the system is a problem; some simulators have been able to use an existing machine with similar architecture as a base for projecting performance. For example, the behavior of a new central processor and memory (IBM 360/195) was simulated with a reported accuracy of 10% when the final product was tested [37].

Simulation provides excellent results for selection evaluation of a new machine and software system, but the effort and cost of preparing simulators for the specific systems is usually prohibitive. Simulation offers the greatest advantages for projecting performance on proposed systems; it is clear that the third generation of computers suffered from the lack of sufficient simulation prior to design [39]. However, it is in projecting the performance of proposed systems that validation problems are the most severe. Simulation is also excellent for performance monitoring as it provides a model of the system on which to try changes.

PERFORMANCE MONITORING

Monitoring is a method of collecting data on the performance of an existing system. It is generally used to locate the bottlenecks limiting performance when either reconfiguring the existing hardware or improving the execution of software. Monitoring is also useful in gathering a profile on the use of a system, for example, the percentage of compute-oriented jobs. Such data can help in determining priorities and which systems should be supported by a computer installation [46, 56]. For example, if statistics show a high proportion of compilation time compared with execution time, an installation should institute faster compilers that produce slower code. Two activities are involved in the monitoring process: the actual collection of statistics during operations and the analysis of the data, usually at a later time. In general, the techniques to be described are the most useful for this type of evaluation, but several of those described above (particularly simulation) can also be used for this purpose.

Hardware techniques for monitoring performance generally use some type of "black box" to measure certain parameters, such as CPU and I/O time, combined with wait and overlapped activities [57]. Given a specific set of readings, it is possible to calculate a number of other parameters, such as total system idle, compute only time, I/O only time, etc. [7]. The fact that the system is not disturbed in any way by the act of taking measurements is the major advantage of hardware monitoring. For example, the transfer of the supervisor from virtual to real store, shared and reentrant program behavior, and channel usage were monitored on the IBM 360/67 without altering the performance of the system [45].

In its simplest form, a software monitor, such as the NASA real-time system [51], may be a job accounting routine. Such a device can provide statistics on I/O device utilization, main storage usage, I/O wait time, idle time, and CPU time, etc. Usually the operating system, itself, must be altered in some way to collect the statistics. The most extreme case is one in which all changes in the status of the CPU are communicated to a special program monitor that collects statistics [31]. Even though software measurement may affect the process being monitored, the degradation of useful compute time can be kept to a minimum (in the NASA system, as low as 1% of CPU usage [51]). The advantage of a software monitor is its flexibility in determining what parameters are to be monitored and in making changes in the statistics to be collected.

A monitoring scheme is fairly easy to implement. This is particularly true of a hardware monitor which merely has to be connected to the appropriate parts of the system [50]. The major difficulty with either type of monitor, however, is the analysis that must be performed on the vast quantity of statistics produced by a comprehensive trace of the system. The interpretation of these data is more difficult than for other techniques of performance evaluation. For example, the monitor may indicate the present limitation on performance, but it provides no information on how much improvement can be made before another factor becomes limiting.

The monitor is primarily oriented toward analyzing the behavior of an existing system in order to improve performance, as shown in Table11-1. Timer runout interrupts can be used to record the program locations currently being executed. These data are then sorted to show the frequency of execution for different instructions. Program traces make it possible to relate execution addresses to program modules. The frequency distributions of address executions and the program trace show what modules are used most often and, hence, what routines have the most leverage for optimization [15]. Attention can then be paid to improving these modules. This procedure drastically reduces the execution time required by the GECOS FORTRAN compiler. Often, in an operating system five to ten modules are the most frequently used, and "tuning" these can result in a great savings.

The technique of monitoring has also been used in the design of a new system. A monitor can help debug the software as it is being developed by examining frequently used program segments to determine whether their performance is according to specifications. However, the analysis during design is not really for the purpose of projecting performance. For design projection, instruction traces have been used (particularly by IBM) as input to simulators in order to provide a more realistic job mix [16, 37, 52]. Such analysis implies that the projected use of instructions and their frequency of execution will be the same as those for an existing machine. Monitoring can be used to compare machine performance for selection evaluation, but it should be combined with other techniques, such as benchmarks or synthetic jobs.

RECOMMENDATIONS

From the above discussion and the summary in Table 11-1, it is apparent that simulation is the most adequate technique for all of the purposes of evaluation. However, it requires a major development effort and has a high cost. It is best suited to making estimates of projected performance, but projects of this type are probably the fewest in number and often quite extensive. Design of the 360/195 and the NASA real-time system were projects of sufficient size and expense to justify the resources that are required in simulation. These large-scale systems also require continual modification, and the presence of a simulator will aid in monitoring performance and evaluating potential changes in the systems.

Although simulation is helpful in monitoring performance, it is not sufficient. It is also unlikely that one would ever construct a simulation just for the purpose of monitoring a system and making changes, whereas the hardware and software monitoring techniques described above may be used fairly easily. The cost of implementing these techniques is not prohibitive, and the benefits can be significant. The next step is to close the loop between the acquisition of data and its analysis, so that results can be fed back to alter performance. Even if this is not feasible at present, all systems should include some provision for performance monitoring, either through hardware devices or as an integral part of the operating system.

Performance measurement is probably undertaken in the majority of cases for the purpose of selection evaluation, i.e., to decide which computer system to obtain. The expense of developing a simulation for each machine or system under consideration is prohibitive, and the existing simulations that purport to measure a variety of systems suffer from certain deficiencies, particularly in the evaluation of software. The most attractive technique for evaluating performance for this purpose, both from the standpoints of cost and capabilities, is the synthetic program.

A series of synthetic programs is needed that adequately represents the various types of computing demands presented by different users. The specifications for the synthetic modules can be developed by a user group or by computing organizations such as the ACM. The individual modules could be coded by the manufacturers for their machines, with suitable refereeing by a third party. The cost of this effort could be borne by the computer manufacturer and ultimately passed on to the user in equipment and software charges. While the expense for development may seem high, it would be amortized over the number of executions of the synthetic programs. Many specifications for bids from vendors now include some type of benchmark requirement that must be uniquely programmed for the individual user. The ability to select from a standard set of synthetic modules for each manufacturer's machine would greatly facilitate performance evaluation and comparison.

Such synthetic programs would have to be extremely comprehensive in the range of activities included. Each synthetic program should consist of a series of modules that would combine to form a program. These modules should be designed to test language compilation and execution, hardware, I/O capabilities, and batch and real-time operating systems. Multicomputer systems, such as a small preprocessor sending messages to an on-line system, would present special problems in interfacing synthetic modules for each machine. The exact content of each module would have to be specified by the group developing standards; some of the areas that should be included are listed in Table 11-2.

Table 11-2. Functional Description of Synthetic Testing.*

Compilation and execution timing
Timings:
Compute-bound routines
I/O-bound routines
I/O and computations together
Library and subroutine testing
Flexibility of execution:
Data moves, bit and byte manipulations
Range of I/O operations
Updating
Simultaneity
Oversized job (segmentation, overlay)
Errors:
Compile errors
Execution errors

Operating system
Job management:
Source deck, compile and go
Compilation
Loading and execution
Data management:
Tape file handling
Disk accessing methods
Telecommunications:
Transmission routines
Buffering and message handling
Control system:
Control and assignment of I/O
Storage allocation
Peripheral operations
Spooling
Library
Job accounting system
Transfer from one job to next
Priority sequencing

Other features:
  Parallel jobs
  Multiprogramming, multiprocessing
  Terminal-based systems
  Restart and recovery
Errors:
  Hardware and software protection
  Execution and I/O errors

---

* Each test is comprised of numerous programs, each consisting of a number of synthetic modules.

Overall recommendations on the use of performance evaluation techniques for the various purposes are diagrammed in Figure 11-2. For selection evaluation, the user must analyze his job mix and develop the appropriate weights for his particular situation. For example, programs can be classified by the ratio of compile to execute times, or the pattern of routines or instructions executed can be analyzed [26, 42]. The evaluator must then select the appropriate modules which would be joined to form a synthetic program. A number of these programs would then be produced in a representative mix and priority of execution for that user, and executed on the machines in question. The results could be weighted according to the user's type of processing, equipment, and unique requirements [26].

For projecting the performance of software systems, it may be possi-

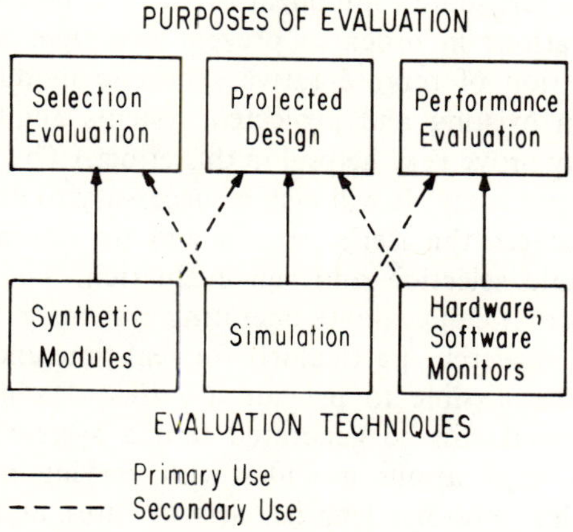

Figure 11-2. Recommended Performance Evaluation Purposes and Techniques.

ble to choose various segments of a synthetic program if the proposed hardware already exists. If not, or if the system involves a complex interaction of hardware and software as many on-line systems do, then the entire proposed system can be evaluated by simulation.

Though performance monitoring is different from the other two types of evaluation, all three are interrelated. Systems of the future should include built-in hardware and software monitors. Existing systems can include aspects of both through the addition of special measuring devices and/or minor changes to the supervisor. The data from the monitor can be used to plan modifications in the system. If a simulation exists, the changes can be tested prior to implementation. If the alteration is only a software routine, then it may be possible to use a synthetic module for testing, provided a representative module exists.

RESEARCH PROBLEMS

The development of a highly parameterized event simulator that makes allowance for varying configuations on different machines will require much further research in simulation. For all types of simulation, validation techniques need to be improved, particularly those for projecting performance. During monitoring, special equipment is needed to permit the feedback of performance data in a closed loop in real-time. It is not easy to generalize as to what data are needed or what type of analysis is suitable. It will probably not be possible to alter software dynamically, though certain modules may be called, depending on the state of the system. For example, a faster compiler producing less efficient output code can be called when the system is confronted with a large number of compilations. The dynamic reconfiguration of hardware should be made easier; some component isolation is now being done during systems operations in order to prevent complete hardware failure.

The specification of representative synthetic modules will require much research on existing and projected systems and loads. (Performance monitors may prove very helpful in this effort.) The linking of modules will also require study. It will also be necessary to develop analytical methods to characterize the user's job mix and to automate the process of synthetic module selection and run evaluation. The development of synthetic modules that can evaluate operating systems is a difficult task. This will require research, particularly for real-time and terminal-based systems. Will it be possible to provide a series of synthetic operating systems modules that can be generated into a system? Will it then be possible to select applications modules with varying response requirements and differing message lengths, arrival rates, and update requirements? Given the importance of performance evaluation, such research is vital.

SUMMARY

Various forms of performance evaluation have been reviewed in light of their contribution to the three major purposes of computer evaluation. Timings, instruction mixes, kernel programs, analytical models, benchmark runs, synthetic programs, and simulations, along with performance monitoring of hardware and software have been discussed. Each of these has been analyzed in terms of its contributions to selection evaluation for existing computer systems, the estimation of projected system performance, and the monitoring of existing systems.

An evaluation technique has been proposed that uses a comprehensive set of synthetic programs as an aid in the most frequent purpose of evaluation — systems selection. This technique can also help in certain types of performance projection and monitoring. For those areas in which synthetic module evaluation is not suitable, such as projecting hardware and software performance for designing new systems, the cost of developing a simulation is generally reasonable, given the extent of the project. It has been stressed that performance monitoring should be an integral part of all computer systems. Not only can improvements be made in the operation of existing systems, but valuable insights are gained for selection evaluation and for projecting the performance of proposed systems. No matter for what purpose, performance evaluation is essential for analyzing past history and planning for the future.

REFERENCES

1. ANACKER, W.; AND C.P. WANG. "Performance evaluation of computing systems with memory hierarchies." *IEEE Trans. Computers EC-16,* 6 (Dec. 1967), 764-773.
2. APPLE, C. T. "The program monitor—a device for program performance measurement." *Proc. ACM 20th Natl. Conf.,* 1965, pp. 66-75.
3. ARBUCKLE, R. A. "Computer analysis and thruput evaluation." *Computers and Automation 15,* 1 (Jan. 1966), 12-15, 19.
4. BAGLEY, P. R. "Two think pieces." *Comm. ACM 3,* 1 (Jan. 1960), 1.
5. BALDWIN, F. R.; W. B. GIBSON; AND C. B. POLAND. "A multiprocessing approach to a large computer system." *IBM Systems J. 1* 1 (Sept. 1962), 64-76.
6. BEMER, R. W.; AND A. L. ELLISON, "Software instrumentation systems for optimum performance." *Proc. IFIP Congress 1968,* Vol. 1, North-Holland Publ. Co., Amsterdam, pp. 520-524.
7. BONNER, A. J. "Using system monitor output to improve performance." *IBM Systems J. 8,* 4 (1969), 290-298.
8. BUCHOLZ, W. "A synthetic job for measuring system performance." *IBM Systems J. 8,* 4 (1969), 309-318.

9. ________. "A selected bibliography on computer system performance evaluation." *Computer Group News* (March 1969), 21-22.
10. BUDD, A. E. "A method for the evaluation of software: general description including benchmark considerations." Mitre Corp. Tech. Rep. 197, vol 1, 1966.
11. ________. "A method for the evaluation of software: procedural language compilers—particularly COBOL and FORTRAN," Mitre Corp. Tech. Rep. 197, vol. 2, 1966.
12. ________. "A method for the evaluation of software: executive, operating and monitor systems." Mitre Corp. Tech. Rep. 197, vol 3, 1966.
13. CALINGAERT, P. "System performance evaluation: survey and appraisal." *Comm. ACM 10,* 1 (Jan. 1967), 12-18.
14. CAMPBELL, D.J.; AND W.J. HEFFNER. "Measurement and analysis of large operating systems during system development." *Proc. AFIPS 1968 FJCC,* Vol. 33, Pt. 1, AFIPS Press. Montvale, N.J., pp. 903-914.
15. CANTRELL, H. N.; AND A. C. ELLISON. "Multiprogramming system performance and analysis." *Proc. AFIPS 1968 SJCC,* Vol. 32. AFIPS Press, Montvale, N.J., pp. 213-221.
16. CHENG, P. S. "Trace-driven system modeling." *IBM Systems J. 8,* 4 (1969), 280-289.
17. DOPPING, O. "Test problems used for evaluation of computers." *BIT 2,* 4 (1962), 197-202.
18. DRUMMOND, M. E. "A perspective on systems performance evaluation." *IBM Systems J. 8,* 4 (1969), 252-263.
19. GLINKA, L. R.; R. M. BRUSH; AND A. J. UNGAR. "Design, thru simulation, of a multiple-access information system." *Proc. AFIPS 1967 FJCC,* Vol. 31, AFIPS Press, Montvale, N.J., pp. 437-447.
20. HERMAN, DONALD J. "SCERT: a computer evaluation tool." *Datamation 13,* 2 (Feb. 1967), 26-28.
21. HERMAN, D. J.; AND F. C. IHRER. "The use of a computer to evaluate computers." *Proc. AFIPS 1964 SJCC,* Vol. 25, Spartan Books, New York, pp. 383-395.
22. HUESMANN, L. R.; AND ROBERT P. GOLDBERG. "Evaluating computer systems through simulation." *Computer J. 10,* 2 (Aug. 1967), 150-155.
23. HUTCHINSON, G. K. "A computer center simulation project." *Comm. ACM 8, 9* (Sept. 1965), 559-568.
24. ________; AND J. N. MAGUIRE. "Computer systems design and analysis through simulation." *Proc. AFIPS 1965 FJCC,* Vol. 27, Pt. 1, Spartan Books, New York, pp. 161-167.
25. IHRER, F. C. "Computer performance projected through simulation." *Computers and Automation 16,* 4 (April 1967), 22-27.
26. JOSLIN, E. O. "Applications benchmarks: the key to meaningful computer evaluations." *Proc. ACM 20th Natl. Conf.* 1965, pp. 27-37.
27. ________. "Cost-value technique for evaluation of computer system proposals." *Proc. AFIPS 1964 SJCC,* Vol. 25, Spartan Books, New York, pp. 367-381.
28. ________; AND JOHN J. AIKEN. "The validity of basing computer selection on benchmark results." *Computers and Automation 15,* 1 (Jan. 1966), 22-23.

29. KATZ, J. H. "Simulation of a multiprocessor computer system." *Proc. AFIPS 1966 SJCC,* Vol. 28, Spartan Books, New York, pp. 127-139.
30. ———. "An experimental model of the System/360." *Comm. ACM 10,* 11 (Nov. 1967), 694-702.
31. KEEFE, D. D. "Hierarchical control programs for systems evaluation." *IBM Systems J. 7,* 2 (1968), 123-133.
32. KNIGHT, K. E. "Changes in computer performance." *Datamation 12,* 9 (Sept. 1966), 40-54.
33. ———. "Evolving computer performance 1963-1967." *Datamation 14,* 6 (Jan. 1968), 31-35.
34. LEHMAN, M. M.; AND J. L. ROSENFELD. "Performance of a simulated multi-programming system." *Proc. AFIPS 1968 FJCC,* Vol. 33, Pt. 2, AFIPS Press, Montvale, N.J., pp. 1431-1442.
35. LUCAS, HENRY C., JR. "Computer evaluation through benchmark testing." Unpublished paper, MIT, Cambridge, Mass., May, 1967.
36. MERIKALLIO, R. A.; AND F. C. HOLLAND. "Simulation design of a multiprocessing system." *Proc. AFIPS 1968 FJCC,* Vol 33, Pt. 2, AFIPS Press, Montvale, N.J., pp. 1399-1410.
37. MURPHY, JESSE O.; AND ROBERT M. WADE, "The IBM 360/195 in a world of mixed job streams." *Datamation 16,* 4 (April 1970), 72-79.
38. NIELSEN, NORMAN R. "The simulation of time-sharing systems." *Comm. ACM 10,* 7 (July 1967), 397-412.
39. ———. "Computer simulation of computer system performance." *Proc. ACM 22nd Natl. Conf.,* 1967, MDI Publns., Wayne, Pa., pp. 581-590.
40. OPLER, ASCHER. "Measurement of software characteristics." *Datamation 10,* 7 (July 1964), 27-30.
41. PATRICK, ROBERT L. "Measuring performance." *Datamation 10,* 7 (July 1964), 24-27.
42. RAICHELSON, E.; AND G. COLLINS. "A method for comparing the internal operating speeds of computers." *Comm. ACM 7,* 5 (May 1964), 309-310.
43. ROSIN, R. F. "Determining a computing center environment." *Comm. ACM 8,* 7 (July 1965), 463-468.
44. SCHERR, ALLAN L. "Time-sharing measurement." *Datamation 12,* 4 (April 1966), 22-26.
45. SCHULMAN, F. D. "Hardware measurement device for IBM System/360 time-sharing evaluation." *Proc. ACM 22nd Natl. Conf.,* 1967, MDI Publns., Wayne, Pa., pp. 103-109.
46. SCHWARTZ, EUGENE S. "Computer evaluation and selection." *J. Data Management 6,* 6 (June 1968), 58-62.
47. SEAMAN, P. H.; AND R. C. SOUCY. "Simulating operating systems." *IBM Systems J. 8,* 4 (1969), 264-279.
48. SHARPE, WILLIAM F. *The economics of computers.* Columbia University Press, New York, 1969.
49. SMITH, J. L. "An analysis of time-sharing computer systems using Markov models." *Proc. AFIPS 1966 SJCC,* Vol. 28, Spartan Books, New York, pp. 87-95.
50. STANG, HAROLD; AND PETER SOUTHGATE. "Performance evaluation of third-generation computing systems." *Datamation 15,* 11 (Nov. 1969), 181-190.

51. STANLEY, W. I. "Measurement of system operational statistics." *IBM Systems J. 8,* 4 (1969), 299-308.
52. ———; AND H. F. HERTEL. "Statistics gathering and simulation for the Apollo real-time operating system." *IBM Systems J. 7,* 2 (1968), 85-102.
53. STATLAND, NORMAN. "Methods of evaluating computer systems performance." *Computers and Automation 13,* 2 (Feb. 1964), 18-23.
54. STIMLER, S.; AND K. A. BRONS. "A methodology for calculating and optimizing real-time system performance." *Comm. ACM 11,* 7 (July 1968), 509-516.
55. TOTARO, J. B. "Real-time processing power: a standardized evaluation." *Computers and Automation 17,* 4 (April 1967), 16-19.
56. WALTER, E. S.; AND V. L. WALLACE. "Further analysis of a computing center environment." *Comm. ACM 10,* 5 (May 1967), 266-272.
57. WHITE, PETER. "Relative effects of central processor and input/output speeds upon throughput on the large computer." *Comm. ACM 7,* 12 (Dec. 1964), 711-714.
58. WILLIAMS, O.; ET AL. "A methodology for computer selection studies." *Computers and Automation 12,* 5 (May 1963), 18-23.
59. YOUCHAH, M.I.; ET AL. "The data processing system simulator (DPSS)." *Proc. AFIPS 1964 FJCC,* Vol. 26, Pt. 1, Spartan Books, New York, pp. 251-276.

Index